THE TIGER OF MYSORE

THE TIGER OF MYSORE

A STORY OF

THE WAR WITH TIPPOO SAIB

BY

G. A. HENTY

Author of "With Clive in India", "Through the Sikh War", "Beric the Briton" "Held Fast for England", "For Name and Fame", & c.

WITH TWELVE ILLUSTRATIONS BY W. H. MARGETSON
AND A MAP

GYAN

Published by

GYAN

Gyan Publishing House
5, Ansari Road
Daryaganj, New Delhi-110002
Phone: 011-47034999, 9811692060
E-mail: books@gyanbooks.com

Distribution Network
gyanbooks.com
India, USA, Canada, UK, Australia, France

ISBN : 978-81-212-4115-1 (PB)
First Published, London, 1896

2nd Impression 2020

Printed at: Gyan Press, Delhi.

The Tiger of Mysore
Author: G. A. Henty

THE TIGER OF MYSORE

A STORY OF

THE WAR WITH TIPPOO SAIB

BY

G. A. HENTY

Author of "With Clive in India", "Through the Sikh War", "Beric the Briton"
"Held Fast for England", "For Name and Fame", &c.

WITH TWELVE ILLUSTRATIONS BY W. H. MARGETSON
AND A MAP

LONDON
BLACKIE & SON, LIMITED, 50 OLD BAILEY, E.C.
GLASGOW AND DUBLIN
1896

PREFACE.

While some of our wars in India are open to the charge that they were undertaken on slight provocation, and were forced on by us in order that we might have an excuse for annexation, our struggle with Tippoò Saib was, on the other hand, marked by a long endurance of wrong, and a toleration of abominable cruelties perpetrated upon Englishmen and our native allies. Hyder Ali was a conqueror of the true Eastern type; he was ambitious in the extreme, he dreamed of becoming the Lord of the whole of Southern India, he was an able leader, and, though ruthless where it was his policy to strike terror, he was not cruel from choice. His son, Tippoo, on the contrary, revelled in acts of the most abominable cruelty. It would seem that he massacred for the very pleasure of massacring, and hundreds of British captives were killed by famine, poison, or torture, simply to gratify his lust for murder. Patience was shown towards this monster until patience became a fault, and our inaction was naturally ascribed by him to fear. Had firmness been shown by Lord Cornwallis, when Seringapatam was practically in his power, the second war would have been avoided and thousands of lives spared. The blunder was a costly one to us, for the work had to be done all over again, and the fault of Lord Cornwallis retrieved by the energy and firmness of the Marquis of Wellesley.

The story of the campaign is taken from various sources, and the details of the treatment of the prisoners from the published narratives of two officers who effected their escape from prisons.

Yours sincerely,

G. A. HENTY.

CONTENTS.

ILLUSTRATIONS.

ILLUSTRATIONS

Yours Truly

G A Henty

THE TIGER OF MYSORE.

CHAPTER I.

A LOST FATHER.

"THERE is no saying, lad, no saying at all. All I know is that your father the captain was washed ashore at the same time as I was. As you have heard me say, I owed my life to him. I was pretty nigh gone when I caught sight of him holding on to a spar; spent as I was, I managed to give a shout loud enough to catch his ear. He looked round. I waved my hand and shouted, 'Good-bye, Captain!' Then I sank lower and lower, and felt that it was all over, when, half in a dream, I heard your father's voice shout, 'Hold on, Ben!' I gave one more struggle, and then I felt him catch me by the arm. I don't remember what happened, until I found myself lashed to the spar beside him. 'That is right, Ben,' he said cheerily, as I held up my head; 'you will do now. I had a sharp tussle to get you here, but it is all right. We are setting inshore fast. Pull yourself together, for we shall have a rough time of it in the surf. Anyhow we will stick together, come what may.'

"As the waves lifted us up I saw the coast with its groves

of cocoa-nuts almost down to the water's edge, and white sheets of surf running up high on the sandy beach. It was not more than a hundred yards away, and the captain sang out, 'Hurrah! There are some natives coming down; they will give us a hand.' Next time we came up on a wave he said, 'When we get close, Ben, we must cut ourselves adrift from this spar, or it will crush the life out of us; but before we do that I will tie the two of us together.'

"He cut a bit of rope from the raffle hanging from the spar, and tied one end round my waist and the other round his own, leaving about five fathoms loose between us.

"'There,' he shouted in my ear. 'If either of us gets chucked well up and the natives get a hold of him, the other must come up too. Now mind, Ben, keep broadside on to the wave if you can, and let it roll you up as far as it will take you; then, when you feel that its force is spent, stick your fingers and toes into the sand and hold on like grim death.' Well, we drifted nearer and nearer until, just as we got to the point where the great waves tumbled over, the captain cut the lashings and swam a little away, so as to be clear of the spar; then a big wave came towering up; I was carried along like a straw in a whirlpool. Then there was a crash that pretty nigh knocked the senses out of me. I do not know what happened afterwards. It was a confusion of white water rushing past and over me. Then for a moment I stopped, and at once made a clutch at the ground that I had been rolling over. There was a big strain and I was hauled backwards as if a team of wild horses were pulling at me. Then there was a jerk, and I knew nothing more till I woke up and found myself on the sands, out of reach of the surf.

"Your father did not come to for half-an-hour; he had been hurt a bit worse than I had, but at last he came round. Well, we were kept three months in a sort of castle place, and then one day a party of chaps with guns and swords came into the yard where we were sitting. The man who seemed the head of the fellows who had been keeping us prisoners, walked up

M 84

THE CAPTAIN AND BEN LASH THEMSELVES TO THE SPAR.

with one who was evidently an officer over the chaps as had just arrived. He looked at us both, and then laid his hand on the captain; then the others came up. The captain had just time to say, 'We are going to be parted, Ben. God bless you! If ever you get back, give my love to my wife, and tell her what has happened to me, and that she must keep up her heart, for I shall make a bolt of it the first time I get a chance.' The next day I was taken off to a place they call Calicut. There I stopped a year, and then the rajah of the place joined the English against Tippoo, who was lord of all the country, and I was released. I had got by that time to talk their lingo pretty well, though I have forgotten it all now, and I had found out that the chaps who had taken your father away were a party sent down by Tippoo, who, having heard that two Englishmen had been cast on shore, had insisted upon one of them being handed over to him. It is known that a great many of the prisoners in Tippoo's hands have been murdered in their dungeons. He has sworn over and over again that he has no European prisoners, but every one knows that he has numbers of them in his hands. Whether the captain is one of those who have been murdered, or whether he is still in one of Tippoo's dungeons, is more than I or any one else can say."

"Well, as I have told you, Ben, that is what we mean to find out."

"I know that is what your mother has often said, lad, but it seems to me that you have more chance of finding the man in the moon than you have of learning whether your father is alive or not."

"Well, we are going to try, anyhow, Ben. I know it's a difficult job, but mother and I have talked it over, ever since you came home with the news, three years ago, so I have made up my mind, and nothing can change me. You see, I have more chances than most people would have. Being a boy is all in my favour; and then, you know, I talk the language just as well as English."

"Yes, of course that is a pull, and a big one; but it is a desperate undertaking, lad, and I can't say as I see how it is to be done."

"I don't see either, Ben, and I don't expect to see until we get out there; but, desperate or not, mother and I are going to try."

Dick Holland, the speaker, was a lad of some fifteen years of age; his father, who was captain of a fine East Indiaman, had sailed from London when he was nine, and had never returned. No news had been received of the ship after she touched at the Cape, and it was supposed that she had gone down with all hands, until, nearly three years later, her boatswain, Ben Birket, had entered the East India Company's office, and reported that he himself, and the captain, had been cast ashore on the territories of the Rajah of Coorg, the sole survivors, as far as he knew, of the *Hooghley*. After an interview with the Directors, he had gone straight to the house at Shadwell inhabited by Mrs. Holland. She had left there, but had removed to a smaller one a short distance away, where she lived upon the interest of the sum that her husband had invested from his savings, and from a small pension granted to her by the Company.

Mrs. Holland was a half-caste, the daughter of an English woman who had married a young rajah. Her mother's life had been a happy one; but when her daughter had reached the age of sixteen she died, obtaining on her deathbed the rajah's consent that the girl should be sent to England to be educated, while her son, who was three years younger, should remain with his father. Over him she had exercised but little influence; he had been brought up like the sons of other native princes, and, save for his somewhat light complexion, the English blood in his veins would never have been suspected.

Margaret, on the other hand, had been under her mother's care, and as the latter had always hoped that the girl would, at any rate for a time, go to her family in England, she had always conversed with her in that language, and had, until her decreasing strength rendered it no longer possible, given her an English education.

In complexion and appearance she took far more after her English mother than the boy had done, and, save for her soft, dark eyes, and glossy, jet-black hair, might have passed as of pure English blood. When she sailed, it was with the intention of returning to India in the course of a few years; but this arrangement was overthrown by the fact that on the voyage, John Holland, the handsome young first mate of the Indiaman, completely won her heart, and they were married a fortnight after the vessel came up the Thames. The matter would not have been so hurried had not a letter she posted on landing, to her mother's sister, who had promised her a home, received an answer written in a strain which determined her to yield at once to John Holland's pressing entreaties that they should be married without delay. Her aunt had replied that she had consented to overlook the conduct of her mother in uniting herself to a native, and to receive her for a year at the rectory, but that her behaviour in so precipitately engaging herself to a rough sailor, rendered it impossible to countenance her. As she stated that she had come over with a sum sufficient to pay her expenses while in England, she advised her to ask the captain—who, by the way, must have grossly neglected his duties by allowing an intimacy between her and his mate—to place her in some school where she would be well looked after until her return to India.

The Indian blood in Margaret's veins boiled fiercely, and she wrote her aunt a letter which caused that lady to congratulate herself on the good fortune that had prevented her from having to receive under her roof a girl of so objectionable and violent a character. Although the language that John Holland used concerning this letter was strong indeed, he was well satisfied, as he had foreseen that it was not probable Margaret's friends would have allowed her to marry him without communicating with her father, and that the rajah might have projects of his own for her disposal. He laid the case before the captain, who placed her in charge of his wife until the marriage took place. Except for the long absences of her husband, Margaret's life had been a very happy one, and she was looking forward to the time when, after another voyage, he would be able to give up his profession and settle down upon his savings.

When months passed by and no news came of the *Hooghley* having reached port, Mrs. Holland at once gave up her house and moved into a smaller one; for although her income would have been sufficient to enable her to remain where she was, she determined to save every penny she was able for the sake of her boy. She was possessed of strong common-sense and firmness of character, and when Ben Birket returned with his tale, he was surprised at the composure with which she received it.

"I have always," she said, "had a conviction that John was still alive, and have not allowed Dick to think of his father as dead; and now I believe as firmly as before that some day John will be restored to me. I myself can do nothing towards aiding him. A woman can do little here; she can do nothing in India, save among her own people. I shall wait patiently for a time; it may be that this war will result in his release. But in the meantime I shall continue to prepare Dick to take up the search for him as soon as he is old enough. I hear once a year from my brother, who is now rajah, and he will be able to aid my boy in many ways. However, for a time I must be patient and wait. I have learnt to wait during my husband's long absences; and besides, I think that the women of India are a patient race. I trust that John will yet come home to me, but if not, when it is time we will try to rescue him."

Ben said nothing at the time to damp her courage, but he shook his head as he left the cottage. "Poor creature," he said. "I would not say anything to discourage her, but for a woman and boy to try to get a captive out of the claws of the Tiger of Mysore is just madness."

Each time he returned from a voyage Ben called upon

Mrs. Holland. He himself had given up every vestige of hope when it was known that the name of her husband was not among the list of those whom Tippoo had been forced to release. Margaret Holland, however, still clung to hope. Her face was paler, and there was a set, pathetic expression in it; so when she spoke of her husband as being still alive, Ben would sooner have cut out his tongue than allow the slightest word indicative of his own feeling of certainty as to the captain's fate, to escape him, and he always made a pretence of entering warmly into her plans. The training, as she considered it, of her son, went on steadily; she always conversed with him in her father's language, and he was able to speak it as well as English. She was ever impressing upon him that he must be strong and active. When he was twelve she engaged an old soldier, who had set up a sort of academy, to instruct him in the use of the sword and in such exercises as were calculated to strengthen his muscles and to give him strength and agility. Unlike most mothers, she had no word of reproach when he returned home from school with a puffed face or cut lips, the signs of battle.

"I do not want you to be quarrelsome," she often said to him, "but I have heard your father say that a man who can use his fists well is sure to be cool and quick in any emergency. You know what is before you, and these qualities are of far more importance in your case than any book learning; therefore, Dick, I say, never quarrel on your own account, but whenever you see a boy bullying a smaller one, take the opportunity of giving him a lesson while learning one yourself. In the days of old, you know, the first duty of a true knight was to succour the oppressed, and I want you to be a true knight. You will get thrashed sometimes, no doubt, but don't mind that; perhaps next time you will turn the tables."

Dick acted upon this advice, and by the time he was fifteen had established a reputation among not only the boys of his own school, but of the district. In addition to his strength and quickness, he had a fund of dogged endurance and imperturbable good-temper that did not fail him, even on the rare occasions when, in combats with boys much older than himself, he was forced to admit himself defeated. The fact that he fought, not because he was angry, but as if it were a matter of business, gave him a great advantage, and his readiness to take up the cause of any boy ill-treated by another was so notorious that "I will tell Dick Holland" became a threat that saved many a boy from being bullied. Ten days before his conversation with Ben his mother had said,—

"Dick, I can stand this no longer; I have tried to be patient for six years, but I can be patient no longer. I feel that another year of suspense would kill me. Therefore I have made up my mind to sail at once. The voyage will take us five months, and perhaps you may have to remain some little time at my brother's before you can start. Now that the time is come, I think that perhaps I am about to do wrong, and that it may cost you your life. But I cannot help it, Dick; I dream of your father almost every night, and I wake up thinking that I hear him calling upon me to help him. I feel that I should go mad if this were to last much longer."

"I am ready, mother," the boy said earnestly. "I have been hoping for some time that you would say you would start soon; and though I have not, of course, the strength of a man, I think that will be more than made up by the advantage I should have as a boy, in looking for my father; and at any rate, from what you tell me, I should think that I am quite as strong as an average native of your country. Anyhow, mother, I am sure that it will be best for us to go now. It must have been awful for you, waiting all this time, and though you have never said anything about it, I have noticed for a long time that you were looking ill, and was sure that you were worrying terribly. What would be the use of staying any longer? I should not be very much stronger in another year than I am now, and a year would seem an age to father."

And so it was settled, and Mrs. Holland at once began to

make preparations for their departure. She had already, without saying anything to Dick, given notice that she should give up the house. She had, during the six years, saved a sum of money amply sufficient for the expenses of the journey and outfit, and she had now only to order clothes for herself and Dick, and to part with her furniture. Ben, on his return, had heard with grave apprehension that she was about to carry out her intention; but as he saw that any remonstrance on his part would be worse than useless, he abstained from offering any, and warmly entered into her plans. After an hour's talk he had proposed to Dick to go out for a stroll with him.

"I am glad to have a talk with you, Ben," Dick said. "Of course, I have heard from mother what you told her when you came home, but I shall be glad to hear it from you, so as to know exactly how it all was. You know she feels sure that father is still alive; I should like to know what your opinion really is about it. Of course it will make no difference, as I should never say anything to her; but I should like to know whether you think there is any possibility of his being alive."

To this Ben had replied as already related. He was silent when Dick asserted that, desperate or not, he intended to carry out his mother's plan.

"I would not say as I think it altogether desperate, as far as you are concerned," he said thoughtfully. "It don't seem to me as there is much chance of your ever getting news of your father, lad; and as to getting him out of prison if you do come to hear of him, why, honest, I would not give a quid of baccy for your chance; but I don't say as I think that it is an altogether desperate job, as far as you are concerned yourself. Talking their lingo as you do, it's just possible as you might be able to travel about in disguise without any one finding you out, especially as the Rajah, your uncle, ought to be able to help you a bit, and put you in the way of things, and perhaps send some trusty chap along with you. There is no doubt you are strong for your age, and being thin and nothing but muscle, you would pass better as a native than if you had been thick and chunky. My old woman tells me as you have a regular name as a fighter, and that you have given a lesson to many a bully in the neighbourhood. Altogether there is a lot in your favour, and I don't see why you should not pull through all right; at any rate, even should the worst come to the worst, and you do get news somehow that your poor father has gone down, I am sure it will be better for your mother than going on as she has done for the last six years, just wearing herself out with anxiety."

"I am sure it will, Ben. I can tell you that it is as much as I can do sometimes not to burst out crying when I see her sitting by the hour, with her eyes open, but not seeing anything or moving as much as a finger—just thinking, and thinking, and thinking. I wish we were going out in your ship, Ben."

"I wish you was, lad; but it will be five or six weeks before we are off again. Anyhow, the ship you are going in—the *Madras*—is a fine craft, and the captain bears as high a character as any one in the Company's fleet. Well, lad, I hope that it will all turn out well. If I could have talked the lingo like a native, I would have been glad to have gone with you and taken my chances. The captain saved my life in that wreck, and it would only have been right that I should risk mine for him, if there was but a shadow of chance of its being of use; but I know that in a job of this sort I could be of no good whatsomever, and should be getting you into trouble before we had gone a mile together."

"I am sure that you would help if you could, Ben; but of course you could be of no use."

"And when do you think of being home again, lad?"

"There is no saying, Ben—it may be years; but however long it takes I sha'n't give it up until I find out for certain what has become of my father."

"And ain't there a chance of hearing how you are getting on, Dick? I shall think of you and your mother often and often when I am on deck keeping my watch at night, and it will seem hard that I mayn't be able to hear for years as to what you are doing."

"The only thing that I can do, Ben, will be to write if I get a chance of sending a messenger, or for my mother to write to you to the office."

"That is it. You send a letter to Ben Birket, boatswain of the *Madeira*, care of East India Company, Leadenhall Street, and I shall get it sooner or later. Of course I shall not expect a long yarn, but just two or three words to tell me how you are getting on, and whether you have got any news of your father. And if you come back to England, leave your address at the Company's office for me, for it ain't an easy matter to find any one out in London unless you have got their bearings right."

Ten days later Mrs. Holland and Dick embarked on the *Madras*. Dick had been warned by his mother to say nothing to any one on board as to the object of their voyage.

"I shall mention," she said, "that I am going out to make some inquiries respecting the truth of a report that has reached me, that some of those on board the *Hooghley*, of which my husband was captain, survived the wreck, and were taken up the country. That will be quite sufficient. Say nothing about my having been born in India, or that my father was a native rajah. Some of these officials—and still more, their wives—are very prejudiced, and consider themselves to be quite different beings to the natives of the country. I found it so on my voyage to England; at any rate, we don't want our affairs talked about; it will be quite sufficient for people to know that we are, as I said, going out to make some inquiries about the truth of this rumour."

"All right, mother. At any rate, the captain has told you that he will look after you and make things comfortable for you, so we need not care about anything else."

"We certainly need not care, Dick; but it is much more agreeable to get on nicely with every one. I was very pleased when Captain Barstow called yesterday and said that, having heard at the office that the Mrs. Holland on the passenger list was the widow of his old shipmate, John Holland, he had come round to see if there was anything that he could do for her, and he promised to do all in his power to make us comfortable. Of course, I told him that I did not regard myself as Captain Holland's widow—that all we knew was that he had got safely ashore, and had been taken up to Mysore, and as I had a strong conviction he was still alive, I was going out to endeavour to ascertain from native sources whether he was still living. 'Well, ma'am, I hope that you will succeed,' he said. 'All this is new to me. I thought he was drowned when the *Hooghley* went ashore. Anyhow, Mrs. Holland, I honour you for making this journey just on the off chance of hearing something of your husband, and you may be sure I will do all I can to make the voyage a pleasant one for you.' So you see we shall start favourably, Dick, for the captain can do a great deal towards adding to the comfort of a passenger. When it is known by the purser and steward that a lady is under the special care of the captain, it ensures her a larger share of civility and special attentions than she might otherwise obtain."

As soon as they went on board, indeed, the captain came up to them.

"Good-morning, Mrs. Holland," he said. "You have done quite right to come on board early. It gives you a chance of being attended to before the stewards are being called for by twenty people at once." He beckoned to a midshipman. "Mr. Hart, please tell the purser I wish to speak to him.——So this is your son, Mrs. Holland? A fine, straight-looking young fellow; are you going to put him in the Service? You have a strong claim, you know, which I am sure the Board would acknowledge."

"Do you know, Captain, it is a matter that I have hardly thought of—in fact, I have for years been so determined to go out and try and obtain some news of my husband, as soon as Dick was old enough to journey about as my protector, that I have not thought, as I ought to have done, what profession he should follow. However, he is only fifteen yet, and there will be time enough when he gets back."

"If he is to go into the service, the sooner the better, ma'am—one can hardly begin too young. However, I don't say there are not plenty of good sailors afloat who did not enter until a couple of years older than he is—there is no strict rule as to age. Only fifteen, is he? I should have taken him for at least a year older. However, if you like, Mrs. Holland, I will put him in the way of learning a good deal during the voyage. He might as well be doing that as loafing about the deck all day."

"Much better, Captain. I am very much obliged to you, and I am sure that he will be, too."

"I should like it immensely, Captain," Dick exclaimed.

At this moment the purser came up.

"Mr. Stevenson," the captain said, "this is Mrs. Holland. She is the wife of my old friend John Holland—we were midshipmen together on board the *Ganges*. He commanded the *Hooghley*, which was lost, you know, five or six years ago, somewhere near Calicut. There were two or three survivors, and he was one of them, and it seems that he was taken up the country; so Mrs. Holland is going out to endeavour to ascertain whether he may not be still alive, though perhaps detained by one of those native princes. Please do everything you can to make her comfortable, and tell the head steward that it is my particular wish she shall be well attended to. Who is she berthed with?"

The purser took the passenger list from his pocket.

"She is with Mrs. Colonel Williamson and the wife of Commissioner Larkins."

The captain gave a grunt of dissatisfaction. The purser went on. "There is a small cabin vacant, Captain. Two ladies who were to have it—a mother and daughter—have, I hear this morning, been unexpectedly detained, owing to the sudden illness of one of them. Their heavy baggage is all in the hold, and must go on, and they will follow in the next ship. Shall I put Mrs. Holland in there?"

"Certainly; this is most fortunate. I don't think that you would have been comfortable with the other two, Mrs. Holland. I don't know the colonel's wife, but Mrs. Larkins has travelled with us before, and I had quite enough of her on that voyage."

"Thank you very much, Captain. It will indeed be a comfort to have a cabin to myself."

Dick found that he was berthed with two young cadets, whose names, he learned from the cards fastened over the bunks, were Latham and Fellows. Half-an-hour after the arrival of the Hollands on board, the passengers began to pour in rapidly, and the deck of the *Madras* was soon crowded with them, their friends, and their luggage. Below, all was bustle and confusion. Men shouted angrily to stewards; women, laden with parcels, blocked the gangway, and appealed helplessly to every one for information and aid; sailors carried down trunks and portmanteaus; and Mrs. Holland, when she emerged from her cabin, having stowed away her belongings and made things tidy, congratulated herself on having been the first on board, and so had not only avoided all this confusion, but obtained a separate cabin, which she might not otherwise have been able to do, as the captain would have been too busy to devote any special attention to her. After having handed her over to the care of the purser, Captain Barstow had spoken to the second officer, who happened to be passing.

"Mr. Rawlinson," he said, "this is the son of my old friend, Captain Holland. He is going out with his mother. I wish you would keep your eye upon him, and let him join the midshipmen in their studies with you in the morning. Possibly he may enter the Service, and it will be a great advantage to him to have got up navigation a bit before he does so; at any rate, it will occupy his mind and keep him out of mischief. A lad of his age would be like a fish out of water among the passengers on the quarter-deck."

"Ay, ay, sir. I will do what I can for him." And he hurried away.

Dick saw that, for the present, there was nothing to be done but to look on, and it was not until the next morning, when the *Madras* was making her way south, outside the Goodwins, that the second officer spoke to him.

"Ah, there you are, lad! I have been too busy to think of you, and it will be another day or two before we settle down to regular work; however, I will introduce you to one or two of the midshipmen, and they will make you free of the ship."

Dick was indeed already beginning to feel at home. The long table, full from end to end, had presented such a contrast to his quiet dinner with his mother, that, as he sat down beside her and looked round, he thought he should never get to speak to any one throughout the voyage. However, he had scarcely settled himself when a gentleman in a naval uniform, next to him, made the remark:

"Well, youngster, what do you think of all this? I suppose it is all new to you?"

"It is, sir. It seems very strange at first, but I suppose I shall get accustomed to it."

"Oh, yes. You will find it pleasant enough by-and-bye. I am the ship's doctor; the purser has been telling me about you and your mother. I made one voyage with your father; it was my first, and a kinder captain I never sailed with. I heard from the purser that there seems to be a chance of his being still alive, and that your mother is going out to try and find out something about him. I hope most sincerely that she may succeed in doing so; but he has been missing a long time now. Still, that is no reason why she should not find him; there have been instances where men have been kept for years by some of these rascally natives—why, goodness only knows, except, I suppose, because they fear and hate us, and think that some time or other an English prisoner may be useful to them. Your mother looks far from strong," he went on, as he glanced across Dick to Mrs. Holland, who was talking to a lady on the other side of her; "has she been ill?"

"No, sir; I have never known her ill yet. She has been worrying herself a great deal; she has waited so long, because she did not like to go out until she could take me with her. She has no friends in England with whom she could leave me. She looks a good deal better now than she did a month ago. I think directly she settled to come out, and had something to do, she became better."

"That is quite natural," the doctor said. "There is nothing so trying as inactivity. I have no doubt that the sea air will quite set her up again. It performs almost miracles on the homeward-bound passengers. They come on board looking pale and listless and washed out; at the end of a month at sea they are different creatures altogether."

The purser had taken pains to seat Mrs. Holland at table next to a person who would be a pleasant companion for her, and the lady she was now talking to was the wife of a chaplain in the army. She had, a year before, returned from India in the *Madras*, and he knew her to be a kind and pleasant woman.

Dick did not care for his cabin mates. They were young fellows of about eighteen years of age; one was a nephew of a Director of the Company, the other the son of a high Indian official. They paid but little attention to him, generally ignoring him altogether, and conversing about things and people in India in the tone of men to whom such matters were quite familiar.

In three or four days Dick became on good terms with the six midshipmen the *Madras* carried; two of them were younger than himself, two somewhat older, while the others were nearly out of their time, and hoped that this would be their last trip in the midshipmen's berth. The four younger lads studied two hours every morning under the second officer's instruction, and Dick took his place at the table regularly with them. Mathematics had been the only subject in which he had at all distinguished himself at school, and he found himself able to give satisfaction to Mr. Rawlinson in his studies of navigation. After this work was over, they had an hour's practical instruction by the boatswain's mate, in knotting and splicing ropes, and in other similar matters.

In a fortnight he had learned the names and uses of what had at first seemed to him the innumerable ropes, and long before that had accompanied one of the midshipmen aloft. On the first occasion that he did so, two of the topmen followed him, with the intention of carrying out the usual custom of lashing him to the ratlines until he paid his footing. Seeing them coming up, the midshipman laughed, and told Dick what was in store for him. The boy had been as awkward as most beginners in climbing the shrouds, the looseness and give of the ratlines puzzling him; but he had for years practised climbing ropes in the gymnasium at Shadwell, and was confident in his power to do anything in that way. The consequence was, that as soon as the sailors gained the top, where he and the midshipman were standing, Dick seized one of the halliards and with a merry laugh came down hand over hand. A minute later, he stood on the deck.

"Well done, youngster," said the boatswain's mate, who happened to be standing by, as Dick's feet touched the deck. "This may be the first time you have been on board a ship, but it is easy to see that it isn't the first, by a long way, that you have been on a rope. Could you go up again?"

"Yes, I should think so," Dick said. "I have never climbed so high as that, because I have never had the chance; but it ought to be easy enough."

The man laughed. "There are not many sailors who can do it," he said. "Well, let us see how high you will get."

As Dick was accustomed to go up a rope thirty feet high, hand over hand, without using his legs, he was confident that, with their assistance, he could get up to the main-top, lofty as it was, and he at once threw off his jacket and started. He found the task harder than he had anticipated; but he did it without a pause. He was glad, however, when the two sailors above grasped him by the arms and placed him beside them on the main-top.

"Well, sir," one said admiringly, "we thought you was a Johnny Newcome by the way you went up the ratlines, but you came up that rope like a monkey. Well, sir, you are free up here, and if you weren't it would not make much odds to you, for it would take half the ship's company to capture you."

"I don't want to get off paying my footing," Dick said, pulling five shillings from his pocket and handing them to the sailors; for his mother had told him that it was the custom on first going aloft to make a present to them, and had given him the money for the purpose. "I can climb, but I don't know anything about ropes, and I shall be very much obliged if you will teach me all you can."

CHAPTER II.

A BRUSH WITH PRIVATEERS.

DICK was surprised when, on descending to the deck, he found that what seemed to him a by no means very difficult feat had attracted general attention. Not only did half a dozen of the sailors pat him on the back with exclamations expressive of their surprise and admiration, but the other midshipmen spoke quite as warmly, the eldest saying, "I could have got up the rope, Holland, but I could not have gone up straight, as you did, without stopping for a bit to take breath. You don't look so very strong, either."

"I think that it is knack more than strength," Dick replied. "I have done a lot of practice at climbing, for I have always wanted to get strong, and I heard that there was no better exercise."

When, presently, Dick went aft to the quarter-deck, Captain Barstow said to him, "You have astonished us all, lad. I could hardly believe my eyes when I saw you going up that rope. I first caught sight of you when you had climbed but twenty feet, and wondered how far you would get at that pace. I would have wagered a hundred guineas to one that you would not have kept it up to the top. Well, lad, whatever profession you take to, it is certain that you will be a good sailor spoilt."

They had now been three weeks out, but had made slow progress, for the winds had been light, and mostly from the south-west. "This is very dull work," the doctor said to Dick one day at dinner. "Here we are, three weeks out, and still hardly beyond the Channel. There is one consolation: it is not the fault of the ship; she has been doing well under the circumstances, but the fates have been against her thus far. I have no doubt there are a score of ships still lying in the Downs, that were there when we passed; and, tedious as it has been beating down the Channel, with scarce wind enough most of the time to keep our sails full, it would have been worse lying there all the time."

"Still, we have gained a good bit on them, sir."

"If the wind were to change round, say to the north-east, and they brought it along with them, they would soon make up for lost time, for it would not take them three days to run here. However, we shall begin to do better soon; I heard the captain say that he should change his course to-morrow. We are somewhere off Cork, and when he makes a few miles more westing, he will bear away south. If we had had a favourable wind, we should have taken our departure from the Start, but with it in this quarter we are obliged to make more westing before we lay her head on her course, or we should risk getting in too close to the French coast; and their privateers are as thick as peas there."

"But we should not be afraid of a French privateer, doctor?"

"Well, not altogether afraid of one, but they very often go in couples; and sometimes three of them will work together. I don't think one privateer alone would venture to attack us, though she might harass us a bit, and keep up a distant fire, in hopes that another might hear it and bear down to her aid. But it is always as well to keep free of them if one can; you see, an unlucky shot might knock one of our sticks out of us, which would mean delay and trouble, if no worse. We had a sharp brush with two of them on the last voyage, but we beat them off. We were stronger then than we are now, for we had two hundred troops on board, and should have astonished them if they had come close enough to try boarding—in fact, we were slackening our fire, to tempt them to do so, when they made out that a large craft coming up astern was an English frigate, and sheered off. I don't know what the end of it was, but I rather fancy they were taken. The frigate followed them, gaining fast, and, later on, we could hear guns in the distance.'

"You did not join in the chase then, doctor?"

"Oh no; our business is not fighting. If we are attacked, of course we defend ourselves; but we don't go a foot out of our way if we can help it."

Three weeks at sea had done wonders for Mrs. Holland. Now that she was fairly embarked upon her quest, the expression of anxiety gradually died out; the sea air braced up her nerves, and, what was of still greater benefit to her, she was able to sleep soundly and dreamlessly, a thing she had not done for years. Dick was delighted at the change in her.

"You look quite a different woman, mother," he said. "I don't think your friends at Shadwell would know you if they were to see you now."

"I feel a different woman, Dick. I have not felt so well and so bright since your father sailed on his last voyage. I am more convinced than ever that we shall succeed. I have been trying very hard for years to be hopeful, but now I feel so without trying. Of course, it is partly this lovely weather and the sea air, and sleeping so well; and partly because every one is so kind and pleasant."

As soon as the *Madras* had been headed for the south, she began to make better way. The wind freshened somewhat, but continued in the same quarter. Grumbling ceased over the bad luck they were having, and hopeful anticipations that after all they would make a quick passage were freely indulged in. On the fourth day after changing her course, she was off the coast of Spain, which was but a hundred and fifty miles distant. At noon that day the wind dropped suddenly, and an hour later it was a dead calm.

"We are going to have a change, Dick," the doctor said, as he stopped by the lad, who was leaning against the bulwark watching a flock of sea-birds that were following a shoal of fish, dashing down among them with loud cries, and too intent upon their work to notice the ship lying motionless a hundred yards away.

"What sort of a change, doctor?"

"Most likely a strong blow, though from what quarter it is too soon to say. However, we have no reason to grumble. After nearly a month of light winds, we must expect a turn of bad weather. I hope it will come from the north. That will take us down to the latitude of Madeira, and beyond that we may calculate upon another spell of fine weather, until we cross the Line."

As the afternoon wore on, the weather became more dull. There were no clouds in the sky, but the deep blue was dimmed by a sort of haze. Presently, after a talk between the captain and the first officer, the latter gave the order, "All hands take in sail."

The order had been expected, and the men at once swarmed up the rigging. In a quarter of an hour all the upper sails were furled. The light spars were then sent down to the deck.

"You may as well get the top-gallant sails off her too, Mr.

Green," the captain said to the first officer. "It is as well to be prepared for the worst. It is sure to blow pretty hard when the change comes."

The top-gallant sails were got in, and when the courses had been brailed up and secured, the hands were called down. Presently the captain, after going to his cabin, rejoined Mr. Green.

"The glass has gone up again," Dick heard him say.

"That looks as if it were coming from the north, sir."

"Yes, with some east in it; it could not come from a better quarter." He turned and gazed steadily in that direction. "Yes, there is dark water over there."

"So there is, sir; that is all right. I don't mind how hard it blows, so that it does but come on gradually."

"I agree with you. These hurricane bursts when one is becalmed are always dangerous, even when one is under bare poles."

Gradually the dark line on the horizon crept up towards the ship. As it reached her the sails bellied out, and she began to move through the water. The wind increased in strength rapidly, and in half-an-hour she was running south at ten or eleven knots an hour. The thermometer had fallen many degrees, and as the sun set the passengers were glad to go below for shelter. Before going to bed Dick went up on deck for a few minutes. The topsails had been reefed down, but the *Madras* was rushing through the water at a high rate of speed. The sea was getting up, and the waves were crested with foam. Above, the stars were shining brilliantly.

"Well, lad, this is a change, is it not?" the captain said, as he came along in a pea-jacket.

"We seem to be going splendidly, Captain."

"Yes, we are walking along grandly, and making up for lost time."

"It is blowing hard, sir."

"It will blow a good deal harder before morning, lad, but

I do not think it will be anything very severe. Things won't be so comfortable downstairs for the next day or two, but that is likely to be the worst of it."

The motion of the ship kept Dick awake for some time, but, wedging himself tightly in his berth, he presently fell off to sleep, and did not wake again until morning. His two cabin mates were suffering terribly from sea-sickness, but he felt perfectly well, although it took him a long time to dress, so great was the motion of the ship. On making his way on deck, he found that overhead the sky was blue and bright, and the sun shining brilliantly. The wind was blowing much harder than on the previous evening, and a heavy sea was running; but as the sun sparkled on the white crests of the waves, the scene was far less awe-inspiring than it had been when he looked out before retiring to his berth. The ship, under closely-reefed main and fore top-sails, was tearing through the water at a high rate of speed, throwing clouds of spray from her bows, and occasionally taking a wave over them that sent a deluge of water along the deck.

"What do you think of this, lad?" Mr. Rawlinson, who was in charge of the watch, asked him, as, after watching his opportunity, he made a rush to the side and caught a firm hold of a shroud.

"It is splendid, sir," he said. "Has she been going like this all night?"

The officer nodded.

"How long do you think it will last, sir?"

"Two or three days."

"Will it be any worse, sir?"

"Not likely to be; it is taking us along rarely, and it is doing us good in more ways than one. Look there;" and as they rose on a wave, he pointed across the water behind Dick. The lad turned and saw a brig running parallel to their course, half a mile distant.

"What of her, sir?"

"That is a French privateer, unless I am greatly mistaken."

"But she has the British ensign flying, sir."

"Ay, but that goes for nothing. She may possibly be a trader on her way down to the Guinea coast, but by the cut of her sails and the look of her hull, I have no doubt that she is a Frenchman."

"We are passing her, sir."

"Oh, yes; in a gale and a heavy sea, weight tells, and we shall soon leave her astern; but in fine weather I expect she could sail round and round us. If the French could fight their ships as well as they can build them, we should not be in it with them."

"Why don't we fire at her, Mr. Rawlinson?"

The officer laughed. "How are you going to work your guns with the ship rolling like this? No, lad, we are like two muzzled dogs at present—we can do nothing but watch each other. I am sorry to say that I don't think the fellow is alone. Two or three times I have fancied that I caught a glimpse of a sail on our starboard quarter. I could not swear to it, but I don't think I was mistaken, and I called the captain's attention that way just before he went down ten minutes ago, and he thought he saw it too. However, as there was nothing to be done, he went down for a caulk; he had not left the deck since noon yesterday."

"But if she is no bigger than the other, I suppose we shall leave her behind, too, Mr. Rawlinson?"

"Ay, lad, we shall leave them both behind presently; but if they are what I think, we are likely to hear more of them later on. They would not be so far off-shore as this unless they were on the look-out for Indiamen, which of course keep much farther out than ships bound up the Mediterranean; and having once spotted us they will follow us like hounds on a deer's trail. However, I think they are likely to find that they have caught a tartar when they come up to us. Ah! here is the doctor. Well, doctor, what is the report below?"

"Only the usual number of casualties,—a sprained wrist, a few contusions, and three or four cases of hysterics."

"Is mother all right, doctor?" Dick asked.

"As I have heard nothing of her, I have no doubt she is. I am quite sure that she will not trouble me with hysterics. Women who have had real trouble to bear, Dick, can be trusted to keep their nerves steady in a gale."

"I suppose you call this a gale, doctor?"

"Certainly; it is a stiff north-easterly gale, and if we were facing it instead of running before it, you would not want to ask the question. That is a suspicious-looking craft, Rawlinson," he broke off, catching sight of the brig now on their port quarter.

"Yes, she is a privateer I have no doubt, and unless I am mistaken she has a consort somewhere out there to starboard. However, we need not trouble about them; travelling as we are, we are going two knots an hour faster than the brig."

"So much the better," the doctor said shortly. "We can laugh at one of these fellows, but when it comes to two of them, I own that I don't care for their company. So the longer this gale holds on, the better."

The mate nodded.

"Well, Dick," the doctor went on, "do you feel as if you will be able to eat your breakfast?"

"I shall be ready enough for it, doctor, but I don't see how it will be possible to eat it, with the vessel rolling like this."

"You certainly will not be able to sit down to it—nothing would stay on the table a minute; there will be no regular breakfast to-day. You must get the steward to cut you a chunk of cold meat, put it between two slices of bread, and make a sandwich of it. As to tea, ask him to give you a bottle and to pour your tea into that; then, if you wedge yourself into a corner, you will find that you are able to manage your breakfast comfortably, and can amuse yourself watching people trying to balance a cup of tea in their hand."

Not more than half a dozen passengers ventured on deck for the next two days, but at the end of that time the force of the wind gradually abated, and on the following morning the

Madras had all her sails set to a light but still favourable breeze. Madeira had been passed, to Dick's disappointment; but, except for a fresh supply of vegetables, there was no occasion to put in there, and the captain grudged the loss of a day while so favourable a wind was taking them along.

"Do you think we shall see anything of that brig again, doctor?" Dick asked, as, for the first time since the wind sprang up, the passengers sat down to a comfortable breakfast.

"There is no saying, Dick. If we gained two knots an hour during the blow (and I don't suppose we gained more than one and a half), they must be a hundred and twenty miles or so astern of us; after all, that is only half a day's run. I think they are pretty sure to follow us for a bit, for they will know that in light winds they travel faster than we do, and if we get becalmed while they still hold the breeze, they will come up hand over hand. It is likely enough that in another three days or so we may get a sight of them behind us."

This was evidently the captain's opinion also, for during the day the guns were overhauled, and their carriages examined, and the muskets brought up on deck and cleaned. On the following day the men were practised at the guns, and then had pike and cutlass exercise. None of the passengers particularly noticed these proceedings, for Dick had been warned by the captain to say nothing about the brig; and as he was the only passenger on deck at the time, no whisper of the privateers had come to the ears of the others. The party were just going down to lunch on the third day when a look-out in the maintop hailed the deck,—

"A sail astern."

"How does she bear?"

"She is dead astern of us, sir, and I can only make out her upper sails. I should say that they are her royals."

Mr. Green ran up, with his telescope slung over his shoulder. "I cannot make much out of her, sir," he shouted to the captain; "she may be anything. She must be nearly thirty miles astern. I think, with Pearson, that it is her royals we see."

"Take a look round, Mr. Green."

The mate did so, and presently called down, "I can make out something else away on the starboard quarter, but so far astern that I can scarce swear to her. Still, it can be nothing but a sail."

"Thank you, Mr. Green; I daresay that we shall know more about her later on."

When the captain joined the passengers at table, one of the ladies said, "You seem interested in that ship astern of us, captain."

"Yes, Mrs. Seaforth; one is always interested in a ship when one gets down as far as this. She may be another Indiaman, and although the *Madras* has no claim to any great speed in a light breeze like this, one never likes being passed."

The explanation was considered as sufficient, and nothing more was said on the subject. By sunset the upper sails of the stranger could be made out from the deck of the *Madras*. Mr. Green again went up and had a look at her.

"She is coming up fast," he said, when he rejoined the captain. "She keeps so dead in our wake that I can't make out whether she is a brig or a three-master; but I fancy that she is a brig, by the size and cut of her sails. I can see the other craft plainly enough now; she is eight or ten miles west of the other and has closed in towards her since I made her out before. I have no doubt that she is a large schooner."

"Well, it is a comfort that they are not a few miles nearer, Mr. Green. There is no chance of their overtaking us before morning, so we shall be able to keep our watches as usual, and shall have time to get ready for a fight if there is to be one."

"The sooner the better sir, so that it is daylight; it is quite certain that they have the legs of us."

In the morning when Dick came up he found that the wind

had quite died away, and the sails hung loosely from the yards. Looking astern, he saw two vessels; they were some six miles away, and perhaps two miles apart. As they lay without steerage way they had swung partly round, and he saw that they were a brig and a schooner. The former he had no doubt, from her lofty masts and general appearance, was the same the *Madras* had passed six days before. As the passengers came up they were full of curiosity as to the vessels.

"Of course, we know no more actually than you do yourselves," the captain said, as some of them gathered round and questioned him, "but I may as well tell you frankly that we have very little doubt about their being two French privateers. We passed them during the gale, and had some hopes that we should not see them again; but in the light breeze we have been having during the last few days they have made up lost ground, and I am afraid we shall have to fight them."

Exclamations of alarm broke from some of the ladies who heard his words.

"You need not be alarmed, ladies," he went on. "We carry twelve guns, you know, and I expect that all of them are of heavier metal than theirs. The *Madras* is a strongly-built ship, and will stand a good deal more hammering than those light craft will, so that I have no doubt we shall give a good account of ourselves."

After breakfast the hatches were opened and the gun-cases belonging to the passengers brought on deck. Scarce one of them but had a rifle, and many had in addition a shot gun. The day passed without any change in the positions of the vessels, for they still lay becalmed.

"Why don't they get out their boats, and tow their vessels up?" Dick asked the doctor.

"Because they would be throwing away their chances if they did so. They know that we cannot get away from them, and we might smash up their boats as soon as they came within range. Besides, their speed and superior handiness give them a pull over us when fighting under sail. They may try to tow up during the night, if they think they are strong enough to take us by boarding, but I hardly think they will do so."

The night, however, passed off quietly, but in the morning a light breeze sprang up from the east, the sails were trimmed, and the *Madras* again began to move through the water. By breakfast-time, the craft behind had visibly decreased their distance. The meal was a silent one. When it was over the captain said, "As soon as those fellows open fire, ladies, I must ask you all to go down into the hold. The sailors have already cleared a space below the water-line large enough for you, and they will take down some cushions and so on to make you as comfortable as possible under the circumstances. Pray do not be alarmed at any noises you may hear; you will be below the water-line and perfectly safe from their shot, and you may be sure that we shall do our best to keep the scoundrels from boarding us; and I will let you know from time to time how matters are going."

The unmarried men at once went up on deck; the others lingered for a short time behind, talking to their wives and daughters, and then followed.

"The wind has strengthened a bit, Mr. Green," the captain said, "and I fancy we shall get more."

"I think so too, Captain."

"Then you may as well get off the upper sails and make her snug. Get off everything above the top-gallant; then, if the wind increases, we shall not want to call the men away from the guns."

The crew had, without orders, already mustered at quarters. The lashings had been cast off the guns, the boatswain had opened the magazines, and a pile of shot stood by each gun, together with cases of canister and grape-shot for close work. Boarding-pikes and cutlasses were ranged along by the bulwarks. The men had thrown aside their jackets, and many of those at the guns were stripped to the waist. Some of them were laughing and talking, and Dick saw, by their air of confidence, that they had no doubt of their ability to beat off the assault of the privateers.

The latter were the first to open the ball. A puff of smoke burst out from the brig's bows, followed almost instantly by one from the schooner. Both shots fell short, and for a quarter of an hour, the three vessels kept on their way.

"We have heavier metal than that," the captain said cheerfully, "and I have no doubt we could reach them; but it is not our game to play at long bowls, for it is probable that both of them carry a long pivot gun, and if they were to draw off a bit, they could annoy us amazingly, while we could not reach them."

Presently the privateers opened fire again. They were now about a mile away, and the same distance from each other. Their shot fell close to the Indiaman, and two or three passed through her sails. Still no reply was made. The men at the guns fidgeted and kept casting glances towards the poop, in expectation of an order. It came at last, but was not what they had expected.

"Double-shot your guns, men," the captain said.

Scarcely was the order obeyed when the brig, which was now on the port quarter, luffed up a little into the wind and fired a broadside of eight guns. There was a crashing of wood: the *Madras* was hulled in three places; two more holes appeared in her sails; while the other shot passed harmlessly just astern of her. There was an angry growl among the sailors as the schooner bore away a little and also fired her broadside. Except that a man was struck down by a splinter from the bulwarks, no damage was done.

"Bear up a little," the captain said to the second officer, who was standing by the helmsman. "I want to edge in a little towards the brig, but not enough for them to notice it. Now, gentlemen," he went on to the passengers, "I have no doubt that most of you are good shots, and I want you, after we have fired our broadside, to direct your attention to the brig's helmsmen. If you can render it impossible for the men to stand at the wheel, we will make mincemeat of this fellow in no time. Directly I have fired our port broadside, I am going to bring her up into the wind on the opposite tack, and give him the starboard broadside at close quarters. Don't fire until we have gone about, and then pick off the helmsmen if you can. Get ready, men." The brig was now but a little more than a quarter of a mile distant. "Aim at the foot of his mainmast," he went on. "Let each man fire as he gets the mast on his sight."

A moment later the first gun fired, and the whole broadside followed in quick succession.

"Down with the helm! Hard down, sheets and tacks!"

The men whose duty it was to trim the sails ran to the sheets and braces. The *Madras* swept up into the wind, and as her sails drew on the other tack she came along on a course that would take her within a hundred yards of the brig. As she approached, three rifles cracked out on her poop. One of the men at the helm of the brig fell, and as he did so, half a dozen more shots were fired; and as his companion dropped beside him, the brig, deprived of her helm, flew up into the wind. Three men ran aft to the wheel, but the deadly rifles spoke out again. Two of them fell; the third dived under the bulwark, for shelter.

"Steady, men!" the captain shouted. "Fetch her mainmast out of her!"

As they swept along under the stern of the brig, each gun of their other broadside poured in its fire in succession, raking the crowded deck from end to end. A moment later the mainmast was seen to sway, and a tremendous cheer broke from the *Madras* as it went over the side, dragging with it the foretopmast with all its gear.

"Down with the helm again!" the captain shouted. "Bring her head to wind, and keep her there!"

The first officer sprang forward to see that the order was carried into effect, and a minute later the Indiaman lay, with her sails aback, at a distance of a hundred yards, on the quarter of the brig.

"Grape and canister!" the captain shouted, and broadside after broadside swept the decks of the brig, which, hampered by her wreckage, was lying almost motionless in the water. So terrible was the fire that the privateer's men threw down the axes with which they were striving to cut away the floating spars, and ran below.

"Double-shot your guns, and give her one broadside between wind and water!" the captain ordered. "Haul on the sheets and braces, Mr. Green, and get her on her course again—the schooner won't trouble us now."

That craft had indeed at first luffed up, to come to the assistance of her consort; but on seeing the fall of the latter's mast, and that she was incapable of rendering any assistance, had again altered her course, feeling her incapacity to engage so redoubtable an opponent single-handed. Three hearty cheers broke from all on board the *Madras*, as, after pouring in a broadside at a distance of fifty yards, she left the brig behind her and proceeded on her way.

"Then you don't care about taking prizes, captain?" one of the passengers said, as they crowded round to congratulate him upon his easy and almost bloodless victory.

"No, taking prizes is not my business; and were I to weaken my crew by sending some of them off in a prize, I might find myself short-handed if we met another of these gentlemen, or fell in with bad weather. Besides, she would not be worth sending home."

"The brig is signalling to her consort, sir," Mr. Green said, coming up.

"Ay, ay; I expect she wants help badly enough. I saw the chips fly close to her water-line as we gave her that last broadside."

"They are lowering a boat," one of the passengers said.

"So they are; I expect they haven't got more than one that can swim. I think she is settling down," the captain said,

M 84

THE *MADRAS* BEATS OFF TWO FRENCH PRIVATEERS.

as he looked earnestly at the wreck astern. "See how they are crowding into that boat, and how some of the others are cutting and slashing to get the wreckage clear of her."

"She is certainly a good bit lower in the water than she was," the first officer agreed. "The schooner has come round, and won't be long before she is alongside of her."

There was no doubt that the brig was settling down fast. Men stood on the bulwarks and waved their caps frantically to the schooner; others could be seen, by the aid of a glass, casting spars, hen-coops, and other articles, overboard, and jumping into the water after them; and soon the sea around the wreck was dotted with heads and floating fragments, while the wreckage of the mainmast was clustered with men. When the *Madras* was a mile away, the schooner was lying thrown up head to wind fifty yards from the brig, and her boats were already engaged in picking up the swimmers. Suddenly the brig gave a heavy lurch.

"There she goes!" the captain exclaimed. A moment later the hull had disappeared, and the schooner remained alone.

By this time the whole of the ladies had ascended from their place of safety to the poop, and a general exclamation broke from the passengers as the brig disappeared.

"The schooner will pick them all up," the captain said. "They must have suffered heavily from our fire, but I don't think any will have gone down with her. The boat which has already reached the schooner must have taken a good many, and the mainmast and foretopmast and spars would support the rest, to say nothing of the things they have thrown overboard. There is one wasp the less afloat."

No further adventure was met with throughout the voyage. They had a spell of bad weather off the Cape, but the captain said it was nothing to the gales they often encountered there, and that the voyage as a whole was an exceptionally good one; for even after the delays they had encountered at the start, the passage had lasted but four months and a half.

They touched at Point de Galle for news, and to ascertain whether any French war-ships had been seen of late along the coast. A supply of fresh vegetables and fruit was taken on board, as the vessel, after touching at Madras, was to go on to Calcutta. A few of the passengers landed at Point de Galle, but neither Dick nor his mother went ashore.

"You will have plenty of opportunities of seeing Indians later on, Dick," Mrs. Holland had said; "and as the gigs will not take all ashore, we may as well stop quietly here. I heard the captain say that he would weigh anchor again in four hours."

Dick was rather disappointed, but as they would be at Madras before long, he did not much mind. Ten days later they anchored off that town. Little was to be seen except the fort, a number of warehouses, and the native town, while the scenery contrasted strongly with that of Ceylon, with its masses of green foliage with hills rising behind. For the last fortnight Mrs. Holland had been somewhat depressed. Now that the voyage was nearly over, the difficulties of the task before her seemed greater than they had done when viewed from a distance, and she asked herself whether, after all, it would not have been wiser to have waited another two or three years, until Dick had attained greater strength and manhood. The boy, however, when she confided her doubts to him, laughed at the idea.

"Why, you know, mother," he said, "we agreed that I had a much greater chance as a boy of going about unsuspected, than I should have as a man; besides, we could never have let father remain any longer without trying to get him out. No, no, mother, you know we have gone through it over and over again, and talked about every chance. We have had a first-rate voyage, and everything is going on just as we could have wished, and it would never do to begin to have doubts now. We have both felt confident all along. It seems to me that of all things we must keep on being confident, at any rate until there is something to give us cause to doubt."

On the following morning they landed in a surf-boat, and were fortunate in getting ashore without being drenched. There was a rush of wild-looking and half-naked natives to seize their baggage; but upon Mrs. Holland, with quiet decision, accosting the men in their own language, and picking out four of them to carry the baggage up to one of the vehicles standing on the road that ran along the top of the high beach, the rest fell back, and the matter was arranged without difficulty. After a drive of twenty minutes, they stopped at a hotel.

"It is not like a hotel, mother," Dick remarked, as they drew up; "it is more like a gentleman's house, standing in its own park."

"Almost all the European houses are built so here, Dick, and it is much more pleasant than when they are packed together."

"Much nicer," Dick agreed. "If each house has a lot of ground like this, the place must cover a tremendous extent of country."

"It does, Dick; but as every one keeps horses and carriages, that does not matter much. Blacktown, as they call the native town, stands quite apart from the European quarter."

As soon as they were settled in their rooms, which seemed to Dick singularly bare and unfurnished, mother and son went out for a drive in one of the carriages belonging to the hotel. Dick had learned so much about India from her that, although extremely interested, he was scarcely surprised at the various scenes that met his eye, or at the bright and varied costumes of the natives. Many changes had taken place during the seventeen years that had elapsed since Mrs. Holland had left India. The town had increased greatly in size. All signs of the effects of the siege by the French, thirty years before, had been long since obliterated. Large and handsome government buildings had been erected, and evidences of wealth and prosperity were everywhere present.

CHAPTER III.

THE RAJAH.

"NOW, mother, let us talk over our plans," Dick said, as, after dinner, they seated themselves in two chairs in the verandah, at some little distance from the other guests at the hotel. "How are we going to begin?"

"In the first place, Dick, we shall to-morrow send out a messenger to Tripataly, to tell my brother of our arrival here."

"How far is it, mother?"

"It is about a hundred and twenty miles in a straight line, I think, but a good bit farther than that by the way we shall go."

"How shall we travel, mother?"

"I will make some inquiries to-morrow, but I think that the pleasantest way will be to drive from here to Conjeveram. I think that is about forty miles. There we can take a native boat, and go up the river Palar past Arcot and Vellore, to Vaniambaddy. From there it is only about fifteen miles to Tripataly. I shall tell my brother the way I propose going. Of course, if he thinks any other way will be better, we shall go by that."

"Are we going to travel as we are, mother, or in native dress?"

"That is a point that I have been thinking over, Dick; I will wait and ask my brother which he thinks will be the best. When out there I always dressed as a native, and never put on English clothes except at Madras. I used to come down here two or three times every year with my mother, and generally stayed for a fortnight or three weeks. During that time we always dressed in English fashion, as by so doing we could live at the hotel and take our meals at public tables without exciting comment. My mother knew several families here, and liked getting back to English ways occasionally. Of course, I shall dress in Indian fashion while I stay at my brother's, so it is only the question of how we shall journey there, and I think I should prefer going as we are. We shall excite no special observation travelling as English, as it will only be supposed that we are on our way to pay a visit to some of our officers at Arcot. At Conjeveram, which is a large place, there is sure to be a hotel of some sort or other, for it is on the main road from Madras south. On the way up by water we shall of course sleep on board, and we shall go direct from the boat to Tripataly. However, we need not decide until we get an answer to my letter, for it will take a very short time to get the necessary dresses for us both. I think it most likely that my brother will send down one of his officers to meet us, or possibly may come down himself. You heard what they were all talking about at dinner, Dick?"

"Yes, mother, it was something about Tippoo attacking the Rajah of Travancore, but I did not pay much attention to it. I was looking at the servants in their curious dresses."

"It is very important, Dick, and will probably change all our plans. Travancore is in alliance with us, and every one thinks that Tippoo's attack on it will end in our being engaged in war with him. I was talking to the officer who sat next to me, and he told me that if there had been a capable man at the head of government here, war would have been declared as soon as the Sultan moved against Travancore. Now that General Meadows had been appointed governor and commander-in-chief, there was no doubt, he said, that an army would move against Tippoo in a very short time—that it was already being collected, and that a force was marching down here from Bengal. So you see, my boy, if this war really breaks out, the English may march to Seringapatam and compel Tippoo to give up all the captives he has in his hands."

"That would be splendid, mother."

"At any rate, Dick, as long as there is a hope of your father being rescued in that way, our plans must be put aside."

"Well, mother, that will be better in some respects, for of course if father is not rescued by our army I can try afterwards as we arranged. It would be an advantage in one way, as I should then be quite accustomed to the country and more fit to make my way about."

A week later an old officer arrived from Tripataly.

"Ah, Rajbullub," Mrs. Holland exclaimed, as he came up with a deep salaam, "I am indeed glad to see you again. I knew you were alive, for my brother mentioned you when he wrote last year."

Rajbullub was evidently greatly pleased at the recognition. "I think I should have known you, lady," he said; "but eighteen years makes more changes in the young than in the old. Truly I am glad to see you again. There was great joy among us who knew you as a child, when the Rajah told us that you were here. He has sent me on to say that he will arrive to-morrow. I am to see to his apartments, and to have all in readiness. He intends to stay here some days before returning to Tripataly."

"Will he come to this hotel?"

"No, lady, he will take the house he always has when he is here; it is kept for the use of our princes when they come down to Madras. He bade me say that he hopes you will remain here, for that none of the rooms could be got ready at such a short notice; he has not written, for he hates writing, which is a thing that he has small occasion for. I was to tell you that his heart rejoiced at the thought of seeing you again, and that his love for you is as warm as it was when you were a boy and girl together."

"This is my son, Rajbullub. He has often heard me speak of you."

"Yes, indeed," Dick said warmly. "I heard how you saved her from being bitten by a cobra when she was a little girl."

"Ah! the young lord speaks our tongue," Rajbullub said, with great pleasure. "We wondered whether you would have taught it to him. If it had not been that you always wrote to my lord in our language, we should have thought that you yourself would surely have forgotten it after dwelling so long among the white sahibs."

"No, we always speak it when together, Rajbullub. I thought that he might some day come out here, and that he would find it very useful; and I, too, have been looking forward to returning for a time to the home where I was born."

There were many questions to ask about her brother, his wife and two sons; they were younger than Dick, for Mrs. Holland was three years senior to the Rajah. At last she said, "I will not detain you longer, Rajbullub. I know that you will have a great deal to do to get ready for my brother's coming. At what time will he arrive?"

"He hopes to be here by ten in the morning, before the heat of the day sets in."

"I shall, of course, be there to meet him."

"So he hoped, lady. He said that he would have come straight here first, but he thought it would be more pleasant for you to meet him in privacy."

"Assuredly it would," she agreed.

"I will bring a carriage for you here at nine o'clock, and take you and my young lord to the Rajah's house."

At the appointed time a handsome carriage and pair drove up to the door of the hotel, and in ten minutes Mrs. Holland and Dick alighted in the courtyard of a large house. Four native servants were at the door, and the old officer led the way to a spacious room. This was carpeted with handsome rugs; soft cushions were piled on the divan running round the room, the divan itself being covered with velvet and silk rugs; looking-glasses were ranged upon the walls; a handsome chandelier hung from the roof; draperies of gauze, lightly embroidered with gold, hung across the windows.

"Why, Rajbullub, you have done wonders—that is, if the house was unfurnished yesterday."

"It is simple," the Hindoo said. "My lord your brother, like other rajahs who use the house when they come down here, has a room upstairs in which are kept locked up everything required for furnishing the rooms he uses. Four of his servants came down here with me. We had but to call in sweepers to clear the house from dust and wash down the marble floors, and then everything was put into its place. The cook, who also came down, has hired assistants, and all will be ready for my lord when he arrives."

In half-an-hour one of the servants ran in and announced that the Rajah was in the courtyard. There was a great trampling of hoofs, and a minute later he ascended the stairs and was met by his sister and Dick at the door of the room. Mrs. Holland had attired herself handsomely, not so much for the sake of her brother, but that, as his sister, those with him would expect to see in her an English lady of position, and Dick thought that he had never seen her looking so well as when, in a dress of rich brocade, and with a flush of pleasure and expectation on her cheeks, she advanced to the door. She was still but a little over thirty-three years old, and although the long years of anxiety and sorrow had left their traces on her face, the rest and quiet of the sea voyage had done much to restore the fulness of her cheeks and to soften the outline of her figure. The Rajah, a young and handsome-looking man of thirty, ascended the stairs with an eagerness and speed that were somewhat at variance with Dick's preconceived ideas of the stateliness of an Eastern prince.

"My sister Margaret!" he exclaimed in English, and embraced her with a warmth that showed that his affection for her was unimpaired by the years that had passed since he last saw her. Then he stood with his hands on her shoulders, looking earnestly at her. "I know you again," he said; "you are changed, but I can recall your face well. You are welcome, Margaret, most welcome. And this is my nephew?" he went on, turning to Dick and holding out both his hands to him. "You are taller than I expected—well-nigh as tall as I am. You are like your mother and my mother, and you are bold and active and strong, she writes me. My boys are longing to see you, and you will be most welcome at Tripataly. I have almost forgotten my English, Margaret"—and indeed he spoke with some difficulty, evidently choosing his words—"I should quite have forgotten it, had not I often had occasion to speak it with English officers. I see by your letters that you have not forgotten our tongue."

"Not in the least, Mortiz. I have for years spoken nothing else with Dick, and he speaks it as well as I do."

"That is good," the Rajah replied, in his own tongue, and in a tone of relief. "I was wondering how he would get on with us. Now let us sit down. We have so much to tell each other, and, moreover, I am ravenous for breakfast, as I have ridden forty miles since sunrise."

Breakfast was speedily served, the Rajah eating in English fashion.

"I cling to some of our mother's ways you see, Margaret. As I have grown older I have become more English than I was. Naturally, as a boy of thirteen, as I was when you last saw me, I listened to the talk of those around me and was guided by their opinions a good deal. Among them there was a feeling of regret that our father had married an English woman, and I of course was ever trying my hardest to show that in riding, or the chase, or in exercises of any kind, I was as worthy to be the son of an Indian rajah as if I had no white blood in my veins. As I grew up I became wiser. I saw how great the English were, how steadily they extended their dominions, and how vastly better off were our people under their sway than they were in the days when every rajah made war against his neighbour, and the land never had rest. Then I grew proud of my English blood, and although I am to my people Rajah of Tripataly, a native prince and lord of their destinies, keeping up the same state as my father, and ruling them in native fashion, in my inner house I have adopted many English ways. My wife has no rival in the zenana. I encourage her to go about as our mother did, to look after the affairs of the house, to sit at table with me, and to be my companion, and not a mere plaything; I am sure, Margaret, your stay with us will do her much good, and she will learn a great deal from you."

"You have heard no news since you last wrote, Mortiz?"

A slight cloud passed across the Rajah's animated face.

"None, Margaret. We have little news from beyond the mountains. Tippoo hates us who are the friends of the English as much as he hates the English themselves, so there is little communication between Mysore and the possessions of the Nabob of Arcot. We will talk later on of the plans you wrote of in your last letter to me."

"You do not think that they are hopeless, Mortiz?" Mrs. Holland asked anxiously.

"I would not say that they are hopeless," he said gently, "although it seems to me that, after all these years, the chances are slight indeed that your husband can be alive; and the peril and danger of the enterprise that, so far as I understood you, you intend your son to undertake, would be terrible indeed."

"We see that, Mortiz; Dick and I have talked it over a thousand times. But so long as there is but a shadow of a chance of his finding his father, he is ready to undertake the search. He is a boy in years, but he has been trained for the undertaking, and will, when the trial comes, bear himself as well as a man."

"Well, Margaret, I shall have plenty of opportunities for forming my own judgment, because of course he will stay with us a long time before he starts on the quest, and it will be better to say no more of this now. Now tell me about London. Is it so much a greater city than Madras?"

Mrs. Holland sighed. She saw by his manner that he was wholly opposed to her plan, and although she was quite prepared for opposition, she could not help feeling disappointed. However, she perceived that, as he said, it would be better to drop the subject for a time, and she accordingly put it aside and answered his questions.

"Madras is large—that is, it spreads over a wide extent;

but if it were packed with houses as closely as they could stand, it would not approach London, in the number of its population."

"How is it that the English do not send more troops out here, Margaret?"

"Because they can raise troops here, and English soldiers cannot stand the heat as well as those born to it. Moreover, you must remember that at present England is at war, not only with France and half Europe, but also with America. She is also obliged to keep an army in Ireland, which is greatly disaffected. With all this on her hands she cannot send a large army so far across the seas, especially when her force here is sufficient for all that can be required of it."

"That is true," he said. "It is wonderful what they have done out here with such small forces. But they will have harder work, before they conquer all India—as I believe they will do—than they have yet encountered. In spite of Tippoo's vauntings, they will have Mysore before many years are over. The Sultan seems to have forgotten the lesson they taught him six or seven years back. But the next time will be the last, and Tippoo, tiger as he is, will meet the fate he seems bent on provoking. But beyond Mysore lies the Mahratta country, and the Mahrattas alone can put thirty thousand horsemen into the field. They are not like the people of Bengal, who have ever fallen, with scarce an attempt at resistance, under the yoke of one tyrant after another. The Mahrattas are a nation of warriors; they are plunderers if you will, but they are brave and fearless soldiers, and might, had they been united, have had all India under their feet before the coming of the English. That chance has slipped from them. But when we—I say 'we' you see, Margaret—meet them, it will be a desperate struggle indeed."

"We shall thrash them, Uncle," Dick broke in; "you will see that we shall beat them thoroughly."

The Rajah smiled at Dick's impetuosity.

"So you think English soldiers cannot be beaten, eh?"

"Well, Uncle, somehow they never do get beaten. I don't know how it is. I suppose that it is just obstinacy. Look how we thrashed the French here, and they were just as well drilled as our soldiers, and there were twice as many of them."

The Rajah nodded.

"One secret of our success, Dick, is that the English get on better with the natives here than the French do—I don't know why, except what I have heard from people who went through the war; they say that the French always seemed to look down on the natives, and treated even powerful allies with a sort of haughtiness that irritated them and made them ready to change sides at the first opportunity, while the British treated them pleasantly, so that there was a real friendship between them."

Dick, finding that the conversation now turned to the time when his mother and uncle were girl and boy together, left them and went downstairs. He found some twenty horses ranged in the courtyard, while their riders were sitting in the shade, several of them being engaged in cooking. These were the escort who had ridden with the Rajah from Tripataly—for no Indian prince would think of making a journey unless accompanied by a numerous retinue. Scarcely had he entered the yard than Rajbullub came up with the officer in command of the escort, a fine-looking specimen of a Hindoo soldier. He salaamed as Rajbullub presented him to Dick. The lad addressed him at once in his own tongue, and they were soon talking freely together. The officer was surprised at finding that his lord's nephew from beyond the sea was able to speak the language like a native. First Dick asked the nature of the country and the places at which they would halt on their way; then he inquired what force the Rajah could put into the field, and was somewhat disappointed to hear that he kept up but a hundred horsemen, including those who served as an escort.

"You see, Sahib, there is no occasion for soldiers. Now that the whites are the masters, they do the fighting for us.

When the Rajah's father was a young man, he could put two thousand men under arms, and he joined at the siege of Trichinopoly with twelve hundred. But now there is no longer need for an army; there is no one to fight. Some of the young men grumble, but the old ones rejoice at the change. Formerly they had to go to the plough with their spears and their swords beside them, because they never knew when marauders from the hills might sweep down; besides, when there was war, they might be called away for weeks, while the crops were wasting upon the ground. As to the younger men who grumble, I say to them, 'If you are tired of a peaceful life, go and enlist in a Company's regiment'; and every year some of them do so. In other ways the change is good. Now that the Rajah has no longer to keep up an army, he is not obliged to squeeze the cultivators; therefore they pay but a light rent for their lands, and the Rajah is far better off than his father was; so that on all sides there is content and prosperity. But even now the fear of Mysore has not quite died out."

"My position, Margaret," the Rajah said, after Dick had left the room, "is a very precarious one. When Hyder Ali marched down here, eight years ago, he swept the whole country from the foot of the hills to the sea coast. My father would have been glad to stand neutral, but was, of course, bound to go with the English, as the Nabob of Arcot, his nominal sovereign, went with them. His sympathies were, of course, with your people, but most of the chiefs were at heart in favour of Hyder; it was not that they loved him, or preferred the rule of Mysore to that of Madras. But at that time Madras was governed by imbeciles; its Council was composed entirely of timid and irresolute men. It was clear to all that before any force capable of withstanding him could be put in the field, the whole country beyond reach of the guns of the forts at Madras would be at the mercy of Hyder. What that mercy was, had been shown elsewhere. Whole populations had been either massacred or carried off as slaves. Therefore, when the storm was clearly about to burst, almost all of them sent secret messages to Hyder, to assure him that their sympathies were with him, and that they would gladly hail him as ruler of the Carnatic.

"My father was in no way inclined to take such a step. His marriage with an English woman, the white blood in my veins, and his long-known partiality for the English, would have marked him for certain destruction; and as soon as he received news that Hyder's troops were in movement, he rode with me to Madras. At that time his force was comparatively large, and he took three hundred men down with us. He had allowed all who preferred it to remain behind; and some four hundred stayed to look after their families. Most of the population took to the hills, and as Hyder's forces were too much occupied to spend time in scouring the ghauts in search of fugitives, when there was so much loot and so many captives ready to their hands on the plains, the fugitives for the most part remained there in safety. The palace was burnt, the town sacked and partly destroyed, and some fifteen hundred of our people who had remained in their homes, killed or carried off.

"My father did some service with our horse, and I fought by his side. We were with Colonel Baillie's force when it was destroyed, after for two days resisting the whole of Hyder Ali's army. Being mounted, we escaped, and reached Madras in safety, after losing half our number. But all that I can tell you about some other day.

"When peace was made and Hyder retired, we returned home, rebuilt the palace, and restored the town. But if Tippoo follows his father's example and sweeps down from the hills, there will be nothing for it but to fly again. Tippoo commanded one of the divisions of Hyder's army last time, and showed much skill and energy, and has, since he came to the throne, been a scourge to his neighbours in the north. So far as I can see, Madras will be found as unprepared as it was last time; and although the chiefs of Vellore, Arcot,

Conjeveram, and other places may be better disposed towards the English than they were before—for the Carnatic had a terrible lesson last time—they will not dare to lift a finger against him until they see a large British force assembled.

"So you see, sister, your position will be a very precarious one at Tripataly, and it is likely that at any time we may be obliged to seek refuge here. The trouble may come soon, or it may not come for a year; but, sooner or later, I regard it as certain that Tippoo will strive to obtain what his father failed to gain—the mastership of the Carnatic. Indeed, he makes no secret of his intention to become lord of the whole of southern India. The Nizam, his neighbour in the north, fears his power, and could offer but a feeble resistance, were Tippoo once master of the south and west coast. The Mahrattas can always be bought over, especially if there is a prospect of plunder. He relies, too, upon aid from France; for although the French, since the capture of Pondicherry, have themselves lost all chance of obtaining India, they would gladly aid in any enterprise that would bring about the fall of English predominance here.

"There are, too, considerable bodies of French troops in the pay of the Nizam, and these would at any rate force their master to remain neutral in a struggle between the English and Tippoo. However, it will be quite unnecessary that you should resume our garb, or that Dick should dress in the same fashion. Did I intend to remain at Tripataly, I should not wish to draw the attention of my neighbours to the fact that I had English relations resident with me. Of course, every one knows that I am half English myself, but that is an old story now. They would, however, be reminded of it, and Tippoo would hear of it, and would use it as a pretext for attacking and plundering us. But as I have decided to come down here, there is no reason why you should not dress in European fashion."

"We would remain here, brother," Mrs. Holland said, "rather than bring danger upon you. Dick could learn the ways of the country here as well as with you, and could start on his search without going to Tripataly."

"Not at all, Margaret. Whether you are with me or not, I shall have to leave Tripataly when Tippoo advances, and your presence will not in any way affect my plans. My wife and sons must travel with me, and one woman and boy, more or less, will make no difference. At present this scheme of yours seems to me to border on madness. But we need not discuss that now; I shall at any rate be very glad to have you both with me. The English side of me has been altogether in the background since you went away; and though I keep up many of the customs our mother introduced, I have almost forgotten the tongue, though I force myself to speak it sometimes with my boys, as I am sure that in the long run the English will become the sole masters of southern India, and it will be a great advantage to them to speak the language. However, I have many other things to see about, and the companionship of Dick will benefit them greatly. You know what it always is out here. The sons of a rajah are spoilt early by every one giving way to them and their being allowed to do just as they like; naturally they get into habits of indolence and self-indulgence, and never have occasion to exert themselves or to obtain the strength and activity that make our mother's countrymen irresistible in battle. They have been taught to shoot and to ride, but they know little else, and I am sure it will do them an immense deal of good to have Dick with them for a time. If nothing comes of this search for your husband, I hope you will take up your residence permanently at Tripataly. You have nothing to go back to England for, and Dick, with his knowledge of both languages, should be able to find good employment in the Company's service."

"Thank you greatly, brother. If, as you say, my quest should come to nothing, I would gladly settle down in my old home. Dick's inclinations at present turn to the sea, but I have no doubt that what you say is true, and that there may be far more advantageous openings for him out here. However, that is a matter for us to talk over in the future."

The Rajah stayed four days at Madras. Every morning the carriage came at nine o'clock to fetch Mrs. Holland, who spent several hours with her brother, and was then driven back to the hotel, while Dick wandered about with Rajbullub through the native town, asking questions innumerable, observing closely the different costumes and turbans, and learning to know at once the district, trade, or caste, from the colour or fashion of the turban and other little signs.

The shops were an endless source of amusement to him, and he somewhat surprised his companion by his desire to learn the names of all the little articles and trinkets, even of the various kinds of grain. Dick, in fact, was continuing his preparations for his work. He knew that ignorance of any trifling detail which would, as a matter of course, be known to every native, would excite more surprise and suspicion than would be caused by a serious blunder in other matters, and he wrote down in a note-book every scrap of information he obtained, so as to learn it by heart at his leisure. Rajbullub was much surprised at the lad's interest in all these little matters, which, as it seemed to him, were not worth a thought on the part of his lord's nephew.

"You will never have to buy these things, Sahib," he said; "why should you trouble about them?"

"I am going to be over here some time, Rajbullub, and it is just as well to learn as much as one can. If I were to stroll into the market in Tripataly, and had a fancy to buy any trifle, the country people would laugh in my face were I ignorant of its name."

His companion shook his head.

"They would not expect any white sahib to know such things," he said. "If he wants to buy anything, the white sahib points to it and asks, How much? Then, whether it is a brass iota, or a silver trinket, or a file, or a bunch of fruit, the native says a price four times as much as he would ask any one else. Then the sahib offers him half, and after protesting many times that the sum is impossible, the dealer accepts it, and both parties are well satisfied. If you have seen anything that you want to buy, sahib, tell me, and I will go and get it for you; then you will not be cheated."

The start for Tripataly was made at daybreak. Dick and his mother drove in an open carriage that had been hired for the journey; the Rajah rode beside it or cantered on ahead; his escort followed the vehicle. The luggage had been sent off two days before, by cart.

The country as far as Arcot was flat; but everything was interesting to Dick, and when they arrived at the city, where they were to stop for the night at the house the Rajah had occupied on his way down, he sallied out, as soon as their meal was over, to inspect the fort and walls. He had, during his outward voyage, eagerly studied the history of Clive's military exploits, and the campaigns by which that portion of India had been wrested from the French; and he was eager to visit the fort whose memorable defence by Clive had first turned the scale in favour of the British. These had previously been regarded by the natives as a far less warlike people than the French, who were expected to drive them, in a very short time, out of the country.

Rajbullub was able to point out to him every spot associated with the stirring events of that time.

"'Tis forty-six years back, and I was but a boy of twelve; but six years later I was here, for our rajah was on the side of the English, although Tripataly was, and is now, under the Nabob of Arcot. But my lord had many causes of complaint against him, and when he declared for the French, our lord, who was not then a rajah, although chief of a considerable district, threw in his lot with the English, and, when they triumphed, was appointed rajah by them; and Tripataly was made almost wholly independent of the Nabob of Arcot. At one time a force of our men was here with four companies of white troops, when it was thought that Dupleix was likely to march against us, and I was with that force and so learned all about the fighting here."

The next day the party arrived, late in the evening, at Tripataly. A large number of men with torches received them in front of the palace, and on entering, Mrs. Holland was warmly received by the Rajah's wife, who carried her off at once to her apartments, which she did not leave afterwards, as she was greatly fatigued by the two long days of travel. Dick, on the contrary, although he had dozed in the carriage for the last two or three hours of the journey, woke up thoroughly as they neared Tripataly. As soon as they entered the house, the Rajah called his two sons, handsome, dark-faced lads of twelve and thirteen.

"This is your cousin, boys," he said. "You must look after him and see that he has everything he wants, and make his stay as pleasant as you can."

Although a little awed by the, to them, tall figure, they evinced neither shyness or awkwardness, but, advancing to Dick, held out their hands one after the other with grave courtesy. Their faces both brightened as he said in their own language,—

"I hope we shall be great friends, cousins. I am older and bigger than you are, but everything is new and strange to me, and I shall have to depend upon you to teach me everything."

"We did not think that you would be able to talk to us," the elder, whose name was Doast Assud, said, smiling. "We have been wondering how we should make you understand. Many of the white officers, who come here sometimes, speak our language, but none of them as well as you do."

"You see, they only learn it after they come out here, while I learnt it from my mother, who has talked to me in it since I was quite a little boy; so it comes as naturally to me as to you."

In a few minutes supper was announced. The two boys sat down with their father and Dick, and the meal was served in

English fashion. Dick had already become accustomed to the white-robed servants at the hotel at Madras, and everything seemed to him pleasant and home-like.

"To-morrow, Dick," his uncle said, "you must have your first lesson in riding."

The two boys looked up in surprise. They had been accustomed to horses from their earliest remembrance, and it seemed to them incredible that their tall cousin should require to be taught. Dick smiled at their look of astonishment.

"It is not with us in England as it is here," he said. "Boys who live in the country learn to ride, but in London, which is a very great town, with nothing but houses for miles and miles everywhere, few people keep horses to ride. The streets are so crowded with vehicles of all sorts, and with people on foot, that it is no pleasure to ride in them, and every one who can afford it goes about in a carriage. Those who cannot, go in hired vehicles, or on foot. You would hardly see a person on horseback once in a week."

"I do not like walking," Doast said gravely.

"Well, you see, you have no occasion to walk, as you always have your horses; besides, the weather here is very hot. But in England it is colder, and walking is a pleasure. I have walked over twenty miles a day many times, not because I had to do it, but as a day's pleasure with a friend."

"Can you shoot, cousin?"

"No," Dick laughed. "There is nothing to shoot at. There are no wild beasts in England, and no game birds anywhere near London."

Dick saw at once that he had descended many steps in his cousins' estimation.

"Then what can you find to do?" the younger boy asked.

"Oh, there is plenty to do," Dick said. "In the first place, there is school; that takes the best part of the day. Then there are all sorts of games. Then I used to take lessons in sword-exercise, and did all sorts of things to improve my muscles and to make me strong. Then, on holidays, three or four of us would go for a long walk, and sometimes we went out on the river in a boat; and every morning early we used to go for a swim. Oh, I can tell you, there was plenty to do and I was busy from morning till night. But I want very much to learn to shoot, both with gun and pistol, as well as to ride."

"We have got English guns and pistols," Doast said. "We will lend them to you; we have a place where we practise. Our father says every one ought to be able to shoot, don't you, father?"

The Rajah nodded.

"Every one out here ought to, Doast, because, you see, every man here may be called upon to fight, and every one carries arms. But it is different in England; nobody fights there, except those who go into the army, and nobody carries weapons."

"What! not swords, pistols, and daggers, father?" Doast exclaimed, in surprise; for to him it seemed that arms were as necessary a part of attire as a turban, and much more necessary than shoes. "But when people are attacked by marauders, or two chiefs quarrel with each other, what can they do if they have no arms?"

"There are no marauders and no chiefs," Dick laughed. "In the old times, hundreds of years ago, there were nobles who could call out all their tenants and retainers to fight their battles, and in those days people carried swords as they do here. There are nobles still, but they have no longer any power to call out any one, and if they quarrel they have to go before a court for the matter to be decided, just as every one else does."

This seemed to Doast a very unsatisfactory state of things, and he looked to his father for an explanation.

"It is as your cousin says, Doast. You have been down with me to Madras, and you have seen that, except the officers in the army, none of the Europeans carry arms. It is the same in England. England is a great island, and as they have many ships of war, no enemy can land there. There is one king over the whole country, and there are written laws by which every one, high and low alike, are governed. So you see, no one has to carry arms: all disputes are settled by the law, and there is peace everywhere; for as nothing would be settled by fighting, and the law would punish any one, however much in the right he might be, who fought, there is no occasion at all for weapons. It is a good plan, for you see no one, however rich, can tyrannise over others; and were the greatest noble to kill the poorest peasant, the law would hang him just the same as it would hang a peasant who killed a lord. And now, boys, you had better be off to bed. Your cousin has had a long day of it, and I have no doubt he will be glad to do so. To-morrow we will begin to teach him to ride and to shoot, and I have no doubt that he will be ready, in return, to teach you a great deal about his country."

The boys got up. But Doast paused to ask his father one last question.

"But how is it, father, if the English never carry weapons and never fight, that they are such brave soldiers? For have they not conquered all our princes and rajahs, and have even beaten Tippoo Sahib and made him give them much of his country?"

"The answer would be a great deal too long to be given to-night, Doast. You had better ask your cousin about it in the morning."

CHAPTER IV.

FIRST IMPRESSIONS.

THE next morning Dick was up early, eager to investigate the place, of which he had seen little the night before. The house was large and handsome, the Rajah having added to it gradually every year. On passing the doors, the great hall was at once entered; its roof, of elaborately carved stone, was supported by two rows of pillars with sculptured capitals. The floor was made of inlaid marble, and at one end was raised a foot above the general level. Here stood a stone chair on which the Rajah sat when he adjudicated upon disputes among his people, heard petitions, and gave audiences; while a massive door on the left-hand side gave entrance to the private apartments. These were all small in comparison with the entrance hall. The walls were lined with marble slabs, richly carved, and were dimly lighted by windows, generally high up in the walls, which were of great thickness. The marble floors were covered with thick rugs, and each room had its divan, with soft cushions and rich shawls and covers. The room in which they had supped the night before was the only exception. This had been specially furnished and decorated in English fashion. The windows here were low and afforded a view over the garden. Next to it were several apartments, all fitted with divans, but with low windows and a bright outlook; they could be darkened during the heat of the day by shutters. With the exception of these windows, the others throughout the house contained no glass, the light entering through innumerable holes that formed a filigree work in the thin slabs of stone that filled the orifices.

The grounds round the palace were thickly planted with trees, which constituted a grove rather than a garden, according to Dick's English notions. This was, indeed, the great object of the planter, and numerous fountains added to the effect of the overhanging foliage. Dick wandered about, delighted. Early as it was, men with water-skins were at work among the clumps of flowers and shrubs that covered the ground wherever there was a break among the trees. Here and there were small pavilions whose roofs of sculptured stone were supported by shafts of marble. The foliage of shrubs and trees alike was new to Dick, and the whole scene delighted him. Half-an-hour later his two cousins joined him.

"We wondered what had become of you," Doast said, "and should not have found you if Rajbullub had not told us that he saw you come out here. Come in now; coffee is ready. We always have coffee the first thing, except in very hot weather, when we have fruit sherbet. After that we ride or shoot till the sun gets hot, and then come in to the morning meal at ten."

On going in, Dick found that his mother and the ranee were both up, and they all sat down to what Dick considered a breakfast, consisting of coffee and a variety of fruit and bread. One or two dishes of meat were also handed round, but were taken away untouched.

"Now come out to the stables, Dick," the Rajah said. "Anwar, the officer who commanded the escort, will meet us there. He will be your instructor."

The stables were large. The horses were fastened to rings along each side, and were not, as in England, separated from each other by stalls. A small stone trough, with running water, was fixed against each wall at a convenient height, and beneath this was a pile of fodder before each horse.

"This is the one that I have chosen for you," the Rajah said, stopping before a pretty creature, that possessed a considerable proportion of Arab blood, as was shown by its small head; "it is very gentle and well trained, and is very fast. When you have got perfectly at ease upon it you shall have something more difficult to sit, until you are able to ride any horse in the stable bare-backed. Murad is to be your own property as long as you are out here."

A syce led the horse out; it was bridled but unsaddled, and Anwar gave a few instructions to Dick and then said, "I will help you up, but in a short time you will learn to vault on to his back without any assistance. See! you gather your reins so, in your left hand, place your right hand on its shoulder, and then spring up."

"I can do that now," Dick laughed, and, placing his hand on the horse's shoulder, he lightly vaulted into his seat.

"Well done, Dick," the Rajah said, while the two boys, who had been looking on with amused faces, clapped their hands.

"Now Sahib," Anwar went on, "you must let your legs

hang easily. Press with your knees, and let your body sway slightly with the movement of the horse; balance yourself rather than try to hold on."

"I understand," Dick said. "It is just as you do on board ship when she is rolling a bit. Let go the reins."

For half-an-hour the horse proceeded at a walk along the road that wound in and out through the park-like grounds. "I begin to feel quite at home," Dick said, at the end of that time. "I should like to go a bit faster now. It is no odds if I do tumble off."

"Shake your rein a little; the horse will understand it," Anwar said.

Dick did so, and Murad at once started at a gentle canter. Easy as it was, Dick thought several times that he would be off. However, he gripped as tightly as he could with his knees, and as he became accustomed to the motion and learned to give to it, acquired ease and confidence. He was not, however, sorry when, at the end of another half-hour, Anwar held up his hand as he approached him, and the horse stopped at the slightest touch of the rein. As he slid off, his legs felt as if they did not belong to him, and his back ached so that he could scarce straighten it. The Rajah and his sons had returned to the palace, and the boys were there waiting for him.

"You have done very well, cousin," Doast said, with grave approval; "you will not be long before you can ride as well as we can. Now you had better go up at once and have a bath, and put on fresh clothes."

Dick felt that the advice was good, as, bathed in perspiration, and stiff and sore in every limb, he slowly made his way to his room. For the next month he spent the greater part of his time on horseback. For the first week he rode only in the grounds of the palace; then he ventured beyond, accompanied by Anwar on horseback; then his two cousins joined the party; and, by the end of the month, he was perfectly at home on Murad's back.

So far, he had not begun to practise shooting. "It would be

of no use," the Rajah said, when he one day spoke of it; 'you want your nerves in good order for that, and it requires an old horseman to have his hand steady enough for shooting straight after a hard ride. Your rides are not severe for a horseman, but they are trying for you. Leave the shooting alone, lad; there is no hurry for it."

By this time the Rajah had become convinced that it was useless to try and dissuade either his sister or Dick from attempting the enterprise for which they had come over. Possibly the earnest conviction of the former that her husband was still alive influenced him to some extent, and the strength and activity of Dick showed him that he was able to play the part of a man. He said little, but watched the boy closely, made him go through trials of strength with some of his troopers, and saw him practise with blunted swords with others. Dick did well in both trials, and the Rajah then requested Anwar, who was celebrated for his skill with the tulwar, to give him, daily, half-an-hour's sword-play, after his riding lesson. He himself undertook to teach him to use the rifle and pistol.

Dick threw himself into his work with great ardour, and in a very short time could sit any horse in the stable, and came to use a rifle and pistol with an amount of accuracy that surprised his young cousins.

"The boy is getting on wonderfully well," the Rajah said one day to his sister; "his exercises have given him so much nerve and so steady a hand, that he already shoots very fairly. I should expect him to grow up into a fine man, Margaret, were it not that I have the gravest fears as to this mad enterprise, which I cannot help telling you, both for your good and his, is, in my opinion, absolutely hopeless."

"I know, Mortiz," she said, "that you think it is folly on my part to cling to hope; and while I do not disguise from myself that there would seem but small chance that my husband has survived, and that I can give no reason for my faith in his still being alive, and my confidence that he will be restored to me some day, I have so firm a conviction that nothing will shake it. Why should I have such a confidence if it were not well founded? In my dreams I always see him alive, and I believe firmly that I dream of him so often because he is thinking of me. When he was at sea, several times I felt disturbed and anxious, though without any reason for doing so, and each time, on his return, I found, when we compared dates, that his ship was battling with a tempest at the time I was so troubled about him. I remember that the first time this happened he laughed at me; but when, upon two other occasions, it turned out so, he said, 'There are things we do not understand, Margaret. You know that in Scotland there are many who believe in second sight, as it is called, and that there are families there, and they say in Ireland also, where a sort of warning is given of the death of a member of the family. We sailors are a superstitious people, and believe in things that landsmen laugh at. It does not seem to me impossible that when two people love each other dearly, as we do, one may feel when the other is in danger, or may be conscious of his death. It may be said that such things seldom happen; but that is no proof that they never do so, for some people may be more sensitive to such feelings or impressions than others, and you may be one of them. There is one thing, Margaret: the fact that you have somehow felt when I was in trouble, should cheer you when I am away, for if mere danger should so affect you, surely you will know should death befall me; and as long as you do not feel that, you may be sure that I shall return safe and sound to you.' Now, I believe that firmly. I was once troubled—so troubled, that for two or three days I was ill—and so convinced was I that something had happened to Jack, and yet that he was not dead, that when, nigh two years afterwards, Ben came home, and I learned that it was on the day of the wreck of his ship that I had so suffered, I was not in the least surprised. Since then I have more than once had the same feelings, and have always been sure that at the time Jack was in special danger; but I have never once felt that he was dead, never once thought so, and am as certain that he is still alive as if I saw him sitting in the chair opposite to me, for I firmly believe that, did he die, I should see his spirit, or that, at any rate, I should know for certain that he had gone. So whatever you say, though reason may be altogether on your side, it will not shake my confidence one bit. I know that Jack is alive, and I believe firmly, although of this I am not absolutely sure, that he will some day be restored to me."

"You did not tell me this before, Margaret," the Rajah said, "and what you say goes for much with me. Here in India there are many who, as is said, possess this power that you call second sight; certainly some of the Fakirs do. I have heard many tales of warnings they have given, and these have always come true. I will not try, in future, to damp your confidence, and will hope with you that your husband may yet be restored to you."

One evening Dick remarked: "You said down at Madras, Uncle, that you would some day tell me about the invasion by Hyder Ali. Will you tell me about it now?"

The Rajah nodded. His sons took their seats at his feet, and Dick curled himself up on the divan by his side.

"You must know," the Rajah began, "that the war was really the result of the intrigues of Sir Thomas Rumbold, the governor of Madras, and his council. In the first place they had seriously angered the Nizam; the latter had taken a French force into his service which the English had compelled Basult Jung to dismiss, and Madras sent an officer to his court, with instructions to remonstrate with him for so doing. At the same time they gave him notice that they should no longer pay to him the tribute they had agreed upon, for the territory called the Northern Circars. This would have led to war, but the Bengal government promptly interfered, cancelled altogether the demands made by the Madras government, and for the time patched up the quarrel. The Nizam professed to be satisfied, but he saw that trouble might arise when the English were more prepared to enforce their demands; he

M84

THE RAJAH TELLS THE STORY OF THE WAR.

therefore entered into negotiations with Hyder Ali and the Mahrattas for an alliance, whose object was the entire expulsion of the British from India.

"The Mahrattas from Poonah were to operate against Bombay; those in Central India and the north were to make incursions into Bengal; the Nizam was to invade the Northern Circars; and Hyder was to direct his force against Madras. Hyder at once began to collect military stores, and obtained large quantities from the French at Mahè, a town they still retain, on the Malabar coast. The Madras government prepared to attack Mahè, when Hyder informed them that the settlements of the Dutch, French, and English, on the Malabar coast, being situated within his territory, were equally entitled to his protection, and that if Mahè were attacked, he should retaliate by an incursion into the province of Arcot. In spite of this threat, Mahè was captured. Hyder for a time remained quiet, but the Madras government gave him fresh cause for offence by sending a force in August 1779 to the assistance of Basult Jung at Adoni.

"To get there this detachment had to pursue a route which led for two hundred miles through the most difficult passes, and through the territories both of the Nizam and Hyder. The Council altogether ignored the expressed determination of both these princes to oppose the march, and did not even observe the civility of informing them that they were going to send troops through their territory. I do not say, Dick, that this made any real difference in the end; the alliance between the three native Powers being made, it was certain that war would break out shortly; still, had it not been for their folly in giving Hyder and the Nizam a reasonable excuse for entering upon hostilities, it might have been deferred until the Madras government was better prepared to meet the storm. The Bengal government fortunately again stepped in and undid at least a part of the evil. It took the entire management of affairs out of the hands of Rumbold's council, and its action was confirmed by the Board of Directors, who censured all the proceedings, dismissed Sir Thomas Rumbold and his two chief associates from the Council, and suspended other members.

"The prompt and conciliatary measures taken by the Bengal government appeased the resentment felt by the Nizam, and induced him to withdraw from the Confederacy. Hyder, however, was bent upon war, and the imbecile government here took no steps whatever to meet the storm. The commissariat was entirely neglected; they had no transport train whatever, and the most important posts were left without a garrison. It was towards the end of June that we received the news that Hyder had left his capital at the head of an army of ninety thousand men, of whom twenty-eight thousand were cavalry. He attempted no disguise as to his object, and moved, confident in his power, to conquer the Carnatic and drive the English into the sea. My father had already made his preparations. Everything was in readiness, and as soon as the news reached him, he started for Madras, under the guard of his escort, with my mother and myself, most of the traders of the town, and the landowners, who had gathered here in fear and trembling.

"It was a painful scene, as you may imagine, and I shall never forget the terrified crowds in the streets and the wailing of the women. Many families who then left reached Madras in safety, but of those who remained in the town all are dead or prisoners beyond the hills. Hyder descended through the pass of Changama on the 20th of July, and his horsemen spread out like a cloud over the country, burning, devastating, and slaughtering. Hyder moved with the main army slowly, occupying town after town and placing garrisons in them. You must not suppose that he devastated the whole country; he was too wise for that. He anticipated reigning over it as its sovereign, and had no wish to injure its prosperity. It was only over tracts where he considered that devastation would hamper the movements of an English army, that everything was laid waste.

"On the 21st of August he invested Arcot, and a week later, hearing that the British army had moved out from Madras, he

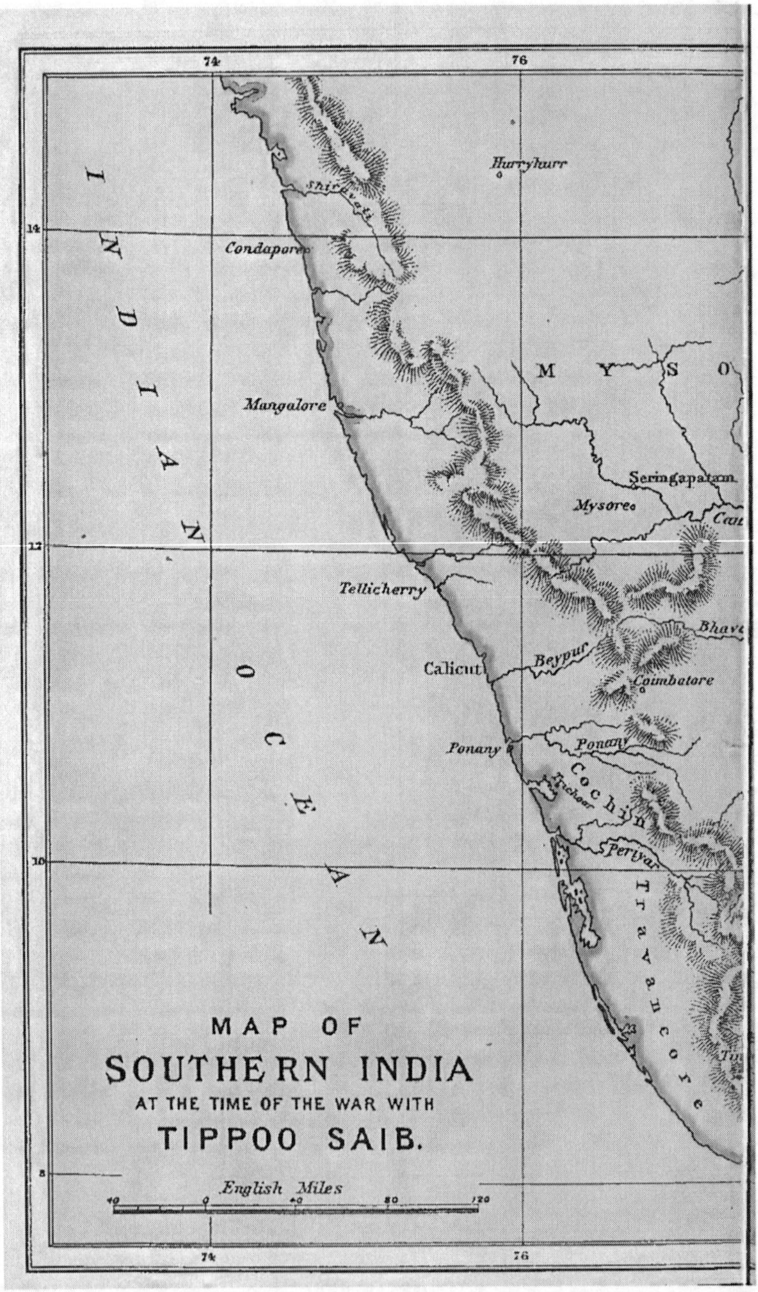

MAP OF
SOUTHERN INDIA
AT THE TIME OF THE WAR WITH
TIPPOO SAIB.
English Miles
INDIAN OCEAN
MYSO
Hurryhurr
Condapore
Mangalore
Seringapatam
Mysore
Tellicherry
Calicut
Beypur
Coimbatore
Ponany
Cochin
Periyar
Travancore
74
76
14
12
10
8

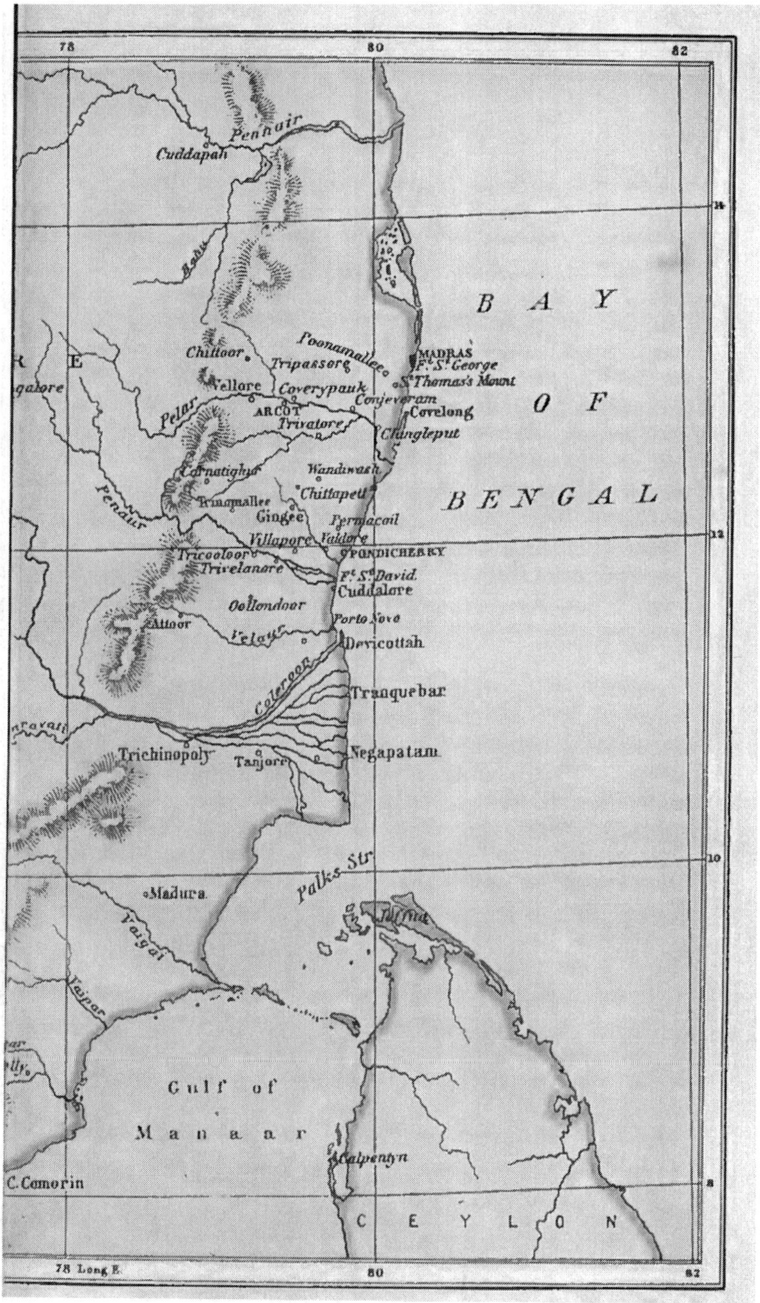
BAY OF BENGAL
Pennair
Cuddapah
MADRAS
Ft. St. George
St. Thomas's Mount
Poonamallee
Chittoor
Tripassore
Vellore
Coverypauk
Conjeveram
Covelong
ARCOT
Trivatore
Chingleput
Pelar
Carnatighur
Wandiwash
Chittapett
Trinomallee
Gingee
Permacoil
Villapore
Valdore
PONDICHERRY
Tricooloor
Trivelanore
Ft. St. David
Cuddalore
Oollondoor
Porto Novo
Attoor
Velaur
Devicottah
Coleroon
Tranquebar
Trichinopoly
Tanjore
Negapatam
Madura
Palks Str
Jaffna
Vaigai
Gulf of Manaar
Calpentyn
C. Comorin
CEYLON
78 Long E.
80
82

broke up the siege and advanced to meet them. Sir Hector Munro, the British general, was no doubt brave, but he committed a terrible blunder; instead of marching to combine his force with that of Colonel Baillie, who was coming down from Guntoor, he marched in the opposite direction to Conjeveram, sending word to Colonel Baillie to follow him. Baillie's force amounted to over two thousand eight hundred men, Munro's to five thousand two hundred. Had they united, the force would have exceeded eight thousand, and could have given battle to Hyder's immense army with fair hope of success. The English have won before now with greater odds against them. My father had marched out with his cavalry one hundred and fifty strong, with Munro. Of course I was with him, and it was to him that the English general gave the despatch to carry to Colonel Baillie. We rode hard, for at any moment Hyder's cavalry might swoop down and bar the road; but we got through safely, and the next morning, the 24th Baillie started.

"The encampment was within twenty-five miles of Madras, and with one long forced march we could have effected a junction with Munro. The heat was tremendous, and Baillie halted that night on the bank of the River Cortelour. The bed was dry, and my father urged him to cross before halting. The colonel replied that the men were too exhausted to move farther, and that as he would the next day be able to join Munro, it mattered not on which side of the river he encamped. That night the river rose, and for ten days we were unable to cross. On the 4th of September we got over; but by that time Tippoo, with five thousand picked infantry, six thousand horse, six heavy guns, and a large body of irregulars, detached by Hyder to watch us, barred the way.

"Colonel Baillie, finding that there was no possibility of reaching Conjeveram without fighting, took up a position at a village, and on the 6th was attacked by Tippoo. The action lasted three hours, and although the enemy were four times more numerous than we were, the English beat off the attacks.

We were not engaged, for against Tippoo's large cavalry force our few horsemen could do nothing, and were therefore forced to remain in the rear of the British line. But though Colonel Baillie had beaten off the attacks made on him, he felt that he was not strong enough to fight his way to Conjeveram, which was but fourteen miles distant, and he therefore wrote to Sir Hector Munro to come to his assistance. For three days Sir Hector did nothing, but on the evening of the 8th he sent off a force composed of the flank companies of the regiments with him. These managed to make their way past the forces both of Hyder and Tippoo, and reached us without having to fire a shot.

"Their arrival brought our force up to over three thousand seven hundred men. Had Munro made a feigned attack upon Hyder, and so prevented him from moving to reinforce Tippoo, we could have got through without much difficulty. But he did nothing; and Hyder, seeing the utter incapacity of the man opposed to him, moved off with his whole army and guns to join his son. Our force set out as soon as it was dark on the evening of the 9th; but the moment we started we were harassed by the enemy's irregulars. The march was continued for five or six miles, our position becoming more and more serious, and at last Colonel Baillie took the fatal resolution of halting till morning, instead of taking advantage of the darkness to press forward. At daybreak fifty guns opened on us. Our ten field-pieces returned the fire until our ammunition was exhausted. No orders were issued by the colonel, who had completely lost his head; so that our men were mowed down by hundreds, until at last the enemy poured down and slaughtered them relentlessly.

"We did not see the end of the conflict. When the colonel gave the orders to halt, my father said to me, 'This foolish officer will sacrifice all our lives; does he think that three thousand men can withstand one hundred thousand, with a great number of guns? We will go while we can; we can do no good here.' We mounted our horses and rode off; in the darkness we came suddenly upon a body of Tippoo's horsemen, but dashed straight at them and cut our way through, but with the loss of half our force, and did not draw rein until we reached Madras. The roar of battle had been heard at Conjeveram, and the fury and indignation in the camp, at the desertion of Colonel Baillie's detachment, was so great that the general at last gave orders to march to their assistance. When his force arrived within two miles of the scene of conflict the cessation of fire showed that it was too late, and that Baillie's force was well-nigh annihilated. Munro retired to Conjeveram, and at three o'clock the next morning retreated, with the loss of all his heavy guns and stores, to Madras.

"The campaign only lasted twenty-one days, and was marked by almost incredible stupidity and incapacity on the part of the two English commanders. We remained at Madras. My father determined that he would take no more share in the fighting until some English general, possessing the courage and ability that had always before distinguished them, took the command. In the meantime Hyder surrounded and captured Arcot after six weeks' delay, and then laid siege to Amboor, Chingleput, and Wandiwash. In November Sir Eyre Coote arrived from England and took the command; confidence was at once restored, for he was a fine old soldier and had been engaged in every struggle in India from the time of Clive; but with the whole country in the hands of Hyder, it was impossible to obtain draft animals or carts, and it was not until the middle of January that he was able to move. On the 19th he reached Chingleput, and on the 20th sent off a thousand men to obtain possession of the fort of Carangooly. It was a strong place, and the works had been added to by Hyder, who had placed there a garrison of seven hundred men. The detachment would not have been sent against it, had not news been obtained on the way that the garrison had fallen back to Chingleput.

"Our troop of cavalry went with the detachment, as my father knew the country well. To the surprise of Captain Davis, who was in command, we found the garrison on the walls.

"'What do you think, Rajah?' Captain Davis, who was riding by his side, asked. 'My orders were that I was to take possession of the place, but it was supposed that I should find it empty.'

"'I should say that you had better try, with or without orders,' my father replied. 'The annihilation of Baillie's force and the miserable retreat of Munro, have made a terribly bad impression through the country, and a success is sorely needed to raise the spirits of our friends.'

"'We will do it,' Captain Davis said, and called up a few English engineers and a company of white troops he had with him, and ordered them to blow in the gate.

"My father volunteered to follow close behind them with his dismounted cavalry, and when the word was given, forward we went. It was hot work, I can tell you. The enemy's guns swept the road, and their musketry kept up an incessant roar. Many fell, but we kept on until close to the gate, and then the white troops opened fire upon Hyder's men on the walls, so as to cover the sappers, who were fixing the powder-bags. They soon ran back to us. There was a great explosion, and the gates fell. With loud shouts we rushed forward into the fort; and close behind us came the Sepoys, led by Captain Davis.

"It took some sharp fighting before we overcame the resistance of the garrison, who fought desperately, knowing well enough that, after the massacre of Baillie's force, little quarter would be given them. The British loss was considerable, and twenty of my father's little company were among the killed. Great stores of provisions were found here, and proved most useful to the army. The news of the capture of Carangooly so alarmed the besiegers of Wandiwash that they at once raised the siege and retreated, and on the following day Sir Eyre Coote and his force arrived there. It was a curious thing that on the same day of the same month Sir Eyre Coote had, twenty-one years before, raised the siege of Wandiwash by a victory over the army that was covering the operation. Wandiwash had been nobly defended by a young lieutenant named Flint, who

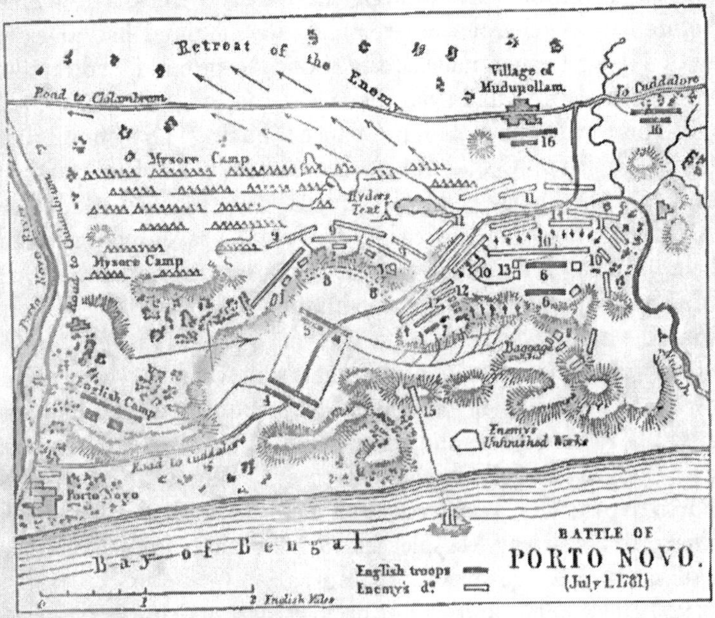

1, 2, 3. The enemy's masked batteries, placed to oppose our march to Cuddalore
4, 5. First and second positions of the English advancing.
6. First English line during the cannonade.
7. Second English line during the cannonade.
8. A chain of Hyder's irregular horse posted as a decoy to the masked batteries.
9. First position of the Mysoreans.
10. Second position of Hyder's infantry, over whom his guns fired from the sand-banks.
11. Position of Hyder's horse during the cannonade.
12. Attempt by Hyder's grenadiers to gain the hill.
13. Attempt by Kiram Saib to charge our line, where he and most of the party were killed.
14. Hyder's station during the action.
15. An armed ship firing upon the enemy.
16. English camp after the battle.

had made his way in through the enemy's lines, a few hours before the treacherous native officer in command had arranged with Hyder to surrender it, and, taking command, had repulsed every attack, and had even made a sortie.

"There was now a long pause; having no commissariat train, Sir Eyre Coote was forced to make for the sea-shore, and, though hotly followed by Hyder, reached Cuddalore. A French fleet off the coast, however, prevented provisions being sent to him, and, even after the French had retired, the Madras government were so dilatory in forwarding supplies that the army was reduced to the verge of starvation. It was not until the middle of June that a movement was possible, owing to the want of carriage. The country inland had been swept bare by Hyder, and, on leaving Cuddalore, Sir Eyre Coote was obliged to follow the sea-coast. When he arrived at Porto Novo, the army was delighted to find a British fleet there, and scarcely less pleased to hear that Lord Macartney had arrived as governor of Madras.

"Hyder's army had taken up a strong position between the camp and Cuddalore, and Sir Eyre Coote determined to give him battle. Four days' rice was landed from the fleet, and with this scanty supply in their knapsacks the troops marched out to attack Hyder. We formed part of the baggage guard and had, therefore, an excellent opportunity of seeing the fight. The march was by the sea. The infantry moved in order of battle in two lines. After going for some distance we could see the enemy's position plainly. It was a very strong one; on its right was high ground, on which were numerous batteries which would take us in flank as we advanced, and their line extended from these heights to the sand-hills by the shore.

"They had thrown up several batteries, and might, for aught we knew, have many guns hidden on the high ground on either flank. An hour was spent in reconnoitring the enemy's position, during which they kept up an incessant cannonade, to which the English field-guns attempted no reply. To me and the officers of this troop it seemed impossible that any force could advance to the attack of Hyder's position without being literally swept away by the cross-fire that would be opened upon it; but when I expressed my fears my father said, 'No; you will see no repetition of that terrible affair with Baillie's column. The English have now got a commander who knows his business, and when that is the case there is never any fear as to what the result will be. I grant that the look-out seems desperate. Hyder has all the advantage of a very strong position, a very powerful artillery, and has six or seven to one in point of numbers; but for all that I firmly believe that before night you will see us in possession of those hills, and Hyder's army in full flight.'

"Presently we saw a movement. The two lines of infantry formed into columns, and instead of advancing towards Hyder's position, turned down towards the sea, and marched along between it and the sand-hills. We were at the same time set in motion, and kept along between the infantry and the sea, so as to be under their protection if Hyder's cavalry should sweep down. All his preparations had been made under the supposition that we should advance by the main road to Cuddalore, and this movement entirely disconcerted his plans. The sand-hills completely protected our advancing columns, and when they had reached a point almost in line with Hyder's centre, the artillery dashed up to the crest of the hills and the first column passed through a break in them and moved forward against the enemy, the guns above clearing a way for them. A short halt was made until the artillery of the second line came up, and also took their position on the hill; then the first column, with its guns, moved forward again.

"Hyder had in the meantime moved back his line and batteries into a position at right angles to that they had before occupied, and facing the passage through the sand-hills by which the English were advancing. As soon as the column issued from the valley a tremendous fire was poured upon it, but it again formed into line of battle, and, covered by the fire of the artillery, moved forward. It was a grand sight. My father and I had left the baggage, which remained by the sea, and had ridden up on to a sand-hill, from which we had a view of the whole of the battle-ground. It was astonishing to see the line of English infantry advancing, under that tremendous fire, against the rising ground occupied by the dense masses of the enemy. Presently there was a movement opposite, and a vast body of cavalry moved down the slope. As they came the red English line suddenly broke up, and, as if by magic, a number of small squares, surrounded by glistening bayonets, appeared where it had stood.

"Down rode Hyder's cavalry. Every gun on our side was turned upon them. But though we could see the confusion in the ranks caused by the shot that swept them, they kept on. It seemed that the little red patches must be altogether overwhelmed by the advancing wave. But as it came closer, flashes of fire spurted out from the faces of the squares. We could see the horses recoil when close to the bayonets, and then the stream poured through the intervals between the squares. As they did so, crackling volleys broke out, while from the batteries on the sand-hills an incessant fire was kept up upon them. Then, following the volleys, came the incessant rattle of musketry. The confusion among the cavalry grew greater and greater. Regiments were mixed up together, and their very numbers impeded their action. Many gallant fellows, detaching themselves from the mass, rode bravely at the squares, and died on the bayonets; others huddled together, confused and helpless against the storm of bullets and shot; and at last, as if with a sudden impulse, they rode off in all directions, and, sweeping round, regained their position in the rear of their infantry, while loud cheers broke from our side.

"The squares again fell into line, which, advancing steadily, drove Hyder's infantry before it. As this was going on, a strong force of infantry and cavalry, with guns, was moved round by Hyder to fall on the British rear. These, however, were met by the second line, which had hitherto remained in reserve, and after fierce fighting were driven back along the sand-hills. But as they were retiring the main body of Hyder's cavalry moved round to support the attack. Fortunately a British schooner, which had sailed from Porto Novo when the troops started, had anchored near the shore to give what protection she could to the baggage, and now opened fire with her guns upon the cavalry as they rode along between the sand-hills and the sea, and with such effect that they halted and wavered; and when two of the batteries on the sand-hills also opened fire upon them, they fell back in haste.

"This was Hyder's last effort. The British line continued to advance until it had gained all the positions occupied by the enemy, and these were soon in headlong flight; Hyder himself, who had been almost forced by his attendants to leave the ground, being with them. It was a wonderful victory. The English numbered but 8,476 men, of whom 306 were killed or wounded. Hyder's force was about 65,000, and his loss was not less than 10,000. The victory had an immense effect in restoring the confidence of the English troops, which had been greatly shaken by the misfortunes caused by the incapacity of Munro and Baillie; but it had no other consequences, for want of carriage, and a deficiency of provisions and equipment, prevented Sir Eyre Coote from taking the offensive, and he was obliged to confine himself to capturing a few forts near the coast.

"On the 27th of August the armies met again, Hyder having chosen the scene of his victory over Baillie's force to give battle, believing the position to be a fortunate one for himself. Hyder had now been joined by Tippoo, who had not been present at the last battle, and his force numbered 80,000 men, while the English were 11,000 strong. I did not see the battle, as we were at the time occupied in escorting a convoy of provisions from Madras. The fight was much better contested than the previous battle had been. Hyder was well acquainted with the ground, and made skilful use of his opportunities, by fortifying all the points at which he could be attacked. The fight lasted eight hours. At last Sir Eyre Coote's first division turned the enemy's left flank by the capture of the village of Pillalore, while his second turned their right, and Hyder was obliged to fall back. But this was done in good order, and the enemy claimed that it was a drawn battle. This, however, was not the case, as the English at night encamped on the position occupied by Hyder in the morning.

"Still the scandalous mismanagement at Madras continued to cripple us. But, learning from the commandant at Vellore that, unless he were relieved, he would be driven to surrender for want of provisions, Sir Eyre Coote marched to his help. He met the enemy on the way. Hyder was taken by surprise, and was moving off when the English arrived. In order to give his infantry time to march away, he hurled the whole of his cavalry against the English. Again and again they charged down with the greatest bravery, and although the batteries swept their ranks with grape, and the squares received them with deadly volleys, they persevered until Tippoo had carried off his infantry and guns, and then, having lost five thousand men, followed him. The English then moved on towards Vellore. Hyder avoided another encounter, and Vellore was relieved. Sir Eyre Coote handed over to its commandant almost the whole of the provisions carried by the army, and, having thus supplied the garrison with sufficient food for six weeks, marched back to Madras, his troops suffering greatly from famine on the way.

"Nothing took place during the winter, except that Sir Eyre Coote again advanced and revictualled Vellore. In March a French fleet arrived off the coast, landed a force of three thousand men to assist Hyder, and informed him that a much larger division was on its way. Fortunately, this did not arrive, many of the ships being captured by the English on their way out. In the course of the year there were several fights, but none of any consequence, and things remained in the same state until the end of the year, when, on the 7th of December, Hyder died, and Tippoo was proclaimed his successor. Bussy arrived with fresh reinforcements from France in April, and took the command of Hyder's French contingent, and in June there was a battle between him and a force commanded by General Stuart, the successor to Sir Eyre Coote, who had been obliged to resign from ill health, and who had died in the spring.

"The French position was a very strong one, and was protected by numerous field-works. The battle was the most sanguinary fought during the war, considering the numbers engaged. The English carried a portion of the works and captured fourteen guns, and, as the French retired during the night, were able to claim a victory. Their loss, however, was over a thousand, while that of the French was not more than a third of that number. During that year there was little fighting down here. A Bombay force, however, under the command of General Matthews, captured Bednore; but Tippoo hastened against him with a great force, besieged Bednore, and forced it to surrender after a desperate defence. Tippoo violated the terms of capitulation, and made the defenders prisoners. Mangalore was next besieged by him, but resisted for nearly nine months, and only surrendered in January 1784.

"Tippoo had, by this time, lost the services of his French auxiliaries, as England and France had made peace at home. Negotiations between Tippoo and the English went on till March, when a treaty was signed. By its provisions, Tippoo should have handed back all his prisoners. He murdered large numbers of them, but 1000 British soldiers and 1600 Sepoys obtained their liberty. No one knows how many were retained of the number, calculated at 200,000, of natives carried off from the countries overrun by Hyder's troops. Only 2000 were released. More British would doubtless have been freed had it not been for the scandalous cowardice of the three men sent up as British commissioners to Tippoo. They were treated with the greatest insult and contempt by him, and, in fear of their lives, were too glad to accept the prisoners he chose to hand over, without troubling themselves in the slightest about the rest, whom they basely deserted and left to their fate."

CHAPTER V.

WAR DECLARED.

"THAT gives you a general idea, Dick, of the war with Tippoo. I saw little of the events after the battle of Porto Novo, as my father was taken ill soon after, and died at Madras. Seeing that there was no probability whatever of the English driving Hyder back until they had much larger forces and a much better system of management, I remained in Madras until peace was made; then I came back here, rebuilt the palace, and have since been occupied in trying to restore the prosperity of my poor people. It is, I feel, a useless task, for it is certain that ere long the English will again be engaged with Mysore, and if they are, it is well-nigh certain that Tippoo's hordes will again sweep down from the hills and carry ruin and desolation everywhere.

"He would, as Hyder had, have the advantage on his side at the beginning of the war. He has a score of passes to choose from, and can descend on to the plain by any one he may select. And even were there a force here capable of giving battle to the whole Mysorean army, it could not watch all the passes, as to do so the army would have to be broken up into a dozen commands. Tippoo will therefore again be able to ravage the plains for weeks, perhaps, before the English can force him to give battle. But there is no army at present in existence of sufficient strength to meet him. The Madras force would have to wait until reinforcements arrived from Calcutta. It was bad before, but it will be worse now Hyder, no doubt, slaughtered many, but he was not cruel by nature. He carried off enormous quantities of people, with their flocks and herds, but he did this to enrich Mysore with their labour, and did not treat them with unnecessary cruelty.

"Tippoo, on the other hand, is a human tiger; he delights in torturing his victims, and slays his prisoners from pure love of bloodshed. He is proud of the title of 'Tiger'; his footstool is a tiger's head, and the uniforms of his infantry are a sort of imitation of a tiger's stripes. He has military talent, and showed great judgment in command of his division—indeed, most of the successes gained during the last war were his work. Since then he has laboured incessantly to improve his army; numbers of regiments have been raised, composed of the captives carried off from here and from the west coast. They are drilled in European fashion by the English captives he still holds in his hands."

"But why, Uncle, instead of giving time to Tippoo to come down here, should we not march up the passes and compel him to keep his army up there to defend Seringapatam?"

"Because, Dick, in the first place, there is not an army strong enough to do so; but even were there a force of fifty thousand men at Madras, they could not take the offensive in time. An English army cannot move without a great train to carry ammunition, stores and provisions; and to get such a train together would be the work of months. As I have been telling you, during the three years the last war lasted, the Madras authorities were never able to collect such a train, and the consequence was that their army was unable to go more than two or three days' march from the city. On the other hand, Tippoo could any day order that three days' supply of rice or grain should be served out to each soldier, and could set out on his march the following morning, as, from the moment he reached the plains, his cavalry would have the whole of the resources of the country at their mercy."

"I see, Uncle. Then, if war broke out, you would at once go to Madras again?"

"There would be nothing else to do, Dick. I should send everything of value down there as soon as I saw that war was inevitable. The traders here have already begun to prepare; the shops are half empty, for they have not replaced goods they have sold, and a very few hours would suffice for everything worth taking to be cleared out of the town. The country round here is comparatively uninhabited, and but a small portion of it tilled, so great was the number carried off by Hyder. Next time they will take to the hills at once, and I believe that many have already stored up grain in hiding-places there. This time it may be hoped that a few weeks, or months at most, may see Tippoo driven back, and for that time the peasants can manage to exist in the hills. No doubt the richer sort, who have large flocks of goats, and many cattle, will, as soon as danger threatens, drive them down to Madras, where they are sure to fetch good prices for the use of the army. I have already told all men who have bullock-carts and teams, that they can, if forced to leave home, earn a good living by taking service in the English transport train. I hope, therefore, that the results will not be so disastrous as before. The town may be burnt down again, but unless they blow up my palace, they can do little harm to it. When I rebuilt it, seeing the possibility of another war, I would not have any wood whatever used in its construction. Therefore, when the hangings are taken down, and the furniture from these rooms cleared out, there will be nothing to burn, and they are not likely to waste powder in blowing it up. As to the town, I warned the people who returned that it might be again destroyed before long, and therefore there has been no solid building. The houses have all been lightly run up with wood, which is plentiful enough in the hills, and no great harm, therefore, will be done if it is again burnt down. The pagoda and palace are the only stone buildings in it. They did some harm to the former last time by firing shot at it for a day or two, and, as you can see for yourself, no attempt has since been made to repair it, and I do not suppose they will trouble to damage it further. So you see, Dick, we are prepared for the worst."

"Will you fight again, as you did last time, Uncle?"

"I do not know, Dick. I show my loyalty to the English rule by repairing to the capital; but my force is too small to render much service. You see, my revenues have greatly diminished, and I cannot afford to keep up so large a force as my father could. Fortunately, his savings had been considerable, and from these I was able to build this palace and to succour my people, and have still enough to keep up my establishment here, without pressing the cultivators of the soil for taxes. This year is the first that I have drawn any revenue from that source; but, at any rate, I am not disposed to keep up a force which, while it would be insufficient to be of any great value in a war like this, would be a heavy tax on my purse."

"Even the force you have, must be that, Uncle."

"Not so much as you would think, Dick, with your English notions. The pay here is very small—so small that it would seem to you impossible for a man to live on it; and yet many of these men have wives and families. All of them have patches of land that they cultivate, only twenty, who are changed once a month, being kept on duty. They are necessary; for I should have but little respect from my people, and less still from other rajahs, did I not have sentries at the gates, and a guard ready to turn out in honour of any visitor who might arrive, to say nothing of an escort of half a dozen men when I ride through the country. Of course, all can be called out whenever I want them, as, for example, when I rode to Madras to meet you. The men think themselves well off upon the pay of three rupees a month, as they are practically only on duty two months each year, and have the rest of the time to cultivate their fields. Therefore, with the pay of the officers, my troop only costs me about four hundred rupees a month, which is, you know, equivalent to forty English pounds; so that you cannot call it an expensive army, even if it is kept for show rather than use."

"No, indeed, Uncle! It seems ridiculous that a troop of a hundred men can be kept up for five hundred pounds a year."

"Of course the men have some little privileges, Dick. They pay no rent or taxes for their lands; this is a great thing for them, and really costs me nothing, as there is so much land lying uncultivated. Then, when too old for service, they have a pension of two rupees a month for life, and on that, and what little land they can cultivate, they are comparatively comfortable."

"Well, it does not seem to me, Uncle, that soldiering is a good trade in this country.'

"I don't know that it is a good trade, in the money way, anywhere. After all, the pay out here is quite as high, in comparison with the ordinary rate of earning of a peasant, as it is in England. It is never the pay that tempts soldiers: among young men there are always great numbers who prefer the life to that of a peasant working steadily from daylight to dark, and I don't know that I altogether blame them."

"Then you think, Uncle, there is no doubt whatever that there will be war?"

"Not a shadow of doubt, Dick—indeed, it may be said to have begun already; and, like the last, it is largely due to the incapacity of the government of Madras."

"I have just received a message from Arcot," the Rajah said, two months later, "and I must go over and see the Nabob."

"I thought," Mrs. Holland said, "that Tripataly was no longer subject to him. I understood that our father was made independent of Arcot?"

"No, Margaret, not exactly that. The Nabob had involved himself in very heavy debts during the great struggle. The Company had done something to help him, but were unable to take all his debts on their shoulders; and indeed, there was no reason why they should have done so, for although during most of the war he was their ally, he was fighting on his own behalf, and not on theirs. In the war with Hyder it was different.

He was then quite under English influence, and, indeed, could scarcely be termed independent. And as he suffered terribly—his lands were wasted, his towns besieged, and his people driven off into slavery—the Company are at present engaged in negotiations for assisting him to pay his debts, which are very heavy. It was before you left, when the Nabob was much pressed for money and had at that time no claim on the Company, that our father bought of him a perpetual commutation of tribute, taxes, and other monies and subsidies, payable by Tripataly; thus I am no longer tributary to Arcot. Nevertheless, this forms a portion of the Nabob's territories, and I cannot act as if I were an independent prince.

"I could not make a treaty with Mysore on my own account, and it is clear that neither Arcot nor the English could allow me to do so, for in that case Mysore could erect fortresses here, and could use Tripataly as an advanced post on the plain; therefore I am still subject to the Nabob, and could be called upon for military service by him. Indeed, that is one of the reasons why, even if I could afford it, I should not care to keep up a force of any strength. As it is, my troop is too small to be worth summoning. The Nabob has remonstrated with me more than once, but since the war with Hyder I have had a good excuse, namely, that the population has so decreased that my lands lie untilled, and it would be impossible for me to raise a larger force. I have, however, agreed that, in case of a fresh war, I will raise an additional hundred cavalry.

"I expect it is in relation to this that he has sent for me to Arcot. We know that the English are bound by their treaty with Travancore to declare war. They ought in honour to have done it long ago, but they were unprepared. Now that they are nearly ready, they may do so at any time, and indeed the Nabob may have learned that fighting has begun. The look-out is bad. The government of Madras is just as weak and as short-sighted as it was during Hyder's war. There is but one comfort, and that is that Lord Cornwallis at Calcutta has far greater power than his predecessors, and as he is an experienced soldier, and is said to be an energetic man, he may bring up reinforcements from Calcutta without loss of time, and also set the troops of Bombay in motion. I expect that, as before, things will go badly at first, but hope that this time we shall end by giving Mysore so heavy a lesson that she will be powerless for mischief in future."

"And release all the captives," Mrs. Holland exclaimed, clasping her hands.

"I sincerely trust so, Margaret," her brother said gravely; "but, after what happened last time, we must not be sanguine. Scattered about as they may be in the scores of little hill-forts that dot the whole country, we can, unhappily, never be sure that all are delivered, when we have only the word of a treacherous tyrant like Tippoo. We know that last time he kept back hundreds of prisoners, among whom, as we may hope, was your husband, and it may be that, however completely he may be defeated, he may yet retain some of them, knowing full well it is impossible that all these hill-forts and their dungeons can be searched. However, doubtless if an English army marches to Seringapatam, many will be recovered, though we have reason to fear that many will, as before, be murdered before our arrival."

When the Rajah returned from Arcot on the following day, he brought back the news that General Meadows had moved to the frontier at Caroor, fifty miles beyond Trichinopoly, and that the war was really about to begin.

"You know," he said, "how matters stand up to now. Tippoo, after making peace with the Nizam and the Mahrattas, with whom he had been engaged in hostilities for some time, turned his attention to the western coast, where Coorg and Malabar had risen in rebellion. After, as usual, perpetrating horrible atrocities, and after sending a large proportion of the population as slaves to Mysore, he marched against Travancore. Now, Travancore was specially mentioned in the treaty of Mangalore as one of the allies of the English, with whom

Tippoo bound himself not to make war; and had he not been prepared to fight the English he would not have attacked their ally. The excuse for attacking Travancore was that some of the fugitives from Coorg and Malabar had taken refuge there.

"Seeing that Tippoo was bent upon hostilities, Lord Cornwallis and his council at Calcutta directed, as I learnt from an official at Madras, the authorities there to begin at once to make preparations for war. Instead of doing so, Mr. Holland, the governor, gave the Rajah the shameful and cowardly advice to withdraw his protection from the fugitives. The Rajah refused to comply with such counsel, and after some months spent in negotiations, Tippoo attacked the wall that runs along the northern frontier of Travancore. That was about six months ago. Yes, it was on the 28th of December—so it is just six months. His troops, fourteen thousand strong, made their way without difficulty through a breach, but they were suddenly attacked by a small body of Travancore men. A panic seized them; they rushed back to the breach, and in the wild struggle to pass through it, no less than two thousand were either killed or crushed to death.

"It was nearly three months before Tippoo renewed his attack. The lines were weak, and his army so strong that resistance was impossible. A breach, three-quarters of a mile in length, was made in the wall, and marching through this he devastated Travancore from end to end. His unaccountable delay before assaulting the position has been of great advantage to us. Had he attacked us at once, instead of wasting his time before Travancore, he would have found the Carnatic as defenceless and as completely at his mercy as Hyder did. He would still have done so had it depended upon Madras, but as the authorities here did nothing, Lord Cornwallis took the matter into his own hands. He was about to come here himself, when General Meadows, formerly Governor of Bombay, arrived, invested by the Company with the offices of both governor and of commander-in-chief.

"He landed here late in February, and at once set to work, to prepare for war. Lord Cornwallis sent from Calcutta a large amount of money, stores, and ammunition, and a battalion of artillerymen. The Sepoys objected to travel by sea, as their caste rules forbade them to do so, and he therefore sent off six battalions of infantry by land, and the Nabob tells me they are expected to arrive in four or five weeks' time. The Nabob of Arcot and the Rajah of Tanjore, both of whom are very heavily in debt to the government, are ordered, during the continuance of the war, to place their revenues at its disposal, a liberal allowance being made to them both for their personal expenses. Tippoo is still in Travancore—at least, he was there ten days ago, and has been endeavouring to negotiate. The Nabob tells me he believes that the object of General Meadows in advancing from Trichinopoly to Caroor, is to push on to Coimbatoor, where he will, if he arrives before Tippoo, cut him off from his return to his capital; and as Meadows has a force of fifteen thousand men, he ought to be able to crush the tyrant at a blow.

"I fear, however, there is little chance of this. The Mysore troops move with great rapidity, and as soon as Tippoo hears that the English army is marching towards Caroor, he is sure to take the alarm, and by this time has probably passed Coimbatoor on his way back. With all his faults, Tippoo is a good general, and the Nabob's opinion—and I quite agree with him—is that, as soon as he regains the table-land of Mysore, he will take advantage of the English army being far away to the south, and will pour down through the passes into this part of the Carnatic, which is at present absolutely defenceless. This being the case, I shall at once get ready to leave for Madras, and shall move as soon as I learn for certain that Tippoo has slipped past the English.

"The Nabob has called upon me to join him with my little body of cavalry, and as soon as the news comes that Tippoo is descending the passes, I shall either join him or the English army. That will be a matter to decide afterwards."

"You will take me with you, of course, Uncle?" Dick asked eagerly.

"Certainly, Dick; if you are old enough to undertake the really perilous adventure of going up in disguise to Mysore, you are certainly old enough to ride with me. Besides, we may hope that this time the war is not going to be as one-sided as it was the last time, and that we may end by reaching Seringapatam; in which case we may rescue your father, if he is still alive, very much more easily than it could be managed in the way you propose."

The news that the English army had marched to Caroor, and that there was no force left to prevent the Mysoreans from pouring down from the hills, spread quickly, and when Dick went out with the two boys into the town, groups of people were talking earnestly in the streets. Some of them came up, and asked respectfully if there was any later news.

"Nothing later than you have heard," Dick said.

"The Rajah is not going away yet, Sahib?"

"No; he will not leave unless he hears that Tippoo has returned with his army to Seringapatam. Then he will go at once, for the sultan might come down through the passes at any moment, and can get here a fortnight before the English army can return from Caroor."

"Yes; it will be no use waiting here to be eaten up, Sahib. Do you think Conjeveram would be safe? Because it is easy to go down there by boat."

"I should think so. Hyder could not take it last time, and the English army is much stronger than it was then. Besides, there will be six thousand men arriving from Bengal in a month's time, so I should think there is no fear of Conjeveram being taken."

"It is little trouble getting there," the trader said, "but it is a long journey to Madras. We could go down with our families and goods in two days in a boat; but there would not be boats enough for all, and it will be best, therefore, that some should go at once, for if all wait until there is news that Tippoo is coming, many will not be able to get away in time."

"No, not in boats," Dick agreed; "but in three days a bullock-cart would get you there."

Next day several of the shops containing the most valuable goods were shut up, and day by day the number remaining open grew smaller.

"It is as I expected," the Rajah said one morning, as he came into the room where the family was sitting. "A messenger has just come in from the Nabob with the news that sickness broke out among the army as soon as they arrived at Caroor, and in twenty-four hours a thousand men were in hospital. This delayed the movement, and when they arrived at Coimbatoor they were too late: Tippoo and his army had already passed, moving by forced marches back to Mysore. Finish your packing, ladies; we will start at daybreak to-morrow morning. I secured three boats four days ago, and have been holding them in readiness. Rajbullub will go in charge of you; there is not the least fear of Tippoo being here for another fortnight at the earliest. I shall ride with the troop; Dick and the boys will go with me. We shall meet you at Conjeveram. I have already arranged with some of our people, who have gone on in their bullock-carts with their belongings, and will unload them there, to be in readiness to take our goods on to Madras, so there will be no delay in getting forward."

By nightfall the apartments were completely dismantled. The furniture was all stowed away in a vault which the Rajah had had constructed for the purpose, when the palace was rebuilt. Access was obtained to it through the floor in one of the private apartments. The floor was of tesselated marble, but some ten squares of it lifted up in a mass, forming together a trap-door, from which steps led down into the vault. When the block was lowered again, the fit was so accurate that, after sweeping a little dust over the joint, the opening was quite imperceptible to any one not aware of the hiding-place. The cushions of the divans were taken down here, as well as the furniture, and all the less valuable carpets, rugs and hangings, while the costlier articles were rolled up into bales for transport.

The silver cups and other valuables were packed in boxes, and were, during the night, carried by coolies down to the boats, over which a guard was placed until morning. Provisions for the journey down the river were also placed on board. The palace was astir long before daybreak. The cushions that had been slept on during the night were carried down to the boats, the boxes of wearing apparel closed and fastened, and a hasty meal was taken. The sun was just rising when they started. One boat had been fitted up with a bower of green boughs, for the use of the two ladies and their four attendants; the other two carried the baggage. After seeing them push off, the Rajah, his sons, and Dick, returned to the palace. Here for a couple of hours he held a sort of audience, and gave his advice to the townspeople and others who came, in considerable numbers, to consult with him. When this was done they went into the courtyard, where all was ready for their departure.

The troop had, during the past week, been raised to two hundred men, many of the young cultivators coming eagerly forward as soon as they heard that the Rajah was going to increase his troop, being anxious to take a share in the adventures that might be looked for, and to avenge the sufferings that had been inflicted on their friends by Hyder's marauders. They were a somewhat motley troop, but this mattered little, as uniformity was unknown among the forces of the native princes. The majority were stout young fellows. All provided their own horses and arms, and although the former lacked the weight and bone of English cavalry horses, they were capable of performing long journeys and of existing on rations on which an English horse would starve.

All were well armed, for any deficiency had been made up from the Rajah's store, and from this a large number of guns had, three days before, been distributed among such of the ryots as intended to take to the hills on the approach of the enemy. Ammunition had also been distributed among them. Every man in the troop carried a shield and tulwar, and on his back was slung a musket or spear; and there were few without pistols in their girdles. They rode half-way to Conjeveram, and stopped for the night at a village—the men sleeping in the open air, while the Rajah, his sons, and Dick, were entertained by the chief man of the place. The next afternoon they rode into Conjeveram, where, just at sunset, the boats also arrived.

The troop encamped outside the town, while the Rajah and his party occupied some rooms that had been secured beforehand for them. In the morning the ladies proceeded in a native carriage with the troop, an officer and ten men following, in charge of the bullock-carts containing the baggage. On reaching Madras, they encamped on the Maidan—a large open space used as a drill-ground for the troops garrisoned there—and the Rajah and his party established themselves in the house occupied by him on the occasion of his last visit. The next day the Rajah went to the Government House and had an interview with the deputy-governor.

"I think," the latter said, after some conversation, "that your troop of cavalry will be of little use to the Nabob. If Tippoo comes down from the hills, he will not be able to take the field against him, and will need all his forces to defend Arcot, Vellore, and his smaller forts, and cavalry would be of no real use to him. Your troop would be of much greater utility to the battalions from Bengal when they arrive; they will be here in three weeks or so, and as soon as they come I will attach you to them. I will write to the Nabob, saying that you were about to join him, but that, in the interest of the general defence, I have thought it better at present to attach you to the Bengal contingent. You see, they will be entirely new to the country, and it will be a great advantage to them to have a troop like yours, many of whom are well acquainted with the roads and general geography of the country. Your speaking English, too, will add to your usefulness.'

"I have a nephew with me who speaks English perfectly, and also Hindustani," the Rajah said. "He is a smart young fellow, and I have no doubt that the officer in command would be able to make him very useful. He is eager to be of service. His father, who was an Englishman, was wrecked some years ago on the west coast, and sent up a prisoner to Mysore; he was not one of those handed over at the time of the peace, but whether he has been murdered, or is still a prisoner in Tippoo's hands, we do not know. My sister came out with the boy, three or four months ago, to endeavour to obtain some news of him."

"I will make a note of it, Rajah; I have no doubt that he will be of great use to Colonel Cockerell."

In the last week in July the Rajah moved with his troop to Conjeveram, and on the 1st of August the Bengal forces arrived there. They were joined at once by three regiments of Europeans, one of native cavalry, and a strong force of artillery, raising their numbers to nine thousand five hundred men. Colonel Kelly took command of the force, and begged the Rajah to advance with his horsemen at once to the foot of the ghauts, to break it up into half-troops, and to capture or destroy any small parties of horse Tippoo might send down by any of the passes to reconnoitre the country and ascertain the movements and strength of the British forces. He was also to endeavour to obtain as much information as he could of what was going on in Mysore, and to ascertain whether Tippoo was still with his army, watching General Meadows in the west, or was moving as if with the intention of taking advantage of the main force of the English being away south to descend into the Carnatic.

The order was a very acceptable one to the Rajah. His troop made a good appearance enough when in company with those of the Nabob of Arcot, but he could not but feel that they looked a motley body by the side of the trained native and European troops; and he was frequently angered by hearing the jeering comments of English soldiers to each other when he rode past them with his troop, and had not a little astonished the speakers more than once by turning round on his horse and abusing them hotly in their own language. He was therefore glad to be off. For such work his men were far better fitted than were even the native cavalry in the Company's service. They were stout, active fellows, accustomed to the hills, and speaking the dialect used by the shepherds and villagers among the ghauts. Proceeding northward through Vellore, he there divided his force into four bodies; he himself with fifty men took up a position at the mouth of the pass of Amboor; another fifty were sent to the pass of Moognee, to the west of Chittoor, under the command of Anwar, the captain of the troop. The rest were distributed among the minor passes.

Dick remained with his uncle, who established himself in a village seven miles up the pass. He was well satisfied with the arrangement, for he was anxious to learn to go about among the hills as a spy, and was much more likely to get leave from his uncle to do so than he would have been from any of the officers of the troop, who would not have ventured to allow the Rajah's nephew to run into danger; in the second place, his especial friend among the officers, a youth named Surajah, son of Rajbullub, was with the detachment. Surajah had been especially picked out by the Rajah as Dick's companion; he generally joined him in his rides, and they had often gone on shooting excursions among the hills. He was about three years Dick's senior, but in point of height there was but little difference between them.

Every day half the troop, under an officer, rode up the pass until within a mile of the fort near the summit, garrisoned by Mysorean troops. They were able to obtain but little information, for the villages towards the upper end of the pass were all deserted and in ruins, the inhabitants never having ventured back since Hyder's invasion. The Rajah was vexed at being able to learn nothing of what was passing on the plateau, and was therefore more disposed than he might otherwise have been to listen to Dick's proposal.

"Don't you think, uncle," the latter said one evening, "that I might try to learn something by going up with Surajah alone? We could strike off into the hills as if on a shooting expedition, just as we used to do from Tripataly, except that I should stain my face and hands. The people in the villages on the top of the ghauts are, every one says, simple and quiet; they have no love for Tippoo or Mysore, but are content to pay their taxes and to work quietly in their fields. There will be little fear of our being interfered with by them."

"You might find a party of Tippoo's troops in one of the villages, Dick, and get into trouble."

"I don't see why we should, uncle. Of course we should not go up dressed as we are, but as shikarees, and when we went into a village, should begin by asking whether the people are troubled with any tigers in the neighbourhood. You see, I specially came out here to go into Mysore in disguise, and I should be getting a little practice in this way, besides obtaining news for you."

"I am certainly anxious to get news, Dick. So far, I have had nothing to send down, except that the reports from all the passes agree in saying that they have learned nothing of any movement on the part of Tippoo, and that no spies have come down the passes, or any armed party whatever. This is good so far as it goes, but it only shows that the other passes are, like this, entirely deserted. Therefore we really know nothing whatever. Even at this moment Tippoo may have fifty thousand men gathered on the crest of the hills, ready to pour down to-morrow through one of the passes; and therefore, as I do not think you would be running any great danger, I consent to your going with Surajah on a scouting expedition on foot among the hills. As you say, you must, of course, disguise yourselves as peasants; you had better, in addition to your guns, each take a brace of pistols, and so armed, even if any of the villagers were inclined to be hostile, they would not care about interfering with you."

"Thank you, uncle. When would you expect us back, if we start to-morrow morning?"

"That must be entirely in your hands, Dick; you would hardly climb the ghauts and light upon a village in one day, and it might be necessary to go farther before you could obtain any news. It is a broken country, with much jungle for some distance beyond the hills, and the villages lying off the roads will have but little communication with each other, and might know nothing whatever of what was happening in the cultivated plains beyond. At any rate, you must not go into any villages on the roads leading to the heads of the passes; for there are forts everywhere and you would be certain to find parties of troops stationed in them. Even before war broke out, I know that this was the case, as they were stationed there to prevent any captives, native or European, escaping from Mysore. You must, therefore, strictly avoid all the main roads, even though it may be necessary to proceed much farther before you can get news. I should think if we say three days going and as many returning, it will be as little as we can count upon, and I shall not begin to feel at all uneasy if you do not reappear for a week. It is of no use your returning without some information as to what is going on in Mysore, and it would be folly to throw away your work and trouble, when in another day or two you might get the news you want. I shall therefore leave it entirely to your discretion."

Greatly pleased at having succeeded beyond his expectations, Dick at once sought out Surajah. The latter was very gratified when he heard that he was to accompany the young Sahib on such an expedition, and at once set about the necessary preparations. There was no difficulty in obtaining in the village the clothes required for their disguises, and one of the sheep intended for the following day's rations was killed, and a leg boiled.

"If we take, in addition to this, ten pounds of flour, a

gourd of ghee, and a little pan for frying the cakes in, we shall be able to get on, without having to buy food, for four or five days; and of course, when we are once among the villages, we shall have no difficulty in getting more. You had better cut the meat off the bone and divide it in two portions, and divide the flour too; then we can each carry our share."

"I will willingly carry it all, Sahib."

"Not at all, Surajah; we will each take our fair share. You see, we shall have a gun, pistols, ammunition, and a tulwar; and that, with seven or eight pounds of food each, and our water-bottles, will be quite enough to carry up the ghauts. The only thing we want now is some stain."

"I will get something that will do, and bring it with me in the morning, Sahib; it won't take you a minute to put on. I will come for you at the first gleam of daylight."

Dick returned to the cottage he occupied with his uncle, and told him what preparations they had made for their journey; and they sat talking over the details for another hour. The Rajah's last words as they lay down for the night were, "Don't forget to take a blanket each; you will want it for sleeping in the open, which you will probably have to do several times, although you may occasionally be able to find shelter in a village."

By the time the sun rose the next morning, they were well upon their way. They had a good deal of toilsome climbing, but by nightfall had surmounted the most difficult portions of the ascent, and encamped, when it became dark, in a small wood. Here they lighted a fire, cooked some cakes of flour, and, with these and the cold meat, made a hearty meal. They had during the day halted twice, and had breakfasted and lunched off some bread, of which they had brought sufficient for the day's journey.

"I suppose there is no occasion to watch, Surajah?"

"I don't know, Sahib; I do not think it will be safe for us both to sleep. There are, as you know, many tigers among these hills, and though they would not approach us as long as the fire is burning brightly, they might steal up and carry one of us off when the fire gets low. I will therefore watch."

"I certainly should not let you do that, without taking my turn," Dick said; "and I feel so tired with the day's work that I do not think I could keep awake for ten minutes. It would be better to sleep in a tree than that."

"You would not get much sleep in a tree, Sahib. I have done it once or twice, when I have been hunting in a tiger-infested neighbourhood, but I got scarcely any sleep, and was so stiff in the morning that I could hardly walk. I would rather sit up all night and keep up a good fire, than do that."

Dick thought for a minute or two, and then got up and walked about under the trees, keeping his eyes fixed upon the branches overhead.

"This will do," he said at last. "Come here, Surajah. There; do you see those two branches coming out in the same direction. At one point they are but five or six feet apart. We might fasten our blankets side by side with the help of the straps of our water-bottles and the slings of the guns, so as to make what are called on board a ship hammocks, and lie there perfectly safe and comfortable."

Surajah nodded.

"I have a coil of leather thong, Sahib; I thought that it might be useful if we wanted to bind a prisoner, or for any other purpose, so I stuffed it into my waist-sash."

"That is good; let us lose no time, for I am quite ready for sleep. I will climb up first."

In ten minutes the blankets were securely fastened side by side, between the branches. Surajah descended, threw another armful of wood on to the fire, placed their meat in the crutch of a bough six feet above the ground, and then climbed the tree again; thus they were soon lying side by side in their blankets. These bagged rather inconveniently under their weight, but they were too tired to mind trifles, and were very soon fast asleep. Dick did not wake until Surajah called him. It was already broad daylight; his companion had slipped down quietly, stirred up the embers of the fire, thrown on more wood, and cooked some chupatties before waking him.

"It is too bad, Surajah," Dick said, as he looked down; "you ought to have woke me. I will unfasten these blankets before I get down; it will save time after breakfast."

Half-an-hour later they were again on their way, and shortly came upon a boy herding some goats; he looked doubtfully at them, but, seeing that they were not Mysorean soldiers, he did not attempt to fly.

"How far is it to the next village, lad?" Surajah asked, "and which is the way? We are shikarees. Are there any tigers about?"

"Plenty of them," the boy said. "I drive the goats to a strong, high stockade every evening, and would not come out before the sun rose for all the money they say the sultan has. Make for that tree, and close to it you will see a spring. Follow that down; it will take you to the village."

After walking for six hours they came to the village. It was a place of some little size, but there were few people about. Women came to the doors to look at Surajah and Dick as they came along.

"Where are you from?" an old man asked, as he came out from his cottage.

"From down the mountain-side. Tigers are getting scarce there, and we thought we would come over and see what we could do here."

"Here there are many tigers," the old man said. "For the last twenty years the wars have taken most of our young men away. Some are forced to go against their will, for when the order comes to the head man of the village, that the sultan requires so many soldiers, he is forced to pick out those best fitted for service. Others go of their own free will, thinking soldiering easier work than tilling the fields, besides the chance of getting rich booty. So there are but few shikarees, and the tigers multiply and are a curse to us. We are but poor people, but if you choose to stay here for a time we will pay something for every tiger you kill, and we will send round to the other villages within ten miles, and doubtless every one of them will contribute, so that you might get enough to pay you for your exertions."

"We will think of it," Surajah replied. "We did not intend to stop in one village, but proposed to travel about in the jungle-covered district; and wherever we hear complaints of a tiger committing depredations, we will stop and do our best to kill the evil beast. We mean first to find out where they are most troublesome, and then we shall work back again. We hear that the sultan gives good prices for those taken alive."

"I have heard so," the old man said, "but none have been caught alive here or by any one in the villages round. The sultan generally gets them from the royal forests, where none are allowed to shoot save with his permission. Sometimes, when there is a lack of them there, his hunters come into these districts and catch them in pitfalls and have nets and ropes with which the tigers are bound and taken away."

A little crowd had by this time collected round them; and the women, when they heard that the strangers were shikarees who had come up with the intention of killing tigers, brought them bowls of milk, cakes, and other presents.

"I suppose now that the sultan is away at war," Dick said, "his hunters do not come here for tigers?"

"We know nothing of his wars," a woman said. "They take our sons from us, and we do not see them again. We did hear a report that he had gone with an army to conquer Travancore. But why he should want to do it, none of us can make out. His dominions are as wide as the heart of man can require. It is strange that he cannot rest contented, but, like his father, should be always taking our sons away to fight. However, these things are beyond the understanding of poor people like us; but we can't help thinking that it would be better if he were to send his armies to destroy all the tigers. If he would do that, we should not grudge the sums we have to pay when the tax-gatherers come round."

After pausing for an hour in the village, they continued on their way. Two or three other small collections of huts were passed, but it was not until the evening of the next day that they issued from the jungle-covered country on to the cultivated plain. At none of the places they had passed was there anything known as to Tippoo or his army, but they were told that there were parties of troops in all the villages along the edge of the plain, as well as in the passes.

"We must be careful now, Surajah," Dick said, as, after a long day's march, they sat down to rest at a distance of half a mile from a large village. "Our tale that we are shikarees will not do here. Had that really been our object, we should have stopped at the first place we came to, and, at any rate, we should not have come beyond the jungle. We might still say that we are shikarees, but that tigers had become scarce on the other side of the hills, and hearing a talk that Tippoo and the English are going to war with each other, we made up our minds to go to Seringapatam and enlist in his army."

"That would do very well," Surajah agreed; "they would have no reason for doubting us, and even if the officer here were to suggest that we should enlist under him, we could do so, as there would be no difficulty in slipping away and making off into the jungle again."

They waited until the sun set, and then walked on into the village. They had scarcely entered when two armed men stopped them, and questioned them whence they came.

Surajah repeated the story they had agreed upon, and the men appeared quite satisfied.

"You will be just in time," one said. "We have news that the sultan has just moved with his army to Seringapatam. Officers came here only yesterday to buy up cattle and grain; these are to be retained here until orders are received where they are to be sent, so I should say that he is coming this way, and will be going down the passes, as Hyder did. We shall be very glad, for I suppose we shall join as he passes along; it has been dull work here, and we are looking forward to gaining our share of the loot. It would be just as well for you to join us here now, as to go on to Seringapatam."

"It would save us a long tramp," Surajah agreed. "We will think it over, and maybe we will have a talk with your officer to-morrow morning."

They sauntered along with the men, talking as they went, and so escaped being questioned by other soldiers. Presently they made the excuse that they wanted to buy some flour and ghee before the shops were closed, and, with a friendly nod to the two soldiers, stopped before the stall of a peasant who had, on a little stand in front of him, a large jar of ghee. Having purchased some, they went a little farther and laid in a fresh supply of flour.

"Things are very dear," Surajah remarked.

"There is very little left in the village," the man said. "All the flour was bought up yesterday for the sultan's army, which, they say, is coming in this direction, and I have only got what you see here; it has been pounded by my wife and some other women, since morning."

"That is good enough," Dick said, as they walked away. "Our work is done, Surajah, and it is not likely that we should learn anything more if we were to stop here for a week. Let us turn down between these houses, and make our way round behind; we might be questioned again by a fresh party of soldiers if we were to go along the street."

They kept along on the outskirts of the village, regained the road by which they had come, and walked on until they reached the edge of the jungle. Going a short distance among the trees, they collected some sticks, lit a fire, and sat down to cook their meal. At the last village or two they had heard but little of tigers, and now agreed that they could safely lie down, and that it would not be necessary for them to rig up their blankets as hammocks, as they had done on the first two nights.

CHAPTER VI.

A PERILOUS ADVENTURE.

THEY retraced their steps without adventure until they reached the village they had first stopped at.

"There are soldiers here," Surajah exclaimed, as they entered.

"We can't help it now," Dick said. "There is nothing for it but to go on boldly. I suppose that Tippoo has sent troops into all these frontier villages to prevent any chance of news of his movements being taken to the plains. Ah! there is the old chap who spoke to us last time; let us stop at once and talk with him."

"So you are back again," the peasant said, as they came up to him.

"Yes," Surajah replied; "we told you we should come back here unless we got news of some tiger being marked down near one of the other villages. We have been as far as the edge of the jungle, and although we have heard of several, not one of them seems to be in the habit of coming back regularly to the same spot, so we thought we could not do better than return here at once and make it our head-quarters. I see you have got some soldiers here."

"Yes," the old man said discontentedly, "and a rough lot they are; they demand food, and instead of paying for it in money, their officer gives us bits of paper with some writing on them; he says that when they go we are to take them to him and he will give us an order equal to the whole of them, for which we can receive money from the treasury at Seringapatam. A nice thing that! None of us have ever been to Seringapatam, and should not know what to do when we got there; moreover, there would be no saying whether one would ever come back again. It is terrible. Besides, we have only grain enough for ourselves, and shall have to send down to the plains to buy more; and where the money is to come from, nobody can tell."

"I think I could tell you how you had better proceed, if you will take us into your house,' Surajah said. "This is not a place for talking; there are four or five soldiers there watching us."

The old man entered the house and closed the door behind them. "How would you counsel us to proceed?" he asked, as soon as they had seated themselves on a divan formed of a low bank of beaten earth with a thick covering of straw.

"It is simple enough," Surajah said. "One of you would take the order on the sultan's treasury to a large village down in the plain; you would go to a trader and say that you wished to purchase so much grain and other goods, and would pay for them with an order on the sultan's treasury. It would probably be accepted as readily as cash, for the trader would send it to a merchant or banker at Seringapatam to get it cashed for him, to pay for goods he had obtained there, and either to send him any balance there might be, or to retain it for further purchases. An order of that kind is better than money for trading purposes, for there would be no fear of its being stolen on the way, as it could be hidden in the hair, or shoe, or anywhere among the clothes of the messenger."

"Wonderful!" the old peasant said. "Your words are a relief indeed to me, and will be to all the village when they hear them."

"And now," Dick broke in, "let us talk about tigers. While you have been speaking, those soldiers have passed the door twice, and have been looking suspiciously at the house. If they take it into their heads to come here and to ask who we are and what is our business, it would not do to tell them that we have been discussing the value of the orders on the sultan's treasury. Now, if our advice has been of any assistance to you in this matter, you, in turn, can render us aid in our business of killing tigers. We want you to find out for us when a tiger was last seen near the village, where its lair is supposed to be, and whether, according to its situation, we should have the best chance of killing it by digging a pitfall on the path by which it usually comes from the jungle, or by getting a kid and tying it up, to attract the tiger to a spot where we shall be stationed in a tree."

"I will assuredly do that, and every one here will be glad to assist when I tell them the advice I have received from you—and would indeed do so in any case, for it will be a blessing to the village if you can kill the tiger that so often carries off some of our sheep and goats."

At this moment there was a loud knocking at the door. On the peasant opening it, a group of soldiers demanded to see the men who had entered.

"We are here," Surajah said, coming forward. "What do you want?"

"We want to know who you are and where you come from."

"Any one in the village could have told you that," Surajah said. "We are shikarees, and have come here to destroy tigers. We were arranging with this old man to find us guides who can point out the tracks of the one which has for some time been preying on their animals."

"Yes, and our children," the old man put in; "for three of them were carried off from the street here within the last month."

The soldiers looked doubtful, but one of them said,—

"This is for our officer to inquire about. The men are strangers to the village, and he will want to question them."

"We are quite ready to be questioned," Surajah said. "Our host here will bear me out in what I say, and there are others in the village who will tell you that we have been arranging with them to kill tigers in this neighbourhood, though as yet we have not settled what they will pay us for each beast we destroy."

Accompanied by the peasant, they went with the soldiers to the guard-house, with which each of the frontier villages was provided. It consisted of a group of huts, surrounded by a thick wall of sunburnt bricks. They were taken into the largest hut, where the officer of the party was seated on a rough divan.

"Who have you here?" he asked irritably, for he had been awakened from a doze by their entry.

"They are two young fellows who are strangers here. They say they are shikarees who have come into the village to gain a reward for killing a tiger that has been troublesome."

"They were here three days ago, Sahib," the villager said, "and asked us many questions about the tigers, and were, when the soldiers came to the door, questioning me as to the tiger's place of retreat, and whether a pitfall, or a kid as a decoy, would be most suitable."

"Where do you come from?" the officer asked Surajah.

"We live in a little village some distance down the ghauts. We heard that tigers were more abundant in the jungle country up here than they are below, and thought that we would for a time follow our calling here. We can get good prices for the skins down below, and with that and what we get from the villages for freeing them from the tigers, we hope in a few months to take back a good store of money."

"Your story is a doubtful one," the officer said harshly. "You may be what you say, and you may be spies."

"If we had been spies," Surajah said, "we should not be here, but at Bangalore or Seringapatam. Those villages are not the places where news is to be gained."

This was so self-evident that the officer had nothing to say against it.

"At any rate," he said, after a pause, "there is no confirmation to your story, and as I have orders to put all suspicious persons under arrest, I shall detain you."

"It is very hard—" Surajah began; but the officer made an impatient gesture, while two of the soldiers put their hands on the shoulders of the prisoners, and led them from the hut.

"You need not look so downcast," one of them said good-naturedly. "I don't suppose you will be kept here long, and will no doubt be released when the sultan has gone down the passes with his army. A week or two here will do you no harm—the tigers can wait for a bit. There, give us your weapons; I daresay you will get them back again when we go on, as I hope we shall do, for there is nothing to eat and nothing to do in this miserable place."

The arms were taken into the officer's hut, and as there was a sentry at the gate, no further attention was paid to them.

"I will get you some provisions and bring them in," the old man said. "It is hard, indeed, that men cannot go about their business without being interfered with."

"Thank you, but we have enough for two or three days. When that is gone we will give you some money to buy more, for we have a few rupees with us, as we knew it might be some time before we should be able to kill a tiger."

As soon as the old man had left them, they seated themselves on a large faggot of wood that had been brought in by the villagers for fuel.

"We cannot stay here, Surajah; it is most important that we should get back with the news, and I have no doubt that pig-headed brute in there will do as he says, and will hold us prisoners until Tippoo has gone down the passes. We must get off to-night if possible. We are not likely to be looked after very sharply; I don't think that fellow really suspects us, but is simply keeping us to show his authority. There ought to be no difficulty in getting out. I suppose we shall be put into one of the soldiers' huts to-night, and if we crawl out when they are asleep, we have only to make our way up those narrow steps to the top of the wall, and then let ourselves down the other side. It is not above fifteen feet high, and even if we dropped we should not be likely to hurt ourselves."

"There will, most likely, be a sentry at the gate," Surajah observed, "and there is a moon to-night."

"There ought to be no difficulty in pouncing on him suddenly, gagging him before he can give the alarm, and then tying him.

We will walk round and see if there is any rope lying about; if not, I will tear my sash into strips; we can use yours to lower ourselves over the wall. I should like to get our weapons if we could; the guns do not matter, but the pistols are good ones. And, if there is an alarm given, we may have to fight; besides, it is not impossible that we may come across a tiger as we go along. I vote that when we have secured the sentry we pay the officer a visit."

Surajah nodded. He was quite ready to agree to anything that Dick might suggest, and felt a strong desire to re-possess himself of his arms, for it seemed to him that it would be a humiliation to go back without them.

"Of course," Dick went on, "if the sentry gives the alarm before we can secure him, we must give up part of our plan; for in that case we should have to bolt. Once over the wall we should be all right. They may fire away at us as we run, but there is no fear of their hitting us, half asleep as they will be, and not quite sure what it is all about. If we get a fair start of them, we need not have much fear of their catching us."

"Not as long as it is straight running, Sahib; but if they follow us far, they may come up within range of us as we are making our way down some of those nasty places where we came up the face of the ghaut."

"If we once get well away from them we will hide up somewhere, and then strike off on another line."

"We might do that," Surajah agreed; "but you know the place where we came up was the only one that seemed to us climbable, and it would be certainly better to make for it again if we can find our way."

"I quite agree with you there, Surajah; it would never do to go and find ourselves on the edge of a precipice that we could not get down, with the soldiers anywhere near us; besides, it is of the greatest importance that we should take the news back as soon as possible, as every hour may be of importance. I only wish we could find out which pass Tippoo means to go by, but

I don't suppose that will be known until he starts for it. Anyhow, our news will be very valuable, for at present he is supposed to be over on the other side, and he would have taken our troops entirely by surprise if he had suddenly poured out on to the plain. So we must give up my idea of hiding up, for if we did so we should have to lie there all day, and it would mean the loss of twenty-four hours; for I would not go down those ghauts for any money, except in daylight. It is a very different thing going down-hill to going up, and if we were to attempt it in the dark we should break our necks for a certainty. If we can get away early to-night we shall be at the edge of that steep place by nine o'clock in the morning, and if we strike the right point we might be back to the Rajah by nightfall."

"It will be difficult to find our way back in the dark," Surajah said.

"No doubt. Still we can keep in the general direction, and even if we do not hit upon the stream to-night, we shall find it in the morning."

It was late in the afternoon when they reached the village, and it was now growing dark; two soldiers came up to them and bade them follow them into one of the huts, and there pointed to the farther corner as their place. They wrapped themselves in their blankets, and at once lay down.

"If they take it into their heads," Dick whispered to Surajah, "to put a sentry on guard at the door, it will upset all our plans. It would not be very difficult to cut our way through the mud wall behind us, but in the first place they have taken away our knives, and even if we had them, it would be risky work trying it. The chances are that they will sit and talk all night; of course, we might surprise the sentry, but it would be a great risk with those fellows close at hand, and we should have to run straight for the steps, and might get a dozen balls after us before we were over the wall."

"I don't think there would be much chance of their

hitting us," Surajah said. "Jumping up from their sleep in confusion, they would be a minute or so before they could find out what had happened, and we should be at the foot of the steps before they saw us, and then they would fire almost at random. But in that case we should lose our weapons," he added regretfully.

"We cannot help that. The arms are of no consequence at all, compared to our getting away—unless, of course, any of them happen to overtake us."

For three or four hours the soldiers, of whom there were ten in the hut, sat eating, talking, and smoking round the fire, which they kept burning on the earthen floor. One by one, however, they left it and lay down. When but three remained, one of them got up with a grumble of discontent, took his musket, which was leaning against the wall, and went out of the hut.

"What a nuisance!" Dick whispered. "He is evidently going on sentry duty."

"Perhaps he has gone to the gate?" Surajah suggested.

"I am afraid not; I expect the other hut is furnishing the sentry there. Listen!"

During the pauses of the low conversation of the two men still sitting by the fire, they could hear a footfall outside.

"That settles the question," Dick said. "Now, the sooner those fellows go to sleep, the better."

"We had better wait for some time after they do," Surajah replied. "One or two of the men who lay down first, are sure to get up and go to the door and look out. They always do that once or twice during the night. The sentry will soon get accustomed to the door being opened, and won't look round sharp."

"That is a good idea," Dick agreed. "The moon is at the back of the hut, so we shall be in the shadow. I will spring upon him, and will try and grip him by the throat, so that he can't holloa. You wrench the musket from his hands, and snatch his belt of cartridges; that will give us a weapon, anyhow. As soon as you have got it, I will give him one sharp squeeze and throw him down; it will be some time before he gets breath enough to holloa."

In half-an-hour the two men by the fire lay down. It was not long before, as Surajah predicted, one of the sleepers sat up and stretched himself; then he rose and walked to the door, opened it, and stood at the entrance; a moment later he was joined by another figure, and for a few minutes they stood talking together. Then he came in again, shut the door, and lay down. During the next hour three of the others followed his example, the last of them leaving the door ajar behind him when he came in.

"Now is our chance, Surajah. We must give him ten minutes to fall asleep again; then we will move. Should one of them be lying awake and notice us—which is not likely, for it is too dark in here to see figures distinctly—and ask where we are going, say, 'To the door to get cool'; they won't imagine that we are thinking of escape, with one sentry at the door and another at the gate."

"Don't you think, Sahib, that it would be safer to kill the sentries?"

"Safer or not, Surajah, we will not do it. At present, they have done us no harm; they are only acting as their officer ordered, and we have no grudge against them. When they take to shooting at us, we must shoot at them; but to kill this sentry would be nothing short of murder."

After waiting a few minutes longer, Dick said, "We had better be off now; if we were to wait longer we should have another fellow getting up."

They rose quietly to their feet, made their way to the door, and opened it noiselessly. The sentry was standing, leaning on his long matchlock, a few feet away. Suddenly a voice behind exclaimed, "Who is that?"

The sentry was in the act of turning round when Dick sprang upon him, and grasped him by the throat. No cry came from the man's lips, but the gun fell from his grasp as he clutched convulsively at Dick's wrists, and went off as it fell.

"Pick it up," Dick shouted, "and run."

He released his grip from the man's throat, snatched the bandolier from his shoulder, and, tripping his feet from under him, threw him heavily to the ground, and then turned to run.

The whole had occupied but a few seconds, but as he started a soldier ran out from the hut, shouting loudly. He had a gun in his hand. Dick changed his mind, turned, threw himself upon him, wrenched the gun from his hold, and, as the man staggered back, struck him with his right hand under the chin. The man fell back through the open door, as if shot. Dick seized the handle and closed it, and then ran at full speed towards the foot of the steps. They were but some twenty yards away.

"Up you go, Surajah. We have not a moment to lose!"

Dick sprang up the steps, Surajah following. As they reached the top of the wall, a shot was discharged at them by the sentry at the gate, who, ignorant of the cause of the sudden uproar, had been standing in readiness to fire. He was, however, too excited to take aim, and the bullet flew harmlessly over their heads. In another instant they sprang over the parapet.

"Lower yourself by your arms, and then drop."

The wall, like many others of its sort, was thicker at the base than on the top, and the foot projected two feet beyond the upper line, so that it was a sharp slide rather than an absolute fall. It was well that it was so, for although only some twelve feet high inside, it was eight feet higher on its outer face, as a dry ditch encircled it. Both came down in a heap on the sand that had crumbled from the face of the wall. As soon as they picked themselves up, Dick exclaimed, "Keep along the foot of the wall, Surajah," and they dashed along until they reached the angle. As they turned the corner, they heard a burst of voices from the wall where they had slid down, and several shots were fired. Dick led the way along the ditch to the next angle, then left it and entered the village, and dashed along the street.

The sound of firing had roused many of the peasants; doors were opening, and men coming out. Exclamations of surprise were heard as the two figures rushed past, but no one thought of interfering with them. As they left the houses behind them, Surajah said,—

"You are going the wrong way, Sahib; you are going right away from the ghauts."

"I know that well enough," Dick panted; "but I did it on purpose. We will turn and work round again. They will hear from the villagers that we have come this way, and will be following us down the road while we are making our way back to the ghauts."

They ran for another hundred yards, then quitted the path, and made across the fields. From the fort and village they could hear a great hubbub, and above it could make out the voice of the officer, shouting orders. They continued to run for another quarter of a mile, and then turned.

"Now we can go quietly," Dick said, breaking into a walk; "this line will take us clear of the fort and village, and we have only to make straight for the ghauts. I think we have thrown them well off the scent, and unless the officer suspects that we have only gone the other way to deceive him, and that we are really making for the ghauts, we shall hear nothing more of them."

"It is capital," Surajah said. "I could not think what you were doing when you turned round the corner of the fort and made for the village, instead of going the other way. But where did you get that gun from?"

Dick told him how it had come into his possession.

"It was not so much that I cared for the gun," he said, "as that I wanted to prevent the man from using it; if he had followed me closely he could hardly have helped hitting one of us as we went up the steps. By shutting the door we gained a few moments, for they were all in confusion in the dim light inside, and would certainly not learn anything, either from the man I pitched in among them, or from the sentry outside. I don't suppose any of them had an idea of what had happened until the sentry shouted to them that we had got over the wall. Then they rushed up and fired at random from the top, thinking that we should be running straight from it."

They walked along for a short distance, and then Dick said,—

"I have got my wind again now; we will go on at a jog-trot. I mistrust that officer; he had a crafty face, and as we said we belonged to a village down the ghauts, he may have a suspicion that we have been trying to throw him off our scent, and think we should be sure to double back and make for home."

They kept on their way, sometimes dropping into a walk, but generally going at an easy trot, until day broke.

"As soon as it gets a little lighter, Surajah, we will go up on to one of these rises, so as to have a good look down over the line we have come. If they are following us, we must go on at the top of our speed; if we see nothing of them, we can take it quietly. Of course, they can't have been following our steps, but it is quite likely that some of the villagers may know that the ghauts can be climbed at the point where we came up. You know we noticed signs of a path two or three times on the way up; in that case, if the officer really did think of pursuing us, he would take one of the villagers as guide."

Half-an-hour later they ascended a sharp rise, and threw themselves down on its crest.

"I don't think that there is the least chance of their coming," Surajah said carelessly; "when they had gone some distance without overtaking us on the road, they may possibly have suspected that we had turned and made this way; but by the time they got back to the village, they would know well enough that there was no chance of overtaking us."

Dick made no answer. He had a sort of uneasy conviction that the officer would at once suspect their plan, and that pursuit would have commenced very shortly after they had re-passed the fort. For some minutes no words were spoken. No sign of life was to be seen; but in so broken a country, covered in many places with jungle or wood, a considerable body of men might be coming up unperceived.

Suddenly Dick grasped Surajah's arm. "There they are. You see that I was right. Look at that clump of bush half a mile away, well to the left of the line we came by. They have just come out from there; there are ten or twelve of them."

"I see them," Surajah said; "they are running, too, but not very fast."

"We will crawl back till we are out of their sight, and then make a run for it. They must have got a guide, and are, no doubt, taking a more direct line than we are, for we may be a good bit off the stream we followed as we came along. I have not seen anything I recognise since it got light, though I am sure we have been going somewhere near the right direction. Now we have got to run for it."

They dashed off at a rate of speed much higher than that at which they had before been travelling, keeping as much as possible in ground covered from the sight of their pursuers, and bearing somewhat to the left, so as to place the latter directly behind them and to strike the path Dick had no doubt their pursuers were keeping.

"It is no use running too fast," he said, a few minutes later. "There is a good long way to go yet—another ten miles, I should think; and anyhow, I don't think we can get down that steep place before they come to the edge of the cliff above. You see, we are not certain as to where it is. We might strike the cliffs a mile or two on either side of it, and I have no doubt they will go straight to the spot. I expect the man they have got as a guide has been in the habit of going down the ghauts, and knows his way. If it were not that we are in such a hurry to get to uncle with the news about Tippoo, it would be much better to turn off altogether and stay in a wood for a day or two. They would not stop very long at the top of the ghauts, for they cannot be sure that we are going that way at all, and when a few hours passed and we didn't come, the officer would suppose that he was mistaken, and that we really kept on in the line on which we started."

They trotted along for some time in silence, and then Surajah said,—

"Do you not think that it would be better for us to make for the pass to the left? It is twenty miles off, but we should be there by the evening, and we should surely find some way of getting into it below where the fort stands."

Dick stopped running. "Why not go the other way and make for the pass we know?" he said. "It can't be more than fifteen miles at the outside, and once below the fort we know our way, and should get down to the village twelve hours sooner than if we went round by the other pass."

"It would be the right plan if we could do it," Surajah agreed; "but you know the rocks rise straight up on both sides of the fort, and the road passes up through a narrow cleft with the fort standing at its mouth. That is why I proposed the other pass."

"I think we had better try it, nevertheless, Surajah; we should not be more than three hours in going straight there, and shall have ample time to follow the edge of the precipice for the last five miles. We may discover some break where we can get down; if we should find it impossible to descend anywhere, we must sleep till sunset, then strike the road above the fort, go down at night and manage to slip past the sentry."

"The only thing is, Sahib, that it seemed as if the fort lay right across the entrance to the gorge, and the road went through it."

"It did look like that, Surajah: certainly the road went through a gateway. But there must be a break somewhere. We could see that in the wet season a lot of water comes down there, so there must be some sort of passage for it; and if the passage is big enough for the storm water to go through, it must be big enough for us."

Surajah agreed, and they turned off from the line that they had before been following; no longer hurrying, but walking at a leisurely pace. They were not pressed for time; there was no chance whatever of pursuit, and as they had been going for some six hours at the top of their speed, they were both feeling exhausted.

After proceeding for two miles, they came upon a small stream. Here they sat down, lighted a fire, mixed some flour and water—for although the ghee had been taken from them when they were disarmed, they had been allowed to retain their supply of flour for their sustenance in prison—and made some small cakes. These they cooked in the glowing embers; they could not be termed a success, for the outside was burned black, while the centre was a pasty mass. However, they sufficed to satisfy their hunger, and after an hour's rest they again went forward. It was not very long before they stood on the edge of the rock wall; they followed this along, but could nowhere find a spot where a descent seemed at all possible. After walking for an hour they saw a road winding up a long valley below them.

"That is our road," Dick exclaimed. "That clump of houses, Surajah, must be the one where we generally turned. I know that from below these rocks looked as steep as walls, so there is no chance of our finding a way down anywhere between this and the fort."

Surajah nodded; to him also the ascent of the ghauts had seemed impracticable.

"It is no use following this line any more," Dick went on. "We may as well strike across until we come on to the edge of the pass somewhere above the fort; find a place where we can descend easily, and then lie down and sleep till it is time to make our attempt."

In another hour they were looking down on the road, a mile or so above the fort. The slopes here were gradual, and could be descended without the least difficulty, even in the dark.

"There; do you see, Surajah, the water-course runs along

by the side of the road; there is a little water in it now. You know we used to meet with it down below, and water our horses at a pool close to that ruined village. When we start we can follow the road until we get close to the fort, and then crawl along in the water-course and take our chances. If we should find it so blocked up that we can't get through, we must then see how we can get past the place in some other way. If the gate is only barred, no doubt we should be able to overpower the sentry, and get the gate open before any alarm is given; if it is locked we must do the best we can. We may calculate upon taking the sentry by surprise, as we did in the prison, and on silencing him at once; then we should have time to break up some cartridges and pour the powder into the keyhole, which is sure to be a big one, make a slow match, and blow the lock open. We could make the slow match before we start, if we had some water."

"Shall I go down to the stream and get some?"

"You have nothing to carry it up in, Surajah; and besides, some one might come along the valley."

"We shall only want a little water. I will take off my sash and dip it in the stream; that will give us plenty when it is wrung out."

"At any rate, Surajah, we will do nothing until it is getting dusk. See! there are some peasants with three bullocks coming down the valley, and there are four armed horsemen riding behind them. We will go back to those bushes a hundred yards behind us, and sleep there until sunset; then we will make our way down to that heap of boulders close to the stream, manufacture our slow match, and hide up there until it is time to start. We want a rest badly; we did not sleep last night, and if we get through, we must push on to-night without a stop, so we must have a good sleep now."

The sun was low when they woke; they watched it dip below the hills, and then, after waiting until it began to get dusk, started for the valley. No one was to be seen on the road, and they ran rapidly down the slope until they reached the heap of boulders. Surajah tore off a strip of cotton six inches long by an inch wide from the bottom of his dress, went forward to the stream and wetted it. When he came back they squeezed the moisture from it, broke up a cartridge, rubbed the powder into the cotton, and then rolled it up longways.

"That will be dry enough by the time we want to start," Dick said. "I hope we sha'n't have to use it, but if there is no other way we must do so."

They remained where they were until they thought that the garrison of the fort would be for the most part asleep; then they crossed the stream and walked along by the side of the road, taking care not to show themselves upon it, as their figures would be seen for a long distance on its white, dusty surface. Presently the sides of the valley approached more closely to each other, and just where they narrowed they could make out a number of dark objects, which were, they doubted not, the houses occupied by the garrison. They at once took to the bed of the stream, stooping low as they went, so that their bodies would be undistinguishable among the rocks. They could hear the murmur of voices as they passed through the village. Once beyond it they entered the gorge. Here there was but room enough for the road and the stream, whose bed was several feet below the causeway; a few hundred yards farther the gorge widened out a bit, and in the moonlight they could see the wall of the fort stretching before them, and a square building standing close to it.

"That is the guard-house, no doubt," Dick said in low tones; "it is too close to be pleasant if we have to attack the sentry."

Very carefully they picked their way among the rocks until close to the wall; then Dick gave a low exclamation of disappointment. The stream ran through a culvert some twelve feet wide and ten feet high, but this was closed by iron bars crossing each other at intervals of only five or six inches, the lower ends of the perpendicular bars being fixed in a stone dam extending across the bed of the stream. Dick waded across the pool formed by the dam, and felt the bars, but found them perfectly solid and strong.

"It is no good, Surajah," he said, when he returned. "There is no getting through there. There is nothing for it but the gate, unless we can find the steps up to the top of the wall and get up unnoticed. Then we might tear up our sashes longways, knot them together, and slip down. The first thing to do is to have a look round. I will get up close to the wall; it is in shadow there."

Entering the pool again, he climbed up the steep bank, which was here faced with stones. He stopped when his eyes were above the level, and looked round. There was the gate twelve feet away, and to his delight no sentry was to be seen. He was about to whisper Surajah to join him, when he heard voices. They came from above, and he at once understood that instead of a man being posted behind the gate, two were on guard on the wall above it. He beckoned to Surajah to join him, and when he did so, whispered what he had discovered.

"If the gate is only barred we are all right now, Surajah, except that we shall have to run the risk of being shot by those fellows on the wall. We shall be a pretty easy mark on that white road by moonlight. Our only plan will be to keep close to the wall when we are through the gate, get down into the bed of the stream again, and then crawl along among the rocks; the bottom will be in shadow, and we may get off without being noticed; the only fear is that we shall make a noise in opening the gate. Now let us try it."

Keeping close to the wall, they crept to the gateway; this projected two feet beyond the gate itself, and standing against the latter they could not be seen, even in the unlikely event of one of the sentries looking down. The only risk was of any one in the guard-house coming out. This, however, could not be avoided, and they at once began to examine the fastenings of the gate, which consisted of two massive bars of wood running across it; these, by their united strength, they removed one after another. But when they tried it they found the gate still immovable.

"The beastly thing is locked," Dick said; "there is nothing to do but to blow it open."

He broke off the ends of three cartridges, poured the powder in at the keyhole, and then inserted the slow match.

"Stand in the corner there, Surajah. I will go down to the stream again to light the tinder. The noise is less likely to be heard there."

He stole back again, sat down at the edge of the water, placed his tinder-box in his lap, took his turban off and put it over his hands so as to deaden the sound, and then struck the steel sharply against the flint. The first blow was successful. The spark fell on the tinder, and at once began to extend. He listened intently. The men on the wall were still talking, and the sound had evidently not reached their ears.

CHAPTER VII.

BESIEGED.

DICK hastily clambered up the wall, ran to the gate, blew the tinder, and then applied it to the slow match. A moment later this began to fizz.

"Round the corner of the wall, Surajah!" he exclaimed, running back himself. A few anxious seconds passed, then came a sharp explosion; in an instant they ran up. The gate stood two or three inches open; it yielded to a push, and they ran out. Loud shouts were heard from the men above, and a hubbub of cries from the guard-house.

"Run, Surajah! We must risk it. Keep on the edge of the road, and dodge as you go. The chances are they will run down below to see what has happened."

At the top of their speed they dashed down the road. No

shot was fired from the wall, Dick's conjecture that the first impulse of the sentries would be to run down below having been justified. They were a couple of hundred yards away before two shots were fired from the gate. The bullets whistled by harmlessly.

"We are all right now," Dick cried. "They can scarcely see us, and we shall soon be out of sight altogether."

Five or six more shots were fired a few seconds later, as the men from the guard-house reached the gate. On looking back when they had gone another hundred yards, they saw a number of figures on the road.

"Not quite so fast, Surajah." Dick said. "It is going to be a long chase now. We have got three hundred yards start, and they won't be able to load again, running at full speed."

For a time their pursuers gained somewhat upon them; then gradually they began to straggle, as the effect of the speed at which they were running told upon them. When they reached the ruined village there were four men running together some three hundred yards behind; the rest were a considerable distance in the rear.

"Another mile or two and they will all give up the chase except these four, Surajah, and if they turn out better runners than we do, we can make a stand; there are some more huts another two miles farther, and we will fight them there."

They were going slower now, for although the downward course of the road helped them a good deal, the run was telling on them. Not a word was spoken until they reached the second village. When they came to the first house they stopped simultaneously and looked round. Their pursuers were not more than two hundred yards behind them.

"In here, Surajah," Dick said, as he ran into the ruined hut. Its roof was gone, its door hung loose on its hinges. It had but one window, a small one, looking up the valley. Dick laid his gun on the sill, which was nearly level with his shoulder.

"I must wait until they get pretty close," he said, "for I

am panting so that I can't keep the barrel steady, even with this rest."

"I will kneel down outside," Surajah said.

"Mind, I will fire first, Surajah. Don't you fire until they are within twenty yards of you; by that time I shall have loaded again."

Dick had more time than he had expected, for as soon as their pursuers saw them enter the hut they slackened their pace considerably. They were within about eighty yards, when Dick held his breath, and standing for a moment immovable, took a steady aim and fired. One of the men stumbled in his run, took a step or two forward, and then fell on his face; the others paused for a moment, and then, with a fierce yell, ran forward. The moment he had fired, Dick dropped the stock of his gun on to the ground, snatched a cartridge from the bandolier, bit off the end, and emptied the powder into the barrel, gave the gun a shake, so as to be sure that it ran into the touch-hole, and then rammed down the bullet. As he was in the act of doing so, Surajah fired, and a loud yell told that his shot had been successful. Dick sprang to the door as Surajah entered. Two shots at the same instant rang out; but, at even so short a distance, the bullets went wide. Dick stepped out, and in turn fired. One of the two men fell; the other threw down his musket, and fled up the road.

"Thank goodness that is over," Dick exclaimed. "I thought they had no chance with us here. Now the first thing is to get our wind again. They stood for two or three minutes breathing heavily; then, as their breath came again, they prepared to move, when Dick exclaimed suddenly, "What is that noise?"

There was a dull, confused sound in the air, and then Surajah, pointing up the road, exclaimed, "Cavalry!"

Far away on the white road a dark mass could be seen. At first, Dick instinctively turned to resume their flight, but then he said,—

"It is of no use, Surajah; the sides of the valley are too steep to climb, and they will be up in five or six minutes. We must fight it out here. Run out to that man I shot, and bring in his gun, bandolier, pistols, if he has any, and sword; I will take them from these two. It will make all the difference having spare weapons."

Surajah, without a word, hurried up the road, while Dick ran over to the house opposite, which seemed to be larger than the one they had first entered. He looked round. It contained only one room, but this was twenty feet square. There were three small windows, one looking into the street, one looking up the valley, and one behind. The floor was littered with the beams of the roof; the door was still in its place. Having ascertained this, he ran back to the bodies of the two men, picked up the three guns, took off their bandoliers, and removed the pistols from their sashes; and with these, and one of their swords, returned to the house, just as Surajah came back.

"This is the best house to defend, Surajah. There are some beams with which we can block up the door."

Laying down the arms inside, they set to work with the beams, and barricaded the door so firmly that, short of its being splintered to pieces, no entry could be effected. This done, they re-charged the six guns, examined the pistols, and finding that they were loaded, placed three of them in each of their sashes, and hung the swords by their sides. Then they went to the window looking up the valley. The horsemen, some twenty in number, were but a short quarter of a mile away, and were coming along at a gallop.

"Don't fire, Surajah," Dick said. "They will have heard from the man who has got away that we are in the house opposite, and if they don't find us there, they will think that we have gone on, and will ride down the valley till they are sure they must be ahead of us. Then they will search the ground carefully as they come back, and altogether we may gain an hour; and every moment is of use. It must be two o'clock now, and our troop generally gets here soon after seven."

As he spoke the horsemen drew up in front of the opposite hut. There was a momentary pause, and then a voice said,—

"It is empty."

Then followed the command, "Ride on, men; they can't have got very far. We shall overtake them in ten minutes."

As soon as they started, Dick said,—

"Take a ramrod, Surajah, and make some holes through the walls to fire through. If we were to show ourselves at the windows we might get shot."

The walls were built of mud and clay, and with the iron ramrods they had no difficulty in making four holes an inch wide and two inches high, on each side of the house.

"Now we are ready for them," Dick said, when they had finished. "They have been gone half-an-hour, and it won't be long before they are back." In a few minutes they heard the clatter of horses' hoofs. It ceased some forty or fifty yards away, and by the sound of voices and orders, it was evident that the other houses were being searched. Voices were also heard at the back of the house, and they guessed that the ground was being closely examined up to the foot of the rock walls which enclosed the valley.

"Now, Surajah, you can take a shot from the window on that side. The others will be here in a minute, and it is just as well to let them know where we are before they get close up to our door."

Surajah went to the window at the back. Four horsemen were making their way at a walk along the level ground between the rocks and the huts; the nearest was but some forty yards away. Surajah fired, and the man at once fell from his horse; the others instantly galloped on at full speed up the valley, and from the window at the end Surajah saw them gather on the road three or four hundred yards away, and then, after a short consultation, cross to the other side of the valley, with the intention, he had no doubt, of rejoining their comrades.

The sound of the gun had been followed by shouts and exclamations from the party in the village. Dick could hear a conference in low tones; then all was silent. He went to the loop-hole at the corner, laid his rifle in it, and waited, looking along the barrel. Two or three minutes later the hole was darkened, and he fired at once. There was a sound of a heavy fall, followed by cries of rage, and a moment later there was a rush of men against the door. Surajah ran across. Two spare guns were pushed through the loop-holes, one on each side of it; these had not been bored straight through the wall, but at angles that would enable them to fire at any one attacking it. Looking along the barrels, each could see one of the group in front, and fired at the same moment. With a yell of rage and surprise, the assailants of the door sprang back and ran down the street.

"There are four less, anyhow," Dick said, as he and Surajah reloaded the empty guns. "Those loop-holes will puzzle them, and I don't think they will care to come on again for a bit."

There was a pause for some minutes, and then from the huts opposite, and from various points higher up the valley and behind, a dropping fire was opened.

"Keep out of the line of the windows, whatever you do, Surajah; and it will be just as well to lie down for a bit, until we see whether any of their shots come through the wall. I think we are quite safe from the distant fire, but from the house opposite it is possible they may penetrate it. Anyhow, don't stand in the line of a loop-hole; a stray ball might find its way in."

For a few minutes the enemy fired away unanswered, and then Dick, who had been seated on the ground with his back against the end wall, got up and went along that facing the street, carefully examining it.

"I don't think any of their balls have come through, Surajah. I should be able to see out into the moonlight if they had done so. Now it is time for us to be doing something. I expect they are getting a little bolder, and will perhaps give us a chance.

You take this loop-hole; it is exactly in a line with the opposite hut, and the fellows in there must come to their door to fire. I will take this slanting hole by the door-post. I can see one of the windows of the next hut to that we were in; I have no doubt that they are firing from there also. Don't wait for them to shoot, but fire directly a figure shows itself."

In a very short time Surajah fired. Dick heard the clatter of a gun as it fell to the ground.

"You have hit him, Surajah."

"Yes, but only wounded him. I think I hit him on the shoulder; he let his gun drop and ran into the house."

"Take a spare gun at once. If there are others there, they will think that you are loading, and may show themselves again."

A moment later Dick saw a gun thrust out through the window he was watching; then the head and shoulders of a man appeared behind it. He fired, and the figure disappeared. Almost at the same instant, Surajah fired again.

"I had one that time, Sahib!"

It was now quiet for some little time; then a horseman dashed suddenly past and galloped up the valley at full speed.

"The end window, Surajah! Bring him down if you can."

Surajah ran there and fired.

"I have missed him!" he said, in a tone of deep disappointment.

"It does not make much difference; if you had hit him, they could have sent another off close to the opposite side of the valley. There is no doubt as to what he has gone for; you see they have lost six killed and one wounded, and they must know that they have not the slightest chance of taking this hut. I have no doubt that he has ridden back to bring down the infantry from the fort. From the number of huts round the gate, and the sound of talking, I should think there were fifty or sixty at least—perhaps a hundred. If they send down fifty we shall have sharp work. Our difficulty will be to prevent them from making a rush at all the windows together. If they were to get there they could riddle us with balls."

"Could we block them up, Sahib?"

"That is just what I was thinking," Dick replied. "We might try, anyhow. It will be an hour and a half before they are down here; it must be past four now, and in another hour daylight will begin to break. There is any amount of the old thatch down on the floor. The best way would be to fill up the window-holes with it first, then to put two or three bits of wood across, and a strong piece down behind it, and to keep that in its place by wedging one of the long beams against it. If they came up and tried to pull the thatch out, we could fire through it with our pistols; and we will make a loop-hole below each when we have got the work done."

It was not so difficult a business as they thought it would be. The windows were little more than a foot across and two feet high; it was but the work of a few minutes to fill these up with the masses of thatch. When this was done, they picked out thick pieces of wood for cross-bars; then they took a beam eight feet long, made a hole with their tulwars in the clay floor close to the wall, put one end of the beam into it, and reared it upright against the window. Dick held it in its place while Surajah hacked a deep notch in it—a by no means difficult matter, for it was half rotten with exposure. The notch was cut just opposite the middle of the window. The three cross pieces were then put into their place, and the upright pressed firmly against them; one end of a long beam was placed in the notch, the other in a slight hole made in the ground, thus forming a strut, which held the rest firmly in their positions.

"That is a good job done," Dick said, "but a very hot one. Now, Surajah, sharpen three or four pieces of wood, and drive them down into the ground at the foot of that strut; then it will be as firm as a rock."

They then proceeded in the same way with the other two windows.

"It is getting light fast," Dick said, as he wiped the perspiration from his face. "Take a look out up the valley; they ought to be coming by this time."

Surajah applied his eye to one of the loop-holes.

"I can see them," he said; "they are half a mile away, There are two mounted men; I expect one is their officer, and the other the man who rode back to fetch them."

"Let us set to work at the loop-holes under the windows, Surajah; it is most important to get them done. You make the one at the end, I will do that one looking into the street; put it as close to the beam as you can."

They worked hard, and it was not long before the walls were pierced.

"Now, Surajah, you do the one at the back. The fellows will soon be within range, and I will give them a lesson to be careful. They will naturally break up, and go round behind the houses opposite, as they can find shelter nowhere else; and, for a bit at any rate, we shall get them all on one side of us, which is what we want."

Dick carried the six guns to the end of the hut, and then applied his eye to the loop-hole there. The enemy were coming along at a run, in a confused mass.

"I can't very well miss them," he muttered to himself, as he thrust his gun through a loop-hole and fired.

Without waiting to see the result, he thrust another gun out, aimed, and fired.

"Never mind the hole, Surajah," he said. "Come here and reload."

The four other shots were discharged in rapid succession. The Mysoreans at first opened an irregular fire on the hut. When the sixth shot was fired they left the road in a body, and ran across the valley, leaving four of their number on the ground behind them.

As soon as the guns were reloaded, Surajah returned to his

work. It was now broad daylight, and the sun was shining upon the hill-tops. A quarter of an hour passed without a movement from the enemy. Dick and his companion occupied the time in further strengthening the door with cross-beams, kept in their place by struts.

"If they break it to splinters," Dick said, when they had finished, "they will hardly be able to force their way in, for if they were to try to crawl in between those cross-beams, they would be completely at our mercy. Now we must get ready for a rush. I expect they will come all together. There are the six guns, and three pistols each; keep one of the latter in reserve. We ought not to waste a shot; and if they lose ten men I should think they will give up the attack on the door. Stand clear of it, Surajah; they will probably fire into it before they charge—keep down below the level of the loop-holes."

Presently a volley of musketry was fired, and the door was riddled by bullets; then a number of figures sprang from between the two opposite houses, and rushed at the door. Two of them carried a long, heavy beam. Two shots flashed out in return from the hut. One of the men carrying the beam fell, as did an officer who was leading them, but instantly another caught up the end of the timber, and in a moment a crowd were clustered round the door. Several caught hold of the beam, and swung it as though they meant to use it as a battering-ram. Two more puffs of smoke spurted out from the loop-holes, and again two of the men fell. The others, however, swung it forward with a crash against the door. The end of the beam went right through the rotten woodwork. Dick and Surajah fired their last musket-shots with as deadly effect as before. The next blow dashed the door from its hinges, and, split and shattered by the former shocks, it fell forward into the road, while a yell of triumph broke from the Mysoreans. This died away, however, when they saw the three cross-bars blocking their entrance. Again two pistol-shots carried death among them.

"Load your guns, Surajah."

But before Surajah had time to do so, the Mysoreans made a rush at the door. The defenders stepped forward and fired between the cross-bars, and then, drawing their tulwars, ran the two men in front through the body. As they dropped, those behind them drew back.

"The last pistols!" Dick shouted, and they fired two shots into the crowd. This completed the consternation of the enemy. It seemed to them that the defenders possessed an unlimited supply of fire-arms. Already twelve shots had been fired, and not one had failed to take effect. With a cry of consternation they fled down the street, leaving the ground in front of the fatal door strewn with bodies. The defenders instantly set about the work of re-charging their fire-arms. They were not interrupted, but presently an irregular fire opened upon them from the jungle that had taken the place of the garden between the opposite houses.

"We may as well lie down at full length," Dick said, setting the example; "there is no use in running risks. You keep that side and listen attentively. It is likely enough that they will work round behind next time and try the windows. By the way they are firing I fancy there are not more than five or six of them opposite."

Another half-hour passed; then Surajah exclaimed, "I can hear them on this side."

Dick got up and crossed at once. "I will take the loop-hole under this window. You go to the one at the end; I expect they will try both windows at once."

Dick placed the muzzle of his gun in the loop-hole, and, glancing along, saw that something dark barred his view. He fired at once. There was a loud cry and a fall, then a rush to the window, and a moment later a hole appeared in the thatch. Dick discharged two pistols through it, and as he did so Surajah fired. The thatch was speedily pulled down, as the enemy had learned to avoid the loop-holes. A yell of rage rose as the fallen thatch showed them that the window was defended with cross-bars in the same way as the door. Immediately afterwards Dick had a narrow escape from a shot fired through a loop-hole close to him.

"Stoop down," he cried, and, crouching below the level of the loop-holes, made his way to the end of the hut. "Recharge the guns first, Surajah. They may fire away through the loop-holes as long as they like. It is lucky we made them so high, except the three under the windows; we must be careful in keeping out of the line of those. You sit down where you can command the end window and the one behind—I will watch the front window and door. A bold fellow might put his musket through and pick one of us off, and that is what we have to prevent, so keep your gun in readiness, and if you see a head appear, don't miss it."

The enemy now kept up a constant fire through the loop-holes at the end and back of the house; but as these were shoulder high, and there was no altering the elevation of the guns, the shots flew harmlessly over the heads of the defenders. Several times Dick went to one or other of the loop-holes, pistol in hand, and, standing close beside it, waited until a shot was fired, and then, thrusting the barrel into the loop-hole, fired before another gun could be inserted, the discharge being generally followed by a sharp cry of pain. After this had gone on for nearly an hour, the assailants evidently became discouraged; the shots came from the loop-holes less frequently, and presently ceased altogether.

"I would give a good deal to know what they are up to," Dick said, after a long pause.

"Shall I look through the loop-hole?" Surajah asked.

"Certainly not; there will be a man standing at each of them, waiting in expectation of our taking a look out."

"But there are none in front," Surajah said.

"That is more than we can say. They have not been firing on that side, but they may have men there now. No, we will leave well alone, Surajah; the longer they delay the better for us. Keep your eye on the top of the wall as well as on the window. They may have made some ladders by this time, and may intend to try a shot."

"Perhaps they are gone?" Surajah suggested.

"It is quite possible; they must know that our troop comes up here early, and as they have four miles to walk back to the fort, and several wounded to carry with them, they certainly won't stay much longer—if, as you say, they have not gone already."

It was indeed well that Surajah had not attempted to look out at one of the loop-holes, for at the time he asked the question a dark figure was standing at each, looking along the barrel of his gun, in readiness to fire the moment the light was obscured. A few minutes later Dick exclaimed,—

"How stupid! We can easily test whether there is any one there, Surajah;" and taking up a piece of thatch he pushed it suddenly across one of the loop-holes. No shot followed the action, and he went round the hut and repeated the experiment at each of them.

"They have all gone," he said confidently; "had they been outside, they would certainly have fired directly the light was obscured."

Standing a short distance back from the end window, he looked out between the cross-beams.

"Hurrah!" he shouted. "There they go up the road; they are a quarter of a mile away; they are not more than half as strong as they were when they came down; they are carrying eight or ten figures on their shoulders, on litters, or doors."

"I don't see the cavalry," Surajah said, as he joined him.

"No; it is likely enough that they may be in hiding among the huts opposite, and are waiting, in hopes that we may be foolish enough to take it for granted that they are all gone, and pull down the bars of the door. I expect they will stay until they see our troop coming up the valley."

They continued to look out from the window, from which they had now removed the bars. Half-an-hour later Dick exclaimed,—

"There they go, up that side of the valley. I have no doubt they see our troop, and that in a few minutes we shall hear them coming."

It was not long before they heard a trampling of horses, and a moment later the Rajah's voice exclaimed, "Why, what is this? Here are a dozen dead bodies; they are Mysoreans, by their dress."

"All right, uncle," Dick shouted, "we will be out as soon as we get these bars down. We have been standing a siege."

It did not take long to remove the bars. The Rajah and his men had dismounted, as soon as some of the latter had gone round the hut and had brought back the report that there were five more dead on that side. As Dick and his companion stepped out, the Rajah exclaimed,—

"What, are you alone?"

"Yes; there is no one with us, uncle."

"Do you mean to say that you two have defended this place alone, and killed sixteen of the enemy, besides some I see lying farther up the road?"

"Yes, uncle. You see, it was a pretty strong position, and we had time to block up the doors and windows, and to make loop-holes to fire through."

"What think you of that, Anwar?" the Rajah exclaimed to the captain of the troop. "My nephew and Rajbullub's son have shown themselves brave fighters, have they not?"

"It is wonderful," the captain said; and exclamations of admiration broke from the men standing round.

"Tell us all about it, Dick," the Rajah went on.

"It is a long story, uncle; but the real news is that Tippoo, with his army, has left the head of the western passes, and has gone to Seringapatam. He is going to march down one of the passes this side at once. Provisions have been collected for his army to consume on the march. No one knows yet which pass he will come down by; but it will not be far from here, for they are buying up cattle in the villages at the top of the ghauts."

"That is important, indeed, Dick, and we must ride off without delay; but first I must have a look at this fortress of yours."

He entered the hut, the soldiers crowding in after him, and examined the defences at the windows, and the loop-holes; while Dick explained how the bars had been arranged to defend the door.

"We began on the other side, uncle. We had a fight with four men who came up with us there, only one of them got away—and he left his gun behind. It was lucky, for their guns and pistols were of immense use to us; we could not have held out with only our own weapons. About twenty of their cavalry came up a few minutes afterwards. We beat them off, and then they sent up to the fort for infantry, and about fifty men came down and attacked us just at sunrise. They kept it up to within half-an-hour ago; then the infantry marched back, knowing, of course, that your troop generally got here about seven. The horsemen stayed here till within a few minutes of your arrival. No doubt they thought that we should suppose they had all gone, and might venture out and let them get a shot at us."

"Why, it must have been a veritable battle, Dick."

"There was a good deal of noise, uncle, though not much danger. So long as we kept below the level of the loop-holes and windows, and out of the line of the door, there was no chance of our being hit."

"They must have made a strong attack on the door," the Rajah said. "I see that the two lying next to it were both killed by sword-thrusts."

"Yes, that was the most critical moment, uncle. We had emptied nearly all our barrels, and if they could have broken down the bars, which I have no doubt they could have done if they had stuck to it, they would have made very short work of us."

"Now let us be going," the Rajah said. "You can tell me the whole story as we go along."

Two of the sowars were ordered to give up their horses to Dick and Surajah, and to mount behind comrades. Then they started down the valley, Dick riding between his uncle and the captain, while Surajah took his place with the two other officers of the troop. They rode so rapidly that Dick's story was scarcely concluded by the time they reached the village where the troops were quartered.

"Well, you have done marvellously well, Dick," his uncle said. "Surajah deserves the highest praise too. Now I will write a note to the British officer with the Nabob, giving the news of Tippoo's movements, and will send it off by two of the troopers at once. Where Colonel Maxwell's force is I have no idea; it marched to join General Meadows on the day we came up here. In the meantime you can have a wash, while breakfast is being cooked. I have no doubt that you are ready for it."

"I am indeed, uncle. We had nothing yesterday but a few cakes made of flour and water, and have had nothing at all since."

"All right, lad. I will be ready almost as soon as breakfast is."

After the meal was over the Rajah lit his hookah, and said,—

"You must go through the story again this evening, Dick. You cut short some of the details as you told it to me on the road, and I want to understand it all thoroughly. You had better turn in now for a long sleep; you must want it badly enough, lad, after the work of the two last nights."

Dick slept until his uncle roused him at six o'clock.

"Dinner will be ready in ten minutes. It is just as well that you should get up for two or three hours. After that you will be good for another sleep till morning. We shall have to look out sharp now, and keep a couple of vedettes always at that village, as, for all we know, this may be the pass by which Tippoo is coming down."

Dick got up rather reluctantly, but he was not long in

shaking off his drowsiness, and after dinner was able to go through the story again, with full details of his adventures.

"I don't know what I should have done without Surajah, uncle. He is a capital fellow, and if ever I go up by myself into Mysore to look for my father, I hope that you will let me take him."

"That I will certainly do, Dick. Ever since I first heard of your plans, I have quite decided that you ought not to go alone. I daresay I should have chosen an older man to accompany you, but after what you and the lad have done together, I don't think you could do better than take him. Of course, such an affair would demand infinitely greater care and caution, though not greater courage, than you had occasion to use on this excursion. It is one thing to enter a village, to ask a few questions, make a purchase or two, and be off again; but it is a very different thing to be among people for weeks, or perhaps months, and to live as one of themselves. However, we may hope that this war will end in our army marching to Seringapatam, when we shall recover many of the prisoners in Tippoo's hands. I do not say all. We know how many hundreds remained in his power last time, in spite of his promise to deliver them all up, and maybe something of the same sort will occur next time. Numbers may be sent away by him to the hill-fortresses dotted all over the country, and we should never be able to obtain news of them. However, we must hope for the best."

The next morning the troopers arrived with a letter from the English resident at Arcot. The Rajah glanced through it, and handed it to Dick, with the remark, "You will not get the honour you deserve, Dick."

The letter ran,—

"DEAR RAJAH,—Your news would be extremely valuable were it correct; but unfortunately it is not so, and doubtless the reports brought down by your nephew were spread by Tippoo for the purpose of deceiving us, or possibly he may have intended to have come that way, but afterwards changed his mind. We have news that just after Colonel Maxwell effected his junction with General Meadows near Caveripatam, and was about to ascend the ghauts by the Tapour pass, Tippoo came down by that very route, slipped past them, and is marching on to Trichinopoly. That being the case, I see no further utility in your remaining with your troop in the passes, but think it were best that you should re-assemble them at once and march here. There is no chance of Tippoo capturing Trichinopoly before Meadows, who is following him, can come up and force on a battle; so it is likely that the Mysore army may continue their march in this direction, in which case every fighting man will be of use to defend this place until it is relieved by the general."

Dick uttered an exclamation of disgust as he laid the letter down.

"It does not matter about my news turning out wrong," he said, "but it is very bad that General Meadows should have allowed Tippoo to pass him, as he may do frightful damage to the country before he can be overtaken."

"He never can be overtaken as long as he chooses to keep ahead. He is hampered with no baggage train; he lives on the plunder of the country he passes through; and the British army, with all its baggage and provision train, has no more chance of overtaking him than it has of flying."

Messengers were at once sent off to call in the scattered portions of the troop. These were assembled in twenty-four hours, and at once started for Arcot, where they arrived after a two days' march. They there learned that Tippoo had appeared before Trichinopoly, and after pillaging and laying waste the sacred island of Seringham, had marched north. Day after day news arrived of the devastation he was committing on his march. At Thiagur, however, he met with a serious repulse. Great numbers of the inhabitants from the surrounding country had crowded into the town with their valuables, and Tippoo, expecting a rich booty, attacked the town; but although its fortifications were insignificant, the little garrison was commanded by Captain Flint, the officer who had so bravely defended Wandiwash in the previous war, and two assaults were repulsed with serious loss. At Trinalee, thirty-five miles farther north, he was more successful, capturing the town, and putting the inhabitants to the sword. Here Tippoo changed his course, and marched for Pondicherry, capturing Permacoil by the way. The news that Tippoo had changed his course to the south-east was received with great joy at Arcot. Although confident that this capital would be able to resist any sudden attack, the belief had been general that the whole territory would be laid waste, as it had been by Hyder, and hopes were now entertained that the British army would arrive in time to bar Tippoo's further progress.

CHAPTER VIII.

THE INVASION OF MYSORE

FOR some time there was a pause in the hostilities. Tippoo remained with his army near Pondicherry, carrying on negotiations with the French governor, and arranging for the despatch of an envoy to France, with a request that the Republic would furnish him with six thousand French troops. While he was thus wasting his time, General Meadows was slowly moving with the army towards an encampment formed at Vellout, some eighteen miles west of Madras. On the 14th of December a messenger arrived with the news that Lord Cornwallis had arrived from Calcutta two days before with considerable reinforcements, and that he was about to assume the supreme command of the army. The news caused unbounded satisfaction. By the extreme dilatoriness of his movements, and especially by the manner in which he had allowed Tippoo to pass him near Caveripatam, when he might easily have attacked him while his army was still struggling through the pass, General Meadows had disgusted his troops; he had frittered away, without striking a single blow, the finest army that the British had, up to that time, ever put into the field in India; and had enabled Tippoo, unmolested, to spread destruction over a large extent of country.

The only countervailing success that had been gained by the British was a brilliant victory won by Colonel Hartley, who was in command of a Bombay force consisting of a European regiment and two battalions of Sepoys. With these he engaged Hossein Ali, who had been left by Tippoo in Malabar with a force of 9000 men, when the sultan first retreated before General Meadows' advance. This force was defeated, with a loss of 1000 men killed and wounded, 900, including Hossein himself, taken prisoners on the field, and 1500 in the pursuit; the total British loss being only 52 men. A few days after this victory, General Abercrombie arrived from Madras with reinforcements, and the whole of Tippoo's fortified places in Malabar were captured one after another, and the entire province conquered.

As soon as Lord Cornwallis reached the camp at Vellout, with a large train of draught animals that had been brought by sea from Calcutta, the Rajah and his troops received orders to join him.

It was on the 29th of January, 1791, that the commander-in-chief arrived at Vellout, and the Rajah arrived there on the 4th of February; as he was the bearer of a letter from the Resident at Arcot, he was at once enabled to have an interview with Lord Cornwallis. On finding that he could speak English, the general received him with much courtesy.

"I am glad, indeed, to have a troop like yours with us, Rajah," he said. "There are few of my officers who know anything of this part of the country, and your local knowledge will be invaluable. Moreover, as I do not speak the language myself, it will be a great advantage to have some one with me through whom I can communicate freely with the people of the country. There is no doubt that such communications are much more effectual when they come through one of their own princes, than through English officers. I shall therefore order that on the march a space be allotted for the encampment of your troop by the side of that occupied by my own escort, and hope that when not employed on scouting or other duties, you will ride with my staff. Your mother, Rajah, was an English lady, I am told."

"She was, sir; my sister, who married an Englishman, is at present in Madras with my family, and her son is with me,—I beg to recommend him to your lordship. He speaks my language perfectly, and having been brought up in his father's country, naturally speaks English as well as Hindustani, and will understand far better than I can do any orders that you may give. He has come out with his mother in the hopes of finding his father, who has, if alive, been a prisoner for several years in the hands of Tippoo. He is a fine young fellow. The other day he made a most dangerous reconnaissance into Mysore, in order to ascertain Tippoo's movements. He had with him a young officer of mine, two or three years older than himself; and when I tell you that the two young fellows held a ruined hut for hours against the attack of some seventy of Tippoo's troops, and beat them off with a loss of upwards of twenty killed, I need hardly say that he has no lack of courage."

"You are right, indeed, Rajah. Let the lad ride beside you with my staff. Some day he will perhaps shorten a long day's march by giving me details of this adventure of his."

On the 5th of February the army started on its march, and on the 11th reached Vellore. Tippoo had for two months been wasting his time at Pondicherry, but upon hearing news that instead of, as he expected, the English general having marched south from Vellout to meet him, he had turned westward, and that Mysore itself was threatened with invasion, he hastily broke up his camp and marched at full speed for the ghauts, and, reaching the table-land, hurried to oppose the British army as it endeavoured to ascend the pass going from Vellore through Amboor, by which he made sure he would come. Lord Cornwallis encouraged him in the idea by sending a battalion a considerable distance up the pass, while he started north and entered the easy pass of Mooglee, leading west from Chittoor to Moolwagle. He pushed rapidly up the pass and gained the summit before Tippoo could reach the spot and oppose him. It took four days longer for the battering train, baggage, and provisions, to reach the top of the pass.

After a delay of a day or two, to rest the animals, which included sixty-seven elephants which had been brought from Bengal, the army set out for Bangalore, the second largest town in Mysore. The Rajah's troops had been busily employed from the time the army moved from Vellout. The men on their tireless little horses carried his messages to the various divisions and brigades, brought up news of the progress of the train, or rode on ahead with the officers of the quartermaster's department, whose duty it was to precede the army, to decide on the camping ground, and to mark off the spots to be occupied by the various corps. In this way they saved the regular cavalry from much fatiguing duty. Surajah and Dick were generally with the party that went on with the quartermasters, and, as soon as the camping ground was fixed upon, aided them in the purchase of forage and food from the natives, as it was most desirable that the forty days' provisions the army carried with it should remain intact until the army had passed up the ghauts. Beyond that it was expected that it would be harassed by the Mysore horse, who would render it impossible for the cavalry to go out to collect forage or provisions from the country through which it marched.

So well did the Rajah's troop perform its duties that Lord Cornwallis ordered it to be taken on the strength of the army and to receive the pay and rations of native cavalry in the service. On the day after leaving Vellore the general sent an orderly to request the Rajah and his nephew to ride with him.

"I have not had an opportunity of hearing of your scouting expedition," he said to Dick, "and shall be glad if you will give me full details of it."

Dick related the adventure from the time they had started.

"You were wonderfully lucky in getting back safely," the general said, when he had finished; "at least, luck is not the proper word, for your safety was due to your quick-wittedness and courage, and your escape with your companion from the guard-house, the manner in which you got through the fort in the pass, and your defence of that hut until the Rajah's troop arrived to your rescue, were all of them admirably managed."

He then proceeded to inquire further into the object for which Dick had come out to India. "I heartily wish you success in your search," he said, "and sincerely hope we may obtain news of your father. I do not know what your intentions may be afterwards, but should you wish to enter the army, I will at once nominate you to a commission in one of our native cavalry regiments."

"I am deeply obliged to your Excellency," Dick replied, "but as, if we learn nothing of my father during the war, I am quite resolved to spend, if necessary, some years in Mysore in the search for him, I must therefore be free to devote my time to that."

"At any rate," the general said, "if at any time you should feel free to accept my offer, it will be open to you; in the meantime I will appoint you one of the interpreters to the army during the expedition, and will attach you to my own staff. It will give you a recognised position, and it is only right that as you are doing good service you should receive pay. You shall be put in orders this evening. You can, of course, continue to camp and live with the Rajah."

The change made very little difference in Dick's duties, and he contined at his former work in the quartermasters' department until the army was ready for its advance to Bangalore. To the general surprise, as the army moved forward nothing was seen of Tippoo's cavalry, by which they had expected to be continually harassed. The sultan had, as soon as he perceived that Bangalore was threatened, hurried the whole army to that city, where he had sent his harem when he started from Seringapatam to attack Travancore, and instead of sending off a few hundred horsemen to escort them to the capital, while with his army he opposed the advance of the British, he took his whole force with him, in order to remove his harem with all the pomp and ceremony with which their passage through the country was generally accompanied. Consequently it was not until after taking, without resistance, the forts of Colar and Ooscotah, and arriving within ten miles of Bangalore, that the army encountered Tippoo's cavalry.

This was on the 4th of March. They made an attempt to reach the baggage trains, but were sharply repulsed, and on the following day the army took up its position before Bangalore. As they approached the town three horsemen dashed out from a small grove and rode furiously towards a little group consisting of Lord Cornwallis, General Meadows, and the staff, who were reconnoitring at some little distance from the head of the column. It was evident that their intention was to cut down the general. The Rajah, who was riding as usual with the staff, dashed forward with four or five other officers and encountered the horsemen before they could reach him. The Rajah cut down one of them, another was killed by one of the staff, and the third knocked off his horse and captured. It was learned that the enterprise was not a planned one, but was the result of a quarrel between the men themselves. One had charged the others with cowardice, and in return they had challenged him to follow them where they dared go. All had prepared themselves for the enterprise by half-intoxicating themselves with bhang, and thus made but a poor fight when they found their object thwarted by the officers who threw themselves between them and their intended victim.

Bangalore was a fine town, situated on a plain so

elevated that the climate was temperate, the soil fertile, and vegetation abundant. The town was of considerable extent, that portion lying within the fortifications being a mile and a quarter long by half a mile broad. It was surrounded by a strong rampart, a thick hedge, and a deep, dry ditch. The wall, however, did not extend across the side facing the fort, whose guns were supposed to render it ample protection. The fort was oval in shape, and about nine hundred yards across at its greatest diameter. It was defended by a broad rampart, strengthened by thirty semicircular bastions and five outworks. The two gates, one at each end, were also protected by outworks. In the fort stood the splendid palace built by Tippoo; here also were immense foundries of cannon, factories for muskets, the arsenal, and large magazines of grain and ammunition.

The position taken up by the army lay to the north-east of the petah or town, and the next morning a reconnoitring party, escorted by Colonel Floyd, with the whole of the cavalry and a brigade of infantry, went out to examine the defences of the town and fort. Seeing a large body of laden elephants and camels, escorted by a strong body of horsemen, Colonel Floyd rode with the cavalry to attack them. The movement was a rash one, as the guns on the fort opened fire, and although at first he defeated the Mysore horse, a heavy fire was poured upon him when entangled in broken ground. He himself was shot by a musket-ball which, striking him in the face, passed through both jaws. It was at first believed that he was dead, but he was carried back to camp and ultimately recovered. This rash attack cost the lives of seventy-one men, and of four times as many horses.

As Tippoo's army was lying at a distance of only six miles away, the general determined that it would be best in the first place to capture the town without delay, and to assault the fort on that side, as he could then do so without any fear of an attack by Tippoo, who would be able to harass him constantly were he to approach the fort from any other direction.

Orders were therefore issued for the 36th Regiment, supported by the 26th Bengal Sepoys, and a party of artillery under Colonel Moorhouse, to prepare to storm the north gate of the town at daybreak the next morning. As soon as dawn broke, the troops rushed forward against the gate. The outside work was speedily stormed, but as they issued from it towards the gate itself, they were received with a very heavy fire from the walls, together with a storm of hand-grenades. Colonel Moorhouse brought forward a six-pounder, receiving two wounds as the piece was run up to the gate.

The first time it was fired it had no effect beyond making a small hole, and the next shot had no greater success. Colonel Moorhouse ordered a twelve-pounder to be brought up, but as he was aiding to put it into position, another ball struck him, and he fell dead. While the artillerymen were pouring shot after shot into the gate, the roar of musketry was unceasing, the 36th keeping up an incessant fire upon the enemy upon the wall, in order to cover as much as possible the operations of the gunners. At last the gate gave way. The troops poured in, cheering loudly, and the enemy at once fled. Many, however, took up their positions in the houses, and kept up a galling fire until their places of refuge were stormed by detachments of troops scattered through the town.

By nine o'clock all was over, and the town completely in the possession of the British. Tippoo, furious at its having been so speedily captured, moved down early in the afternoon with a strong force of infantry, and marching along by the side of the fort, endeavoured to force his way into the town through the open space at that end. He was aided by the guns of the fort, while his artillery kept up a heavy cannonade upon the British encampment. When the sultan was seen marching towards the town, with the evident intention of endeavouring to retake it, the 76th Regiment was sent in to reinforce the garrison, and the three battalions opposed so steady a resistance to Tippoo's infantry that the latter were forced to fall back, after sustaining a loss of five hundred men. The troops began next morning to erect batteries.

The position was a singular one. A small army was undertaking the siege of a strong fortress, while an army vastly outnumbering it was watching them, and was able at any moment to throw large reinforcements into the fort through the Mysore gate, which was at the opposite end of the fort to that attacked, the efforts of the British being directed against the Delhi gate, which faced the town.

The advantage which had been gained by the employment of the great train carrying the provisions for the troops was now manifest, for unless the army had been so provided it would have been forced to retreat, as in the face of Tippoo's army, with its great host of cavalry, it would have been impossible to gather provisions. The first batteries erected by the engineers proved to be too far distant from the wall of the fort to effect any material damage, and others were commenced at a much shorter range. The work was performed with great difficulty, for the guns of the defenders were well served, and a storm of missiles were poured night and day into the town and against the batteries. The garrison, which consisted of eight thousand men, were frequently relieved by fresh troops from the sultan's army, and were thus able to maintain their fire with great vigour.

On the 17th, Tippoo cannonaded the British camp from a distance, but without doing great damage. In the meantime the fire of our siege guns was steadily doing its work, in spite of the heavy fire kept up on them. The stone facing of the bastion next to the gateway was soon knocked away, but the earth-banks behind, which were very thick and constructed of a tough red clay, crumbled but slowly. Still, the breach was day by day becoming more practicable, and Tippoo, alarmed at the progress that had been made, moved his army down towards the east side of the fort, and seemed to meditate an attack upon our batteries. He placed some heavy guns behind a bank surrounding a large tank, and opened some embrasures through which their fire would have taken our trenches, which were now pushed up close to the fort, in flank.

Lord Cornwallis at once directed a strong force to advance, as if with the intention of attacking the new work, and Tippoo ordered his troops to retire from it. It was evident, however, that he had determined to give battle in order to save the fort, and the English general therefore determined to storm the place that very night, the 21st of March. The preparations were made secretly, lest the news should be taken to Tippoo by one of the natives in the town, and it was not until late in the evening that orders were issued to the troops which were to take part in the assault. The column was to be composed of the grenadier and light companies of all the European regiments, and these were to be followed and supported by several battalions of Sepoys. The force, commanded by Colonel Maxwell, at eleven o'clock issued from the town and advanced through the trenches. The besieged were vigilant, and the instant the leading company sprang from the trenches and, in the bright moonlight, ran forward to the breach, a number of blue lights were lighted all along the ramparts, and a heavy musketry fire was opened.

The scene was eagerly watched by the troops in the camp, every feature being distinctly visible. The storming party could be seen rushing up the breach and mounting by ladders over the gateway, which was the central object of attack. The enemy gathered in masses at the top of the breach, but as soon as the stormers collected in sufficient strength, and charged them with the bayonet, they broke and dispersed. The grenadiers moved along the ramparts to the right, clearing it of its defences as they went along; the light companies did the same along the ramparts to the left; while the Sepoys descended into the body of the fort. The whole of the defenders fled towards the Mysore gate at the other end of the fort, and when the three bodies of troops met there, they found the gate blocked by the masses of fugitives.

They charged them on all sides. The governor, a brave old soldier, and a great favourite of the sultan, died fighting gallantly to the last. Six hundred of the garrison fell, and three hundred, for the most part wounded, were taken prisoners. The British loss was only fifty officers and men killed and wounded. The body of the governor was found next morning among the slain, and Lord Cornwallis sent a message to Tippoo, with an offer to have the body carried to his camp for burial. Tippoo, however, replied that the proper place for a soldier to be buried was where he fell, and accordingly the brave old soldier was laid to rest in the fort by the Mohammedan troops in the Sepoy regiments, with all military honours.

While the assault was going on, Tippoo—who, in spite of the precautions taken, had received news of the intention of the general, and had warned the garrison of the fort to be prepared—despatched two heavy columns, as soon as the fire opened, to attack the British camp on its flank. The movement had been foreseen and prepared against, and the attacks were both repulsed with heavy loss.

The capture of the fort was effected but just in time, for the provisions were almost entirely consumed, and the scanty rations were eked out by digging up the roots of grasses and vegetables within the circuit of our pickets. The draught and carriage cattle were dying daily by hundreds, the few remaining, intended for food, were in so emaciated a state that the flesh was scarcely eatable, and, worst of all, the supply of ammunition was almost exhausted. The news of the fall of the fortress, considered by the natives to be almost impregnable, under the very eyes of the sultan himself and his great army, produced a widespread effect, greatly depressing the spirit of Tippoo's adherents, while it proportionately raised those of the British troops and excited the hopes of the peoples conquered by Tippoo and his father. One result was that the polagars, or chiefs, of a tribe that had but recently fallen under the yoke of Mysore, were at once emboldened to bring in provisions to the town. As great stores were found in the magazines in the fort, the starving animals regained some of their condition during the ten days that the troops were occupied in repairing the breaches, burying the dead, and placing the fort in a condition to stand a siege, should Tippoo return during the absence of the army.

When this was done and the stores of ammunition replenished from the magazines, the army started on its march north to Deonhully, where they were to effect a junction with the cavalry that the Nizam had agreed to furnish. As it marched, it passed within three miles of Tippoo's army, which was proceeding in a westerly direction. Tippoo could here have brought on a general engagement, had he wished it; but the capture of Bangalore had for the time cowed his spirit, and he continued his march at a rate that soon placed him beyond the reach of the British. At Deonhully a junction was effected with the Nizam's horse, ten thousand in number. These proved, however, of no real utility, being a mere undisciplined herd, who displayed no energy whatever, except in plundering the villagers. The united force now moved south-east, to guard a great convoy which was advancing up the pass of Amboor, and when this had been met, returned to Bangalore.

During the operations of the siege the Rajah's troop had remained inactive, and Dick's duties as interpreter had been nominal. At Bangalore no English prisoners had been found, and he was heartily glad when he heard that it was the intention of Lord Cornwallis to march directly upon Seringapatam. It was, indeed, a necessity for the English general to bring the campaign to a speedy termination. The war was entailing a tremendous strain upon the resources of the Company; the Nizam and Mahrattas were not to be depended upon in the slightest degree, and might at any moment change sides. The French revolution had broken out, and all Europe was alarmed, and many of the English regiments might at any moment be ordered to return home. Therefore, anything like a thorough conquest of Mysore was impossible, and there was only time to march to Seringapatam, to capture Tippoo's capital, and to dictate terms to him. Immense exertions were made to restore the efficiency of the baggage train, and on the 3rd of May the army marched from Bangalore.

Tippoo, devoured alike by rage and fear, had taken no efficient steps to meet the coming storm. His first thought was to prevent the English from discovering the brutal cruelty with which his white captives had been treated. He had over and over again given the most solemn assurances that he had no white prisoners in his hands, and he now endeavoured to prevent their obtaining evidence of his falsehood and cruelty, by murdering the whole of those who remained in his hands at Seringapatam. Having effected this massacre, he next ordered all the pictures that he had caused to be painted on the walls of his palace and other buildings, holding up the English to the contempt and hatred of his subjects, to be obliterated, and he also ordered the bridge over the northern loop of the Cauvery to be destroyed. He then set out with his army to bar the passage of the British to Seringapatam.

The weather was extremely bad when the British started. Rain-storms had deluged the country, and rendered the roads well-nigh impassable, and the movement was in consequence very slow. Tippoo had taken up a strong position on the direct road, and in order to avoid him Lord Cornwallis took a more circuitous route, and Tippoo was obliged to fall back. The whole country through which the English passed had been wasted; the villages were deserted, and not an inhabitant was to be met with.

Suffering much from wet, and the immense difficulties of bringing on the transport, the army, on the 13th of May, arrived on the Cauvery nine miles east of Seringapatam. Here it had been intended to cross the river, but the rains had so swollen the stream that it was found impossible to ford it. It was therefore determined to march to a point on the river, ten miles above Seringapatam, where it was hoped that a better ford could be found, and where a junction might be effected with General Abercrombie's Bombay army, which was moving up from the Malabar coast, and was but thirty or forty miles distant. To effect this movement, it was necessary to pass within sight of the capital. Tippoo came out, and took up a strong position on a rugged and almost inaccessible height.

In front was a swamp stretching to the river, while batteries had been thrown up to sweep the approaches. By a night march, accomplished in the midst of a tremendous thunder and rain-storm, Lord Cornwallis turned Tippoo's position. The confusion occasioned by the storm, however, and the fact that several of the corps lost their way, prevented the full success hoped for from being attained, and gave Tippoo time to take up a fresh position.

Colonel Maxwell led five battalions up a rocky ledge, held by a strong body of the Mysore troops, carried it at the point of the bayonet, and captured some guns. Tippoo immediately began to fall back, but would have lost the greater portion of his artillery had not the Nizam's horse moved forward across the line by which the British were advancing. Here they remained in an inert mass, powerless to follow Tippoo, and a complete barrier to the British advance. So unaccountable was their conduct that it was generally believed in the army that it was the result of treachery, and it was with difficulty that the British troops could be restrained from firing into the horde of horsemen, who had, from the time they joined the force, been worse than useless.

As soon as the British could make their way through or round the obstacle to their advance, they pursued the retreating force of Tippoo until it took refuge under the guns of the works round Seringapatam. Their loss had been 2000, that of the British 500; but the success was of little benefit to the latter. The terrible state of the roads, and the want of food, had caused the death of great numbers of draught animals, and the rest were so debilitated as to be absolutely useless, and during the two days' marches that were required to reach the point on the river previously determined upon, the battering train, and almost the whole of the carts, were dragged along by the troops.

The position of the army was bad in the extreme. Neither food nor forage were to be obtained from the country round. The troops were almost on famine rations, worn out by fatigue, and by the march through heavy rains, and nights spent on the sodden ground. Tippoo's horsemen hovered round them. The cavalry of the Nizam, which had been specially engaged to keep the foe at a distance, never once ventured to engage them. It was absolutely impossible to communicate with General Abercrombie, and after remaining but a couple of days in his new camp, Lord Cornwallis felt that the army could only be saved from destruction by immediate retreat. No time was lost in carrying out the decision when once arrived at. Some natives were paid heavily to endeavour to make their way to Abercrombie, with orders for him to retire down the ghauts again into Malabar. Then the whole of the batttering train, and the heavy equipments, were destroyed, and on the 26th of May the army started for its long march back to Bangalore.

It had made but six miles when a body of horsemen, some two thousand strong, were seen approaching. Preparations were instantly made to repel an attack, when a soldier rode in and announced that the horsemen were the advance party of two Mahratta armies close at hand. This was welcome news indeed, for Lord Cornwallis had no idea that the Mahrattas were within two hundred miles of him, and had come to believe that they had no intention whatever of carrying out their engagements. They had, it appeared, sent off a messenger every day to inform him of their movements; but so vigilant were Tippoo's cavalry that not one of them ever reached the British. In a few hours the junction was completed, and the sufferings of the army were at an end. Stores of every kind were abundant with the Mahrattas, and not only food, but clothing, and every necessary of life, could be purchased in the great bazaars occupied by the Mahratta traders who accompanied the army.

Had the two Mahratta armies arrived a couple of days earlier, the destruction of the siege train would have been avoided, Seringapatam would have been besieged, Abercrombie's army of eight thousand men have joined, and the war brought at once to a conclusion. It was now, however, too late; the means for prosecuting the siege of so powerful a fortress were altogether wanting, and the united armies returned by easy marches to Bangalore. On the march, the future plan of operations was decided upon. Lord Cornwallis sent orders for the sum of ₨1,500,000, that had been intended for China, to be at once despatched to Bangalore for the use of the army and the allies. The larger of the Mahratta forces, under Purseram Bhow, with a detachment of Bombay troops that had accompanied it, were to march to the north-west and reduce some of the forts and towns still held by the troops of Mysore; the other Mahratta force, consisting chiefly of cavalry, under Hurry Punt, were to remain at Bangalore.

The cause of the long delay on the part of the Nizam and the Mahrattis was now explained. The Nizam's troops had spent six months in the siege of the fortress of Capool, while an equal time had been occupied by Purseram Bhow in the siege of Durwar, a very strong place, garrisoned by ten thousand men.

Tippoo began negotiations immediately after his defeat near Seringapatam, and these were continued until July, when they were finally broken off. Some months were occupied in reducing a number of the hill-forts commanding the entrances to the various passes. Among these, two, deemed absolutely impregnable, Savandroog and Nundidroog, were captured, but the attack upon Kistnagherry was repulsed with considerable loss. By the capture of these places Lord Cornwallis obtained access to supplies from the Malabar and Carnatic coasts, and was thus free from the risk of any recurrence of the misfortunes that had marred his previous attempt to lay siege to Seringapatam; and, on the 5th of February, 1792, he again came within sight of Tippoo's capital.

CHAPTER IX.

NEWS OF THE CAPTIVE.

DURING the nine months that had elapsed since the retreat from before Seringapatam, Dick had been occupied in following out the main object of his presence in Mysore. Finding that Purseram Bhow's army was the first that would be engaged in active service, he asked permission from the general to join it. This was at once granted, and Lord Cornwallis introduced him to the officer in command of the Bombay troops attached to that army, informing him of the object that he had in view.

"He will not be of much use as an interpreter," he said, "for as the country in which you are going to operate, formed, until lately, a part of the Mahratta dominions, Mahratti will be principally spoken. He will therefore go simply as an officer of my staff, attached for the present to your command. He has asked me to allow him to take with him twenty men belonging to the troop of his uncle, the Rajah of Tripataly. His object in doing so is that he will be able to traverse the country independently, and can either rejoin me here or go to one of the other columns operating against the hill-forts, if it should seem to him expedient to do so. Should you desire to make a reconnaissance at any time while he is with you, you will find him useful as an escort, and will not be obliged to ask Purseram Bhow for a party of his cavalry."

Dick was sorry to leave his uncle, whose tent he had now shared for the last ten months. He found himself, however, very comfortable with the Bombay troops, being made a member of the mess consisting of the officer in command and the four officers of his staff. Wishing to have some duties with which to occupy himself, he volunteered to act as an aide-de-camp; and although the work was little more than nominal, it gave him some employment. When not otherwise engaged he generally rode with Surajah, whom his uncle had appointed to command the twenty troopers. In the year that had elapsed since his arrival in India, Dick had grown considerably and broadened out greatly, and was now a powerful young fellow of over seventeen. He had, since the troop joined the army of Lord Cornwallis, exchanged his civilian dress for the undress uniform of an officer, which he had purchased at the sale of the effects of a young lieutenant on the general's staff, who had died just as the army arrived before Bangalore. It was, indeed, necessary that he should do this, riding about, as he did, either on the staff of the general, or with the officers of the quartermasters' department. There would be no difficulty in renewing his uniform, for hardship, fever, and war, had carried off a large number of officers as well as men, and the effects were always sold by auction on the day following the funeral.

Many hill-fortresses were captured by the Mahrattis, but few offered any resistance, as their commanders knew well that there was no chance of their being relieved, while the men were in most cases delighted at the prospect of an escape from their enforced service, and of freedom to return to their homes. In a few of these forts, English captives were found. Some had been there for years, their very existence being apparently forgotten by the tyrant. Some had been fairly treated by the Mysore governor, and where this was the case, the latter was furnished by the British officers with papers testifying to the kindness with which they had treated the prisoners, and recommending them to the officers of any of the allied forces they might encounter on their way home, or when established there. Upon the other hand, some of the prisoners were found to have been all but starved, and treated with great brutality.

In two cases, where the captives said that some of their companions had died from the effects of the ill-treatment they had received, the governors were tried by court-martial and shot, while some of the others they sentenced to be severely flogged. Every captive released was closely scrutinised by Dick and eagerly questioned. From one of them he obtained news that his father had certainly been alive four years previously, for they had been in prison together in a hill-fort near Bangalore.

"I was a civilian and he a sailor," he said, "consequently neither of us were of any use in drilling Tippoo's battalions, and had been sent up there. Your father was well then. The governor was a good fellow, and we had nothing much to complain of. Mr. Holland was a favourite of his, for, being a sailor, he was handy at all sorts of things; he could mend a piece of broken furniture, repair the lock of a musket, and make himself generally useful. He left there before I did, as the governor was transferred to some other fort—I never heard where it was—and he took your father with him. I don't know whether he had Tippoo's orders to do so, or whether he took him simply because he liked him. At any rate he was the only prisoner who went with him; the rest of us remained there till a few months back, when the fort was abandoned. It was just after the capture of Bangalore, and the place could have offered no resistance if a body of troops had been sent against it. At any rate, an order arrived one morning, and a few hours afterwards the place was entirely abandoned, and we and the garrison marched here."

"My father was quite well?"

"Quite well. He used to talk to me at times of trying to make his escape. Being a sailor, I have no doubt that he could have got down from the precipice on which the fort stood; but he knew that if he did so we should all suffer for it, and probably be all put to death as soon as Tippoo heard that one of us had escaped—for that was always done, in order to deter prisoners from trying to get away."

"Do you think that there is any chance of his being still alive?"

"That is more than I can possibly say. You see, we have not known much of what is passing outside our prison. Some of the guards were good-natured enough, and would occasionally give us a scrap of news; but we heard most from the ill-tempered ones, who delighted in telling us anything they knew that would pain us. Three or four months ago we heard that every white prisoner in Seringapatam had been put to death by Tippoo's orders, and that doubtless there would be a similar clearance everywhere else. Then again we were told that the English had retreated, beaten, from before Seringapatam, and that the last of them would soon be down the ghauts. But whether the prisoners have been killed in other hill-forts like this I cannot say, although I suppose not, or we should not have escaped."

"Certainly no such orders can have been sent to the forts here, for we have found a few prisoners in several of them. Of course it may be otherwise in the forts near the capital, which Tippoo might have thought were likely to fall into our hands, while he may not have considered it worth while to send the same orders to places so far away as this, where no British force was likely to come. Still, at any rate, it is a great satisfaction that my father was alive four years ago, and that he was in kind hands. That is all in favour of my finding him still alive in one of the places we shall take, for Lord Cornwallis intends to besiege some of the fortresses that command the passes, because he cannot undertake another siege of Seringapatam until he can obtain supplies freely and regularly from beyond the ghauts, as nothing whatever can be obtained from the country round, so completely is it wasted by Tippoo's cavalry. I have, therefore, great hopes that my father may be found in one of these forts."

"I hope, indeed, that you may find him. I am convinced that the governor would save his life if he could do so; though, on the other hand, he would, I am sure, carry out any order he might receive from Tippoo. Of course he may not be in charge of a fort now, and may have been appointed colonel of one of the regiments. However, it is always better to hope that things will come as you wish them, however unlikely it may seem that they will do so. We have been living on hope here, though the chances of our ever being released were small indeed; of course we did not even know that Tippoo and the English were at war until we heard that an English army was besieging Bangalore, and even then we all felt that, even if Tippoo were beaten and forced to make peace, it would make no difference to us. He kept back hundreds of prisoners when he was defeated before, and would certainly not surrender any he now holds unless compelled to do so; and no one would be able to give information as to the existence of captives in these distant forts. And yet, in the teeth of all these improbabilities, we continued to hope, and the hopes have been realised."

The capture of forts by the Mahratta army was abruptly checked. Having, so far, met with such slight opposition, Purseram Bhow became over-confident, and scattered his force over a wide extent of country, in order that they might more easily find food and forage. In this condition they were suddenly attacked by Tippoo, who took advantage of the English being detained at Bangalore while the transport train was being re-organised, to strike a blow at the Mahrattas. The stroke was a heavy one; many of the detached parties were completely destroyed, and the Mahratta general, after gathering the rest to his standard, was forced to retreat until strong reinforcements were sent him from Bangalore. Learning from them that it was probable Lord Cornwallis would advance as soon as they rejoined him, Dick determined to go back to Bangalore, as it was unlikely that, after the severe check they had received, the Mahrattas would resume the offensive for a time.

Surajah and the men were glad to return to the troop, and as soon as the Mysorean force returned to Seringapatam,

Dick, without waiting for the infantry to get in motion, rode rapidly across the country with his little party. He accompanied the English army during their operations, obtaining permission to go with the columns engaged in the siege of the hill-fortresses, and was present at the capture of all the most important strongholds. To his bitter disappointment, no English prisoners were found in any of them, and it was but too certain that all who might have been there had been massacred by Tippoo's orders on the first advance of the British against Seringapatam.

Great indeed was the satisfaction of the army when they at last came in sight of the city. The capital of Mysore stood on an island in the river Cauvery. This was four miles in length and two in breadth; the town stood in its centre, the fort at the northern end. The island was approached by two bridges, one close to the fort, the other at the south, both being defended by strong batteries. There were also three fords, two of these being at the north end of the island, and also defended by batteries; the third was near the centre of the island, a mile below the fort, and leading to the native town. The fort was separated from the rest of the island by a deep ditch cut across it; it was defended by numerous batteries. There were two gardens on the island full of large trees, one of them being the burial-place of Hyder Ali; this was connected with the fort by two avenues of trees. The country round was flat, a considerable portion being almost level with the river, and devoted to the cultivation of rice, while at other points a forest extended almost to the bank.

After obtaining a view, from some high ground, of the city and of Tippoo's army encamped beyond its walls, the British force took up its position six miles to the north-west of the city. No sooner had the army reached their camping ground than Lord Cornwallis, with his staff, reconnoitred the approaches. A thick hedge, formed by a wide belt of thorny shrubs interlaced and fastened together by cords, extended from the bank of

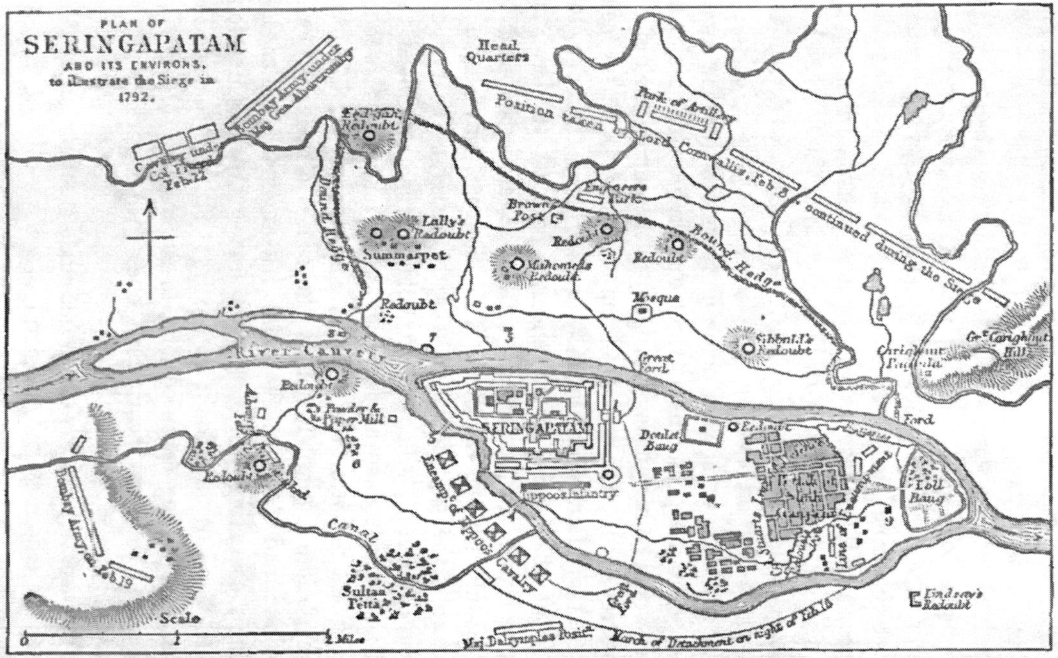

1, Bangalore Gate. 2, Mysore Gate. 3, Old Bridge. 4, New Bridge. 5, Place for breaching Batteries. 6, Place intended for the enfilading Battery. 7, Battery to defend the Bridge. 8, Montresor's Redoubt. 9, Hyder Ali's Tomb.

the river about a thousand yards above Seringapatam, and, making a wide sweep, came down to it again opposite the other end of the island. It was within the shelter of this formidable obstacle that Tippoo's army was encamped. Within the enclosed space were seven or eight eminences, on which strong redoubts had been erected. Fearing that Tippoo might, as soon as he saw the position taken up by the assailants, sally out with his army, take the field, and, as before, cut all his communications, Lord Cornwallis determined to strike a blow at once.

At sunset, orders were accordingly issued for the forces to move in three columns at three o'clock, by which time the moon would be high enough to light up thoroughly the ground to be traversed. The centre column, consisting of 3,700 men, under Lord Cornwallis himself, was to burst through the hedge at the centre of the enemy's position, to drive the enemy before them, and, if possible, to cross the ford to the island with the fugitives. This, however, was not to be done until the centre column was reinforced by that under General Meadows, which was to avoid a strong redoubt at the north-west extremity of the hedge, and, entering the fence at a point between the redoubt and the river, drive the enemy before it until it joined the centre column. Colonel Meadows had 3,300 men under his command. The left column, consisting of 1,700 men under Colonel Maxwell, was first to carry a redoubt on Carrygut Hill just outside the fence, and, having captured this, to cut its way through the hedge, and to cross the river at once with a portion of the centre column.

Unfortunately, owing to a misunderstanding as to the order, the officer guiding General Meadow's column, instead of taking it to a point between the north-western redoubt and the river, led it directly at the fort. This was stoutly defended, and cost the British eighty men and eleven officers. Leaving a strong garrison here, the column advanced, but came upon another redoubt of even greater strength and magnitude;

and the general, fearing that the delay that would take place in capturing it would entirely disarrange the plan of the attack, thought he had better make his way out through the hedge, march round it to the point where the centre column had entered it, and so give Lord Cornwallis the support he must need, opposed as he was to the whole army of Tippoo.

In the meantime, Colonel Maxwell's force had stormed the work on Carrygut Hill, and had made its way through the hedge, suffering heavily as it did so from the fire of a strong body of the enemy concealed in a water-course. The head of the centre column, under General Knox, after cutting its way through the hedge, pushed on with levelled bayonets, thrust its way through the enemy's infantry, and, mingling with a mass of fugitives, crossed the main ford close under the guns of the fort, and took possession of a village half-way between the town and the fort.

Unfortunately, in the confusion but three companies had followed him; the rest of the regiment and three companies of Sepoys crossed lower down and gained possession of a palace on the bank of the river. The officer in command, however, not knowing that any others had crossed, and receiving no orders, waited until day began to break. He then re-crossed the river and joined Lord Cornwallis, a portion of whose column, having been reinforced by Maxwell's column, crossed the river nearly opposite the town. As they were crossing, a battery of the enemy's artillery opened a heavy fire upon them; but Colonel Knox, with his three companies, charged it in the rear, drove out the defenders, and silenced the guns.

All this time Lord Cornwallis was with the reserve of the central column, eagerly waiting the arrival of General Meadows' division. This, in some unaccountable way, had missed the gap in the hedge by which the centre column had entered, and, marching on, halted at last at Carrygut Hill, where it was not discovered until daylight. The Mysore army on its left was still unbroken, and had been joined by large numbers of troops from the centre. On discovering the smallness of the force under Lord Cornwallis, they attacked it in overwhelming numbers, led by Tippoo himself. The British infantry advanced to meet them with the bayonet, and drove them back with heavy loss. They rallied, and returned to the attack again and again, but were as often repulsed, continuing their attacks, however, until daylight, when Lord Cornwallis, discovering at last the position of General Meadows, joined him on Carrygut Hill.

When day broke the commanders of the two armies were able to estimate the results of the night's operations. On the English side the only positions gained were the works on Carrygut Hill, the redoubt at the north-west corner of the hedge, another redoubt captured by the centre column, and the positions occupied by the force under Colonels Stuart and Knox at the eastern end of the island. The sultan found that his army was much reduced in strength, no less than twenty-three thousand men being killed, wounded, or missing. Of these the missing were vastly the most numerous, for ten thousand Chelahs, young Hindoos whom Tippoo had carried off in his raids, and forced to become soldiers, and, nominally, Mohammedans, had taken advantage of the confusion, and marched away with their arms to the Forest of Coorg.

Tippoo made several determined efforts to drive Colonel Stuart's force off the island and to re-capture the redoubts, but was repulsed with such heavy loss that he abandoned the attempt altogether, evacuated the other redoubts, and brought his whole army across on to the island.

Tippoo now attempted to negotiate. He had already done so a month before, but Lord Cornwallis had refused to accept his advances, saying that negotiation was useless with one who disregarded treaties and violated articles of capitulation. "Send hither," he wrote, "the garrison of Coimbatoor, and then we will listen to what you have to say." Lord Cornwallis alluded to the small body of troops who, under Lieutenants Chalmers and Nash, had bravely defended that town when it had been attacked by one of Tippoo's generals. The gallant little garrison had surrendered at last, on the condition that they should be allowed to march freely away. This condition had been violated by Tippoo, and the garrison had been marched as prisoners to Seringapatam. The two officers had been kept in the fort, but most of the soldiers and twenty-seven other European captives who had lately been brought in from the hill-forts, were lodged in the village that Colonel Knox had first occupied on crossing the river, and had all been released by him. Some of these had been in Tippoo's hands for many years, and their joy at their unexpected release was unspeakable.

Preparations were now made for the siege. General Abercrombie was ordered up with a force of six thousand men, but before his arrival, Lieutenant Chalmers was sent in with a letter from Tippoo, asking for terms of capitulation. Negotiations were indeed entered into, but, doubting Tippoo's good faith, the preparations for the siege were continued, and upon the arrival of General Abercrombie's force on the 15th of February, siege operations were commenced at the end of the island still in British possession. A few days afterwards the army was astounded at hearing that the conditions had been agreed upon, and that hostilities were to cease at once. So great was the indignation, indeed, that a spirit of insubordination, and almost mutiny, was evinced by many of the corps. They had suffered extreme hardships, had been engaged in most arduous marches, had been decimated by fever and bad food, and they could scarce believe their ears when they heard that they were to hold their hands now that, after a year's campaigning, Seringapatam was at their mercy, and that the man who had butchered so many hundred English captives, who had wasted whole provinces and carried half a million people into captivity, who had been guilty of the grossest treachery, and whose word was absolutely worthless, was to escape personal punishment.

Still higher did the indignation rise, both among officers and men, when the conditions of the treaty became known, and it was discovered that no stipulation whatever had been made for the handing over of the English prisoners still in Mysore, previous to a cessation of hostilities. This condition, at least, should have been insisted upon, and carried out previous to any negotiations being entered upon. The reasons that induced Lord Cornwallis to make this treaty, when Seringapatam lay at his mercy, have ever been a mystery. Tippoo had proved himself a monster unfitted to live, much less to rule, and the crimes he had committed against the English should have been punished by the public trial and execution of their author. To conclude peace with him now was to enable him to make fresh preparations for war, and to necessitate another expedition at enormous cost and great loss of life. Tippoo had already proved that he was not to be bound either by treaties or oaths. And, lastly, it would have been thought that, as a general, Lord Cornwallis would have wished his name to go down to posterity in connection with the conquest of Mysore and the capture of Seringapatam, rather than with the memorable surrender of York Town, the greatest disaster that ever befell a British army.

The conditions were in themselves onerous, and had they been imposed upon any other than a brutal and faithless tyrant, might have been deemed sufficient. Tippoo was deprived of half his dominions, which were to be divided among the allies, each taking the portions adjacent to their territory. A sum of £3,300,000 was to be paid for the expenses of the war; all prisoners of the allied powers were to be restored. Two of Tippoo's sons were to be given up as hostages. Even after they had been handed over, there were considerable delays before Tippoo's signature was obtained, and it was not until Lord Cornwallis threatened to resume hostilities that, on the 18th of March, a treaty was finally sealed. Of the ceded territory the Mahrattis and the Nizam each took a third as their share, although the assistance they had rendered in the struggle had been but of comparatively slight utility. It may, indeed, be almost said that it was given to them as a reward for not accepting the offers Tippoo had made them of joining with him against the British.

The British share included a large part of the Malabar coast, with the forts of Calicut and Cananore, and the territory of our ally, the Rajah of Coorg. These cessions gave us the passes leading into Mysore from the west. On the south we gained possession of the fort of Dindegul and the districts surrounding it, while on the east we acquired the tract from Amboor to Caroor, and so obtained possession of several important fortresses, together with the chief passes by which Hyder had made his incursions into the Carnatic.

Dick felt deeply the absence of any proviso in the treaty that all prisoners should be restored previous to a cessation of hostilities, at the same time admitting the argument of his uncle that although under such an agreement some prisoners might be released, there was no means of insuring that the stipulation would be faithfully carried out.

"You see, Dick, no one knows, or has indeed the faintest idea, what prisoners Tippoo still has in his hands. We do not know how many have been murdered during the years Tippoo has reigned. Men who have escaped have from time to time brought down news of murders in the places where they had been confined, but they have known little of what has happened elsewhere. Moreover, we have learned that certainly fifty or sixty were put to death at Seringapatam before we advanced upon it the first time; we know, too, that some were murdered in the hill-forts that we have captured. But how many remain alive at the present time we have not the slightest idea. Tippoo might hand over a dozen, and take a solemn oath that there was not one remaining; and though we might feel perfectly certain that he was lying, we should be in no position to prove it.

"The stipulation ought to have been made, if only as a matter of honour, but it would have been of no real efficiency. Of course, if we had dethroned Tippoo and annexed all his territory, we should undoubtedly have got at all the prisoners, wherever they were hidden. But we could hardly have done that. It would have aroused the jealousy and fear of every native prince in India. It would have united the Nizam and the Mahrattis against us, and would even have been disapproved of in England, where public opinion is adverse to further acquisitions of territory, and where people are, of course, altogether ignorant of the monstrous cruelties perpetrated by Tippoo, not only upon English captives, but upon his neighbours everywhere.

"Naturally I am prejudiced in favour of this treaty, for the handing over of the country from Amboor to Caroor with all the passes and forts will set us free at Tripataly from the danger of being again over-run and devastated by Mysore; my people will be able to go about their work peacefully and in security, free alike from fear of wholesale invasion or incursions of robber-bands from the ghauts; all my waste lands will be taken up; my revenue will be trebled. There is another thing: now that the English possess territory beyond that of the Nabob of Arcot, and are gradually spreading their power north, there can be little doubt that before long the whole country of Arcot, Travancore, Tanjore, and other small native powers, will be incorporated in their dominions. Arcot is powerless for defence, and while, during the last two wars, it has been nominally an ally of the English, the Nabob has been able to give them no real assistance whatever, and the burden of his territory has fallen on them. They took the first step when, at the beginning of the present war, they arranged with him to utilise all the resources and collect the revenues of his possessions, and to allow him an annual income for the maintenance of his state and family. This is clearly the first step towards taking the territory into their own hands and managing its revenues, and the same will be done in other cases. Lord Cornwallis the other day, in thanking me for the services that you and I and the troop have rendered, promised me that an early arrangement should be made by which I should rule Tripataly under the government of Madras, instead of under the Nabob.

This, you see, will be virtually a step in rank, and I shall hold my land direct from the English instead of from a prince who has become in fact a puppet in their hands."

A few days later the army set off on its march from Mysore, and the same day the Rajah, after making his adieus to Lord Cornwallis, started with his troop for Tripataly, making his way by long marches instead of following the slow progress of the army. After a couple of days at Tripataly, they went down to Madras, and brought back the Rajah's household. The meeting between Dick and his mother was one of mixed feeling. It was twenty months since the former had left with his uncle, and he was now nearly eighteen. He had written whenever there was an opportunity of sending any letters; and although his position as interpreter on the staff of the general had relieved her from any great anxiety on his account, she was glad indeed to see him again. Upon the other hand, the fact that, as the war went on and fortress after fortress had been captured, no news came to her that her hopes had been realised, and that the war had now come to a termination without the mystery that hung over her husband being in any way cleared up, had profoundly depressed Mrs. Holland, and it was with mingled tears of pleasure and sorrow that she fell on his neck on his return to Madras.

"You must not give way, mother," Dick said, as she sobbed out her fears that all hope was at an end. "Remember that you have never doubted he was alive, and that you have always said you would know if any evil fate had befallen him; and I have always felt confident that you were right. There is nothing changed. I certainly have not succeeded in finding him, but we have found many prisoners in some of the little out-of-the-way forts. Now, some of them have been captives quite as long as he has; therefore there is no reason whatever why he should not also be alive. I have no thought of giving up the search as hopeless. I mean to carry out our old plans; and certainly I am much better fitted to do so than I was when I first landed here. I know a great deal about Mysore, and although I don't say I speak the dialect like a native, I have learnt a good deal of it, and can speak it quite as well as the natives of the ghauts and outlying provinces. Surajah, who is a great friend of mine, has told me that if I go he will go too, and that will be a tremendous help. Anyhow, as long as you continue to believe firmly that father is still alive, I mean to continue the search for him."

"I do believe that he is alive, Dick, as firmly as ever. I have not lost hope in that respect. It is only that I doubt now whether he will ever be found."

"Well, that is my business, mother. As long as you continue to believe that he is still alive, I shall continue to search for him. I have no other object in life at present. It will be quite soon enough for me to think of taking up the commission I have been promised when you tell me that your feeling that he is alive has been shaken."

Mrs. Holland was comforted by Dick's assurance and confident tone. and, putting the thought aside for a time, gave herself up to the pleasure of his return. They had found everything at Tripataly as they had left it, for the Mysore horsemen had not penetrated so far north before Tippoo turned his course east to Pondicherry. The people had, months before, returned to their homes and avocations.

One evening the Rajah said, as they were all sitting together,—

"I hear from my wife, Dick, that your mother has told her you still intend to carry out your original project."

"Yes, uncle; I have quite made up my mind as to that. There are still plenty of places where he may be, and certainly I am a good deal more fitted for travelling about in disguise in Mysore than I was before."

The Rajah nodded. "Yes; I think, Dick, you are as capable of taking care of yourself as any one could be. I hear that Surajah is willing to go with you, and this will certainly be a great advantage. He has proved himself thoroughly intelligent and trustworthy, and I have promised him that some day he shall be captain of the troop. You are not thinking of starting just yet I suppose?"

"No, uncle; I thought of staying another month or two before I go off again. Mother says she cannot let me go before that."

"I fancy it will take you longer than that, Dick, before you can pass as a native."

Dick looked surprised.

"Why, uncle, I did pass as a native eighteen months ago."

"Yes, you did, Dick; but for how long? You went into shops, bought things, chatted for a short time with natives, and so on; but that is not like living among them. You would be found out before you had been a single day in the company of a native."

Dick looked still more surprised.

"How, uncle? What do I do that they would know me by."

"It is not what you do, Dick, but it is what you don't do. You can't sit on your heels—squat, as you call it. That is the habitual attitude of every native. He squats while he cooks; he squats for hours by the fire, smoking and talking; he never stands for any length of time, and except upon a divan or something of that sort he never sits down. Before you can go and live among the natives and pass as one for any length of time, you must learn to squat as they do for hours at a stretch; and I can tell you that it is not by any means an easy accomplishment to learn. I myself have quite lost the power. I used to be able to do it as a boy, but from always sitting on divans or chairs in European fashion I have got out of the way of it, and I don't think I could squat for a quarter of an hour to save my life."

Dick's mother and cousins laughed heartily, but he said, seriously, "You are quite right, uncle; I wonder I never thought of it before; it was stupid of me not to do so. Of course, when I have been talking with Surajah or other officers, by a camp fire, I have sat on the ground; but I see that it would never do in native dress. I will begin at once."

"Wait a moment, Dick," the Rajah said, "there are other things which you will have to practise. You may have to move in several disguises, and must learn to comport yourself in accordance with them. You must remember that your motions are quicker and more energetic than are those of people here; your walk is different; the swing of the arms, your carriage, are all different from theirs; you are unaccustomed to walk either barefooted or in native shoes. Now, all these things have to be practised before you can really pass muster, therefore I propose that you shall at once accustom yourself to the attire, which you can do in our apartments of an evening. The ranee and the boys will be able to correct your first awkwardness and to teach you much.

"After a week or two you must stain your face, arms, and legs, and go out with Rajbullub in the evening. "You must keep your eyes open and watch everything that passes, and do as you see others do. When Rajbullub thinks that you can pass muster, you will take to going out with him in the daylight, and so you will come in time to reach a point that it will be safe for you to begin your attempt. Do not watch only the peasants. There is no saying that it may not be necessary to take to other disguises. Observe the traders, the soldiers, and even the fakirs. You will see that they walk each with a different mien. The trader is slow and sober; the man who wears a sword walks with a certain swagger; the fakir is everything by turns; he whines, and threatens; he sometimes mumbles his prayers and sometimes shrieks at the top of his voice. When you are not riding or shooting, lad, do not spend your time in the garden, or with the women; go into the town and keep your eyes open. Bear in mind that you are learning a lesson, and that your life depends upon your being perfect in every respect. As to your first disguise, I will speak to Rajbullub and he will get it ready by to-morrow evening. The dress of the peasant of Mysore differs little from that here, save that he wears rather more clothing than is necessary in this warm climate."

CHAPTER X.

IN DISGUISE.

ON the following evening Dick appeared in the room where the others were sitting, in the dress Rajbullub had got for him, and which was similar to that of other peasants. The boys had already been told that he was shortly going on a journey, and that it would be necessary for him to travel in disguise, but had been warned that it was a matter that was not to be spoken of to any one. The early respect that Dick's strength and activity had inspired them with had been much shaken when they discovered that he was unable either to ride or shoot; but their father's narrative of his adventures when scouting with Surajah had completely reinstated him in their high opinion. When he entered, however, they burst out laughing. The two ladies could not help smiling, and Dick was not long before he joined in the laugh against himself. He had felt uncomfortable enough when he started in an almost similar dress with Surajah, although there was then no one to criticise his appearance; but now, in the presence of his mother and aunt, he felt strangely uncomfortable.

"Never mind, Dick," his uncle said encouragingly. "The boys would feel just as uncomfortable as you do now, if they were dressed up in European fashion. Now, while we are talking, make your first attempt at sitting on your heels."

Dick squatted down until his knees nearly touched his chest, and a moment later lost his balance and toppled over, amid a roar of laughter. Next time he balanced himself more carefully.

"That is right, Dick; you will get accustomed to it in time. But you must see already that there is a good deal more to be done than you thought of, before you can pass as a native. Remember you must not only be able to balance yourself while sitting still, but must be able to use your hands—for cooking purposes, for example, for eating, or for doing anything there may be to do—not only without losing your balance, but without showing that you are balancing yourself."

"It is much more difficult than I thought, uncle. Of course I have always seen the natives squatting like this, but it seemed so natural that it never struck me it was difficult at all. I say, it is beginning to hurt already; my shin-bones are aching horribly."

"Yes; that is where the strain comes, my boy. But you have got to stick to it until your muscles there, which have never been called into play in this way before, get accustomed to the work."

"I understand that, uncle; it was just the same with my arms when I began to climb. But I can't stand this any longer. I can no more get up than I can fly;" and Dick rolled over on to his side. Again and again he tried, after a short rest between each trial. As he gave it up and limped stiffly to the divan, he said, "I feel as if some one had been kicking me on the shins until he had nearly broken them, mother. I have been kicked pretty badly several times in fights by rough fellows at home in Shadwell, but it never hurt like this;" and he rubbed his aching legs ruefully. "Well, uncle, I am very much obliged to you for putting me up to practising this position. It seemed to me that it would be quite a simple thing to walk along quietly, and to move my arms about as they do; but I never thought of this. I wonder, mother, you never told me that above all things I should have to learn to squat on my heels for any time; it would not have been so difficult to learn it five or six years ago, when I was not anything like so heavy as I am now."

"It never once occurred to me, Dick; I wish it had. I thought I had foreseen every difficulty, but it never once came into my mind that in order to pass as a native you must be able to sit like one."

"Ah, well, I shall learn in time, mother," Dick replied cheerfully. "Every exercise is hard at first, but one soon gets accustomed to it."

Dick threw himself with his usual energy into his new work. Although of a morning when he first woke his shins caused him the most acute pain, he always spent half-an-hour in practice; afterwards he would sit for some time allowing the water from the tap at the side of the bath to flow upon the aching muscles; then he would dress, and, as soon as breakfast was over, go for a run in the garden. At first it was but a shamble, but gradually the terrible stiffness would wear off, and he would return to the house comparatively well. Of an evening the practice was longer, and was kept up until the aching pain became unendurable. At the end of four or five days he was scarcely able to walk at all, but after that time matters improved, and three weeks later he could preserve the attitude for half-an-hour at a time.

In other respects his training had gone on uninterruptedly every day. He went out into the town, accompanied sometimes by Rajbullub, sometimes by Surajah, in the disguises of either a peasant, a soldier, or a trader, and learnt to walk and carry himself in accordance with his dress. Before putting on these disguises, he painted himself with a solution that could easily be washed off on his return to the palace, where he now always wore a European dress.

"You cannot be too careful," the Rajah said. "There are of course Mohammedans here, and, for aught we know, some may act as agents or spies of Tippoo, just as the English have agents and spies in Mysore. Were one of them to send word that you had taken to Indian attire, and that it was believed that you were about to undertake some mission or other, it would add considerably to your difficulties and dangers. As it is, no one outside our own circle ever sees you about with me or the boys, except in your European dress, and Rajbullub tells me that in no single instance while you have been in disguise has any suspicion been excited, or question asked by the people of various classes with whom you and he converse in the streets."

Another month passed, and by this time Dick could,

without any great fatigue, squat on his heels for an hour at a time. As the date for his departure drew near, his mother became more and more nervous and anxious.

"I shall never forgive myself if you do not come back," she said one day when they were alone. "I cannot but feel that I have been selfish, and that really, on the strength of a conviction which most people would laugh at as whimsical and absurd, I am risking the substance for a shadow, and am imperilling the life of my only boy upon the faint chance that he may find my husband. I know that even your uncle, although he has always been most kind about it, and assisted in every way in his power, has but little belief in the success of your search, although, as he sees how bent I am upon it, he says nothing that might dash my hopes. If evil comes of it, Dick, I shall never forgive myself; I shall feel that I have sacrificed you to a sort of hallucination."

"I can only say, mother," Dick replied, "that I came out here and entered into your plans only because I had the most implicit faith that you were right; I should now continue it on my own account, even if to-morrow you should be taken from me. Of course, I see plainly enough that the chances are greatly against my ever hearing anything of father; but from what has taken place during the campaign, I have seen that there must be many British captives still hidden away among the hill-forts, and it is quite possible he may be among them. I do not even say that it is probable, but the chances are not so very greatly against it; and even if I thought they were smaller—much smaller than I believe them to be—I should still consider it my duty to go up and try and find him. So, even if it should happen that I never come back again, you will not have yourself to blame, for it is not you that are sending me, but I who am going of my free will; and indeed, I feel it so much my duty that even were you to turn round now and ask me to stay, I should still think it right to undertake this mission.

"But indeed, mother, I see no great danger in it; in fact,

scarcely any danger at all—at any rate, unless I find father. If I do so, there might certainly be risk in attempting to get him away; but this, if I am lucky enough in discovering him, will not weigh with me for an instant. If I do not find him, it seems to me that the risk is a mere nothing. Surajah and I will wander about, enlisting in the garrisons of forts; then, if we find there are no prisoners there, we shall take an early opportunity of getting away. In some places, no doubt, I shall be able to learn from men of the garrison whether there are prisoners, without being forced to enter at all; for although in the great forts, like Savandroog and Outradroog, it is considered so important the defences should be kept secret that none of the garrison are allowed to leave until they are discharged as too old for service, there is no occasion for the same precaution in the case of less important places. Thus, you see, we shall simply have to wander about, keeping our eyes and ears open, and finding out, either from the peasants or the soldiers themselves, whether there are any prisoners there."

"I wish I could go with you, Dick. I used to think that when the work of searching for your father had begun I could wait patiently for the result, but instead of that I find myself even more anxious and more nervous than I was at Shadwell."

"I can quite understand, mother, that it is very much more trying work sitting here waiting, than it is to be actively engaged. The only thing is, that you must promise me not to trouble more than you can help, for if I think of you as sitting here fretting about me, I shall worry infinitely more than I otherwise should over any difficulties we may have to encounter. You must remember that I shall have Surajah with me; he is a capital companion, and will always be able to advise me upon native business. He is as plucky as a fellow can be, and I can trust him to do anything just as I would myself."

The preparations for departure now began in earnest. There was some discussion as to the arms that were to be taken, but at last it was decided that with safety they could carry nothing beyond a matchlock, a pistol, and a sword each. Great pains were taken in the selection of the matchlocks. In the armoury were several weapons of high finish, with silver mountings, that had belonged to the Rajah's father and grandfather. These were tried against each other, and the two that were proved to be the most accurate were chosen. Dick found, indeed, that at distances up to a hundred yards, they were quite equal to the English rifle he had brought out. The silver mountings were taken off, and then the pieces differed in no way in appearance from those in general use among the peasantry. The pistols were chosen with equal care. The swords were of finely tempered steel, the blades being removed from their jewelled handles, for which were substituted rough handles of ordinary metal.

Ten gold pièces were sewn up underneath the iron bands encircling the leathern scabbard, as many under the bosses of their shields, and five pieces in the soles of each of their shoes. In their waist-sashes, the ordinary receptacle of money, each carried a small bag with native silver coins. At last all was ready, and an hour before daybreak Dick took a cheerful farewell of his mother and a hearty one of his uncle, and, with Surajah, passed through the town and struck up into the hills. Each carried a bag slung over his shoulder, well filled with provisions, a small water-bottle, and, hung upon his matchlock, a change of clothing. In the folds of his turban Dick had a packet of the powder used for making dye, so that he could at any time renew the brown shade, when it began to fade out. For a time but few words were spoken. Dick knew that although his mother had borne up bravely till the last, she would break down as soon as he left her, and the thought that he might never see her again weighed heavily upon him.

Surajah, on the contrary, was filled with elation at the prospect of adventures and dangers, and he was silent simply because he felt that for the present his young lord was in no humour for speech. As soon as the sun rose, Dick shook off his depression. They were now a considerable distance up the hill-side. There was no path, for the people of Tripataly had no occasion to visit Mysore, and still less desire for a visit from the Mysoreans. Periodically, raids were made upon the villages and plains by marauders from the hills, but these were mostly by the passes through the ghauts, thirty or forty miles left or right from the little state which, nestling at the foot of the hills, for the most part escaped these visitations—which, now that the British had become possessed of the territories and the hills, had, it was hoped, finally ceased. Nevertheless, the people were always prepared for such visits. Every cultivator had a pit in which he stored his harvest, except so much as was needed for his immediate wants. The pit was lined with mats, others were laid over the grain; two feet of soil was then placed over the mats, and, after the ground had been ploughed, there was no indication of the existence of the hiding-place.

The town itself was surrounded by a wall of sufficient strength to withstand the attacks of any parties of marauders, and the custom of keeping a man on a watch-tower was still maintained. At the foot of the tower stood a heavy gun, whose discharge would at once warn the peasants for miles round of an enemy, calling those near to hasten to the shelter of the town, while the men of the villages at a distance could hurry, with their wives and families, to hiding-places among the hills.

Dick and Surajah had no need of a path, for they were well acquainted with the ground, and had often wandered up nearly to the crest of the hills in pursuit of game. An hour before noon they took their seats under a rock that shaded them from the sun's rays and, sitting down, partook of a hearty meal. There was no occasion for haste, and they prepared for rest until the heat of the day was passed.

"We are fairly off now, Surajah," Dick said, as he stretched himself out comfortably. "I have been thinking of this almost as long as I can remember, and can hardly believe that it has come to pass."

"I have thought of it but a short time, my lord."

"No, no, Surajah," Dick interrupted. "You know it was arranged that from the first you were to call me Purseram, for unless you get accustomed to it, you will be calling me 'my lord' in the hearing of others."

"I had forgotten," Surajah replied with a smile, and then went on. "It is but a short time since I was sure I was going with you, but I have ever hoped that the time would come when, instead of the dull work of drilling men and placing them on guard, I might have the opportunity of taking part in war and adventure, and indeed had thought of asking my lord your uncle to permit me to go away for a while in one of the Company's regiments, and there to learn my business. Since the English have become masters, and there is no longer war between rajah and rajah, as there used to be in olden times, this is the only way that a man of spirit can gain distinction. But this adventure is far better, for there will be much danger, and need for caution as well as courage."

Dick nodded. "More for caution and coolness than for courage I think, Surajah; it will only be in case we find my father, or if any grave suspicion falls on us, that there will be need for courage. Once well into Mysore, I see but little chance of suspicion falling upon us. We have agreed that we will first make for Seringapatam, avoiding as much as possible all places on the way where inquiries whence we come may be made of us. Once in the city, we shall be safe from such questions, and can travel thence where we will; and it will be hard if we do not, when there, manage to learn the places at which any prisoners there may be, are most likely to be kept. Besides, my father is as likely to be there as anywhere, for Tippoo may, since our army marched away, have ordered all prisoners to be brought down from the hill-forts to Seringapatam."

When the sun had lost its power they proceeded on their way again. Their start had been timed so that for the first week they would have moonlight, and would therefore be able to travel at night until they arrived at Seringapatam. It was considered that it was only necessary to do this for the first two or three nights, as, after that, the tale that they were coming from a village near the frontier, and were on their way to join Tippoo's army, would seem natural enough to any villagers who might question them. They continued their course until nearly midnight, by which time they were both completely fatigued, and, choosing a spot sheltered by bushes, lay down to sleep. It took another two days before they were clear of the broken country, and the greater portion of this part of the journey they performed in daylight. Occasionally they saw in the distance the small forts which guarded every road to the plateau; to these they always gave a very wide berth, as although, according to the terms of peace, they should all have been evacuated, they might still be occupied by parties of Tippoo's troops. Indeed, all the news that had arrived since the army left, represented Tippoo as making every effort to strengthen his army and fortresses, and to prepare for a renewal of the war.

Several times they saw bears, which abounded among the ghauts, and once beheld two tigers crossing a nullah. They had, however, other matters to think of, and neither the flesh nor the skins of the bears would have been of any use to them. The work was severe, and they were glad when at last they reached the level country. In some of the upper valleys opening on to this they had seen small villages. Near one of these they had slept, and as in the morning they saw that the inhabitants were Hindoos, they fearlessly went out and talked with them, in order to gain some information as to the position of the forts, and to learn whether any bodies of Tippoo's troops were likely to be met with. They found the people altogether ignorant on these matters. They were simple peasants; their whole thoughts were given to tilling their land and bringing in sufficient to live upon and to satisfy the demands of the tax-gatherers when they visited them. They had little communication with other villages, and knew nothing of what was passing outside their own. They evinced no curiosity whatever concerning their visitors, who bought from them some cakes of ground ragee, which formed the chief article of their food.

The country through which they passed on emerging from the hills was largely covered with bush and jungle, and was very thinly populated. It was an almost unbroken flat, save that here and there isolated masses of rock rose above it; these were extremely steep and inaccessible, and on their summits were the hill-forts that formed so prominent a feature in the warfare of both Mysore and the Nizam's dominions to the north. These forts were, for the most part, considered absolutely impregnable, but the last war with the British had proved that they were not so, as several of the strongest had been captured, with comparatively slight loss. Whenever they passed within a few miles of one of these hill-fortresses, Dick looked at it with anxious eyes, for there, for aught he knew, his father might be languishing.

After two days' walking across the plain they felt that there was no longer any necessity for concealment, except that it would be as well to avoid an encounter with any troops. Although, therefore, they avoided the principal roads, they kept along beaten paths, and did not hesitate to enter villages to buy food. They no longer saw caste marks on the foreheads of the inhabitants. The Hindoos had been compelled by force to abandon their religion, all who refused to do so being put to death at once. Dick and Surajah found that their dialect differed much more from that of the country below the ghauts than they had expected, and, although they had no difficulty in conversing with the peasants, they found that their idea that they would be able to pass as natives of one of these villages was an altogether erroneous one.

"This will never do, Surajah," Dick said, as they left one of the villages. "We shall have to alter our story somehow, for the first person we meet in Seringapatam will see that we are not natives of Mysore. We must give out that we come from some village far down on the ghauts—one of those which have been handed over to the English by the new treaty. You know the country well enough there to be able to answer any questions that may be asked. We must say that, desiring to be soldiers, and hating the English raj, we have crossed the hills to take service of some sort in Mysore. This will be natural enough: and of course there are many Mohammedans down in the plains, especially among the villages on the ghauts.

"I think that would be best, Purseram."

"There is one comfort," Dick went on: "it is evident that Tippoo is hated by all the Hindoos. He has forced them to change their religion, and we need have no fear of being betrayed by any of them, except from pressure, or from a desire to win Tippoo's good-will."

"Yes, that might be the case with those who are fairly well off, but would scarcely be so among the poorer classes; besides, even they, were we living among them, would have no reason for suspecting our story. There seems no doubt, from what they say, that Tippoo is preparing for war again, and I think that we shall do well, as soon as we enter the city, to change our attire, or we might be forced into joining the army, which would be the last thing we want. What I should desire above all things, is to get service of some kind in the Palace."

After six days' travel they saw the walls of Seringapatam.

Dick had made many inquiries at the last halting-place as to the position of the fords on that side of the town, and learned that only those leading to the fort were guarded. The ford opposite the town was freely open to traffic, and could be crossed without question by country people, although a watch was kept to see that none of the very numerous prisoners escaped by it. It was here, therefore, that they crossed the river, the water being little more than knee-deep. No questions were asked by the guard as they passed, their appearance differing in no way from that of the peasants of the neighbourhood. After a quarter of a mile's walk they entered the town. It was open, and undefended by a wall; the streets were wide, and laid out at right angles. The shops, however, were poor, for the slightest appearance of wealth sufficed to excite the cupidity of Tippoo or his agents, and the possessor would be exposed to exorbitant demands, which, if not complied with, would have entailed first torture and then death. The streets, however, presented a busy appearance. They were thronged with soldiers; battalions of recruits passed along, and it was evident that Tippoo was doing all in his power to raise the strength of his army to its former level. They wandered about for some time, and at last, in a small street, Dick went up to an old man whose face pleased him; he was standing at the door of his house.

"We desire to find a room where we can lodge for a time," he said. "Can you direct us where we can obtain one?"

"You are not soldiers?" the old man asked.

"No; we desire to earn our living, but have not yet decided whether to join the army."

"You are from the plains?" the native said sharply, in their own dialect.

"That is so," Dick replied.

"And yet you are Mohammedans?"

"Every one is Mohammedan here."

"Ah! because it is the choice of 'death or Mohammed.' How comes it that two young men should voluntarily leave their homes to enter this tiger's den? You look honest youths. How come you here?"

"I trust that we are honest," Dick said. "We have assuredly not ventured here without a reason, and that reason is a good one; but this is not a city where one talks of such matters to a stranger in the street, even though his face tells one that he can be trusted with a secret."

The old man was silent for a minute; then he said, "Come in, my sons; you can, as you say, trust me. I have a room that you can occupy."

They followed him into the house, and he led them into a small room at the back. It was poorly furnished, but was scrupulously clean. A pan of lighted charcoal stood in one corner, and over this a pot of rice was boiling.

"I bid you welcome," he said gravely. And as the salutation was not one in use by the Mohammedans, Dick saw that his idea that the old man was a Hindoo who had been forced to abjure his religion, was a correct one. The old man motioned to them to take their seats on the divan.

"I do not ask for your confidence," he said, "but if you choose to give it to me it will be sacred, and it may be that, poor as I am, I am able to aid you. I will tell you at once that I am a native of Conjeveram and, of course, a Hindoo. I was settled as a trader at Mysore the old capital; but when, four years ago, the tyrant destroyed that town, I, with over a hundred thousand of our religion, was forced to adopt Mohammedanism. I was of high caste and, like many others, would have preferred death to yielding, had it not been that I had a young daughter; and for her sake I lived, and moved here from Mysore. I gained nothing by my sin. I was one of the wealthiest traders in the whole city, and I had been here but a month when Tippoo's soldiers burst in one day; my daughter was carried off to the Tiger's harem, and I was threatened with torture unless I divulged the hiding-place of my money. It was useless to resist. My wealth was now worthless to me, and without hesitation I complied with their demands; and all I had was seized, save one small hoard which was enough to keep me thus to the end of my days. My wants are few: a handful of rice or grain a day, and I am satisfied. I should have put an end to my life, were it not that according to our religion the suicide is accursed; and, moreover, I would fain live to see the vengeance that must some day fall upon the tyrant. After what I have said, it is for you to decide whether you think I can be trusted with your secret, for I am sure it is for no slight reason that you have come to this accursed city."

Dick felt that he could safely speak, and that he would find in this native a very valuable ally. He therefore told his story without concealment. Except that an exclamation of surprise broke from his lips when Dick said that he was

English, the old man listened without a remark until he had finished.

"Your tale is indeed a strange one," he said, when he had heard the story. "I had looked for something out of the ordinary, but assuredly for nothing so strange as this. Truly you English are a wonderful people. It is marvellous that one should come all the way from beyond the black water to seek for a father lost so many years ago. Methinks that a blessing will surely alight upon such filial piety, and that you will find your father yet alive. Were it not for that, I should deem your search a useless one. Thousands of Englishmen have been massacred during the last ten years; hundreds have died of disease and suffering; many have been poisoned. Many officers have also been murdered, some of them here, but more in the hill-forts; for it was there they were generally sent when their deaths were determined upon. Still, he may live. There are men who have been here as many years and who yet survive."

"Then this is where the main body of the prisoners were kept?" Dick asked.

"Yes; all were brought here, native and English. Tens of thousands of boys and youths, swept up by Tippoo's armies from the Malabar coast and the Carnatic, were brought up here and formed into battalions, and these English prisoners were forced to drill them. It was but a poor drill. I have seen them drilling their recruits at Conjeveram, and the difference between the quick sharp order there and the listless command here was great indeed. Consequently the Englishmen were punished by being heavily ironed, and kept at starvation point for the slackness with which they obeyed the tyrant's orders. Sometimes they were set to sweep the streets, sometimes they were beaten till they well-nigh expired under the lash. Often would they have died of hunger, were it not that Tippoo's own troops took pity on them and supplied them from their store. Some of the boys, drummer-boys, or ship's-boys, or little ship's officers, were kept in the Palace and trained as singers and dancers for Tippoo's amusement. Very many of the white prisoners were handed over to Tippoo by Admiral Sufferin. Though how a Christian could have brought himself to hand over Christians to this tiger, I cannot imagine.

"Others were captured in forays, and there were till lately many survivors of the force that surrendered in Hyder's time. There are certainly some in other towns, for it was the policy of Hyder, as it is of Tippoo, always to break up parties of prisoners. Many were sent to Bangalore, some to Burrampore, and very many to the fort of Chillembroom; but I heard that nearly all these died of famine and disease very quickly. While Tippoo at times considers himself strong enough to fight the English, and is said to aim at the conquest of all southern India, he has yet a fear of Englishmen, and he thus separates his captives, lest, if they were together, they should plot against him and bring about a rising. He knows that all the old Hindoo population are against him, and that even among the Mohammedans he is very unpopular. The Chelah battalions, who numbered twelve or fourteen thousand, made up entirely of those he has dragged from their homes in districts devastated by him, would assuredly have joined against him, were there a prospect of success, just as they seized the opportunity to desert six months ago, when the English attacked the camp across the river.

"Now, if you will tell me in what way I can best serve you, I will do so. In the first place, sturdy young peasants are wanted for the army, and assuredly you will not be here many days before you will find yourselves in the ranks, whether you like it or not; for Tippoo is in no way particular how he gets recruits."

CHAPTER XI.

A USEFUL FRIEND.

"I AGREE with you that it would be a disadvantage to go as a soldier," Dick said, after a pause; "but what disguise would you recommend us to choose?"

"That I must think over. You both look too straight and active to be employed as the assistants of a trader, or I could have got some of my friends to take you in that capacity. The best disguise will be a gayer attire, such as would be worn by the retainers of some of the chiefs; and were it not that, if questioned, you could not say who was your employer, that is what I should recommend."

"I saw a number of men working at a battery they are erecting by the river side; could we not take service there until something better presents itself?"

"I should not advise that," the native replied, "for the work is very hard and the pay poor; indeed, most of those employed on it are men driven in from the country round and forced to labour, getting only enough pay to furnish them with the poorest food. There would also be the disadvantage that if you were so employed you would have no opportunity of seeing any English captives who may have been brought here of late. All that I can at present do myself, is to speak to some of my friends who have been here for a long time, and ask them whether they can remember an English captive being sent up here from Coorg, some eight years ago, and whether they ever heard what was his fate. I should say, of course, that I have received a message from friends at Conjeveram, that some of the man's relations have sent out to make inquiries concerning him, and asking me if I can find any news as to his fate. My friends may not know themselves, but they may be able to find out from others. Very many of our people were forced into the ranks of the army, and there is not a regiment which has not some men who, although regarded as Mohammedans, are still at heart, as we all are, as true to our faith as ever.

"It is from these that we are more likely to obtain information than in any other way. You will not be very long before you will be able to satisfy yourself as to whether or not he whom you seek is in this city; and if he should not be here, there remain but the two towns that I have named, and the hill-forts. As to these, it will be well-nigh impossible to obtain an entrance, so jealously are they all guarded. None save the garrisons are allowed to enter. The paths, which are often so steep and difficult that men and provisions have to be slung up in baskets, are guarded night and day, and none are allowed to approach the foot of the rocks within musket shot lest, I suppose, they might find some spot where an ascent could be made. The garrisons are seldom changed. The soldiers are allowed to take their wives and families up with them, but once there, they are as much prisoners as those in the dungeons. That is one reason why captives once sent up there never come down again, for were they to do so they might, if by chance they escaped, be able to give information as to the approaches that would assist an assailing force.

"I do not say that all are killed, though undoubtedly most of them are put to death soon after they arrive; but it may be that some are retained in confinement, either from no orders being sent for their execution, or from their very existence being in time forgotten by the tyrant here. Some of these may languish in dungeons, others may have gained the good-will of the commanders of the fort—for even among the Mohammedans there are doubtless many good and merciful men. Now for the present: this house has but one storey in front, but there is a room over this, and that is at your service. Furniture it has none, but I will, this evening, get a couple of trusses of straw. It is but a loft, but you will not want to use it, save to sleep in. You need not fear interruption in this house. There is scarce a man here that is not, like myself, a Hindoo, for when we were brought here from Mysore the piece of ground on which the street stands was assigned to us, and we were directed to build houses here.

"Few besides ourselves ever enter it, for those who still carry on trade have booths in the market-place. There is one thing I will tell you at once. We, the persecuted, have means of recognising each other: outward signs there are none, neither caste mark nor peculiarity of dress; but we know each other by signs. When we salute we turn in the thumbs as we raise our hands to our turbans—so. If we have no occasion to salute, as we move our hands, either to stroke our faces, or to touch the handles of our daggers, or in other way, we keep the thumb turned in. If the man be one of ourselves, he replies in the same way; then, to prevent the possibility of error, the one asks the other a question—on what subject it matters not, providing that before he speaks, he coughs slightly. You must remember that such communication is not made lightly; were it to be so it would soon attract notice. It is used when you want to know whether you can trust a man. It is as much as to say, Are you a friend? can I have confidence in you? will you help me?—and you can see that there are many occasions on which such knowledge may be most useful, even to the saving of life."

"I do indeed see it," Dick said, "and greatly are we indebted to you for telling us of it."

They remained talking with their host, whose name was, he told them, Pertaub, until darkness came on. They had shared his rice with him, and had requested him to lay in such provision as was necessary for them; and as soon as it became dark they went out, leaving their guns behind them. Busy as the main streets were when they had before passed through them, they were very much more so now; the shops were all lighted up by lanterns or small lamps, and the streets were filled with troops, now dismissed from duty, and bent, some on amusement, some in purchasing small additions to their rations with the scanty pay allowed to them. In the open spaces the soldiers were crowded round performers of various kinds. Here was a juggler throwing balls and knives into the air; there was a snake-charmer—a Hindoo, doubtless, but too old and too poor to be worth persecuting; a short distance off was an acrobat turning and twisting himself into strange postures. Two sword-players, with bucklers and blunted tulwars, played occasionally against each other, and offered to engage any of the bystanders; occasionally the invitation would be accepted, but the sword-players always proved too skilful for the rough soldiers, who retired discomfited, amid the jeers of their comrades. More than one party of musicians played what seemed to Dick most discordant music, but which was appreciated by the soldiers, as was evident from the plaudits and the number of small coins thrown to the players. In the great open space by the side of the market the crowd was thickest. Here were large numbers of booths gay with lamps; in one were arranged, on tables, trays of cheap trinkets, calicoes, cloths, blankets, shoes, and other articles of dress; in another were arms, matchlocks, pistols, tulwars, and daggers. On the ground were lines of baskets filled with grain of many kinds, the vendors squatting patiently behind them. Some of the traders volubly accosted passers-by; others maintained a dignified silence, as if they considered the excellence of their wares needed no advertisement. It was not new, but it was very amusing to Dick, and it was late before they returned to their lodging.

"I wish," he said, as they strolled back, "that I were a good juggler or musician. It seems to me that it would be an excellent disguise, and we could go everywhere without question, and get admittance into all sorts of places we could not get a chance of entering into in any other way."

"Yes, that would be a good thing," Surajah agreed; "but I am sure that I could not do anything, even if you could."

"No, I quite see that, and I am not thinking of trying; but it would have been a first-rate plan."

"You are very good at sword-play," Surajah suggested, although somewhat doubtfully.

Dick laughed. "The first really good swordsman that came along would make an exhibition of me. No; one would have to do something really well."

The subject was renewed after they had seated themselves with Pertaub.

"It would be an excellent disguise," he agreed; "a good juggler could gain admission to the Palace, and might even enter forts where no others could set foot; for life there is dull indeed, and any one who could amuse the soldiers would be certain of a welcome, and even a governor might be willing to see his feats."

"Could one bribe a conjurer to let one pass as his assistant?"

"That would be impossible," the Hindoo said, "for an assistant would have opportunities for learning the tricks, and no money would induce a really good juggler to divulge his secrets, which have been passed down from father to son for centuries."

"If one had thought of it," Dick said, "one could have bought in London very many things which would have seemed almost magical to the people here. I am afraid that we must go on, on our old line; it is a pity, for the other would have been first-rate."

"I have obtained for you this evening two suits of clothes such as we spoke of; in them you can pass as followers of some petty rajah, and are not likely to attract attention. I have inquired among some of my friends, and hear that the Rajah of Bohr left here to-day with his following; he is but a petty chief, and Bohr lies up north, close to the Nizam's frontier. Thus, if you should be asked in whose service you are, you will have a name to give, and there will be no fear of your being contradicted. If you are still further questioned by any one with a right to ask, you can say that you were told to remain here, in order to see how fast the drilling of the troops went on, and to send the Rajah a report when it is time for him to return here to accompany Tippoo on his march. You will, of course, account for your dialect by keeping to your present story that you came from a village on the ghauts in order to enter the service of one of our rajahs, and that your father having, years ago, been a soldier in the pay of the Rajah of Bohr, you made your way there direct, instead of coming to the capital."

"That will do excellently, Pertaub. It was a fortunate moment indeed that brought us to your door."

"I have done nothing as yet, Sahib; but I hope that in

time I may be able to be of use to you. It was fortunate for me as well as for you, perhaps, that you stopped at my door. Of late I have had nothing to think of save my own grief and troubles, but now I have something to give an interest to my life, and already I feel that I need not merely drag it on until I am relieved of its burden. And now, Sahibs, I am sure that rest must be needful for you, and would recommend that you seek your beds at once."

On the following morning Pertaub brought up the garments that he had bought for them. Nothing could be more irregular than the dress of the armed retainers of an Indian rajah. All attire themselves according to their fancy. Some carry spears and shields, others matchlocks; some wear turbans, others iron caps. The cut and colour of their garments are also varied in the extreme. Dick's dress consisted of a steel cap with a drooping plume of red horsehair, and a red tunic with a blue sash. Over it was worn a skirt of linked mail, which, with leggings fitting tightly, completed the costume. Surajah had a red turban, a jerkin of quilted leather with iron scales fastened on to protect the shoulders and chest. A scarlet kilt hung to his knees, and his legs were enclosed in putties or swathes of coarse cloth, wound round and round them. He wore a blue-and-gold girdle. Dick laughed as he surveyed the appearance of himself and Surajah.

"We are a rum-looking couple," he said, "but I have seen plenty of men just as gaudy in the train of some of the rajahs who visited the camp when we were up here. I think that it is a much better disguise than the one we wore yesterday. I sha'n't be afraid that the first officer we meet will ask us to what regiment we belong; there were scores of fellows lounging about in the streets last night, dressed as we are."

Sticking their swords and pistols into their girdles, they sallied out, and were pleased to find that no one paid the slightest attention to them. They remained in the town until some battalions of recruits poured out from the fort to drill on the grounds between it and the town. The first four that passed were, as Dick learnt from the remarks of some of the bystanders, composed entirely of boys—some of them Christians, thirty thousand of whom had been carried off by Tippoo in his raid on Travancore; and the young men were compelled to serve after being obliged to become, nominally, Mohammedans. After the Chelah battalions came those of Tippoo's army.

"These fellows look as if they could fight," Dick said. "They are an irregular lot, and don't seem to have an idea of keeping line or marching in step, but they are an active-looking set of fellows, and carry themselves well. As to the Chelahs, I should say they would be no good whatever, even if they could be relied on, which we know they cannot be. They look dejected and miserable, and I suppose hate it all as much as their officers do. I should back half a regiment of English to lick the twelve battalions. I wonder Tippoo himself does not see that troops like these must be utterly useless."

"I don't expect he thinks they would be of much use," Surajah agreed. "He only turned them into soldiers to gratify his hatred of them."

Leaving the troops, they walked on and entered the great fort, which enclosed an area of nearly two square miles. In this were Tippoo's palace, his storehouses,—containing grain sufficient for the garrison for a siege of many months,—mosques, the residences of Tippoo's officials and officers, the arsenals, and the huts for the troops. There was also a street of shops similar to those in the town. Wandering about, unquestioned, they came presently upon a scene that filled Dick with indignation and fury. Two white officers, heavily ironed, were seated on the ground; another, similarly ironed, lay stretched beside them. He was naked from the waist up; his back was covered with blood, and he had evidently been recently flogged until he fell insensible. Half a dozen savage-looking men, evidently executioners of Tippoo's orders, were standing round, jeering at the prisoners and refusing their entreaties to bring some water for their comrade.

"You brutes!" one of the captives exclaimed in English. "I would give all my hopes of liberty for ten minutes face to face with you, with swords in our hands."

"They would not be of much use to us," the other said quietly. "It is four days since we had a mouthful of food, and they would make very short work of us."

"All the better," the other exclaimed. "Death would be a thousand-fold preferable to this misery."

Dick felt that if he remained longer he would be unable to contain himself, and turning hastily away, walked off, accompanied by Surajah.

"It is awful!" he exclaimed, with tears running down his cheeks; "and to be able to do nothing! What must father have gone through! I think, Surajah, that if we were to come upon Tippoo I should go for him, even if he were surrounded by guards. Of course it would cost me my life. If I could kill him I think I should not mind it. Such a villain is not fit to live; and at any rate, whoever came after him, the prisoners could not be worse off than they are now. Let us go back; I have had enough for this morning."

When they returned Dick told Pertaub of the scene that he had witnessed.

"Many of them have been starved to death," the old man said. "Possibly one of their companions may have tried to escape. It is to prevent this that Tippoo's greatest cruelties are perpetrated. It is not so very difficult to get away and take to the jungle. Some have succeeded, but most of them are retaken, for a watch is vigilantly kept up at every village and every road leading on to the frontier, and if caught they are hung or forced to take poison. But whether they are caught or not, Tippoo's vengeance falls upon their companions. These are flogged, ironed, and kept without rations for weeks,—living, if they do live, upon the charity of their guards. This is why there are so few attempts at escape.

A man knows that, whether he himself gets off or not, he dooms his companions to torture, perhaps death. One case I remember in which an English sailor, one out of nine, attempted to get away. He was captured and killed at once, and his eight companions were all hung. So you see, even if one of the captives sees a chance of escape, he does not take it, because of the consequences that would fall upon his companions."

"It is horrible," Dick said, "and I can quite understand why so few escape. The question for me now is whether there are any prisoners kept in dungeons here."

"Not here, I think; Tippoo's policy is to make all his captives useful, and though one might be ironed and confined for a time, I do not think that any are so kept permanently here. There were, of course, some confined to the fort by illness, and some in irons. It may need some little search before you are quite sure that you have seen every one. However, I will try to find out how many there are there, and to get as many of the names as possible. Some of my friends who keep shops in the fort may be able to do this for me. This would shorten your task. But I cannot hold out any hopes that you will find him whom you seek in the city; it is among the hill-forts you will find him, if he be alive. I have been turning the matter over since you spoke to me last night, and the best plan I can think of is, that you should go as a travelling merchant, with Surajah as your assistant. You would want a good assortment of goods: fine muslins and silks, and a good selection of silver jewellery from different parts of India. All these I could purchase for you here. If by good luck you could obtain a sight of the commander of one of these forts, you might possibly obtain permission from him to go up and show your wares to the ladies of his establishment, and to those of other officers. The present of a handsome waist-sash, or a silver-mounted dagger, might incline him favourably to your petition."

"I think that the idea is an excellent one," Dick said

warmly. "If we cannot get in in that way, there seems to me to be no chance, save by taking a careful survey of the fortress, to discover where the rocks can be most easily climbed. There must surely be some spots, even among the steepest crags, where active fellows like Surajah and myself would be able to scale them. Of course, we should have to do it after dark; but once up there, one ought to be able to move about in the fort without difficulty, as we should, of course, be dressed as soldiers, and could take dark blankets to wrap round us. We ought then to be able to find where any prisoners who may be there are confined. There might be a sentry at the door, or, if there were no other way, one might pounce upon some one, force him by threats to tell us what prisoners there are, and where they are confined, and then bind and gag him and stow him away where there would be no chance of his being discovered before daylight."

"There would be a terrible risk in such a matter," Pertaub said, shaking his head gravely.

"No doubt there would be risk, but we came here prepared to encounter danger, and if it were well managed I don't see why we should be found out. Even if we were, we ought to be able to slip away in the darkness and make our way to the point where we went up. Once down on the plain we could renew our disguise as traders, and, however hotly they scoured the country, pass without suspicion through them. I think that there will be more chance in that way than in going in as traders, for we should, in that case, have little chance of walking about, still less of questioning any one. However, it is worth trying that first; we can always fall back upon the other if it fails. We might on our first visit obtain indications that would be very useful to us on our second."

CHAPTER XII.

A TIGER IN A ZENANA.

ANOTHER week passed, and by the end of that time Dick was perfectly assured that his father was not at Seringapatam. It was then a question which of the hill-forts to try first. Pertaub had already procured for them an assortment of goods and dresses suitable for travelling merchants, and the purchase of these things had drawn heavily on their stock of money, although several of the traders, on receiving a hint from Pertaub of the purpose for which the goods were required, had given many articles without charge, while for the majority of the goods Dick gave an order on his mother, who had told him that he could draw up to five hundred pounds. On the day before they were about to start, their plans were interrupted by the issue of a proclamation, saying that sports with wild beasts would take place on the following day; and they agreed that, as one day would make no difference, they would stop to see them, especially as Tippoo himself would be present. Hitherto, although they had several times seen him being carried in his palanquin, they had had no opportunity of observing him closely, as he was always surrounded by his guards.

The sports were held in a great square in the fort. A strong network was erected in a semi-circle, of which the Palace formed the base; behind the network the spectators ranged themselves. Tippoo occupied a window in the Palace looking down into the square. There were always a number of wild beasts in Seringapatam available for these purposes, as a regular supply of tigers, leopards, and wild elephants, was caught and sent in every month. Six of the largest tigers were always kept in cages in the courtyard in front of the Palace, and to these were thrown state criminals or officials who had offended the tyrant, and were devoured by them.

In his younger days, Tippoo had been very fond of the chase, but he was now too fat and heavy, and seldom ventured on horseback. Dick and Surajah, who had arrived early, had placed themselves at the corner, where the network touched the Palace. Some thirty yards in front of them a balcony projected; it was enclosed by a thick lattice-work; from behind this the ladies of Tippoo's harem viewed the sports. These began with a contest of fighting rams. The animals were placed some fifty yards apart. As soon as they saw each other, both showed extreme anger, uttering notes of defiance; then they began to move towards each other, at first slowly, but increasing in speed until, when within a few yards of one another, each took a spring, meeting in mid air, forehead to forehead, with a crash that could be heard far away. Both fell back, and stood for a moment shaking their heads, as if half stupified with the blow; then they backed two steps, and hurled themselves at each other again. After this had been repeated once or twice, they locked forehead to forehead, and each strove to push the other back. For some time the struggle continued on equal terms; then the weaker began to give way, and was pushed back step by step until its strength failed altogether, and it was pushed over on to the ground, when the attendants at once interfered and separated them.

Some thirty pairs of rams fought, the affair being to Dick extremely monotonous; the natives, however, took great interest in the contests, wagering freely on the issues, shouting loudly to the combatants, and raising triumphant cries when one was adjudged victor. Then elephants were brought in: but the struggle between these was even tamer than between the rams; they pushed each other with their foreheads until one gave way, when the other would follow it, beating it with its trunk, and occasionally shoving it.

When this sport was over, two parties of men entered the arena amid a shout of satisfaction from the crowd. After prostrating themselves before Tippoo, they took up their ground facing each other; each man had on his right hand four steel claws fixed to the knuckles. Approaching each other cautiously, they threw with their left hands the garlands of flowers they wore round their necks into the faces of their opponents, trying to take advantage of the moment to strike a blow or to obtain a grip. Each blow laid open the flesh as by a tiger's claws. The great object was to gain a grip, no matter where, which would completely disable the opponent, and render him incapable of defending himself. When this was done, the combat between that pair came to an end. After the ghetties, as these men were named, had retired, a buffalo was matched against a tiger. The latter was averse to the contest, but upon some fire-crackers being thrown close behind him, he sprang at the buffalo, who had been watching him warily. As the tiger launched itself into the air, the buffalo lowered its head, received it on its sharp horns, and threw it a distance of ten yards away. No efforts could goad the wounded tiger to continue the fray, so it and the buffalo were taken out and two others brought in.

The second tiger was a much more powerful beast than its predecessor, and was, indeed, larger than any of those in the cages of the Palace. It had been captured four days before, and was full of fight; it walked round the buffalo three or four times, and then, with the speed of lightning, sprang upon it, breaking its neck with a single blow from its powerful fore-paw. Six buffaloes in succession were brought in and were killed one after the other by the tiger. Satisfied with what it had done, the tiger paid no attention to the seventh animal, but walked round and round the arena, looking for a means of escape; then, drawing back, it made a short rush and sprang at the net, which was fourteen feet high. Strong as were the poles that supported the net, it nearly gave way under the impact. The tiger hung ten feet above the ground until some of the guards outside ran up, discharging their muskets into the air, when it recommenced its promenade round the foot of the net, roaring and snarling with anger.

As it neared the Palace it stopped and uttered a roar of

M84

"DICK TOOK STEADY AIM, AND FIRED AT THE TIGER."

defiance at those at the windows. Then, apparently, something moving behind the lattice-work caught its eye; it moved towards it, crouching, and then, with a tremendous spring, launched itself against it. The balcony was ten feet from the ground, but the tiger's spring took it clear of this. The woodwork gave way like paper, and the tiger burst through. A shout of dismay arose from the multitude, but high above this sounded the screams of the women.

"Quick Surajah!" Dick cried, and drawing his keen dagger, he cut through the network and dashed through, followed by his companion. "Stand here," he cried, as they arrived below the balcony. "Steady! Put your hands against the wall." Then he sprang on to Surajah's back, and thence to his shoulder. Drawing his pistols, he put one between his teeth, grasping the other in his right hand. "Steady, Surajah," he said; "I am going to stand on your head."

He stepped on to his companion's turban, put his left arm on the balcony, and raised himself by it until his arms were above its level. The tiger was standing with its paw upon a prostrate figure, growling savagely, but evidently confused and somewhat dismayed at the piercing screams from the women, most of whom had thrown themselves down on the cushions of the divan. Dick stretched his right hand forward, took a steady aim, and fired. A sharp snarl showed that the shot had taken effect; he dropped the pistol, snatched the other from his mouth, waited for a moment until he could make out the tiger, fired again and at once dropped to the ground, just as a great body flashed from the window above him. He and Surajah had both had their matchlocks slung over their shoulders, and before the tiger could recover from its spring, they levelled and fired. The tiger rolled over, but regained its feet and made towards them. One of the bullets had, however, struck it on the shoulder and disabled the leg; its movements were therefore comparatively slow, and they had time to leap aside. Surajah discharged his pistol into its ear, while Dick brought down his keen sword with all his strength upon its neck, and the tiger rolled over dead.

A mighty shout rose from the crowd.

"We had better be off," Dick said, "or we shall have all sorts of questions to answer." They slipped through the hole in the net again, but were so surrounded by people cheering and applauding them that they could not extricate themselves, and a minute later some soldiers ran up, pushed through the crowd to them, and surrounded them.

"The sultan requires your presence," they said; and as resistance was out of the question, Dick and Surajah at once accompanied them to the entrance of the Palace. They were led through several large halls, until they entered the room where Tippoo was standing. He had just left the women's apartment; where he had hurried to ascertain what damage had been done by the tiger. Dick and his companion salaamed to the ground, in accordance with the custom of the country.

"You are brave fellows," the sultan said graciously, "and all the braver that you risked death, not only from the tiger, but for daring to look upon my women unveiled."

"I saw nothing, your Highness," Dick said humbly, "save the tiger. That he was standing over a fallen figure I noticed. As soon as my eye fell on him I fired at once, and the second time as soon as the smoke cleared so that I could catch a glimpse of him."

"I pardon you that," Tippoo said; "and in faith you have rendered me good service, for had it not been for your interference, he might have worked havoc in my harem, and that before a single one of my officers or men had recovered his senses;" and he looked angrily round at the officers standing near him. "How comes it that you were so quick in thought and execution?" he asked Surajah, as the elder of the two.

"My brother and myself have done much hunting among the hills, your Highness, and have learned that in fighting a tiger one needs to be quick as well as fearless."

"Whence come you?" Tippoo asked. "By your tongue you are strangers."

Surajah gave the account that they had agreed upon as to their birth-place, but he was quick-witted enough to see that it would not be safe to say they were in the service of the Rajah of Bhor, as inquiries might be made, and he therefore said, "We came hither to take service either with your Royal Highness, or with one of your rajahs, but have as yet found no opportunity of doing so."

"It is well," Tippoo said. "Henceforth you are officers in my service; apartments shall be assigned to you in the Palace. Here is the first token of my satisfaction;" and he took out a heavy purse from his girdle and handed it to Surajah. "You are free to go now. I will later on consider what duties shall be assigned to you. When you return, report yourselves to Fazli Ali, my chamberlain;" and he indicated a white-bearded official among the group standing beside him.

Salaaming deeply again, they left the apartments. Not a word was spoken until they were outside the precincts of the Palace.

"This makes a sudden change in our plans," Dick said; "whether for better or worse I cannot say yet."

"I was right in not saying we were in the service of the Rajah of Bhor, was I not? I thought that Tippoo would offer to take us into his service, and he might have caused a letter to be sent to the Rajah, saying that he had done so."

"Yes, you were quite right, Surajah; I had thought of that myself, and was on thorns when you were telling your story, and felt not a little relieved when you changed the tale. I think that it has turned out for the best. As officers of the Palace we may be able to obtain some information as to what Christian captives there are, and the prisons where they are confined."

"Still more," Surajah said; "when we get to be known as being his officers, we might present ourselves boldly at any of the hill-fortresses, as sent there with some orders.

"You are right," Dick said. "I had not thought of that. Indeed, we might even produce orders to inspect the prisoners, in order to render an account to Tippoo of their state and fitness for service, and might even show an order for my father to be handed over to us, if we should find him. This is splendid, and I am sure I cannot be too grateful to that tiger for popping into the harem. He has done more for us in a few minutes than we could have achieved in a year. Well, Surajah, if my father is alive, I think now that we have every chance of rescuing him."

As they walked through the streets, many of those who had been present at the sports recognised them as the heroes in the stirring episode there, and, judging they would gain a high place in Tippoo's favour, came up to them and congratulated them on their bravery, and made offers of service. They replied civilly to all who accosted them, but were glad when they turned off to the quiet quarter where Pertaub lived. The Hindoo was surprised indeed when they told him what had happened and that they were already officers in the Palace, and might consider themselves as standing high in Tippoo's favour.

"It is wonderful," he said, when they brought their story to a conclusion. "Surely Providence must have favoured your pious object; such good fortune would never have occurred to you had it not been that it was destined you should find your father still alive. But if good fortune befalls you it is because you deserve it. That you should face a great tiger without hesitation, and slay him, shows how firm your courage is; and the quickness was still more to be admired. No doubt there are many others there who, to gain the favour of the sultan, would have risked their lives, but you alone of them were quick enough to carry it out."

"We were nearest to the spot, Pertaub; had we been among the crowd farther back we could have done nothing."

"Let praise be given where it is due," Surajah said. "I had nothing to do with the affair. I saw the tiger bound

DICK AND DINAH MAKE THEIR ESCAPE.

through the window and heard screams, and stood frozen with horror. I did not even see my lord cut through the net. I knew nothing until he seized me by the arm and pulled me after him, and it was not until he sprang upon my back and then upon my shoulders that I knew what he was going to do. I simply aided in despatching the tiger when he sprang, wounded, down into the courtyard."

"And yet you are a hunter and a soldier," Pertaub said. "This is how it is that the English have become lords of so wide a territory. They are quick: while we hesitate and spend great time in making up our minds to do anything, they decide and act in a moment; they are always ready, we are always slow; they see the point where a blow has to be struck, they make straight to it and strike. The English sahib is very young, and yet to him comes in a moment what is the best thing to be done. He does not stop to think of the danger; while all others stand in consternation he acts, and slays the tiger before one of them has so much as moved from his place. But indeed, as you say Tippoo himself told you, your danger was not only from the tiger. The tyrant must indeed have been alarmed for the safety of his harem, when he forgave you what, in the eyes of a Mohammedan, is the greatest offence you can commit. This will, of course, change all of your plans."

"For the present, at any rate. It may be that later on we shall still find occasion for our disguises, as possibly we may fall into disfavour and have to assume them to make our escape. We may, as Tippoo's officers, manage to obtain entrance into one or two of the hill-fortresses, but unless absolutely sent by him, that is the utmost we could hope for; for were we missing, messengers would be sent all over the country to order our arrest, and in that case we should have to take to some disguise. The first thing now is to procure our dresses. How much is there in that purse, Surajah? It seems pretty heavy."

Surajah poured the gold out on the table.

"There are fifty tomauns. That will be more than enough to clothe you handsomely," the Hindoo said.

"Much more than enough, I should think, Pertaub."

"Tippoo likes those round him to be well dressed. It is not only a proof of his generosity, but he likes to make a brave show on great occasions, and nothing pleases him more than to be told that neither the Nizam, nor any other Indian prince, can surpass him in the magnificence of his Court. Therefore, the better dressed you are, the more he will be satisfied, for it will seem to him that you appreciate the honour of being officers of the Palace, and that you have laid out his present to the best advantage, and have not a mind to hoard any of it. I will take the matter in hand for you. You will need two suits, one for Court ceremonies and the other for ordinary wear in the Palace."

"I shall be very much obliged to you, Pertaub, for indeed I have no idea what ought to be got. Had we better present ourselves at the Palace this evening or to-morrow morning?"

"This evening, certainly. Did he take it into his head to inquire whether you were in the Palace, and found that you were not, it might alter his humour towards you altogether. He is changeable in his moods; the favourite of one day may be in disgrace and ordered to execution the next. You will soon feel that it is as if you were in a real tiger's den, and that the animal may at any moment spring upon you. Take with you the clothes you now wear and those in which you came, so that at any moment, if you see a storm gathering, you can slip on a disguise and leave the Palace unobserved. In that case hasten here, and you can then dress yourselves as merchants."

"The worst of it is, Pertaub, that our faces will soon become known to so many in the Palace that they would be recognised, whatever our dress."

"A little paint and some false hair and a somewhat darker stain to your skin would alter you so that those who know you best would pass you without suspicion. I trust that no such misfortune will befall, but I will keep everything in readiness to effect a transformation should it be required. Now I will go out at once to get the clothes."

In two hours he returned, followed by a boy carrying the goods he had purchased, and in a few minutes Dick and his companion were arrayed in Court dresses. The turbans were pure white, and the tunic was of dark, rich stuff, thickly woven with gold thread; a short cloak or mantle, secured at the neck by a gold chain three or four inches in length, hung from the back, but could, if necessary, be drawn round the shoulders. A baldric, embroidered with gold, crossed the chest, and from this hung a sword with an ivory handle. The waist-sash was of blue and gold in Dick's case, purple and gold in that of Surajah. Silver-mounted pistols and daggers were stuck into the sashes. The dresses were precisely alike, except that they differed in colour. The trousers were white.

Surajah was greatly delighted with his dress. Dick laughed.

"Of course it comes naturally to you," he said, "but I feel as if I were dressed up for a masquerade."

The other suits were similar in style, but the tunics were of richly figured damask instead of cloth of gold. Half-an-hour later they started for the Palace, a coolie carrying a box containing their second suits and the simple dresses they had worn on their arrival. Dick could not help smiling at the manner in which the people in the streets obsequiously made way for them.

"I shall be very glad," he said, as they traversed the space that divided the town from the fort, "when we have got over the next day or two, and have settled down a bit; it all seems so uncertain, and I have not the most remote idea of what our duties are likely to be. Hitherto we have always had some definite plan of action and had only ourselves to depend upon; now everything seems doubtful and uncertain. However, I suppose we shall soon settle down; and we have the satisfaction of knowing that if things do not turn out well, we can go off to our good friend Pertaub, and get out of the place altogether."

On arriving at the Palace they inquired for the chamberlain.

"He is expecting you, my lord," one of the attendants said, coming forward. "I will lead you first to the room that is prepared for you, and then take you to Fazli Ali."

The room was a commodious one, and the richness of the covering of the divan and the handsome rugs spread on the floor, were satisfactory signs that the chamberlain considered them prime favourites of the sultan. Having seen the box placed in a corner, and paid the coolie, they followed the attendant along some spacious corridors and passages, until they entered a room where Fazli Ali was seated on a divan. The attendant let the curtains that covered the door drop behind them as they entered. They salaamed to the chamberlain, who looked at them approvingly, and motioned to them to take their seats on the divan beside him.

"I see," he said kindly, "that you possess good judgment as well as courage and quickness. The former qualities have won you a place here, but judgment will be needed to keep it. You have laid out your money well, as the sultan loves to see all in the Palace well attired, and quiet also and discreet in behaviour."

"Can you give us any idea what our duties will be?" Surajah asked, as Dick had requested him always to be the spokesman if possible.

The chamberlain shook his head. "That will be for the sultan himself to decide. For a time probably you will have little to do but to attend at the hours when he gives public audeinces. You will, doubtless, occasionally carry his orders to officers in command of troops, at distant places, and will form part of his retinue when he goes beyond the Palace. When he sees that you are worthy of his favour, prompt in carrying out his orders, and in all respects trustworthy, he will in time assign special duties to you; but this will depend upon yourselves. As one who admires the courage and promptness that you showed to-day, and who wishes you well, I would warn you that it is best when the sultan has had matters to trouble him, and may blame somewhat unjustly, not to seek to excuse yourselves; it is bad to thwart him when he is roused. You can rely upon me to stand your friend, and when the storm has blown over to represent the matter to him in a favourable light. The sultan desires to be just, and in his calm moments assuredly is so; but when there is a cloud before his eyes, there is no saying upon whom his displeasure may fall. At present, however, there is little chance of your falling into disgrace, for he is greatly impressed with the service you have rendered him, and especially by the promptness with which you carried it out.

"After you had gone he spoke very strongly about it, and said that he would he were possessed of a hundred officers capable of such a deed; he would in that case have little fear of any of the foes of his kingdom. It is fortunate that you came here this afternoon; it is well-nigh certain that he will ask for you presently, and though he could hardly blame you had you required until to-morrow to complete your preparations, your promptitude will gratify him, and he will, I am sure, be still more pleased at seeing that you have so well laid out his gift. He gave you no orders on the subject, and had you appeared in the dresses you wore this morning, he would, doubtless, have instructed me to provide you with more suitable attire. The fact that you have so laid out the money will show that you have an understanding of the honour of being appointed to the Palace, and a proper sense of fitness. The sultan himself dresses plainly, and, save for a priceless gem in his turban and another in his sword-hilt, there is nothing in his attire to lead a stranger to guess at his rank; but while he does this himself, he expects that all others in the Palace should do justice to his generosity. And now you had best return to your room and remain there until sent for; if he does not think of it himself, I shall, if opportunity occurs, inform him that you have already arrived."

They had some difficulty in finding their way back to their room, and had, indeed, to ask directions of attendants they met before they discovered it. A native was squatting at the door; he rose and salaamed deeply as they came up.

"Your slave is appointed to be your attendant, my lords," he said. "Your servant's name is Ibrahim."

"Good," Surajah said, as he passed him and entered the room. "Now, Ibrahim, tell us about the ways of the Palace, for of these we are altogether ignorant. In the first place about food: do we provide ourselves, or how is it?"

"All in the Palace are fed from the sultan's kitchen. At each meal every officer has so many dishes, according to his rank; these vary from three to twelve. In the early morning I shall bring you bread and fruit and sherbet; at ten o'clock is the first meal, and at seven there is supper; at one o'clock the kitchens are open, and I can fetch you a dish of pillau, kabobs, a chicken, or any other refreshment that you may desire; at present I have no orders as to how many dishes your Excellencies will receive at the two meals."

"We shall not be particular about that," Surajah said; "it is evident we shall fare well, at any rate."

"I am told to inform you, my lords, that the sultan has ordered two horses to be placed at your service. A ghorrawalla has been appointed to take charge of them; his name is Serfojee. If you ask for him at the stable you will be directed to him, and he will show you the horses. In an hour supper will be served, but this evening I shall only be able to bring you three dishes each; such is always the rule until the sultan's pleasure has been declared."

Ibrahim then proceeded to light two lamps hanging from the ceiling, for it was now getting dusk, and then, finding that his masters had no further need of his services, he retired.

"So far, so good, Surajah; we are certainly in clover as far as comfort is concerned, and the only drawback to the situation is Tippoo's uncertain temper. However, we must try our best to satisfy him; we have every reason to stand well with him, and if he sees that we are really anxious to please him, we ought to be able to avoid falling into disgrace, even when he is in his worst moods."

Their attendant presently brought up the six portions of food, and they enjoyed their meal heartily. Each had an ample portion of a pillau of rice and chicken, a plate of stew, which Dick thought was composed of game of some kind, and a confection in which honey was the predominating flavour. With this they drank water, deliciously cooled by being hung up in porous jars. Surajah ate his food with the dexterity of long habit, but Dick had not yet learned to make his bread fulfil the functions of spoon and fork, for at his uncle's table European methods of eating were adopted.

Half-an-hour after they had finished, an officer presented himself at the door, and said that he was ordered to conduct them to the sultan. Tippoo had supped in the harem, and was now seated on a divan in a room of no great size, but richly hung with heavy silken curtains, and carpeted with the richest rugs. Two or three of his chief officers were seated beside him; seven or eight others were standing on either side of the room. A heavy glass chandelier of European manufacture hung from the richly carved ceiling, and the fifty candles in it lighted up the room. The chamberlain met them at the door and advanced with them towards Tippoo.

"Great Sultan," he said, "these are the young men whom it has pleased your Highness to appoint officers in the Palace."

The two lads salaamed until their turbans touched the ground.

"Truly they are comely youths," Tippoo said, "and one would scarcely deem them capable of performing such a feat as that they accomplished this morning. Well, my slayers of tigers, you have found everything fitly provided?"

"Far more so than our deeds merit, your Highness," Surajah replied. "We have found everything that heart could desire, and only hope for an opportunity to show ourselves worthy of your favours."

"You have done that beforehand," Tippoo said graciously, "and I am glad to see, by your attire, that you are conscious that, as my officers, it is fitting you should make a worthy appearance. It shows that you have been well brought up, and are not ignorant of what is right and proper. At present you will receive orders from Fazli Ali, and will act as assistant chamberlains until I decide in what way your services can be made most useful. Now follow me; there are others who wish to see you."

Rising, Tippoo led the way through a door with double hangings, into a room considerably larger than that which they had just left. The chandeliers at the end of the room where they stood were all lighted, while the other end was in comparative darkness. Leaving them standing alone, Tippoo walked towards the other end and clapped his hands. Immediately a number of closely veiled figures entered, completely filling the end of the room.

"These are the young men," Tippoo said to them. "It is the one on the right to whom it is chiefly due that the tiger did not commit havoc among you; it was he who climbed up the balcony and fired twice at the beast. You owe your lives to him and his companion, for among all my officers and guards there was not one who was quick-witted enough to move as much as a finger."

There was a faint murmur of surprise among the veiled figures at the youth of their preserver.

"Hold your heads fully up," Tippoo went on, for Dick and his companion, after making a deep salaam, had stood with bent heads and with eyes fixed upon the ground. Then two of the attendants, girls of thirteen or fourteen years old, came forward from behind the others, each bearing a casket. "These are presented to you with my permission by the ladies whose lives you saved," Tippoo said; "and should you at any time have a favour to ask, or even should you fall under my displeasure, you can rely upon their good offices in your behalf."

There was another low murmur from the other end of the

hall, then Tippoo clapped his hands, and the women moved out as noiselessly as they had entered.

"You can retire now," Tippoo said, as he moved towards the door into the other room. "Be faithful, be discreet, and your fortune is assured." He pointed to another door, and then rejoined his councillors. Dick and his companion stood in an attitude of deep respect until the hanging had fallen behind the sultan, and then went out by the door he had pointed to, and made their way back to their own room.

"Truly, Surajah, fortune is favouring us mightily. This morning we walked the streets in fear of being questioned and arrested; this evening we are officers of the Palace, favoured by Tippoo, and under the protection of the harem. I wonder what the ladies have given us."

They opened the caskets, which were of considerable size. As they examined the contents, exclamations of surprise broke from them. Each contained some thirty or forty little parcels done up in paper, and, on these being opened, they were found to contain trinkets and jewels of all kinds. Some were very costly and valuable. All were handsome. It was evident that every one of the ladies who had been in the room when the tiger burst in, had contributed a token of her gratitude. Many of the more valuable gems had been evidently taken from their settings, as if the donors did not care that jewels they had worn should be exposed to view. One parcel contained twenty superb pearls, another a magnificent diamond and ten rubies, and so on, down to the more humble gifts—although these were valuable—of those of lower rank. Dick's presents were much more costly than those of his companion, and as soon as this was seen to be the case, Dick proposed that they should all be put together, and divided equally. This, however, Surajah would not hear of.

"The whole thing is due to you," he said. "It would never have occurred to me to interfere at all. I had no part in the matter, beyond aiding to kill a wounded tiger, and it was no more than I have done many times among our hills, and thought nothing of. These jewels are vastly more than I deserve for my share in the affair. I do not know much about the value of gems, but they must be worth a large sum, and nothing will induce me to take any of those that you have so well earned."

"I wonder whether Tippoo knows what they have given us," Dick said, after in vain trying to alter his companion's decision.

"I don't suppose he troubled himself about it," Surajah replied. "No doubt he was asked for permission for each to make a present to us. The jewels in the harem must be of enormous value, as for the last fifteen years Tippoo has been gathering spoil from all southern India, having swept the land right up to the gates of Madras. They say that his treasures are fabulous, and no doubt the ladies of his harem have shared largely in the spoils. The question is, What had we best do with these caskets? We know that, in the course of our adventures, it may very well happen that we shall be closely searched, and it would never do to risk having such valuables found upon us."

"No; I should say that we had best bury them somewhere. Some of these merchants here may be honest enough for us to leave the jewels in their care without anxiety, but as they themselves may at any moment be seized and compelled to give up their last penny, these things would be no safer with them than with us. As to Pertaub, I have absolute faith in him, but he himself is liable to be seized at any moment. However, I should say we had better consult him. If we were to bury them, say, under the floor of his house, we might leave them there for a time. If we saw any chance of this place being some day captured by our people, we could wait till then for their recovery; but the war may not be renewed for years. Possibly Pertaub may be able to arrange to send them down, only entrusting a portion at a time to a messenger, so that, if he got into trouble, we should only lose what he had upon him. We will put the caskets into our box and lock it up for the present, and take them down to Pertaub to-morrow evening, after it gets dark. It will be as well to get them off our minds as soon as possible, for although just at present we are in high favour, there is no saying how long it may last, or when it may be necessary for us to move."

CHAPTER XIII.

OFFICERS OF THE PALACE.

THE next morning, just as they had finished their early breakfast, they were sent for by Fazli Ali.

"You had better accompany me on my rounds," he said. "I shall not commit any special duties to you until I see whether the sultan intends that you shall remain with me, or whether, as is far more likely, he assigns other work to you. Were you placed in separate charges in the Palace, I should have to fill your places if you left; therefore I propose that at present you shall assist me in general supervision. We will first go to the kitchens; these give me more trouble than any other part of my duties. In the first place, one has to see that the contractors do their work properly, that the number of carcases sent in is correct, the flesh of good quality, and that the list of game is correct. Then one has to check the amount of rice and other grain sent in from the storehouses, the issue of spices, and other articles of that kind. These matters do not require doing every day; the kitchen officers are responsible for them: but once or twice a week I take care to be present to see that all is right. Then I ascertain that everything is in good and proper order in the kitchen, listen to complaints, and decide disputes.

"When we have done there, we will see that the requisitions from the harem are properly complied with, and that the sweetmeats, perfumes, silks, and muslins, as required, are furnished. The payment of salaries does not come into my department; that is one of the functions of the treasurer of the Palace, who also discharges all accounts upon my signature that they are correct. Then I take a general tour of the Palace, to see that the attendants have done their duties, and that everything is clean and in order. As a rule, I have finished everything before the morning meal is served. The details of making up the accounts are of course done by clerks. After that my duties depend entirely upon the sultan. If there is any state ceremonial in the Palace I summon those whose duty it is to attend, and see that everything is properly arranged and in order; if not, I am generally at his Highness's disposal.

"Unless you receive any instructions from me, you will be free to occupy yourselves as you like. You will, of course, take part in all public ceremonials. You will be among the officers who accompany the sultan when he goes out, and will be liable to be summoned to attend him at all times. Therefore, although free to go into the town or ride beyond the island, it is well that you should never be long absent, and that, if you wish to be away for more than two hours at a time, you should first let me know, as I may be able to tell you if the sultan is likely to require you. He has fixed your pay at four hundred rupees a month."

Dick, as he accompanied the chamberlain on his tour through the Palace, was struck with the order and method that prevailed in every department, and the chamberlain told him that Tippoo himself inquired closely into details, and that, large as was the daily expenditure, no waste of any kind was allowed. The splendour of some of the apartments was surprising, especially the throne-room. The throne itself was of extraordinary magnificence; it was of gold, thickly inlaid with gems. On the apex stood a jewelled peacock, covered entirely with diamonds, emeralds, and rubies, with pendants of pearls. In front of it stood a golden tiger's head, which served as a footstool. On either side were standards of purple silk, having a sun with gold rays in the centre. The spear-heads were of gold set with jewels.

When the work of inspection was finished, they went back to their room, where their attendant, soon afterwards, with an air of great exultation, brought their meal, which consisted of nine dishes each, a proof of the high favour with which Tippoo regarded them. After this meal was eaten they went down to the stables and were pleased indeed with the mounts provided for them. They were fine animals, with handsome saddles and trappings, and Dick and Surajah at once mounted and rode through the town to the other extremity of the island. As they wore scarves that had been furnished them by Fazli Ali, showing that they were officers of the Palace, they were everywhere greeted with deep salaams.

"I hope," Dick said, as they returned from their ride, "that Tippoo will not be long before he finds us some other duties; there is nothing very interesting in counting carcases, or seeing rice measured."

"That is true enough," Surajah agreed. "But we must not be impatient. Fortune has befriended us marvellously, and I have great faith that it will continue to do so. We must be content to wait."

"Yes, I know that, Surajah, but I think it is all the more difficult to do so because we have done so much in a short time. It seems as if one ought to go on at the same rate."

That evening they went down, as they had arranged, with ordinary wraps round their gay attire, to Pertaub's, taking with them the caskets of gems. The Hindoo received them warmly.

"I saw you ride through the streets this morning, although you did not notice me; truly, you made a good appearance, and were well-mounted. I have heard from one of our people, who is a servant in the Palace, that you stand in high favour."

"We have brought you down these two caskets of gems,"

Dick said; "they were given us by the ladies of the harem, and many of the stones Surajah thinks are very valuable. We don't know what to do with them, and wanted to know whether you could arrange to send them down to Tripataly for us."

"I would not undertake to do so if they are valuable," Pertaub said. "The prospects of fresh troubles are stronger every day, and the roads are so closely watched, especially those through the passes, that it would be running a terrible risk to trust valuables to any one."

"In that case, Pertaub, we thought you might bury them in the ground under your house. But first look at some of the stones, and tell us what you think of them."

The Hindoo opened Surajah's casket, and undid many of the little parcels.

"Assuredly they are valuable," he said; "some of them much more so than others; but if all are like these that I have opened, they must be worth at least fifty thousand rupees."

"Now look at this casket, Pertaub."

The Hindoo uttered an exclamation of surprise as he opened some of the packets, and, taking out some of the larger gems, he examined them by the light of his lamp.

"I could not place a value on these," he said at last. "The ladies must indeed have felt that they owed their lives to you. The gems are a fortune. Doubtless they are the spoils of a score of districts, and Tippoo must have distributed them lavishly among his wives, or they could never have made such rich presents. I would bury them, Sahib, for surely they could not be entrusted even to the most faithful messengers, in times like these. But though, if you like, I will hide them here, I think it would be far safer for you to take them across the river and bury them in a wood, marking well the trees, that you may know the place again; for although methinks Tippoo's agents believe that they have squeezed the last rupee from me, one can never tell—I might again be tortured, and none can say that they are brave enough to bear the agonies that Tippoo's executioners inflict. I will bury them for to-night; but I pray you give me notice the first time you cross the river. I will be at the other side of the ford with the jewels hidden in a sack on an ass; this I will drive forward when I see you crossing the ford. You will follow me till I enter a wood. I will have the tools, and when you join me, you can go on a short distance and bury them. I do not wish to see where you hide them, but will move about to make sure that none come near you when so engaged. You had best take out a few small stones, which you will find as good as money, and much more easily concealed, for in every town or large village you will find a jeweller who will give you silver for them."

"I think that will be a very good plan, Pertaub, and will certainly carry it out."

A month passed without any change in their work. They rode with other officers behind Tippoo's palanquin when he went out, which he did almost every day, to inspect the progress of the fortifications, and were among the brilliant circle behind his throne when he gave orders. By this time they had come to know most of the other Court officials, and were able to inquire cautiously about the prisons. They could learn nothing, however, of any English prisoners in Seringapatam, save those they had seen in the hut in the fort.

Six weeks after their appointment as Palace officers, Dick and Surajah were sent for by Tippoo.

"I am about to employ you," the sultan said, when they appeared before him, "on a mission. You are strangers here and are unconnected with any of my officers, and I can, therefore, place greater reliance on your reports than upon those of men who have other interests than my own to serve. I desire you to go and inspect the hill-forts, to see how the repairs of the fortifications injured by the English are progressing, and to make sure that the cannon are in good order, and the supply of ammunition plentiful. You have shown that you are quick-sighted and sharp; look round the defences, and if you see aught that can be done to strengthen them, confer with the governors, learn their opinions on the subject, and if they agree with you, they will be authorised to take men from the country round to strengthen the fortifications, and I will forward at once such guns and stores as may be required. After the inspection of each fort you will despatch a mounted messenger to me with your report; and you will state which fort you will next visit, in order that I may despatch there any order that I may have to give you.

"Do your duty well, and I shall know how to reward you. In order that your authority may be increased, you are both named colonels in the army. Fazli will furnish you with a written copy of the orders I have given you and with authority under my seal to enter and inspect all fortresses and to consult with the governors as to everything considered by them as necessary for their better defence. The last time the English came they captured Nundidroog and other hill-fortresses that we had regarded as impregnable, simply because the governors were over-confident, and the defences had been neglected. This must not occur again, and if there is failure in the defences I shall hold you responsible. Therefore, take care that you do not neglect not only to see that the repairs are being well carried out, but to recommend additions to the fortifications wherever it seems to you that there is even a possibility of an enemy making his way up. You will take with you twenty troopers as an escort, but these are not to enter any of the fortresses with you, for treachery is always possible, and no one save the garrisons must be acquainted with the defences of the hill-forts."

Surajah expressed his thanks to the sultan for entrusting them with the mission, and assured him that their inspection of the forts should be careful and complete, and that they would start in an hour's time.

When they reached their own room, Dick threw up his turban in delight.

"Was there ever such a stroke of good fortune?" he exclaimed. "The tiger business was as nothing to this; Tippoo has given us the mission of all others that will enable us to carry out our search. Our work is as good as done; that is to say," he added, more gravely, "we are at least pretty sure to find my father out, if he is alive. Besides, we may get information that will be of great use if the war is renewed. Now we had better, in the first place, go and see Fazli and get our instructions; we will order our horses to be in readiness to start as soon as we have had our meal—we may not get another chance of eating to-day. I should like to take Ibrahim with us. He is a capital servant and a strong, active fellow; I believe he is fond of us, and we shall want some one who can cook for us, and buy things, and so on. I will speak to Fazli about it."

The chamberlain looked up as they entered the room where he was engaged in dictating to a clerk.

"I congratulate you on your mission," he said. "It will involve a great deal of hard work, but as you have told me how you longed for some duty outside the Palace, you will not mind that; Tippoo consulted me before sending for you. I told him you were diligent in the service, and I felt sure you would do your best in the present matter, and that as you were accustomed, in the pursuit of game, to ascend mountains and scale precipices, you were far more likely to find the weak spots in the forts than an old officer, who would be likely to take everything for granted. There is no doubt that many of the garrisons are very far from being efficient. They have been stationed in the forts for many years; discipline, both among officers and men, is sure to have become lax, and there will be much that young men, going freshly into the matter, will see needs amendment. That the walls are often weak, and the cannon so old as to be almost useless, I am well aware, for sometimes newly-appointed governors have sent in strong protests and urgent requests that they might be furnished with new cannon, and that walls and defences might be renewed. But what with the wars, the removal of the capital, and the building and fortification of this place, these matters have been neglected; and it is only now that the sultan sees the necessity of putting the fortifications of all these places in good repair. I have had the papers prepared and signed; your escort has been ordered. Is there anything else you can think of?"

"We should like to take our Palace attendant with us," Surajah said; "he is a good man, and, starting so suddenly, we should have a difficulty in hiring servants we could rely on."

"I have thought of that," the chamberlain replied, "and have ordered a horse to be got in readiness for him, together with a spare animal to carry food and necessaries for your journey. You will need them on your marches, and may even be glad of them in some of the smaller forts, where the fare will be very rough."

When they returned to their room they found Ibrahim awaiting them. He was evidently delighted at the prospect of accompanying them.

"My lords," he said, "I have the pack-horse saddled in the stable, with two great sacks and ropes. Is it your pleasure that I should go down at once to the market and buy flour and rice, spices, and other things necessary?"

"Certainly, Ibrahim. But it will not be necessary to buy much meat; it will not keep, and we ought always to be able to buy a sheep or a fowl from villagers. Get some thick, wadded sleeping rugs, some cooking pots, and whatever you think is necessary. Do not waste any time, for we shall start immediately after our meal."

As soon as the man had left, Dick said to Surajah, "I will hurry down to the town and see Pertaub. You had best remain here, in case Tippoo should send for us to give us final instructions. You can say, should he ask, that I have gone down to the town to get a supply of powder and ball for our pistols, writing materials, and other things that we may require, which will be true enough. It is most lucky that we buried our jewels in the forest ten days ago, for we should not have had time to do it now."

Dick returned in time for the meal, which was brought up by another servant.

"Pertaub was delighted to hear of our good fortune," he said, on his return. "He will keep our disguises by him, and if we have occasion for them will either bring them himself with the merchandise, or will send them by a trusty messenger, to any place we may mention, directly he hears from us. I do not think there is any chance of our wanting them, but it is as well to prepare for any contingency that may occur."

Half-an-hour later they started at the head of an escort of twenty troopers, Ibrahim riding in the rear, leading the pack-horse, which carried a change of clothes, and thick cloths to keep out the night dews, as well as the stock of provisions. Ibrahim had also purchased two very large, dark blankets that could be used for a temporary shelter. Surajah now felt quite at home, for he was engaged in the same sort of duty he performed at Tripataly, and more than one pair of dark eyes glanced admiringly at the two young officers as they rode down to the ford. They had been furnished by Fazli with a list of the forts they were to visit, and the order in which they were to take them, the first on the list being Savandroog, fifty miles north-east of the city. After a ride of twenty miles, they halted at a village. To the surprise of the troopers, Surajah gave orders that nothing was to be taken by force, as he was prepared to pay for all provisions required. As soon as the villagers understood th s, ample supplies were brought in. Rice, grain, and fowls were purchased for the soldiers, and forage for the horses, and after seeing that all were well provided for, the two officers went to a room that had been placed at their service in the principal house in the village. Ibrahim justified his assertion that he was a good cook, by turning out an excellent curry. By the time they had finished this it was getting dark, and after again visiting the troopers and seeing that their own horses were fed and well groomed, they retired to bed.

An early start was made, and at ten o'clock they approached Savandroog. It was one of the most formidable of the hill-forts of Mysore, and stood upon the summit of an enormous mass of granite, covering a base of eight miles in circuit and rising in ragged precipices to the height of 2,500 feet. The summit of the rock was divided by a deep chasm into two peaks, each of which was crowned with strong works, and capable of separate defence. The lower part of the hill was, wherever ascent seemed possible, protected by walls one behind the other. The natives had regarded the fort as absolutely impregnable until it was stormed by the troops under Lord Cornwallis.

Dick looked with intense interest at the great rock with its numerous fortifications. The damages committed by the British guns could not be seen at this distance, and it seemed to him well-nigh impossible that the place could have been captured. They rode on until they neared an entrance in the wall that encircled the fort at the side at which alone access was considered possible.

They were challenged as they approached. Ordering the troopers to remain behind, Dick and Surajah rode forward. "We are the bearers," Surajah cried out, as they reined in their horses within twenty yards of the gate, "of an order from the sultan for our admittance, and of a letter to Mirzah Mohammed Bukshy, the governor."

"I will send up word to him," an officer on the wall replied. "I can admit no one until I have received his orders to do so."

"How long will it be before we receive an answer?"

"An hour and a half at the earliest. I regret that your Excellencies will be inconvenienced, but my orders are absolute."

"I do not blame you," Surajah replied. "It is necessary that you should always be vigilant;" and they retired under the shade of a tree, a hundred and fifty yards from the gate.

Ibrahim spread out the rugs, and then proceeded to light the fire and to prepare a pillau of rice and fowl, while Dick and his companion regarded the rock with fixed attention, and conversed together as to the possibility of ascending at any of the points so steep as to be left undefended by walls. They concluded at last that it would be next to impossible to climb the rock anywhere on the side that faced them, save by scaling several walls. They had just finished their luncheon when the gate opened and an officer and four soldiers issued out. They at once rose and went to meet them.

"I have the governor's order to admit you on the production of the sultan's pass."

Surajah produced the document. The officer at once recognised the seal, and carried it to his forehead, salaaming deeply. "Your troopers can enter at the gate, but cannot proceed farther than the second wall."

"Can we ride up, or must we walk?" Dick asked.

"You can ride," he replied. "The road is steep, but nowhere so steep that horses cannot mount it."

After the party had entered the gate it was at once closed and bolted. The troopers dismounted, and were led to a small barrack, while Surajah and Dick, accompanied by the officer and four soldiers on foot, rode on. The road was a better one than Dick had expected; it was just wide enough for a cart to proceed up it, and was cut out of the solid rock. It turned and zigzagged continually, and at each angle was a small fort whose guns swept the approach. They passed under a score of gateways, each defended by guns, and after upwards of an hour's climbing, at a quick pace, they approached one of the forts on its summit. The governor met them at the gate.

"You will pardon my not descending to meet you below," he said, "but I am not so young as I used to be, and the journey up and down fatigues me much."

Dick and Surajah dismounted, and the former presented the two documents. The governor, after reading the pass, bowed, and led the way into the interior of the fort, and they were soon seated on a divan in his quarters, when he read the circular letter.

"I am glad indeed," he said, when he had finished, "that the sultan is pleased to take into consideration the many demands I have made for cannon and ammunition. A large number of the pieces are past service, and they would be as dangerous to those who fired them as to those at whom they were aimed; while I have scarcely powder enough to furnish three rounds for each. As to the defences, I have done my best to strengthen them. Idleness is bad for all men, most of all for soldiers, and I have kept them well employed at repairing the effects of the English fire. Still, there is much to do yet before they are finished, and there are points where fortifications might be added with advantage; these I will gladly point out to you. They have been beyond our means here, for, as you will perceive, it will need blasting in many places to scarp the rock, and to render inaccessible several points at which active men can now climb up. For this work powder is required. And I would submit that for such hard work it will be needful to supply extra rations to the troops, for the present scale scarcely suffices to keep the men efficient, especially as most of them have their wives and families dependent on them."

"I have no doubt that the sultan will accede to any reasonable requests, your Excellency; he is anxious that the walls of the forts should be placed in the best possible condition for defence. No one doubts that we shall ere long be again at war with England, and although the sultan relies much upon large reinforcements that have been promised by France, with whom he has entered into an alliance, they have not yet arrived, and he may have to bear the brunt of the attack of the English by himself."

"I have heard of this," the governor said, "and regret that we shall again have the Feringhees upon us. As for the Mahrattas or the Nizam, I heed them not—they are dust, whom the sultan could sweep from his path; but these English are terrible soldiers. I have fought against them under Hyder, and in the last war they again showed their valour; and the strangest thing is that they make the natives under them fight as bravely as they do themselves. As to forts, nothing is safe from them. Were all the troops of the Nizam and the Mahrattas combined to besiege us, I should feel perfectly safe, while were there but five hundred Englishmen, I should tremble for the safety of the fortress. You have come up the hill and have seen for yourselves how strong it is; and yet they took the place without the loss of a single man. I was not here, for I was in command of Kistnagherry at that time, and succeeded in holding it against their assaults. When the war was over, and Kistnagherry was ceded to them, I was appointed to this fortress, which seems to me to be even stronger than that was.

"The commander was a brave man, the garrison was strong, there was no suspicion of treachery; and though at last the troops were seized with a panic, as they might well be when they saw that they were unable to arrest the advance of the enemy, the defence up to that time had been stout. The English brought up guns where it was thought no guns could be taken; they knocked the defences to pieces; and, after winning their way to the top, in one day captured this fort and that on the hill yonder. It seems miraculous."

Coffee was brought in, and pipes, for although Tippoo was violently opposed to smoking, and no one would venture upon the use of tobacco in the Palace or fort, old officers like the governor, in distant commands, did not relinquish tobacco.

"It is necessary here," the governor said, as he filled his pipe. "The country round is terribly unhealthy, and the air is full of fever. I do not discourage its use among the men, for they would die off like flies did they not smoke to keep out the bad air. The climate is indeed the best protection to the fort, for an army that sat down for any length of time before it, would speedily melt away." He opened a box that stood on the divan beside him. "I have copies here," he said, taking some papers out, "of the memorials that I have sent in to the sultan, as to the guns. This is the last; it was sent in two months ago. You see I asked for forty-nine heavy pieces. Of these, thirty are to replace guns that are honeycombed, or split; the other eleven are for new works. I asked for thirty-two lighter ones, or howitzers, and a hundred wall guns. Of course I could do with less; but to place the fort in a perfect state of defence, that is the number that I and my artillery officer think are requisite. Of powder we have not more than a ton and a half, and if the siege were to be a long one we might require ten times as much; we have not more than eight rounds of shot for each gun, and we ought to have at least fifty for the heavy pieces, and twenty for those defending the path up the hill."

Dick made a note of the figures in a pocket-book he had bought for the purpose.

"As for provisions," the governor went on, "we ought to have large stores of rice and grain. The magazines are nearly empty, and as we have eight hundred men in garrison, and perhaps twice as many women and children, we should require a large store were we blockaded for any time."

"Are the troops in good condition?" Surajah asked.

The governor shook his head. "Many of them are past the term of service; but until I get reinforcements to supply their places, I shall not venture to discharge them. Many others are wasted by fever, and, I must say, from insufficient rations, which not only weakens their bodies, but lowers their spirits. As long as there was no fear of attack this mattered little; but if the English are coming again we shall want well-fed and contented men to oppose them. I see by the stars on your turbans that you are both colonels as well as officers of the Palace. You are fortunate in obtaining that rank so young."

"It was due to the sultan's favour," Surajah said. "The other day at the sports a tiger burst into the sultan's zenana, and we were lucky enough to kill it—that is, my friend did most of the killing; I only gave the brute the final *coup*."

"Ah, it was you who performed that deed!" the governor said warmly. "I heard the news from one of my officers who was on leave, and returned yesterday.. Truly it was a gallant action, and one quickly done. No wonder that you obtained the sultan's favour and your rank as colonel. I was a sportsman in my young days. But I think I should have been more frightened at the thought of taking a peep into the sultan's zenana than I should have been of fighting the tiger."

"I did not think anything about it," Dick said, "until it was all over. I heard some women scream, and, being quite close, went to their assistance, without a thought whether they might be the ladies of the zenana or servants of the Palace; but indeed, I saw nothing save the tiger, and only vaguely observed that there were women there at all."

"It was well that the sultan took the view he did of the matter," the governor said. "I have known men put to death for deeds that were but trifles in comparison to looking into the zenana. Now, Colonel, I will send for my artillery officer and the horses, and we will ride round the fortifications on the brow of the hill, inspect the two forts closely, and will point out to you the spots where it appears to us the defences ought to be strengthened.'

CHAPTER XIV.

A SURPRISE.

DICK was much pleased with the governor. He was evidently an outspoken old soldier, and, though rough, his bearded face had an honest and kindly expression, and he thought to himself,' "If my father fell into his hands I don't think he would be treated with any unnecessary hardship, though no doubt the sultan's orders would be obeyed." When a soldier came in to say that the horses were at the door they went out. An officer was standing beside them, and the governor presented him as his chief artillery officer.

"You have not brought your horse," he said.

"No, your Excellency, the distance is not great, and we should need to dismount so many times to get a view from the walls that it would not be worth while to ride."

"In that case, we may as well walk also," Dick said.

"I would rather do so too," the governor said. "I proposed riding because I thought you might be tired. As Bakir Meeram says, the distance is not great; the walls themselves, with the exception of those of the two forts, are not more than half a mile in extent, for in most places the rocks go sheer down, and there defences are of course unnecessary. We will inspect this fort first."

They went the round of the walls, Dick and his companion listening to the suggestions of the two officers. The principal one was that a wall should be raised inside the gate.

"The English last time got in here by rushing in at the tail of the fugitives from below. They were in before the gates could be closed, and took our men so completely by surprise that they were seized with a panic. Were we to raise a semicircular wall behind the gateway, such a thing could not occur again," the governor said. "Of course there would be a gate in the inner wall, but not immediately behind the outer gate-way, as if so placed it might be destroyed by the cannon-shots that battered the outer gate in. I should, therefore, put it at one end of the inner wall. This gate would be generally open, but in case of a siege I should have it blocked up with stones piled behind it, placing a number of ladders by which men, running in, could get on to the walls, and, however closely they were pursued, could make a stand there until the ladders were pulled up."

"That would be an excellent idea," Surajah said gravely, "and I will certainly lay it before the sultan. I suppose you would propose the same for the other fort?"

"Just the same."

"The only thing that I would observe," Dick said, "is that if an enemy once got a footing on the top here, you could not hope to make a long defence of these forts."

"That is so," the governor agreed. "The strength of the defence is not here, but on the upward road, and if the English once gained the top the forts must fall; but at least it shall not be said, as long as I am governor, that Savandroog fell almost bloodlessly. In these forts we can at least die bravely and sell our lives to the last. It is for that reason I desire that they shall be so defended that they cannot be carried, as they were before, by a sudden rush."

The other fort was then visited and a tour made round the walls. The suggestions offered by the governor and the officers were all noted down and approved; then they made what was to Dick the most important part of the inspection, namely, an examination of the undefended portion of the rock. The result showed him that the builders of the defences had not acted unwisely in trusting solely to nature. At many points the rock fell away in precipices hundreds of feet deep. At other points, although the descent was less steep, it was, as far as he could see from above, altogether unclimbable; but this he thought he would be able to judge better from below.

"Do you have sentries round here at night?" he asked the governor.

"No; it would not be necessary, even if an enemy were encamped below. If you will ride round the foot of the hill when you leave, you will see for yourself that, save from the side you came up, the place is absolutely inaccessible."

The view from the top of the hill was superb. Away to the north-east the governor pointed out the pagodas of Bangalore, twenty-two miles away, the distance, in the clear air, seeming comparatively trifling.

"Are there many troops there?" Dick asked.

"There are about five battalions of the regular troops and three Chelah battalions. These can hardly be counted as troops; they have never been of the slightest use. In the last war they ran like sheep. It is a fancy of the sultan's. But indeed he can hardly expect men to fight who have been forced into the ranks and made to accept Mohammedanism against their will. Naturally they regard an invader, not as an enemy, but as a deliverer. Of course the sultan's idea was, that since the native troops, drilled and led by Englishmen, fought so well, the Chelahs, who were also drilled and led by Englishmen, would do the same. But the Company's troops are willing soldiers, and it is the English leading more than the English drill that makes them fight. If the Chelahs were divided among the hill-fortresses they might do good service; and I could, as far as fighting goes, do with a battalion of them here, for, mixed up with my men, they would have to do their duty. But of course they will never be placed in the hill-forts, for one would never be safe from treachery. Even if all the lower walls were in the hands of my own men, some of the Chelahs would be sure to manage to desert and give information as to all the defences."

A considerable portion of the upper plateau of the rock was occupied by the huts of the troops, for the forts were much too small to contain them and their families. On their way back they passed through these. Dick looked anxiously about for white faces, but could see none, nor any building that seemed to him likely to be used as a prison. When they returned to the governor's quarters they found that a room had been placed at their disposal, and they presently sat down to dinner with him.

"I suppose you have no English prisoners here?" Dick said carelessly, when the meal was over.

The governor paused a moment before he replied.

"I don't want any of them here," he said shortly. "Batches are sent up sometimes from Bangalore, but it is only for execution. I am a loyal subject of the sultan, but I would that this work could be done elsewhere. Almost all the executions take place in the hill-forts, in order, I suppose, that they may be done secretly. I obey orders, but I never see them carried out. I never even see the captives. They have done no harm, or, at most, one of their number has tried to escape, for which they are not to be blamed. I always have them shot, whether that is the mode of execution ordered or not. It is a soldier's death, and the one I should choose myself, and so that they are dead it can matter little to the sultan how they die. If they were all shot as soon as they were taken I should not think so much of it; but after being held captive for years, and compelled to work, it seems to me that their lives should be spared. As far as giving up my own life is concerned, I would willingly do it at the orders of the sultan, but these executions make me ill. I lose my appetite for weeks afterwards. Let us talk of something else." And the governor puffed furiously away at the hookah he had just lighted. Then the conversation turned to the forts again.

"No, I do not find the life dull," he said, in answer to a remark of Dick's. I did so at first, but one soon becomes accustomed to it. I have my wife and two daughters, and there are ten officers, so that I can have company when I choose. All the officers are married, and that gives society. Up here we do not observe strictly the rules of the plains, and although the ladies of course wear veils when they go beyond the house, they put them aside indoors, and the families mix freely with each other, so that we get on very well. You see, there are very few changes ever made, and as many of the ladies are, like my wife, no longer young, we treat them as comrades."

In the morning Dick and Surajah mounted their horses, took a hearty farewell of the governor, and rode down to the gate. A soldier had been sent down half-an-hour before, and they found their escort in readiness to move. They had decided that before going to the next fort they would ride round the foot of the hill of Savandroog. This they did, going at a foot-pace, and scanning the cliffs and slopes as they passed. Sometimes they reined up their horses and rode a little farther back, so as to have a view to the very summit. When they completed the round they agreed that there were but two spots where it seemed to them that an ascent was barely possible, and they were very doubtful whether the difficulties, when examined more closely, would not prove to be absolutely insurmountable.

"That is not a satisfactory outlook," Dick said, "but fortunately there is now no motive for climbing the precipice; certainly those places would be of no use to a party wanting to make an attack. In the first place, though you and I might get up with soft shoes on, I am sure that English soldiers, with muskets and ammunition-pouches, could never do it, especially at night; and in the daytime, even if a body of troops strong enough to be of any use could get up, those who first arrived at the top would be killed before the others could come to their assistance, and a few stones rolled down would sweep all behind them to the bottom. I don't like turning my back on the place," he went on, as they turned their horses' heads to the south; for Savandroog was the farthest north of the forts they were to visit; "it seems to me that even now my father may be there."

"How can that be, Dick?" Surajah said in surprise. "Nothing could be more straightforward than the governor seemed to be. I thought that he was even rash in speaking as frankly as he did to us."

"I think he saw there was no fear of our repeating what he said, Surajah. He is a frank, outspoken old soldier, and has evidently been so disgusted at the treatment of the prisoners that he could not mince his words; and yet you know he did not absolutely say that he had no prisoners."

"No; I noticed that he did not reply directly to your question."

"On the contrary, he distinctly hesitated before he spoke. Now, why should he have done that? He might just as well have said, 'No, I have no prisoners; they are only sent up here for execution.' That would have been his natural answer. Instead of that he hesitated and then began, 'I don't want any of them here; batches are sent up sometimes from Bangalore.' Now, why did he shirk the question? If it had been any other subject I might not have noticed that he had not really answered it, but of course, as it was so important a one I was listening most anxiously for his reply, and noticed his hesitation at once, and that he gave no direct answer at all. Now, think it over, Surajah: why should he have hesitated, and why should he have turned the question off without answering it, unless there had been some reason? And if so, what could the reason be?"

Surajah had no suggestion to make, and they rode on for some distance in silence.

"It is quite evident," Dick went on, after a long pause, "that he is a kind-hearted man, and that he objects altogether to Tippoo's cruelty to the prisoners; therefore, if he had any captives, his reason for not answering was most likely a kindly one."

"Yes, I should think so."

"You see, he would consider that we should report to the sultan all particulars we had gathered about the fortress. His remarks about the execution of the prisoners and the worthlessness of the Chelah battalions, and so on, was a private conversation, and was only a matter of opinion. But supposing he had had some prisoners and had said so, we might, for anything he knew, have had orders to inspect them, and to report about them as well as about the garrisons and defences."

"Yes, he might have thought that," Surajah agreed; "but after all, why should he mind that?"

Dick did not answer for some time; he was trying to think it out. Presently he reined in his horse suddenly.

"This might be the reason," he said excitedly. This governor may be the very one who we heard had taken my father with him when he was moved from that fort up in the north. He was in command at Kistnagherry before he came here, after the war, and he may have gone to Kistnagherry from that fort in the north. You see there have been executions, but they have been those of fresh batches sent up, and the governor would not include the captive he had brought with him. In time, his very existence may have been forgotten, and he may still be living there. That would account for the governor's objection to answering the question, as he would be sure that, did Tippoo hear there was a prisoner there, he would send orders for him to be executed at once. This may be all fancy, Surajah, but I cannot think of any other reason why he should have shirked my question."

He took up the reins again, and the horse at once started forward. They rode for some little time in silence, Dick thinking the matter over again and again, and becoming more and more convinced he was right, except that, as he admitted to himself, the prisoner whom the governor wished to shield might not be his father.

He was roused at last by Surajah asking the question, "Is there anything that you would like us to do?"

"Not now," Dick replied; "we could not go back again. We must visit the other forts on our list, and see what we can find out there. When we have quite assured ourselves that my father is not in any of them, we can think this over again; but at present we must put it aside. However, I sha'n't rest until I get to the bottom of it."

During the next ten days they inspected the forts of Navandroog, Sundradroog, Outradroog, and Chitteldroog. Few of these were as extensive, and none so strong, as Savandroog. They did the official part of their business, and assured themselves that no English captives were contained in any of them. The governors all said that prisoners were never kept there many days, and that it was only when Tippoo wished to get rid of them that they were sent there. None of the governors made any objection to answering Dick's questions on the subject, generally adding an expression of satisfaction that prisoners were never left long under their charge.

"It entails a lot of trouble," the governor of Outradroog said; "they have to be watched incessantly, and one never feels certain they may not slip away. Look at this place. You would think that no one could make his escape; and yet, some ten years ago, fourteen of them got away from here.

They slid down a precipice, where no one would have thought a human being could have got down alive. They were all of them retaken, except one, and executed the following day; but the sultan was so furious that, although it was no fault of the governor, who had sentries placed everywhere, he sent for him to Seringapatam and threw him to the tigers, declaring that there must have been treachery at work. You may be sure that I have no desire to hold English prisoners after that, and, when they have been sent here, have been glad indeed when orders came for their execution.

"A good many were ordered to be starved to death. But I never waited for that; it took too long. Do what I could, the guards would smuggle in pieces of bread, and they lingered on for weeks; so that it was more merciful to finish with them at once, besides making me feel comfortable at the knowledge that there was no chance of their making their escape. There were sentries at their doors, as well as on the walls when the fourteen I have told you about escaped, but they dug a passage out at the back of their hut, chose a very dark night, and it was only when the sound of some stones, that they dislodged as they scrambled down the precipice, gave the alarm to the sentries, that their escape was discovered.

"No, I do not want any prisoners up here, and when they do come there is no sleep for me until I get the order to execute them. But they do not often come now. Most of the prisoners who were not given up have been killed since, and there are not many of them left."

Upon finishing their round, they returned to Seringapatam, where Dick drew up a full report of the result of their investigations. The sultan himself went through it with them, questioned them closely, cut off a good many of the items, and gave orders that the other demands should be complied with, and the guns and ammunition sent off at once to the various forts, from the great arsenal at the capital. Dick was depressed at the result of their journey. His hopes had fallen lower and lower, as, at each fort they visited, he heard the same story—that all prisoners sent up to the mountain-fortresses had, in a short time, been put to death. It was possible, of course, that his father might still be at one of the towns where new levies had been drilled, but he had not, from the first, thought it likely that a merchant-sailor would be put to this work; and had it not been that he clung to the belief that there was a prisoner at Savandroog, and that that prisoner was his father, he would have begun to despair.

It was true that there were still many hill-forts scattered about the country unvisited, but there seemed no reason why any of the prisoners should have been allowed to survive in these forts, when they had all been put to death in those they had visited, among which were the places that had been most used as prisons.

"I would give it up," he said to Surajah, "were it not that, in the first place, it would almost break my mother's heart. Her conviction that my father is still alive has never been shaken; it has supported her all these years, and I believe that were I to return and tell her that it was no longer possible to hope, her faith would still be unshaken. She would still think of him as pining in some dungeon, and would consider that I had given up the search from faint-heartedness. That is my chief reason. But I own that I am almost as much influenced by my own conviction that he is in Savandroog. I quite admit that I can give no reason whatever why, if there is a prisoner there, it should be my father, and yet I cannot get it out of my mind that it is he. I suppose it is because I have the conviction that I believe in it. Why should I have that impression so strongly, if it were not a true one? I tell myself that it is absurd, that I have no real grounds to go upon, and yet that does not shake my faith in the slightest. It is perhaps because we have been so fortunate. Altogether everything has turned out so favourably that I can't help thinking he is alive and that I shall find him. What do you think, Surajah? Ought we to give it up?"

"Why should we?" Surajah replied stoutly. "I think you are right, and that we are destined to find your father. There is no hurry. We have not been anything like so long a time as we expected to be, and Fortune has, as you say, befriended us wonderfully. We are well off here; we have positions of honour. For myself, I could wish for nothing better."

"Well, at any rate we will wait for a time," Dick said; "we may be sent to Savandroog again, and if so I will not leave the place until I find out from the governor whether he has still a prisoner, and if so, manage to obtain a sight of him."

The next day Dick was informed by the chamberlain that the officer who was in charge of the wild beasts had fallen into disgrace, and that the sultan had appointed him to the charge. Dick was well pleased in some respects. The work would suit him much better than examining stores and seeing that the servants of the Palace did their duty; but, on the other hand, it lessened his chance of being sent to Savandroog again. However, there was no choice in the matter, and Surajah cheered him by saying,—

"You must not mind, Dick. Has not everything turned out for the best? And you may be sure that this will turn out so also."

It was indeed but two days later that Dick congratulated himself upon the change, for Surajah was sent by Tippoo with an order for the execution of four English prisoners. Dick knew nothing of the matter until Surajah, on his return, told him that he had been obliged to stop and see the orders carried out, by poison being forced down the unfortunate officers' throats.

"It was horrible," he said, with tears in his eyes.

"Horrible!" Dick repeated. "Thank God I have been put to other work, for I feel that I could not have done it. And yet to have refused to carry out the tyrant's orders would have meant death to us both, while it would not have saved the lives of these poor fellows. Anyhow, I would not have done it. As soon as I had received the order I would have come to you and we would have mounted and ridden off together, and taken our chance."

"Let us talk of something else," Surajah said. "Are the beasts all in good health?"

"As well as they can be when they are fed so badly and so miserably cooped up. I made a great row this morning, and have kept the men at work all day in cleaning out the places; they were all in a horrible state, and before I could get the work done I had to threaten to report the whole of them to Tippoo, and they knew what would come of that. I told Fazli last night that the beasts must have more flesh, and got an order from him that all the bones from the kitchens should be given to them."

That evening when Dick, on his way to the apartments of one of the officers, was going along a corridor that skirted the portion of the Palace occupied by the zenana, a figure came out suddenly from behind the drapery of a door, dropped on her knees beside him, and seizing his hand pressed it to her forehead. It was to all appearance an Indian girl in the dress of one of the attendants of the zenana.

"What is it, child?" he said. "You must have mistaken me for some one else."

"No Bahador," she said, "it is yourself I wanted to thank. One of the other attendants saw you go along this corridor some time ago, and ever since I have watched here of an evening, whenever I could get away unobserved, in hopes of seeing you. It was I, my lord, whom the tiger was standing over when you came to our rescue; I was not greatly hurt, for I was pushed down when the tiger burst in, and, save that it seized me with one of its paws, and tore my shoulder, I was unhurt. Ever since I have been hoping that the time would come when I could thank you for saving my life."

"I am glad to have done so, child. But you had best retire into the zenana. It would not be good for you or me, were I found talking to you."

M84

THE WHITE SLAVE-GIRL THANKS DICK FOR SAVING HER LIFE.

The girl rose to her feet submissively, and he now saw her face, which, in the dim light that burnt in the corridor, he had not hitherto noticed.

"Why," he exclaimed, with a start, "you are English!"

"Yes, Sahib; I was brought here eight years ago; I am fourteen now. There were other English girls here then, but they were all older than me, and have been given away to officers of the sultan. I am afraid I shall be too, ere long. I have dreaded it so much! But oh, Sahib, you are a favourite of the sultan; if he would but give me to you, I should not mind so much."

Dick was about to reply when he heard a distant footfall.

"Go in," he exclaimed. "Some one is coming. I will speak to you again in a day or two."

When he returned to his room, he told Surajah what had happened.

"It will, at any rate, give me a fresh interest here," he said. "It is terrible to think that a young English girl should be in Tippoo's power, and that he can give her, whenever he likes, to one of his creatures. Of course, according to our English notions, she is still but a young girl, but as your people out here marry when the girls are but of the age of this child, it is different altogether."

"She does not suspect that you are English?"

"No. As I told you, I had only just discovered that she was so when I heard a footstep in the distance. But I shall see her again to-morrow or next day."

"You will be running a great risk," Surajah said gravely.

"Not much risk, I think," Dick replied. "She is only a little slave girl, and as the tiger was standing over her when I fired, no doubt I did save her life, and it would be natural enough that she would, on meeting me, speak to me and express her thanks."

"That would be a good excuse," Surajah agreed. "But a suspicious tyrant like Tippoo might well insist that this was only a pretence, and that the girl was really giving you a letter or message from one of the inmates of the zenana."

Dick was silent for a time. "I will be very careful," he said. "I must certainly see her again, and it seems to me at present that whatever risk there may be, I must try to save this poor girl from the fate that awaits her. I cannot conceal from myself that, however much I may refuse to admit it, the hopes of my finding and saving my father are faint indeed; and although this girl is nothing to me, I should feel that my mission had not been an entire failure if we could take her home with us and restore her to her friends.

"No, I don't think," he went on, in answer to a grave shake of Surajah's head, "that it would add to our danger in getting away. We know that if we try to escape and are caught, our lives will be forfeited in any case, and if she were disguised as a boy we could travel with her without attracting any more observation than we should alone. She would not be missed for hours after she had left, and there would be no reason whatever for connecting her departure with ours. I don't say, Surajah, that I have made up my mind about it—of course it has all come fresh to me, and I have not had time to think it over in any way; still, it does seem to me that when the time for our leaving comes, whether we ride off openly as Tippoo's officers or whether we go off in disguise, there ought to be no very great difficulty in taking her away with us. You see that yourself, don't you?"

"I can't give any opinion about it at present," Surajah replied. "I do think that it will add to our difficulties, however we may go, but I don't say it cannot be managed."

"I should think not, Surajah, and it would be worth doing, however great the difficulties might be. Just think of the grief that her parents must feel at her loss, and the joy when she is restored to them. You see, it would be no great loss of time if we were obliged to take her down to Tripataly first, and then come back again to renew our search. It would take but a week going and returning, and now that the passes are all open to us, the difficulties would be nothing to what they were when we went back after our scouting expedition. Besides, at that time they were more vigilant all along the frontier than they will be now, because there was war between the two countries, and Tippoo was anxious that no news of his movements should be taken down. There is no talk of war now, for though Tippoo makes no disguise of his fury at his losses, especially at Coorg being taken from him, and is evidently bent upon fighting again, it will take a very long time to get his army into an efficient state, to repair his fortresses, to complete all the new works of defence he is getting up here, and to restore the confidence of his soldiers.

"I should think it will be fully four or five years before he is ready to fight again. At any rate, if we once get well away from here with the girl, we ought to have no difficulty in getting across the frontier; it would mean but a fortnight lost in the search for my father, and, anyhow, we are not making any progress that way as long as we stop here. The only drawback would be, so far as I can see, that we should lose the benefit of our official positions, but unless we happen to be sent off with orders to other hill-forts, that position will only hamper our movements; besides, we should still have our badges of office and Tippoo's official orders to the governors. Possibly the news that we had disappeared might reach the governors of some of the forts in this neighbourhood, but it would not be likely to travel very far. His officers so frequently fall into disgrace, and are either killed or thrown to the tigers, that the fact of our being missing would scarce excite a remark, and those who heard of it would suppose that we had either been secretly made away with, or that, having learned that Tippoo was displeased with us, we had fled."

Surajah nodded. His confidence in his leader was complete, and he was always ready to follow unquestioningly.

"There is one thing, Surajah," Dick concluded: "this state of things cannot last much longer anyhow, for next time it might be me he ordered to see to the execution of an English prisoner, and that would mean that I should, as soon as I received the command, make a bolt for it. So you see our stay here, in any case, may not last many days. I would rather run any risks than carry out such an order."

Two evenings later, Dick went down the corridor at the same hour as that on which he had before met the English girl. She came out from behind the hangings at once when he passed.

"I knew you would come, Bahador!" she said joyfully. "I could see that you were as kind as you were brave, and would have pity upon a poor little white slave!"

"I have much that I want to say to you, child. This is not a good place for speaking; some one might come along at any moment. How long can you be away without fear of your absence being noticed?"

"Not long now," she said. "In the morning I am sent out on messages, and could meet you anywhere."

"Very well; I will remain in my room all the morning to-morrow, and if you do not come then, I will stay in next day."

"I will come," the girl said unhesitatingly.

He then gave her full instructions how to find his room, and made her repeat them to him, in order to be sure that she had them correctly.

"Do you know my companion by sight?" he asked.

"Oh, yes; I have seen him often."

"Well, either he or I will be standing at my door. It is as well that you should look carefully round before you enter, so as to be sure there is no one in the corridor, and that you can slip in unobserved. You may be sure that I am asking you to come for no idle freak, but because I have something very important to say to you. I fancy I hear footsteps. Good-night."

Dick was sure that he and Surajah would both be at liberty next day, for Tippoo had that morning started for Bangalore, where a large number of men were at work repairing the fortifications and removing all signs of the British occupation from the fort and palace. He was likely to be away for at least a fortnight. As soon as Ibrahim had swept the room after their early breakfast, Dick gave him a number of small commissions to be executed in the town and told him that he should not require him again until it was time to bring up their meal from the kitchen. Then he and Surajah by turns watched at the door. An hour later Surajah, who was upon the watch, said, "The girl is coming."

There was no one else in sight, and when Surajah beckoned to her she hurried on, and, passing through the curtains at the door, entered the room. It had been arranged that Surajah should remain on watch, so that should by any chance one of the officials of their acquaintance come along, he might go out and talk with him in the corridor, and, on some excuse or other, prevent his entering the room, if he showed any intention of doing so.

"Now, in the first place," Dick said, as he led the girl to the divan and seated her there, "what is your name?"

"My name is Goorla."

"No; I mean your proper name?"

"My name used to be Annie—Annie Mansfield, Bahador."

"And my name is Dick Holland," he said, in English. She gave a start of surprise. "Yes, Annie, I am a countryman of yours."

She looked at him almost incredulously, and then an expression of aversion succeeded that of confidence in her face. She sprang from the divan and drew herself up indignantly. "Please let me go," she said haughtily. "You have saved my life, but if you had saved it twenty times, I could not like a man who is a deserter!"

Dick had at first been speechless with astonishment at the girl's change of manner and at her reception of the news he had thought would have been very pleasant to her. As her last words threw a light upon the matter, he burst into a merry laugh.

"I am no deserter, Annie. Save my friend at the door and yourself, there is no one here who knows that I am English. Sit down again, and I will tell you how I come to be here. My father was the captain of an English ship. She was wrecked on the west coast, and he was seized and brought up here a prisoner, eight years ago. My mother, who is a daughter of the late Rajah of Tripataly, who married an English lady, taught me to speak Hindustani, so that when I got old enough I could come out here and try to find out if my father was still alive, and if so, to help him to escape. I had only just come up here with my friend, who is an officer of the Rajah's, when that affair with the tiger took place. Then, as you know, Tippoo made us both officers in the Palace. Of course, while we are here we can do nothing towards finding out about my father, and we should not have remained here much longer anyway, and may have to leave at any moment. Since you met me and I found that there was an English girl captive here, it has of course changed my plans, and I feel that I could not go away and leave you to the fate you told me of, and that if possible, I must take you away with me; that is, of course, if you are willing to go with us, and prepared to run a certain amount of risk.

"Do not take on so," he continued, as the girl threw herself on her knees, and, clinging to him, burst into a passion of tears. "Do not cry like that;" and, stooping down, he lifted her, and placed her in a corner of the divan. "There," he said, patting her on the shoulder as she sobbed almost convulsively; "try and compose yourself. We may be disturbed at any moment, and may not have an opportunity of talking again, so we must make our arrangements, in readiness to leave suddenly. I may find it necessary to go at an hour's notice; you may, as you said, be given by Tippoo to one of his favourites at any time. Fortunately he has gone away for a fortnight, so we have, at any rate, that time before us to make our plans. Still, it is better that we should arrange now as much as we can."

CHAPTER XV.

ESCAPE.

ANNIE MANSFIELD was not long before she mastered her emotions. She had learned to do so in a bitter school. Beaten for the slightest fault, or at the mere caprice of one of her many mistresses, she had learned to suffer pain without a tear, to assume a submissive attitude under the greatest provocation, to receive, without attempting to defend herself, punishment for faults she had not committed, and to preserve an appearance of cheerfulness when her heart seemed breaking at the hopelessness of any deliverance from her fate. For the last six months she had been specially unhappy, for when Seringapatam had been besieged she had hoped that when it was captured her countrymen would search the Palace and see that this time no English captive remained behind. Her disappointment, then, when she heard that peace had been made, and that the English army was to march away without even an attempt to see that the condition for the release of captives was faithfully carried out, had for a time completely crushed her, and all hope had forsaken her.

Thus, then, while she had been for a moment overwhelmed at finding that her preserver from the tiger was a countryman in disguise, and that he was willing to make an attempt to rescue her, yet in a few minutes she stifled her sobs, hastily thrust back the hair that had fallen over her face, uncoiled herself from her crouching position in the angle of the divan, and rose to her feet.

"I can hardly believe it to be true," she said, in a low voice. "Oh, Sahib, do you really mean what you say? and are you willing to run the risk of taking me away with you?"

"Of course I am," Dick said heartily. "You don't suppose that an Englishman would be so base as to leave a young countrywoman in the hands of these wretches? I do not think that there is much risk in it. Of course you will have to disguise yourself, and there may be some hardships to go through, but once away from here we are not likely to be interfered with. You see, my friend and I are officers of the Palace, and no one would venture to question us, as we should be supposed to be travelling upon the sultan's business. There is peace at present, and although Tippoo may intend some day or other to fight again, everything is settling down quietly. Traders go about the country unquestioned; there is plenty of traffic on the roads from one town to another; and so long as your disguise is good enough to prevent your being recognised as a white, there is no greater danger in travelling in Mysore than there would be down in the Carnatic."

Annie stood before him with her fingers playing nervously with each other. Long trained in habits of implicit obedience, and to stand in an attitude of deep respect before her numerous mistresses, she was in ignorance whether she ought to speak or not. She had been but a child of six when she had been carried off; her remembrance of English manners had quite died out, and the habit of silent submission had become habitual to her. Dick was puzzled by her silence.

"Of course, Annie," he said, at last, "I don't want you to go with me if you would rather stay here, or if you are afraid of the risk of travelling."

She looked up with frightened eyes.

"Oh, Sahib, it is not that; I would go even if I felt sure I should be found out and cut to pieces. Anything would be better than this. I am not afraid at all. But forgive me, Sahib, I don't know how to thank you; I don't know what is proper to say, it is all so strange and so wonderful."

"Oh, that is all right, Annie," Dick said cheerfully. "Of course you will feel it a little strange just at starting. Well, in the first place, you must call me Dick, instead of calling me sahib; and in the next place, you must talk to me freely, as a friend, and not stand as if I were your master. While we are on this journey together, consider me as a sort of big brother. When we get down the ghauts I shall hand you over to the care of my mother, who is living at present at Tripataly with her brother, the Rajah. Now sit down again and let us make our arrangements. When we have done that we can talk, if there is time. Now, how am I to let you know if I have to go away suddenly? Do you always get out at this time of a morning?"

"Not always, but very often. I always go down at twelve o'clock, with some of the other slave girls, to fetch the food and sweetmeats for the ladies of the harem."

"Well, you must always manage, even if you are not sent out, to look out through that doorway where you met me, at eight o'clock in the morning. If we have anything particular to say to you, Surajah,—that is my friend, you know,—will be there. Which way do you go out from the harem to fetch the food?"

"Not from that door, but from the one nearest to the kitchen. You go right down that corridor, and then take the first turning to the right. There is a flight of stairs at its end. We come out at the door just at its head. At the foot of the stairs there is a long passage, and at the end of that is a large room, with tables, on which the dishes are placed in readiness for us to bring back."

"Well, if it is necessary to speak to you at once, one of us will meet you in the passage between the bottom of the stairs and the room where the food is; if you see one of us, you will know that the matter is urgent, and as soon as you can possibly slip away, you must come here. In the evening you had better again look out from the door where you first met me. Now as to the disguise: it will be better for you to go as a boy; it would be strange to see a girl riding behind two of the officers of the Palace. You won't mind that, will you?"

"Not at all, Sahib."

"Not at all, Dick," he corrected. "Well, I will have a dress ready for you here. You will find it in that corner, and there will be a bottle of stain on the table; it will be only necessary for you to colour your neck, hands, and feet, but you must cut off your hair behind to a level with your ears, so that none of it will show below the turban. You must do that of course before you stain your neck, and must stain the skin where you have cut off your hair also. I am giving you these instructions now, because when the time comes there may not be a minute to spare, though of course I hope there will be no desperate hurry."

"I understand," she said, "and will look out for you three times a day."

"Of course," he went on, "if you are suddenly told that you are to be given to any one, you must slip out at once, and come here. You will find everything ready for you to disguise yourself, and you must do that at once and wait here till one of us comes. Even if you are missed, it will be some time before any search is made, and it would be thought much more likely that you had gone down into the town than that you were hiding in the Palace, so there would be no chance of their looking for you here before we return. Anyhow, we shall be able to have another talk before Tippoo comes back; we shall be here every morning until nine, and if you are able to get away again, come and see us. It will be better perhaps for you not to wait any longer now; I suppose you have been charged with some message or other, and it would not do for you to be too long gone."

The girl stood up at once. "I have to go down to the Pettah to get some sewing silk to match this;" and she drew out a small fragment of yellow silk.

"Very well, then, you had better go and do it, or they may think that you are too long away. Good-bye, Annie. I hope that in another week or ten days at the latest I shall have you out of this;" and he held out his hand to her.

She took it timidly, and would have raised it to her forehead, but Dick said, laughing,—

"That is not the way, Annie. English girls don't treat their friends as if they were lords and masters; they just shake hands with them, as if it were two men or two girls."

"I shall know better in time," she said, with a faint smile, though her eyes were full of tears. "I want to do something, though I don't know what. You saved my life from the tiger, and now you are going to save me again. I should like to throw myself down and kiss your feet."

"You would make me horribly uncomfortable if you did anything of the sort, Annie. I can understand that you feel strange and out of your element at present, but you will soon get over that when you come to know me better. There, good-bye, lassie, I hope to see you again to-morrow or next day, and then you will be able to tell me more about yourself. Is the coast clear, Surajah?"

Surajah looked out through the curtains.

"There is no one in sight," he said a moment later.

The girl passed silently out and went down the corridor. Surajah returned from his post by the door.

"The poor girl is shy and awkward as yet," Dick said, "but I think she will be plucky enough when the time comes. You heard what we said; the first thing will be to get her disguise ready for her. What do you think? Had we better take Ibrahim with us? I think he is to be trusted."

"I am sure he is," Surajah agreed; "he is a Hindoo of Coorg, and was carried away as a slave six years ago. In the first place, he will be delighted at the prospect of getting away, and in the next, I am sure that he is very fond of you; but there is no occasion to tell him that you are English."

"No, it will be time enough to do that when we get over the ghauts. It will be better that he should get the disguise. In the first place he will know exactly what is wanted, and in the next, it would look rum for either of us to be buying such a thing. Of course we could ask Pertaub to get it for us, but if we take Ibrahim with us he may as well buy it. We shall want a couple more horses; these, of course, we can buy ourselves, and saddles and things. When we have got them we had better leave them at some place on the other side of the river. Pertaub would help us there; he is sure to know some one who will look after them for a few days. Then Ibrahim and the girl can start together, go over there and saddle them, so as to be in readiness to mount directly we come along. We will stop at the wood and dig up the caskets; there is nothing like taking them away with us when there is a chance, and it is not likely that we shall come back to Seringapatam again—it would be like putting our heads into a tiger's den."

When Ibrahim brought in the dishes for their meal, Dick said,—

"Go down and get your own food, Ibrahim, and when you have done come back here again; I want to have a talk with you."

They had just finished their meal when Ibrahim returned.

"Ibrahim, would you be glad of a chance of getting away from here, and returning to your own country?"

"I would have given anything to do so, my lord," Ibrahim said, "before I was ordered to attend upon you. But I am happy now; you are kind to me, and I should not like to leave your service."

"But if I were going too, Ibrahim?"

"Then, my lord, I would go with you anywhere, if you would take me."

"Well, Ibrahim, we feel sure that we can trust you, and so I may tell you that I think it likely we shall very shortly go away. You know what the sultan is: one day he gives you honours and rewards, the next he disgraces you, and perhaps sends you into the ranks of the army, perhaps has you thrown to the tigers. We do not care to live under such conditions, and we mean in a few days to slip away and go to our friends down the ghauts. You can come with us if you like."

"I would go with you to the end of the world, my lord," Ibrahim exclaimed earnestly. "To go with you and be a free man, and not a slave, would be almost too great happiness."

"Very well, then, that is settled. Now, Ibrahim, we are

not going alone; we are going to take with us a young white slave in the harem, and restore her to her friends. I want you to get a disguise for her; let it be a dress like your own—long white trousers to the ankle, a shirt and tunic with waist-belt, also the stuff for a turban. That you must wind in proper folds, as she would not be able to do it herself. I also want a bottle of stain for the skin."

"I will get them, my lord. How tall is she?"

"About half a head shorter than you are. She is about the size of an average Hindoo woman."

"Shall I get the things at once, my lord?"

"Yes, you had better get them to-day; we may leave at any time, and it is as well to have them in readiness. We shall buy two horses, one for each of you, and have them taken across the river. You can ride, I suppose?"

"Yes; I used to ride when I was a boy, before Tippoo came down and killed my father and mother and brought me up here. Will my lord want me to take the horses across?"

"I will tell you that in the morning, Ibrahim. We are going down into the town now to inquire about them, but we shall not buy any until to-morrow, as we shall have to make arrangements for them to be kept for us until we want them."

They did not go out until it was dark, and then took their way to Pertaub's house. The old Hindoo was in.

"I am glad to see you, Sahibs," he said to Dick as they entered. "I have always fears that ill may in some way befall you."

"We are going to leave, Pertaub. Surajah had, two days ago, to go up to see four English prisoners put to death at one of the hill-forts. Next time I may be ordered on such a duty; I could not carry it out, and you know that refusal would probably mean death. Moreover, we are convinced that we have no means here of finding out what captives may still be in Tippoo's hands, and have therefore determined to leave. We are going to take with us our servant Ibrahim, who is a slave from Coorg and will, we know, be faithful to us, and also a young English girl who has for eight years been a slave in Tippoo's harem. She will go with us in the disguise of a boy; this Ibrahim is getting for us. We are going to buy a couple of horses for them, and shall make straight down the ghauts, where I shall leave the girl in my mother's care."

"It is a good action," the Hindoo said gravely.

"Now, in the first place, Pertaub, would you like to go with us? Riding as we shall do, as two of the officers of the Palace, it is not likely that any questions whatever will be asked, and certainly we shall have no difficulty until it comes to crossing the frontier."

"No, Sahib; I thank you, but I am too old now for any fresh change. I have friends here, and have none below the ghauts. Nothing save the rescue of my daughter from the harem would induce me to move now, and of that there is little chance; she will by this time have become reconciled to her fate, and would probably not care to escape were an opportunity offered to her. Besides, with only me to protect her, what would she do elsewhere? A few months and she might be left alone in the world."

"As to that," Dick said, "I could promise her the protection of my aunt, the wife of the Rajah of Tripataly. After the kindness that you have shown to us she would, I am sure, gladly take her into her service. And there would be no difficulty about a dowry for her; I would see to that."

The old man shook his head.

"There could be no question of marriage," he said; "but should I ever hear from her that she is unhappy and I can arrange to fly with her, I will assuredly avail myself of your offer, and take her to Tripataly, rejoiced indeed that at my death there will be a shelter open to her. And now, can I aid you in any way, Sahib? One of my friends, a merchant, could get the horses for you without difficulty; he has often occasion to buy them for the purposes of his trade."

"Thank you, Pertaub. I had intended to buy them myself,

but doubtless it will be safer for somebody else to do so. What I was going to ask you was to let me know of some place on the other side of the river where the horses could be kept until I want them."

"That I can do, Sahib. I have a friend a cultivator; his house stands by itself on this side of the first village—the one half a mile beyond the ford. It is the only house this side of the village, so you cannot mistake it; it lies about a hundred yards back from the road. I will go over and arrange with him that when two horses arrive they shall be placed in his stalls and remain there until one arrives who will say to him, after greeting, the word 'Madras'; to him he is to deliver the horses at once, whether he comes by night or day."

"That would do admirably, Pertaub. Of course I shall also want saddles and bridles. How much do you think it will come to altogether? I do not want showy horses, but they must be animals capable of performing a long journey and of travelling at a fair rate of speed—the faster the better; we are likely to get seven or eight hours start at least, but must, of course, travel fast. As long as all goes well I shall keep the main roads, but if there is a breakdown, or an unforeseen accident occurs, I may have to leave the road and take to by-paths."

"The cost of such horses would be about eighty rupees each; the saddles and bridles another fifteen or twenty."

"Then here are two hundred rupees, Pertaub."

"Have you given up all hope of finding your father, Sahib? I have felt so sure that you would be successful. It seemed to me that such brave efforts could not go unrewarded."

"No, Pertaub, I have not given it up at all. I intend to stay at Tripataly for a fortnight with my mother, and shall then come up the ghauts again. That is another matter I want to speak to you about. Of course we should not dare to return to Seringapatam, and I think that we had better settle to go to Bangalore. Could you forward our packs with the merchandise to some one in that town?"

"There will be no difficulty in that, Sahib. There are many Hindoo merchants there who have been forced to change their religion, and who have frequent dealings with traders here. One of my friends will, I am sure, forward your goods with the next consignment that he sends to Bangalore; that also I will arrange to-morrow, and when you come in the evening will give you the name of the trader there, together with a letter from the one here, telling him that you are the person to whom the goods are to be given up."

"Thank you, Pertaub. I don't know what we should have done without your assistance."

"It has been a pleasure to me to be of use to you, Sahib. I had thought my time of usefulness was over, and it has given a real pleasure to my life to have been able to aid you. You will let me know, Sahib, if ever you find your father?"

"Certainly, Pertaub. I will in any case send word to you, either that I have found him or that I have given up all hope and have abandoned my efforts."

The next morning a lad brought Dick a message from Pertaub that he had fulfilled all his commissions, and on the following morning Annie Mansfield again came to Dick's room.

"Everything is going on well, Annie," Dick said, as he shook hands with her. "The horses have been bought. There is your disguise in that corner, and we can start any moment at a quarter of an hour's notice. Now I want you to tell me how you came to be brought up here."

"I have not much to tell," she said. "You see, I was only six years old. I can remember there was a great deal of firing of guns, and that lasted for a long time; then the firing stopped. I suppose the place surrendered."

"Do you know what place it was, Annie?"

She shook her head. "I do not know at all. I suppose I did know then, but I do not remember ever to have heard the name. I remember quite well that there were soldiers, and father and mother, and servants, and many other people, and every one was very miserable, and we all went together out of a gate, and on each side there were a great many natives with guns and swords, some on horse and some on foot; and there were elephants. I don't think I had ever seen one before, for I noticed them particularly. We went on and on, and I know one of the soldiers carried me. At night we stopped somewhere. I think it was in a wood, and there were fires, and we lay down to sleep on the ground. Then I woke up suddenly, and there was a great noise and firing of guns, and some one caught me up and threw something over my head, and I don't remember anything more for a long time. I know that presently I was on horseback before a fierce-looking man. There were a good many of them, and when I cried for my father and mother they said they would cut off my head if I were not quiet.

"I do not know how long we were travelling, but after the first day there was only the man who carried me and another. I was brought here, and there were many people, and I was very much frightened. Then I found myself only among women, and they took off my clothes and dressed me in their fashion. I think I was very happy when I once got accustomed to it. The ladies made a sort of pet of me, and I was taught to dance and to sing little native songs. There were other white girls here, and they were all very kind to me, though they always seemed very sad, and I could not make out why they cried so often, especially when they were beaten for crying. As I grew bigger I was not so happy. I had ceased to be a plaything, and little by little I was set to work to sweep and dust, and then to sew, and then to do all sorts of work, like the other slave-girls. The other white girls gradually went away, the oldest first. The last two, who were two or three years older than I was, went about three years ago.

"At first I used to wonder why they cried so when they went, and why the others all cried too; but by the time the last two left I had come to know all about it, and knew that they had been given by the sultan to his favourite officers. There were many white men here when I first came. When I went out with one of the slaves into the town I saw them often. Sometimes they would burst into tears when they saw me. Then I used to wonder why, but I know now that I must have reminded them of girls of their own, whom they would never see again. Then, till three years ago, there were about twenty white boys who had been taught to dance and sing, and who used to come sometimes, dressed up like women, to amuse the ladies of the harem; but I heard that they were all killed when the sultan first thought that the English might come here. One of the slave-girls told me that it was done because the sultan had often sworn to the English that there were no white captives here, and so he did not wish that any should be found if they came. I don't think that I have anything else to tell you."

"Well, I hope that what you have told me will be enough to enable us some day to find out who you belong to. Evidently you were in some place that was besieged eight years ago, and had to surrender. The garrison were promised their lives and liberty to depart. They were attacked at night by an armed party, who may have been Hyder's horsemen, but who were perhaps merely a party of mounted robbers, who thought that they might be able to take some loot. Most likely they were defeated, especially as you saw no other captives in the party, but in the confusion of the night attack, one of them probably came upon you, and carried you off, thinking you would be an acceptable present here, and that he would get a reward for you from the sultan. Are you not noticed when you go into the streets on errands?"

"No; I always go veiled. Except the slaves who are old and ugly, all the others wear veils when they go outside the Palace, and we all wear a red scarf, which shows we are servants in the harem; and so, even when the town is full of rough soldiers, no one ventures to speak to us. Now tell me, Dick—you see I have not forgotten—all about how you came to be here."

Dick told her briefly how he had come out with his mother; and how, finding war had broken out, he had joined the army; and how, at the end of the war, having been able to learn nothing about his father, he had come up with Surajah to search for him.

"And then you saw that tiger break in," the girl said eagerly; "that was dreadful. I will tell you how it was the tiger came to seize me. I was standing behind a lady, and could not see anything. Suddenly they all began screaming, and ran, some to one side some to the other, of the window, and I, who could not think what was the matter, remained where I was, when there was a great cry, and before I had time to move, or even to wonder, some great thing knocked me down. It was only from the screams of the ladies, and their cries of 'Tiger!' that I knew what had happened. I felt something heavy standing on me—so heavy that I could hardly breathe; and indeed, I did not try to breathe, for I knew many stories of tigers, and had heard that sometimes, when a man shams being dead, the tiger will walk away and kill some one else.

"The tiger was keeping up an angry growl, and I felt that unless it took its paw off me I should soon die, when I heard a shot, and a fierce growl from the tiger, and then the weight was gone, and I think I fainted. When I came round I was lying where I fell, for many of the ladies were insensible, and every one was too busy with them to think anything of me. When I got up, one of the other slave girls, who had been brave enough to look out of the window, told me that it had been killed by two young men, one of whom must have been the one who had fired the shot in at the window. I went and looked out, and saw it lying there. After that every one talked, and laughed, and cried, and then the sultan's chief wife said that every one must make a present to the young men who had saved us, and that each one ought to give one of her best jewels. Of course every one did. I had nothing to give except a little cross of gold filigree work that hung round my neck when I was carried off; it had been hidden by my dress; the men had not noticed it, and they had not taken it away when I was brought here. It was such a poor little gift, but it was all I had."

"I noticed it Annie," Dick said; "there was a little flat plate behind it with the letters 'A. M.,' and I thought then that it must be some little ornament taken from one of the Englishwomen Hyder's troops killed. It is fortunate you kept it, for it may be useful some day in proving that you are Annie Mansfield."

"Now I must be going," she said. "I was slapped and pinched last time for being so long, but I have several things to get to-day, so that if I hurry I can be back again as soon as they expect me. You have not settled when you are going yet?"

"No; but we rather think of going the day after to-morrow. It will be better to do so before Tippoo comes back, for we might be ordered away so quickly as to have no time to make arrangements; besides, there will be ten times as many people about in the Palace, and more guards at the entrances when he returns. So, altogether, it will be better to go before he does so. If we settle it so, I will come along past your door to-morrow evening; and if I say, 'To-morrow morning,' get here as soon as you can in the morning, and directly you have stained your skin and put on your disguise, we will start. My servant, who is going with us, will act as your guide, and will take you to the place where the horses are, and where we shall join you almost as soon as you get there."

At the appointed time next evening Dick told Annie that they should start in the morning. He and Surajah then went down and said good-bye to Pertaub, and Dick gave him a letter to his aunt, to give to her should he ever go to Tripataly with his daughter.

"It may be," he said, "that neither Surajah nor I may be there, but I shall speak to her about you, and of course tell her how much you have done for us; so you may be sure of the heartiest welcome from her."

"And you will also find a hearty friend in my father, Rajbullub," Surajah said. "He is principal officer in the Rajah's household, and will treat you as a brother, and your daughter as if she were my sister."

Then they returned to the Palace, where they had a final talk over the route that it would be best to pursue.

The nearest point to the new frontier was the territory ceded to the English on the Malabar coast. But this would entail a long sea voyage, and they therefore determined to make for Caveripatam, going by the road that led through Anicull, and then through Ryacotta, which stood just outside the line of territory ceded to England, and from whence a road led direct down the passes. Anicull lay nearly due south of Bangalore, but the road they would follow would not be the one by which Tippoo would return, as he would come by the main road, which ran in a direct line between the two cities.

Ibraham was informed of their plans, and was told to warn the syce to get their horses saddled and in readiness at eight o'clock, and that, as they were going for a long day's ride, he would not be required to accompany them—as he always did when they rode only into the town, for then he might be wanted to hold the horses if they dismounted and went into a shop.

He was also to give notice in the kitchen that they would not return to the mid-day meal, and that dishes for them would therefore not be required. Thus it would be unlikely that any suspicion would be aroused by their absence until they had been gone twenty-four hours, by which time they would be more than half-way to the frontier.

They went to bed at their usual time, and slept soundly, for it seemed to them both that there was practically no risk whatever to be run, and that they would be across the frontier before any active search was made for them. Even when it was discovered that they had left the Palace, it would be thought that they had received some order from Bangalore, either to join the sultan, or to go on some mission for him that had occupied more time than they had anticipated on starting. The idea that two officers, who were considered to stand high in Tippoo's favour, should desert, would scarcely occur to any one.

In the morning they were up early, completed their slight preparations, and took their early breakfast, reserving a portion for Annie, who, they thought, would not improbably have eaten nothing before coming to them.

She was a quarter of an hour late in arriving, and looked somewhat pale and flurried.

"They did not send me out this morning," she said, "and so I had to stay until I could slip out without being noticed; but they may miss me at any moment."

"That will be all right," Dick said confidently. "They will search all the rooms in the harem for you first, and certainly won't look for you outside until there has been a lot of talk over your absence. But even if they do search, you will be able in a few minutes to walk through the middle of them without being suspected. However, we will lose no time; and to begin with, I will cut off what hair is necessary. I shall do it a good deal quicker than you would. Then we will leave you to yourself, to stain your skin and put on your disguise. When you have finished, clap your hands. Ibrahim will come in and see that your disguise is all right, and that your turban covers your hair; then he will go with you. We shall be waiting near the gate; there is practically no chance of your being asked any questions, but if you are, and there is any difficulty, we will pass you through all right. Having seen you on your way, we shall mount and follow you."

The operation of cutting off Annie's hair to the line of her ears was speedily done; then, with a few reassuring words, Dick joined Surajah in the corridor. As they walked down it he said,—

"I don't like leaving them to themselves. Look here, Surajah, you go down to the stable and mount at once; tell the syce I shall come for my horse in a few minutes, then ride out and take your post where you can see them come out of the gate, and then follow them closely. I will stay here and see them safely through the gate, and then mount and follow you. I shall overtake you before you get to the ford."

"That will perhaps be safest," Surajah agreed, "though I should think there is no chance of her being suspected, seeing that she will be with Ibrahim. Even if they met one of the Palace officers, and he asked Ibrahim who he had with him, he could say it was a lad who had come to you respecting some horses you had bought."

"Yes, that would do very well."

Dick returned to Ibrahim, who was squatting down in the corridor near the door.

"I am going to follow you until you are through the gate, and shall keep a short distance behind you. If you should meet any officer on your way out, who may ask you who you have with you, say he has come with a message to me from a trader in the town. By the time you have told him that, I shall be up."

"There is no chance of being questioned, my lord; people come and go all day."

"That is so, Ibrahim, but one cannot be too careful."

They stood talking together until they heard Annie clap her hands within. Ibrahim entered at once, and in two or three minutes came out again with the girl. Ibrahim carried a bundle.

"You will do very well," Dick said to Annie. "I should not know you in the least; you make a capital boy. What bundle is that, Ibrahim? I thought you took our other disguises on yesterday to the stable where the horses are."

"Yes, my lord, I took them on; these are the things she has taken off. I thought perhaps it would be better not to leave them here, as, if they were found, it would be known that she had gone with you."

"I don't think it makes much difference, Ibrahim, but

perhaps it is as well to bring them away; we can leave the bundle in the wood. Now go along; I will follow. Perhaps I had better go first; keep a few paces behind me."

They passed through the long passages of the Palace without attracting the slightest attention. Once or twice Dick paused to speak to some officials of his acquaintance, the others stopping respectfully a few paces away; then he went out into the courtyard and across to the gate, and as the sentries saluted he stopped and asked them a few questions as to the regiment they belonged to, until Ibrahim and his companion, who had passed straight through, were well away. He saw Surajah sitting upon his horse a couple of hundred yards away, and then went to the stables.

CHAPTER XVI.

THE JOURNEY.

THE syce brought out his horse as soon as he saw Dick approaching.

"You need not wait up for us after nine o'clock," Dick said, as he mounted. "It is possible that we may be detained and shall not return until to-morrow evening. If we come we shall certainly be back by nine at the latest, and we shall not be back before seven at any rate, so that until then you are free to do as you like."

He rode quietly off, and did not quicken his pace until he had got beyond the fort; then he touched the horse with his heel and cantered down to the ford. Surajah was half-way across the river when he reached it; the other two figures were just ascending the road up the other bank. Surajah checked his horse when he got across, and waited till Dick joined him.

"Shall we go on with them to the farmhouse?" he asked.

"We may as well do so as halt in the road; besides, there are the things Ibrahim took over yesterday, to put into our saddle-bags. There is another thing that I never thought of. Of course, the girl has never been on a horse, and that may give us a good deal of trouble. I wonder I did not think of it, though if I had I don't see that anything else could have been done. We must see how she gets on, and if she cannot manage I must take her before me whenever we see that the road is clear for a good distance ahead. Of course it does not matter about country people, but if we see a body of troops coming in the distance she must mount her own horse again, and follow us at a walk. If we find that things don't go well, we must halt in a wood somewhere and ride only by night."

They cantered on now and overtook the others just as they reached the farmhouse. The farmer was at his door, and looked a little surprised at seeing two of the officers of the Palace come up; he salaamed deeply.

"We have not come to requisition anything," Dick said, with a smile, as he saw that the farmer looked alarmed as well as surprised. "We have only come for the two horses that we have bought for our servants, as we are going on a journey."

"Can I assist you in any way, my lords?"

"No, our men will saddle the horses," Dick said, and, dismounting, went into the stable with Ibrahim and Annie.

"You are not afraid of riding I hope, Annie?" he said.

"I am not afraid of anything, Dick, so that I can but get away."

"We will go quietly at first, anyhow. Mind, as you mount put your left foot in the stirrup. When you are seated, carry yourself as easily as you can. The pony looks quiet enough, but if, when we get fairly off, you find that you cannot sit comfortably, you must get up before me, and Ibrahim must lead your pony. When we are fairly on the road I will fasten a bit of rope to your bridle to act as a leading-rein, and you can ride by my side, unless we see people coming along; then you must drop behind with Ibrahim."

"I won't give more trouble than I can help," she said.

Ibrahim had taken some rugs over with him on the previous afternoon, which had been bought in case they should sleep out at night. When the horses were saddled Dick rolled two of these up, strapped one on the high peak and the other on the cantle of the saddle upon which the girl was to ride.

"That will wedge you in pretty tightly," he said. "Now, Ibrahim, put the things into the saddle-bag, and then we shall be ready."

When this was done the two horses were led outside. The farmer had gone back into the house, and Dick, helping the girl into her seat, arranged the stirrups the right length for her.

"Now," he said, "you must keep your knees pressed against the roll of blankets in front, and hold on as well as you can with them, but the principal thing is for you to balance yourself with your body; don't sit up stiffly, but as if you were in a chair. Now we will start at a walk. Ibrahim will keep quite close to you, so as to be able to catch hold of your rein should there be any occasion for him to do so."

Then, mounting, he and Surajah rode off at a walk, the others following a length or two behind them. Dick looked round from time to time, and saw that Annie exhibited no signs of nervousness.

"I am quite comfortable," she said, in reply to one of his glances.

When they got into the road again Dick said, "We will go at an easy canter now, Annie. If you feel as if you could not keep on, call out, and we will stop directly; but first come up between Surajah and myself, and we will take the leading reins, so that you will have nothing to attend to but holding on."

Two cords had been attached to the bridle before setting out, and Surajah and Dick each taking one, they started again, the horses instinctively breaking into a canter, which was their usual pace. Annie at first grasped the strap of the rug in front of her, but as soon as she became accustomed to the motion, she let go. A small rug had been strapped over the saddle before she mounted, and this afforded her a much better hold than she would have had of the leather; and as the pace of the horse was a gentle one, she found it much more easy to keep her seat than she had expected. Moreover, the fact that Dick and Surajah rode close by her side, and would be able to catch her at once if she swayed in the saddle, gave her confidence.

"It is much better than I thought it would be," she said; "it is quite a pleasant motion. I will go faster if you like."

"No, there is no occasion for that," Dick replied. "This is the pace the horses are most accustomed to, and they will go on longer at it than at any other. There is no fear of pursuit, and we have all day before us."

After a quarter of a mile's riding they came to a wood.

"We must turn in here," Dick said. "We are going treasure hunting; we hid those caskets that were given us by the ladies directly after we got them, and we are going to dig them up now and take them with us."

They rode at a walk now till they came to a very large baobab tree growing by the path they were following.

"Here we turn off."

"There is a man there," Surajah exclaimed, when they had ridden a few yards farther.

Dick checked his horse. "It is Pertaub," he said, a moment later, and in a minute they were beside the Hindoo.

"I could not sleep, thinking of you, Sahib," the latter said, as they came up, "so I came across here, partly to help you dig up the caskets, and partly that I might see you and assure myself that so far all had gone well."

"Thank you, Pertaub. You have, I see, brought a pick-axe; it will save us half-an-hour's work; and besides, I am glad to say good-bye again. All has gone well; this is the young lady."

"She is well disguised," Pertaub said, bowing his head to Annie. "She looks so like a boy that, even now you tell me,

I can scarce believe she is a white girl. Truly you can go on without fear that any one will suspect her."

Leading the way to the spot where the caskets had been buried, Dick looked on while Surajah and Ibrahim dug them up. They were then wrapped up in rugs and strapped securely behind their owners' saddles. Then, after a warm adieu to the kind old man, they turned their horses' heads and rode back out of the woods. After riding for three hours at a canter, Dick saw that, although Annie still spoke cheerfully, her strength was failing her, and on arriving at a wood, he said,—

"We will wait here till the heat of the sun has abated. We have done very well, and the horses, as well as ourselves, will be glad of a few hours' rest."

He alighted from the saddle, gave his horse to Ibrahim, and then lifted Annie from her seat. As he set her down on her feet and loosed his hold of her, she slipped down on to the ground. Dick and Surajah at once raised her, and placed her so that as she sat she could lean against a tree. Here Dick supported her, while Surajah ran and fetched his water-bottle. Annie drank a little, and then said, with a nervous laugh, "It is very silly of me. But I feel better now. My legs seemed to give way altogether."

"It was not silly at all," Dick said. "You have held on most bravely. I can tell you there are not many girls who would have ridden four or five and twenty miles the first time they sat on a horse. Why, I can tell you the first time I mounted I did not do a quarter as much, and I was so stiff I could hardly walk when I got down. I should have stopped before, but you kept talking so cheerfully that it seemed to me you could not be anything like as tired as I was then. I was a brute not to have known that you must be thoroughly done up, although you did not say so. We have got some food with us. Do you think you could eat a little?"

She shook her head. "Not just yet."

"All right. I have brought a couple of bottles of wine I got at one of the traders' stores yesterday. You must take a sip of that, and then we will leave you to yourself for a bit, and you must lie down and have a good nap."

Dick took a bottle from his holster, opened it, and gave her some in a tin cup. Then one of the rugs was spread on the ground, with another one rolled up as a pillow, and then they led the horses farther into the wood, leaving Annie to herself.

"She won't be able to ride again to-night," Surajah said, as they sat down, while Ibrahim took out the provisions that he had on the previous day carried across to the farm.

"No, I must carry her before me. We will shift my saddle a little farther back, and strap a couple of rugs in front of it, so as to make a comfortable seat for her. There is no doubt she will not be able to ride again by herself. I am sure that after my first day's riding I could not have gone on again for anything. We won't start until it begins to get dusk. Of course she ought to have a good twenty-four hours' rest before she goes on, but we dare not risk that. I don't think there is any chance of pursuit for days, or, indeed, of any pursuit at all, for by the time they begin to suspect that we have really deserted, they will know that we have had time to get to the frontier. Still, I don't want to run the slightest risk, and at any rate, if we have to halt it would be better to do so fifty miles farther on than here. When we mount again we will put the saddle-bags from my horse on to hers, and Ibrahim must lead it. Her weight won't make much difference to my horse, and if I find it tiring I will change with you. You may as well put your saddle-bags on to her horse also."

"It would be better, would it not," Surajah said, "if you change to her horse, which will have carried nothing?"

"Yes, of course that would be best, so you had better not shift your saddle-bags."

After they had had their meal they stretched themselves out for a sleep, and when they woke it was already becoming dusk. The horses had had a good feed, and were now given a drink of water from the skin. They were then saddled again, the blankets carefully arranged for Annie's use, and then they went back to the place where she was lying still asleep.

"Put the provisions into the wallet again, Ibrahim. We will see if we can get her up without waking her; she is so dead beat that perhaps we may do so. I don't suppose she would be able to eat anything if we woke her. I had better mount first; then you, Surajah, can lift her up to me. I can stoop down and take her from your arms, and put her in front of me; she is no weight to speak of."

Very gently Surajah put his arms under the sleeping girl, and lifted her.

"That is right," Dick said, as he placed her on the blankets before him, and held her with his right arm, with her head against his shoulder. "She is dead asleep."

The blankets were strapped on to the horses again, the others mounted, and they started at a walk out of the wood. As soon as they were on the road, the horses broke into a canter again. Annie moaned uneasily, but did not open her eyes. Dick drew her still more closely to him.

"She will do now, Surajah," he said, in a low voice. "I hope that she will sleep till morning."

Half-an-hour later they rode through Sultanpetta. It was quite dark now, and although there were people in the streets, Dick knew that at the rate they were riding, in the darkness, the fact that he was carrying a lad in front of him would scarce be noticed; nor would it be of any consequence if it was, as. Even if they met any officer who should stop and question them, it would suffice to say that the lad had been taken ill, and that as their business was urgent, they were taking him on with them. Four hours later they passed through Conkanelly, and crossed the bridge over a branch of the Cauvery. Here Dick felt that his horse was flagging. Halting, he dismounted, and lifted Annie down. This time the movement woke her; she gave a little cry.

"Where am I?' she asked.

"You are quite safe, child," Dick said cheerfully. "Just

lie quiet in my arms. We have come five hours' journey, and as my horse is getting tired, I am changing to yours. Ibrahim is shifting the rugs that you have been sitting on."

"I can go on by myself," she said, making a little struggle to get down.

"You must be good, and do what you are told," he said, with a laugh. "Remember that you are a slave, and I am your master at present."

She said nothing more until they were seated afresh, and had got into motion.

"Oh, you are good, Dick!" she sighed softly. "Only to think of your carrying me like this for five hours, without waking me!"

"Well, it was much better for us both that you should sleep," he said, "and it is the horse that is carrying you, not I. I have been very comfortable, I can assure you. We shall go on for another four hours; after that we shall hide up in a wood, and sleep till the afternoon. Then it will depend upon you: if you can sit your horse, we shall ride on through Anicull; if not, we must wait till it gets dark again, and then go on as we are now. Are you comfortable, child?"

"Very comfortable, Dick." They were talking in English now, for the first time since they started. "I have almost forgotten how to talk English," she said. "We white girls always used to talk it when we were together, so as not to forget it; and since the last one went, three years ago, I have always talked it to myself for a bit before going to sleep, so as to keep it up; but it does not come anything like so easy as the other. Still, I like talking it to you; it almost seems as if I were at home again. You see, I have never heard a man talk English since I was carried away; even now, I can hardly believe this is not a happy dream, and that I shall not wake up presently and find myself a slave-girl in the harem."

"It is pleasant to me to talk English, too," Dick said, "though it is only a few months since I last spoke it. Now, the best thing you can do is to try and get off to sleep again

When we stop you shall have breakfast. I am sure you must want something; you have had nothing since you ate a mouthful or two in my room before starting."

"Oh, I have slept hours and hours!" she said. "I shall not want to sleep any more."

However, before long the easy motion lulled her off again, and she did not wake until, at about four o'clock in the morning, they entered a wood that was, as Dick supposed, some three or four miles from Anicull.

"Well, how do you feel now?" Dick asked, as he set her on her feet.

"I feel stiff," she said; "but that will soon wear off when I have run about a little. Oh how tired you must be after carrying me all these hours!"

"There has not been much to hold," Dick said with a laugh, "especially since we started the last time. Before that, you were so dead asleep that I did have to hold you, but you see you nestled up more comfortably when we changed horses, and needed very little support since then."

"Now, what can I do?" she asked, with a little laugh. "Please order me to do something. I am your slave, you know, and I want to be helping you."

"Well, then, I command you to aid me to gather some sticks for a fire. We have nothing to cook, but it will be cheerful, and the air is cool."

They picked up sticks while Surajah and Ibrahim loosened the girths of the horses, took off their bridles, and poured out another feed from the bag of grain they had brought with them. In a few minutes a fire was blazing, and the wallet of provisions brought out.

"I wish I had a cup of coffee to offer you, Annie," Dick said, as he poured her out some wine and water, "but we must wait for that until we get down to Tripataly."

"I have forgotten all about coffee, Dick, and what it tastes like. The white girls used to talk about it, and say how they longed for a cup. It seems to me funny to drink anything

M 84

DICK POURS OUT SOME WINE AND WATER FOR ANNIE.

hot. I have never tasted anything but water that I can remember, until you gave me that wine yesterday."

"It is very nice and very refreshing. There is another drink that is coming into fashion; it is called tea. I have tasted it a few times, but I don't like it as well as coffee, and it is much more expensive."

"The sultan says that all the English get drunk, and there used to be pictures of them on the walls. They used to make me so angry."

"I don't say that no English get drunk, Annie, because there is no doubt that some do; but it is very far from being true of the great proportion of them. Tippoo only says it to excite the people against us, because, now that he has made them all Mohammedans, they cannot drink wine—at any rate, openly. When I bought these two bottles, the trader made a great mystery over it, and if I had not given him a sign he understood, and which made him believe that I was a Hindoo and not a Mussulman, he would not have admitted that he kept it at all. He did say so at first, for I have no doubt he thought that as I was an officer of the Palace it was a snare, and that if he had admitted he had wine I should have reported him, and it would have served as an excuse for his being fined and perhaps having all his goods confiscated. When I made the sign that an old Hindoo had taught me, his manner changed directly, and he took me to the back of his little shop and produced the wine. I told him I wanted it for medicine and that was quite true, for I thought it was a drug you were very likely to need on your journey."

"How much farther have we to ride?" she asked, after a pause.

"Only about thirty-five miles—that is to say, it is only that distance to the frontier. There is a road that is rather more direct, but it passes through Oussoor, a large town, which we had better avoid. It is not more than fifty miles from the frontier to Tripataly, but once across the line we can take matters easily and stop whenever you get tired."

"It will be all very strange to me, Dick. I sha'n't mind it as long as you are with me, but it will be dreadful when you go. I am afraid your mother won't like me. You see, I know nothing of English ways, and I am oh! so ignorant. I cannot even read—at least, very little. One of the girls used to teach me from a book she had when she was carried off; it was a Bible—she used to tell me stories out of it. But one day they found it, and she was beaten very much for venturing to have it; I am afraid I have quite forgotten even my letters; but she and the other girls used to teach me about religion, and told me I must never forget that I was a Christian, whatever they might do to me, and I was to say my prayers every night after I lay down and every morning before I got up. Of course I have always done it."

"You need not be afraid of my mother, Annie. She is very kind, and I am sure she will take to you very much and will be very glad that I have brought you to Tripataly, for, you see, she has no girls of her own. She will teach you to read and write, and if we go back to England I dare say you will go to school for a time, so as to learn things like other girls."

"I can work very nicely," she said; "the ladies of the harem all used to say that."

"Well, you will find that very useful, no doubt."

"And what else is there to learn?" she asked.

"No end of things, Annie—at least, there are no end of things for boys to learn; I do not know anything about girls. But of course you will have to get to know something of history and geography."

"What is geography, Dick?"

"Well, geography is where countries and places are. For instance, you know something of the geography of India without ever having learnt it. You know that Madras and the Carnatic lie to the east, and Travancore to the south-west, and Malabar to the west, and the Mahratta country and the Nizam's dominions to the north. Well, that is the geography of this part of the country—that and the names of the towns and rivers. In the same way there are a lot of nations in Europe, and you want to know all about them, and where they lie with respect to each other, and the names of their principal towns. Then there are America, and Africa, and Asia, and all the countries in them. If you don't know about these things, you can't follow what people are talking about."

"And did you like learning geography, Dick?" she asked, a little anxiously.

"Well no, I can't say that I did, Annie. I think I used to hate geography; it was very hard to remember where all the places were, and what rivers they stood on. I know very little about it now, except the principal towns and places. But then, I never was very fond of learning anything; I was a very stupid boy at school."

"Oh, I am sure you could not have been that, Dick," she said confidently.

"I was indeed, Annie. I think the only thing I could do well was fighting. I was a beggar to fight—not because I used to quarrel with fellows, but because it made me hard and tough, and my mother thought that it would make me more fit to carry out this search for my father."

"What did you fight with—swords?" Annie asked.

Dick laughed.

"No, no, Annie, when we quarrel in England we fight with our fists."

"What is a fist? I never heard of that weapon."

"That is a fist, Annie. You see, it is hard enough to knock a fellow down, though it does not very often do that; but it hurts him a bit without doing him any harm, except that it may black his eyes or puff up his face for a day or two—and no boy minds that. It accustoms one to bear pain, and is a splendid thing for teaching a boy to keep his temper, and I believe it is one reason why the English make such good soldiers. It is a sort of science, you see, and one learns it just as people here learn to be good swordsmen. I had lessons when I was twelve years old from a little man who used to be a champion light-weight—that is, a man of not more than a certain weight."

Annie looked doubtful for a minute, and then exclaimed, "Ah, yes, I understand now. That is how it is you came to our help so quickly and bravely, when the tiger burst in."

"I daresay it had something to do with it," Dick said, with a smile. "There is no doubt that boxing, as we call it, does make you quick. There is not much time to waste in thinking how you are to stop a blow, and to return it at the same moment. One gets into the habit of deciding at once what is the best thing to be done; and I have no doubt that I should not have seen at once that one must cut through the netting, run to the window, jump on to Surajah's shoulders, and fire at the tiger, unless I had been sharpened up by boxing. I only say I suppose that, because there were no doubt hundreds of men looking on who had pluck enough to face the tiger, and who would have gladly done the thing that we did if the idea had occurred to them. The idea did not occur to them, you see, and I have no doubt that it was just owing to that boxing that I thought of it. So you see, Annie, it was in a way the fights I had with boys at Shadwell—which is the part of London where I lived—that saved you, and perhaps half a dozen ladies of the sultan's harem, from being killed by that tiger.

"Now I should advise you to walk about the wood for at least an hour, to get rid of your stiffness. The longer you walk the better. When you have tired yourself come back here; by that time I daresay you will be ready for another sleep. We will start about three o'clock, and shall cross the frontier before it gets quite dark. Once across, we can camp comfortably where we like, or put up at a village, if we should light upon one. I should not go far away from here," he went on, as the girl at once rose and prepared to start. "Very likely the wood may get thicker farther in, and you might lose your way, or come across a snake; so I should not go far out of sight. The great thing is to keep moving. It is getting broad daylight now."

As soon as Annie had started, Dick lay down.

"I feel dog-tired, Surajah. This right arm of mine is so stiff that I can hardly lift it. I did not feel it at the time, and her weight was nothing, but I certainly feel it now."

"You have a good sleep, Dick. Ibrahim and I will keep watch by turns."

"I don't think there is any occasion for that," Dick said, "No one is likely to come into the wood."

"Not very likely," Surajah agreed; "but a body of travellers might turn in here for a halt in the middle of the day, and it would look strange were they to find two of the Palace officers, and their attendants, all fast asleep."

"They would only think we came in for a rest a short time before they did," Dick said drowsily. "Still, if you don't mind, perhaps it would be best."

In two minutes Dick was sound asleep.

"Now, Ibrahim, you lie down," Surajah said. "I will call you in three hours."

In half-an-hour Annie returned. She looked pitifully at Dick, and then seated herself by Surajah.

"He must be tired," she said. "It was too bad of me, letting him carry me like that all night. I thought so, over and over again, when he believed I was fast asleep, but I knew that it was of no use asking him to let me ride for a bit. You don't mind my sitting here for a little, do you? I am going away again presently; I only came back so soon because I thought he might wonder what had become of me if I did not. I could have gone on walking for a long time. It was very hard work at first, for my back ached dreadfully, and every step hurt me so, it was as much as I could do to keep on walking; but gradually it got better, and at last I had a long run, and after that I scarcely felt it. How long have you known him, Surajah?" and she nodded towards Dick.

"It is about two years and a half since he came to Tripataly, and I have seen a great deal of him ever since. I love him very much; he is always the same; he never seems to get angry, and is kind to every one."

"Did he fight when he was with the army?"

"Not much. He was one of the general's own officers, and used to ride with the others behind him. He fought in the battle before Seringapatam, for the general and every one else had to fight then."

"How is it you come to be always with him?" she asked.

"It first began when we went out on a scouting expedition together, before the English army went up the ghauts. We volunteered to find out, if we could, which way the sultan's army was going. We went through a good deal of danger together, and some hard fighting, and the Sahib was pleased with me; and since then we have always been together."

"Tell me about that, Surajah?"

Surajah related the story of their capture and escape, of their making their way through the fort, and the subsequent pursuit, and their defence of the ruined hut. Annie listened almost breathlessly.

"How I should like to have been with you," she said, when he finished. "At least, I think I should have liked it. I should have been dreadfully in the way, but I could have sat down in the hut and loaded the guns while you were both fighting. You could have shown me how to do it. How brave of you both to have fought fifty or sixty men!"

"It was not so very brave," Surajah said. "We knew we should be killed if they took us; there is nothing brave in doing your best when you know that. But it was not so much the fighting as arranging things, and he did all that, and I only carried out his orders. He always seemed to know exactly what was best to be done, and it was entirely his doing our getting through the fort, and taking to the hut, and making the loop-holes, and blocking up the windows, just as it was his doing entirely that we killed that tiger. Whatever he says is sure to be right, and when he tells me to do a thing I do it directly, for I trust him entirely, and there is no need for me to think at all. If he had told me to go up to the sultan and shoot him in the middle of his officers, I should have done it, though they would have cut me in pieces a minute afterwards."

"I will go away again now," Annie said, getting up. "He told me to keep on walking about, and he would not like it if he were to wake up and find me sitting here."

And she got up and strolled away again. By the time she returned Surajah had lain down to sleep, and Ibrahim was on watch. Annie was by this time tired enough to be ready for sleep again, and, wrapping herself in a rug, she lay down at a short distance from the others. It was two o'clock when she awoke, and she sprang to her feet as she saw Dick and Surajah standing by the fire, talking.

"I was going to wake you soon," Dick said, as she joined them, "for we must have another meal before we start. I hope you feel all the better after your walk and sleep?"

"Ever so much better. I scarcely feel stiff at all, and shall be ready to ride as soon as you like. How do you feel, Dick?"

"Oh, I am all right, Annie. I was all right before, though I did feel I wanted a sleep badly; and you see I have been having a long one, for I only woke up ten minutes ago. I own, though, that I should like a good wash. I don't suppose I can look dirty through this stain, but I certainly feel so."

"There is a pool," she said, "a few hundred yards away there, on the right. I found it the second time I went away, and I did enjoy a wash."

"I thought you were looking wonderfully tidy," Dick said, smiling. "Well, I will go there at once. I shall feel a new man after a bath."

"I will come with you," Surajah said—for he had learned to speak a good deal of English during his companionship with Dick.

They returned in half-an-hour. Ibrahim had warmed up some of the chupatties over the ashes, and they all thoroughly enjoyed their meal. The horses were saddled, and were taken to the pool for a good drink. Then Annie was helped into her saddle, and they started again. They rode at a canter to Anicull, their badges of office securing them from any questioning from the soldiers at the guard-houses when they entered and left the town.

"I don't know whether there is any post established at the frontier," Dick said, as Annie, who had ridden behind with Ibrahim as they passed through the town, took her place again between him and Surajah. "I have no fear that they will be erecting a fort, for after our capturing Bangalore and the hill-fortresses they will know very well that nothing they could build on the flat would be of the slightest use in stopping an army advancing by this line. Still, there may be a guard placed there. How do you think we had better get past, Surajah? We have still got the order to the governors of forts, and it is likely enough that the officer in charge may not be able to read. Very few of those we met before were able to do so; the sight of the sultan's seal at the bottom was quite enough for them, and I should think it would suffice to pass us here. Still, it would look suspicious our leaving the the country altogether, and we must give some explanation if they ask us."

"I might say that we are charged with a mission to the English commander at Kistnagherry."

"That might do, Surajah; the fort is only eight or ten miles on the other side of the frontier, and we might very well be sent on some message. A complaint of some of the villagers that their rights have not been respected as agreed by the treaty, or that they have been robbed by men from this side of the frontier—there are plenty of things about which Tippoo might be sending a message to Kistnagherry. The worst of it is that Tippoo has not given us a mission, and I do hate your having to say what is not true."

Surajah was not so particular, and he replied,—

"Well, he has given us a mission to visit the hill-forts, and as Kistnagherry is a hill-fort it is not a very great stretch to include it."

Dick laughed.

"That is ingenious, Surajah. Anyhow I don't see any better excuse for crossing the frontier, and so we must make the best of it; but I hope we sha'n't be asked at all."

"I think if I say we are going to Kistnagherry, and then show Tippoo's order and seal, that will be sufficient; and the story will be quite true, for we shall go by Kistnagherry, as the road passes close to the fortress."

"Yes, that will be quite true, Surajah, and the officers are not likely to ask any further questions. How are you getting on, Annie?"

"Oh, much better than I did yesterday," she said. "I would much rather not halt until we are across the frontier. I am getting accustomed to the motion now, and am not at all afraid of falling off. I dare say I shall be rather stiff when we halt, but that will not matter then."

The sun was just setting when they arrived at a newly erected house, round which ten or twelve tents were arranged. An officer came out of the house as they approached. He salaamed on seeing two officials of the Palace, wearing the emblems of the rank of colonels. Surajah returned the usual Moslem salutation.

"We are going to Kistnagherry," he said. "Here is the sultan's order."

The officer glanced at the seal, placed it to his forehead, and then stood aside.

"Will you return to-night, my lord? I ask that I may give orders to the sentries."

"No; there is no chance of our being able to be back before morning."

He touched his horse, and then trotted on again. Not a word was spoken until they had gone a few hundred yards, and then Dick checked his horse, and, as Annie came alongside, held out his hand and said,—

"Thank God, Annie, that we have got you safely back on to English territory."

CHAPTER XVII.

BACK AT TRIPATALY.

ANNIE'S lips moved as Dick announced that they had crossed the Mysore boundary, but no sound came from them. He saw her eyes close, and she reeled in the saddle.

"Hold her, Surajah," Dick exclaimed, "or she will fall."

Leaning over, Surajah caught her by the shoulder, and Dick, leaping to the ground, stopped her horse, and, lifting her from the saddle, seated her upon a bank and supported her.

"Some water, Surajah!" he exclaimed. Surajah poured a little water from the skin into the hollow of Dick's hand, and the latter sprinkled the girl's face with it.

"I have not fainted," she murmured, opening her eyes, "but I turned giddy. I shall be better directly."

"Drink a little wine," Dick said. Surajah poured some into a cup, but with an effort she sat up and pushed it from her.

"There is nothing the matter," she said, "only, only——" and she burst suddenly into a passion of sobbing. The spirit that she had shown so long as there was danger, had deserted her now that the peril had passed and she was safe.

Dick looked at her helplessly. A girl in tears was a creature wholly beyond his experience, and he had no idea what he ought to do in such an emergency. He therefore adopted what was doubtless the best course, had he but known it, of letting her alone. After a time the violence of her crying abated, and only short sobs broke from her as she sat with her face hidden in her hands.

"That is right, Annie," he said, putting his hand on her shoulder. "It is quite natural for you to cry after the excitement and fatigue you have gone through. You have been very brave, and have not said a word of complaint to-day about your fatigue, although you must be desperately tired. Now try and pull yourself together. It is getting dark already and we ought to be moving on to Ryacotta, which cannot be much more than a mile away. You shall ride in front of me when we get there."

"I would rather not," she said, getting up with a painful effort. "I am awfully foolish, and I am so sorry that I broke down, but I felt so delighted that I could not help it. You said we could camp safely when we once got across the frontier. Would you mind doing so? for I don't think I could go much farther."

"Certainly we can camp," Dick said cheerfully. "But we must get a little bit farther from that post we passed. If they were to see a fire here they would be sure to suspect something. I see a clump of trees a quarter of a mile on; we can make our camp there, and I would rather do that myself than go on to Ryacotta, where our appearance in the Mysore uniform would excite a stir, and we should have no end of questions to answer. But I am sure that you are not fit to walk even that distance. Now, I will lift you on my saddle and you can sit sideways. There, I will walk by your side and you can put your hand to my shoulder to steady yourself. Surajah can lead your horse and his own, and Ibrahim can take mine."

In this way they performed the journey to the trees, and then halted. Annie was lifted down and laid on a rug. Dick insisted on her drinking some wine, and then, covering her with another rug, they left her and lighted a fire fifty yards away.

"Look here, Ibrahim, put that whole chicken into the pan, cover it with water, and let it stew. Don't let it boil fast, but just simmer until it falls all to pieces; then I will wake her, if she has gone to sleep, and make her drink the broth; it will do her ever so much more good than wine, and she will be all right in the morning, though no doubt she will be desperately stiff again. Still, it has not been a longer ride than she had yesterday. I expect it is the excitement more than the fatigue that has upset her. To-morrow she must ride in front of me again."

An hour and a half later Dick went across with the cup full of strong broth.

"Are you asleep, Annie?" he said, when he reached her side.

"No, I am not asleep. There is so much to think of, and it is such happiness to know that I am free, that I feel quite wide awake; besides, you know, I have been asleep for hours to-day, and I slept all night as I was riding before you."

"Then sit up and drink this hot broth; it will do you good. And after that I hope you will go off; you won't be fit for anything to-morrow if you don't have a good night. You will have plenty of time to think as we ride along."

The girl did as she was told.

"It is very nice," she said, as she handed the cup back to him. "Oh, Dick, I do hope that we shall find my father and mother. I don't want to for some things, but I do for others, and most of all that they may thank you for all your goodness to me, which I shall never be able to do myself."

"Nonsense, child!" he said cheerfully. "I have done what every one would do if they found a little countrywoman in distress. I should have gone away from Seringapatam anyhow, if I had not met you, and getting you down is a good excuse for me to go back and spend a fortnight witn my mother. Now get off to sleep as quickly as you can. We will see what we can do to make things comfortable for your ride to-morrow."

It was late when Annie awoke. The sun was some distance above the horizon, and she saw her companions occupied with the horses. In a few minutes she joined them.

"I am ashamed at sleeping so long," she said.

"We were glad to find that you did," Dick replied. "If you went to sleep soon after I brought you the broth, you have had ten hours of it, and ought to feel all the better."

"I do," she said. "I am very stiff, but not so stiff as I was yesterday morning. How you are both altered!"

"Yes. It would never have done to have gone on in our gay dresses and Tippoo's badges. These are the clothes we came up in, and we shall attract no attention whatever. You won't have to ride far to-day. It will be as well for you to keep to your own horse until we have passed through Ryacotta, which is not much more than half a mile away. After that you must sit on this pad I have fastened behind my saddle. You can sit sideways, you know, and put your arm around me, just as ladies used to ride in England a couple of hundred years ago."

As soon as they had eaten something they started, and rode at a good pace to the little town. People looked at them somewhat curiously as they passed through the street, wondering that they should have come from Mysore; but as they did not halt, no one asked any questions. The population were at present a good deal divided. The great majority by no means regretted their change of masters. Some of the Mohammedans had left when the place was taken over by the English, and had crossed into Mysore. Others had remained, and hoped that ere long Tippoo would drive back the British, and regain his former dominions. Before mounting, the rich housings and the silver work on the bridles had been removed and hidden among the rugs, and there was nothing beyond the excellence of two of the horses, and the direction from which they came, to attract attention. When well beyond the town, they halted. The saddle-bags were all packed upon Annie's horse; Dick lifted the girl on to the pad behind his saddle, and then mounted.

"Now hold tight by me," he said, "and mind, whenever you are tired we will halt for an hour's rest. We will not go more than twenty miles to-day, and then it will only be as much more down to Tripataly to-morrow. We will walk for a bit until you get quite accustomed to your seat."

After a while the horses broke into a gentle canter. For a time Annie felt very doubtful as to whether she could retain her seat, and so held tight with one arm to Dick, while with the other hand she kept a firm hold of the crupper. Presently, however, she was able to release her hold of the latter, and it was not long before she was able honestly to assure Dick that she felt quite comfortable, and had no fear of falling off. In two hours they passed near the hill on which stood the fortress of Kistnagherry, which had successfully resisted the attack of the English, but above which now flew the British flag. Skirting round the foot, they came, in the course of an hour and a half's ride, on to the direct road which they had left at Anicull, in order to avoid passing through the town of Oussoor. Here they came upon a large village, and Dick found no difficulty in hiring a light native cart to take Annie, who was, as he felt by the relaxation of her hold, unable to proceed farther on horseback or continue straight through to Tripataly. A thick layer of straw was placed at the bottom of the car, a couple of rugs spread over it, and on this Annie was enabled to lie down at her ease. The horses were fed and watered, and had an hour's rest, and then they started for the last twenty miles of their journey.

Annie had, while the horses were resting, a chat with a native woman, and had gone into her house with her. When they were ready for the start, she returned, dressed in the costume she had worn in the Palace. It had originally been intended to get rid of the clothes after starting, but Annie had asked for them to be taken on.

"I can change again before I get to Tripataly," she said. "I should not like to appear before your mother for the first time dressed as a boy." And Dick had at once fallen in with her wishes.

The turban was gone, and her head was covered in the fashion of native women, with a long cotton cloth of a deep red colour. Where the road was good the cart proceeded at a fair pace, but in the pass down the ghauts they could go only at a walk, and the sun had set before they reached Tripataly.

Dick, seeing that Annie was growing very nervous as they

neared their destination, had ridden all the way by the side of the cart, chatting cheerfully with her.

"Why, Annie," he said, "you look as solemn as if you were just going into slavery, instead of having escaped from it."

"It is not that I feel solemn, Dick; it is that everything is so new and strange. Of course, after your saving my life, I have never felt that you were a stranger, and as long as there were only you and Surajah I did not mind, and I have felt quite at home with you; but now that I am going to a new place, where I don't know any one, I can't help feeling desolate."

"You will feel quite as much at home with them in twenty-four hours as you have done with me, Annie. You are tired now and quite worn out with your journey, and so you take a gloomy view of things. I will guarantee that before I go away again you will be good friends with every one, and will wonder how you could have thought it to be anything dreadful to come among them."

When they got within a mile of Tripataly, Dick said,—

"Now I will ride on ahead, Annie, and prepare my mother for your coming. It will be pleasant to have no questions or explanations when you arrive, and I am sure she will carry you straight off to bed and keep you there until you have quite got over the effects of your journey."

He did not wait to hear Annie's faint protest against his leaving her, but telling Surajah to take his place beside the cart, and to keep talking to the girl, he galloped on ahead.

He sprang from his horse in the courtyard, threw the reins to a servant, and ran in. The party had just sat down to their evening meal, and as he entered he was greeted by exclamations of astonishment and welcome.

His mother had received two letters, sent through Pertaub by traders going down from Seringapatam. In these he had told her first of his arrival and of the adventure with the tiger, and of his obtaining the post in the Palace; and in the second of the non-success that had attended his visits to the hill-forts. He had told her that he should probably leave Seringāpatam shortly, and continue the search, but that she must not anticipate any result for a long time.

"Well, mother," he said, after the first embrace and greetings were over, "I have left Tippoo's service, you see, and am no longer a colonel or an officer of the Palace. I have come down to spend a fortnight with you before I set out again on my travels."

"Has Surajah come back with you, Dick?" the Rajah asked.

"Yes; he will be here in a few minutes with a cart. That is one of the reasons why I came down here. I found among the slaves of the harem a white girl about fourteen years old. She is the daughter of a British officer named Mansfield, and was carried away from her parents eight years ago; she was the only white captive left in the Palace. There have been other girls in a similar position, but they have all, at about fourteen or fifteen, been given by Tippoo to his officers, as would have been her fate before long, so I determined to carry her off with me, and bring her to you until we could find her parents. She is a very plucky girl, and, although she had never been on a horse before, rode all the way down until we got this side of Kistnagherry. But as you may imagine, the poor little thing is completely knocked up, so we brought her down from there in a cart. It is something, mother, to have saved one captive from Tippoo's grasp, even though it is not the dear one that I was looking for; and I promised that you would be a mother to her until we could restore her to her friends."

"Certainly I will, Dick," Mrs. Holland said warmly. "Will you tell the girls, Gholla," she said to her sister-in-law, "to have a bed made up for her in my room?"

"I will do so at once," the ranee said. "Poor little thing, she must have had a journey indeed."

"She will be here directly, mother," Dick said, as his aunt gave the necessary directions for the bed to be prepared, and a dish of rice and strong gravy. "She is very nervous, and I am sure it will be best if you will meet her when she arrives, and take her straight to her room."

"That is what I was going to do, Dick," his mother said, with a smile. "Well, I will go down with you at once."

Two or three minutes later the cart entered the courtyard. Mrs. Holland was on the steps. Dick ran down and helped Annie from the cart. The girl was trembling violently.

"Don't be afraid, Annie," Dick whispered, as he lifted her down. "Here is my mother waiting to receive you. This is the young lady," he went on cheerfully, as he turned to his mother. "I promised her a warm welcome in your name."

Mrs. Holland had already come down the steps, and as the girl turned towards her she took her in her arms and kissed her in motherly fashion. "Welcome indeed," she said. "I will be a mother to you, poor child, till I can hand you over to your own. I thank God for sending you to me. It will be a comfort to me to know that, even if my son should never bring my husband back to me, he has at least succeeded in rescuing one victim from Tippoo, and in making one family happy."

The girl clung to her, crying softly. "Oh, how good you all are!" she sobbed. "It seems too much happiness to be true."

"It is quite true, dear. Come with me; we will go up the private stairs, and I will put you straight to bed in my room, and no one else shall see you or question you until you are quite recovered from your fatigue."

"I am afraid——" Annie began faintly. She did not need to say more. Mrs. Holland interrupted her.

"Dick, you must lift her up and carry her into my room. Poor child, she is utterly exhausted, and no wonder."

A couple of minutes later Dick returned to the dining-room. He had run down first to tell Surajah to come up with him, but found that he had already gone to his father's apartments.

"Well, Dick," the Rajah said, as he entered, "I was prepared, after hearing of that tiger adventure, and of you and Surajah being colonels in Tippoo's household, for almost anything; but I certainly never dreamt of your returning here with an English girl."

"I suppose not, uncle. Such a thing certainly never entered into my calculations. I did not even know there was a white girl in the Palace, until one day she stopped me as I was passing along the corridor near the harem, to thank me for saving her life—for it was this girl that the tiger had struck down, and was standing upon, when I fired at him. Of course she had no idea that I was English. We only said a few words then, for if I had been seen talking to a slave-girl belonging to the harem, I might have got into a scrape. However, I saw her afterwards, and she told me about herself, and how she was afraid that she would be given away to one of Tippoo's officers. Of course I could not leave her to such a fate as that. There was really no difficulty in getting her away. She was dressed as a boy, and only had to ride with our servant after us. We had arranged so that our absence would not be noticed until we had been away for at least twenty-four hours, and of course, as officers of the Palace, no one questioned us on the journey, so that it is a very simple affair altogether, and the only difficulty there was rose from her being completely tired out and exhausted by the journey, as she was utterly unaccustomed to travelling. I had to carry her one night in front of me on my saddle, for she was scarce able to stand."

"I am not surprised at that. A journey of a hundred and fifty miles, to any one who has never been on horseback, would be a terrible trial, especially to a young girl. I really wonder that she did not break down altogether. Why, you can remember how stiff you were yourself the first day or two you were here, and that after riding only an hour or two."

"I know, uncle, and I should not have been in the least surprised if she had collapsed. I talked it over with Surajah, and we agreed that if she could not go on we must hire a vehicle of some sort, and let her travel every day in front of us with Ibrahim, and that if it delayed us so much that there was any possibility of our being overtaken, we would have put on our peasant's dresses, got rid of our horses, and have gone forward on foot. However, she kept up wonderfully well, and always made the best of things."

"We won't ask you to tell us anything more, Dick, till your mother joins us, or you will have to go over the story twice."

"No, uncle; and I can assure you I don't want to tell the story until I have had my supper, for our meals have not been very comfortable on the road, and I have not eaten anything since early this morning."

"What is Tippoo doing, Dick?"

"Well, as far as I can see, uncle, he is preparing for war again. He is strengthening all his forts, building fresh defences to Seringapatam, and drilling numbers of fresh troops."

"The English general made a great mistake in not finishing with him when he was there. We ought to have taken the city, sent Tippoo down a prisoner to Madras, and there tried him for the murder of scores of Englishmen, and hung him over the ramparts. We shall have all our work to do over again in another four or five years. However, it will not be such a difficult business as it was last time, now that we have the passes in our hands."

"There is no doubt, uncle, that a considerable part of the population will be heartily glad when Tippoo's power is at an end. You see, he and Hyder were both usurpers, and had no more right to the throne than you had."

"Quite so, Dick, and that makes our letting him off, when we could have taken the capital easily, all the more foolish. If he had been the lawful ruler of Mysore, it might not have been good policy to push him too hard, for he would have had sympathy from all the native princes of India. But as being only the son of an adventurer who had deposed and ill-treated the lawful ruler of Mysore, it would seem to them but a mere act of justice if the English had dethroned him and punished him—provided, of course, they put a native prince on the throne, and did not annex all his dominions.

"It has all got to come some day. I can see that in time the English will be the rulers of all India, but at present they are not strong enough to face a general coalition of the native states against them, and any very high-handed action in Mysore might well alarm the native princes throughout India into laying aside their quarrels with each other, and combining in an attempt to drive them out."

Just as they had finished their meal Mrs. Holland entered.

"The poor child is asleep," she said. "She wanted to talk at first, and to tell me how grateful she was to you, Dick, but of course I insisted on her being quiet, and said that she should tell me all about it in the morning. She ate a few mouthfuls of the rice, and not long after she lay down she fell asleep. I have left Sundra sitting there, in case she should wake up again, but I don't think it is likely that she will do so. Now, Dick, you must tell us all about it."

Dick was not a great hand at writing letters, so he had not entered with any fulness into the details of what he was doing, the principal point being to let his mother know that he was alive and well.

"Before he begins," the Rajah said, "I will send for Rajbullub and Surajah. Master Dick is rather fond of cutting his stories short, and we must have Surajah here to fill up details."

Surajah and his father soon appeared. The former was warmly greeted by the Rajah, and when they had seated themselves on a divan, Dick proceeded to tell the story. He was not interrupted until he came to the incident of the killing of the tiger, and here Surajah was called upon to supplement the story, which he did, doing full credit to the quickness with which Dick had, without a moment's loss of time, cut the netting and ascended to the window. When Dick came to the incident of the ladies of the harem presenting them, in Tippoo's presence, with the two caskets, Mrs. Holland broke in,—

"You did not say anything about that in your letter, Dick. Let me see your casket. Where is it?"

"It is in one of the saddle-bags," Dick said.

"They are in my room," Rajbullub corrected. "Surajah brought them up at once."

"Then he had better get them," the Rajah said. "What do they contain, Dick?" he asked, as Surajah left the room.

"All sorts of things—necklaces and rings. Some of them are stones, as if they had been taken out of their settings. Pertaub said they had done this because they thought perhaps that Tippoo would not allow the jewels they had worn to be sold, or worn by any one else."

"Then I should think that they must be valuable," the ranee said.

"Pertaub said they were worth a good deal, but I don't know whether he really knew about the cost of precious stones. Some of the things were of small value, being, I suppose, the trinkets of the slave-girls. All gave something, and there is a little cross there that belonged to Annie; it has her initials on it, and she had it on her neck when she was captured. It was the thing she valued most, and therefore she gave it. I don't suppose she had anything else, except the usual trinkets she would wear, when she went out on special occasions with the ladies of the harem. I thought it would be useful to us, to prove who she was."

Surajah now returned with the casket.

"You had better look at Surajah's first," Dick said. "I don't know anything about it, but it looks as if mine were the more valuable. I wanted Surajah to put them all together, and divide fairly, but he would not."

"My son was perfectly right," Rajbullub said. "If it had not been for the young lord, the deed would never have been done at all. Surajah aided in killing the tiger, but that was nothing more than he has done on the hills here. It is to you the merit is entirely due. The purse that the Sultan gave my son was in itself an ample reward for the share he took in it. Now, Surajah, open your casket; the ladies are waiting to see the contents."

The whole of the little packets, some fifty in number, were opened and examined, many of them eliciting exclamations of admiration from the ranee and Mrs. Holland.

"There is no doubt that many of them are worth a good deal of money," the Rajah said. "It is certain that Tippoo's treasuries are full of the spoils he has carried off from the states he has overrun, and the ladies of the harem, no doubt, possess a store of the jewels, and could afford to be liberal to those whom they considered had saved their lives. Those seven which you put together as the best must alone be worth a large sum. I should think that the total value of the whole cannot be less than forty or fifty thousand rupees, so that if those in your casket are handsomer than these, Dick, they must be valuable indeed."

Dick's casket was next examined.

"Some of these stones are magnificent, Dick. Those three great diamonds could only be valued by a jeweller accustomed to such things, for their value depends upon their being of good lustre, and free from all flaws; but according to my judgment, I should say that at the very least they must be worth ten thousand rupees each. That pearl necklace is worth at least as much; those rubies are superb. I should say, lad, that the value of the whole cannot be less than fifteen thousand pounds. The harem must be rich in jewels indeed to be able to make such gifts. Not that I am surprised at that. Tippoo had all the jewels belonging to the lawful rulers of Mysore. He has captured all those of Coorg, Travancore, and the other states on the Malabar coast. He and his father have looted all the Carnatic from Cape Comorin to the north of Madras. He has captured many of the Nizam's cities, and several Mahratta provinces.

"In fact, he has accumulated at Seringapatam the spoils of the whole of southern India, and those of the Hindoo portion of his own people. The value of the jewels alone must be millions of pounds, and as he himself, as they say, dresses simply, and only wears one or two gems of immense value, he may well have bestowed large quantities upon his harem, especially as these would be, in fact, only loans, as at the death of their wearers they would revert to him, or, indeed, could be reclaimed at any moment in a freak of bad temper. I have no doubt they had to ask his permission to give you the presents, and as you, at the moment, were in high favour with him, I daresay he suffered them to give what they chose, without inquiring at all into their value. The gold he gave you was simply to procure your outfits, and he left it to the harem to reward you as they chose for the service you had rendered.

"Well, Dick, I congratulate your heartily. It places your future beyond doubt, and leaves you free to choose any mode of life that you may prefer. I congratulate you too, Margaret, on the lad's good fortune, which he has well deserved by his conduct. See this, my sons: here you have a proof of the advantages of the training your cousin has had; the quickness and coolness he has acquired by it enabled him to make his way down through the fort at the top of the pass, and to defend the ruined hut against fifty enemies. Now it has enabled him to seize the opportunity opened by the attack of the tiger on Tippoo's harem, thereby gaining the Sultan's favour, his appointment to the rank of colonel in the Mysore army, a post in his Palace, and this magnificent collection of gems. Without that quickness and decision, his courage alone would have done little for him. We in India have courage; but it is because our princes and nobles are brought up in indolence and luxury that the English, though but a handful in point of numbers, have become masters of such wide territories. Surajah is as brave as Dick, but he would be the first to tell you that it is to Dick he owes it that, on their first excursion together, he escaped with his life, and that in this last adventure he attained rank and position, and has returned with these valuable gifts."

"It is indeed, my lord," Surajah said. "The young lord

has been my leader, and I have tried to carry out his orders. Alone I could never have got through the gate in the fort, and should no more have thought of going to the assistance of the ladies of the Sultan's harem than did any other of the thousands of men who were there looking on."

"So you see, boys," the Rajah went on, "that though when he came out here your cousin was able neither to shoot nor to ride, and can neither shoot nor ride as well now as can tens of thousands of natives, he has acquired from his training in rough exercises qualities of infinitely greater value than these accomplishments; and I do hope that his example will stir you up to take much greater interest than, in spite of my advice, you have hithert done in active sports and exercises. Your grandmother was an Englishwoman, and I want to see that, with the white blood in your veins, you have some of the vigour and energy of Englishmen."

It was some days before Annie Mansfield left her room. For the first two she had been completely prostrated; after that she rapidly gained strength; but Mrs. Holland thought it best to insist upon her remaining perfectly quiet until she had quite recovered. Either she or the ranee were constantly with her, so that when, at the end of a week, she made her first appearance at the breakfast table, she was already at home with three of the party. Before long her shyness completely wore off, and she seemed to have become really a member of the family. Mrs. Holland had altered two of her own dresses to fit her, but she preferred, for a time, to dress in Indian costume, to which she was accustomed, and which was indeed much better suited to the climate than the more closely fitting European dress. Mrs. Holland, however, bargained that she should of an evening wear the frocks she had made for her.

"You must get accustomed to them, my dear, so that when you find your own people you will not be stiff and awkward, as you certainly will be when you dress in English fashion for the first time."

The day after his arrival Dick had written to the military

secretary of the governor of Madras, with whom he was well acquainted, to tell him that, having gone up in disguise to Seringapatam to endeavour to ascertain the fate of his father, he had discovered a young English girl detained as a slave in Tippoo's harem, and that he had enabled her to effect her escape, and had placed her in the charge of his mother. He then repeated the account Annie had given of her capture, and asked if the circumstances could be identified, and if the officer of the name of Mansfield concerned in it was still alive, and if so, was he still in India? Annie was secretly dreading the arrival of the answer. After her life as a slave, her present existence seemed to her so perfectly happy that she shrank from the idea of any fresh change. She had no memory whatever of her parents, and had already a very strong affection for Mrs. Holland.

She liked the ranee very much also, and the absence of all state and ceremony in the household of the Rajah was to her delightful. She was already on good terms with the boys, and as to Dick, she was always ready to go out with him if he would take her, to run messages for him, or to do anything in her power, and, indeed, watched him anxiously, as if she would discover and forestall his slightest wish.

"One would think, Annie," he said one day, "that you were still a slave, and that I was your master. I don't want you to wait on me, child, as you waited on the ladies of the harem. However, as I shall be going away in a few days now, it does not matter; but I should grow as lazy as a young rajah if this were to go on long."

"What shall I do when you go away, Dick?"

"Well, I hope that you will set to work hard to learn to read and write, and other things my mother will teach you. You would not like, when you find your own people, to be regarded by girls of your own age as an ignorant little savage; and I want you to set to and make up for lost time, so that, if you are still here when I come back, I shall find you have made wonderful progress."

"Oh, I do hope I sha'n't be gone before that, Dick!"

"I am afraid you must make up your mind to it, Annie, for there is no saying how long I may be away next time. You see, there is not much chance of my lighting upon another white slave-girl, and having to bring her down here; and I shall go in for a long, steady search for my father."

"I don't want you to find another slave-girl, Dick," she said earnestly, "not even if it brought you down here again. I should not like that at all."

"Why not, Annie?"

"Oh, you might like her ever so much better than me. I should like you to do all sorts of brave things, Dick, and to save people as you have saved me, but I would rather there was not another girl."

Dick laughed.

"Well, I don't suppose that there is much chance of it. Besides, I can't turn my uncle's palace into a Home for Lost Girls."

Two days before Dick and Surajah started again, the reply from the military secretary arrived. It stated that the time and circumstances pointed out that the place besieged and forced to surrender, eight years before, was Corsepan; and this was indeed rendered a certainty by the fact that the officer in command was Captain Mansfield. He had with him a half-company of Europeans and three companies of Sepoys. On looking through the official papers at the time, he had found Captain Mansfield's report, in which he stated that, on the night after leaving the fort, the troops, which had been reduced to half their original strength, had been attacked by a party either of dacoits or irregular troops. Fearing that some such act of treachery might be attempted, he had told his men to conceal a few cartridges under their clothes when they marched out with empty cartridge-pouches. They had, on arriving at their halting-place, loaded, and, when the dacoits fell upon them, had opened fire. The robbers doubtless expected to find them defenceless, and speedily fled. In the confusion, some of them had penetrated far into the camp, and had carried off the captain's daughter, a child of six years old. When peace was signed with Tippoo, three weeks afterwards, the commissioners were ordered to make special inquiries as to this child, and to demand her restoration. They reported that Tippoo denied all knowledge of the affair, and neither she nor any of the other girls there were ever given up. The letter went on:—

"There can be no doubt that the young lady you rescued is the child who was carried off, and the initials you speak of on the cross may certainly be taken as proof of her identity. Her father retired from the Service last year with the rank of colonel. I am, of course, ignorant of his address. As you say that Mrs. Holland will gladly continue in charge of her, I would suggest that you should write a letter to Colonel Mansfield, stating the circumstances of the case, and saying that as soon as you are informed of his address the young lady will be sent to England. I will enclose the letter in one to the Board of Directors, briefly stating the circumstances, and requesting them to forward the enclosure to Colonel Mansfield."

To Annie the letter came as a relief. It would be nearly a year before a letter could be received from her father; until then she would be able to remain in her new home.

CHAPTER XVIII.

A NARROW ESCAPE.

MRS. HOLLAND undertook to write the letter to Annie's father, and did so at very much greater length than Dick would have done, giving him the story of the girl's life at Seringapatam, the circumstances of her meeting Dick, and the story of her escape. She assured him that his daughter was all that he could wish her to be.

"She is of a very affectionate disposition; she is frank, outspoken, and natural—qualities that are wonderful, considering the years she has passed as a slave in the harem. Now that she has been with us for a fortnight, and has recovered from the fatigue of her flight, and is beginning to feel at home, she has regained her natural spirits after their long repression.

"Personally she is of about the average height, and of a more graceful figure than is usual with girls of her age. The stain has now worn off her face, and I should say she will, as she grows up, be pretty. She is fair rather than dark, has expressive eyes and a nice mouth. Altogether, had I a daughter, I should be well content if she resembled your Annie. I shall, I can assure you, do my best to supply the place of a mother to her until I receive a letter from you, and shall part from her with regret. She is, of course, at present entirely uneducated, but she has already begun to learn with me, and as she is quick and intelligent I hope that before I resign my charge, her deficiencies will be so far repaired that she will be able to pass muster in all ordinary matters."

"You will be back before I go, won't you, Dick?" Annie said, as she sat by his side on a seat in the garden, on the evening before he was to start.

"I think so," he said. "We can calculate on your being here ten months anyhow. I have been talking it over with my mother. If it had not been for those jewels I should have given up the search for my father after another six months, because it would have been high time for me to get to work in some profession. I had, indeed, made up my mind to enter the Company's service, for Lord Cornwallis promised me a commission, and my uncle received a letter some time ago from the governor of Madras, saying that on the very strong recommendation of Lord Cornwallis, and his report of my services, he was authorised to grant me one; it was to be dated back to the time I joined Lord Cornwallis, more than two years ago. However, now that I am really made independent of a profession, I shall probably continue my search for a somewhat longer time. But at any rate, I will promise to come back at the end of ten months from the present time, so as to say good-bye to you before you start."

The girl's face brightened.

"Thank you, Dick. I don't think I should go, anyhow, until I saw you again—not even if I got a letter saying that I was to sail by the next ship."

"My uncle would take you down bodily and put you on board," Dick laughed. "Mind, Annie, when I come back at the end of ten months I shall expect to find you quite an educated young lady. I shall think of all sorts of hard questions in geography and history to put to you."

"I will try hard, Dick, really hard, to please you. I have had three lessons, and I have learnt all the letters quite well."

"That is a good beginning, Annie. It took me a lot longer than that, I know."

The next morning Dick and Surajah started. They were to ride up the ghauts to the frontier line at Amboor, two troopers accompanying them to bring back their horses. There they were to disguise themselves as traders, and make their way direct to Bangalore. Dick said good-bye to his mother up in her own room.

"You must not be down-hearted, mother," he said, as she tried in vain to keep back her tears. "You see, I have come back to you twice safely, and after passing unsuspected in Tippoo's palace there is no fear of my being detected elsewhere; besides, of course, every month I am there I become better acquainted with the people, and can pass as a native more easily."

"I am not really afraid, my boy. You have got on so well that it seems to me God will surely protect you and bring you back safely. And I can't help thinking that this time your search may be successful. You know why I feel convinced that your father is still alive, and, in spite of past disappointments, I still cling to the belief."

"Well, mother, if he is to be found I will find him. There are still many hill-forts where he may be living, and his very existence forgotten, and until I have visited every one of them I don't mean to give up the search. Anyhow, I shall come back at the end of ten months, whether I have heard of him or not. I have promised Annie that I will be back before she sails. It is not a very long journey down here, and I shall drop in for a fortnight's stay with you, as I have done this time."

"She is in the next room crying her eyes out, Dick. You had better look in there, and say good-bye to her. She is not fit to go down to the door."

After parting with his mother, Dick went in to see Annie.

"You must not cry so, child," he said, as she rose from the divan with her face swollen with crying. "I am sure that you will be very happy here until I come back."

"I know, Dick; but it won't be at all the same without you."

"Oh, you will have plenty to do, and you will soon fall into regular ways; besides, you know you have got to comfort my mother, and keep up her spirits, and I quite rely upon you to do that."

"I will try, Dick," she said earnestly.

"Now, good-bye, Annie."

He held out his hand, but she threw her arms round his neck and kissed him.

"You have never kissed me, not once," she said reproachfully, "and you were going away without it now. Your mother kisses me, and the English girls in the harem always used to do so."

"But that is different, Annie. Girls and women do kiss each other, but boys and girls do not kiss unless they are brothers and sisters, or are relations, or something of that sort."

"But you are not a boy; you are a great big man, Dick."

"I am not much more than a boy yet, Annie. However, there is no harm in kissing when one is saying good-bye, so there. Now be a good girl, and don't fret;" and he ran downstairs to the door where his uncle and the two boys were standing.

"Take care of yourself, lad," the Rajah said, as, after

bidding them good-bye, Dick sprang upon his horse. "Whenever you get a chance, send down a letter as we arranged last night, to the care of Azul Afool, trader, Tripataly. That will seem natural enough, whoever you send it by, while a letter directed to me might excite suspicion. Good-bye."

"Good-bye, uncle;" and with a wave of his hand Dick rode off and joined Surajah, who was waiting for him a short distance off, and then, followed by Ibrahim—who had begged so earnestly to be allowed to accompany them that Dick had consented to take him, feeling indeed that his services would be most useful to them—and the two troopers, they rode off at a sharp pace.

At Amboor they assumed their disguises. Dick purchased a pack-pony and some goods suitable to their appearance as pedlers, and then they started up the pass on foot. They passed the frontier line without any interruption, stopped and chatted for a few minutes with the guard, and then passed on up the valley.

"There is the house where we had our fight, Surajah," Dick said, as they reached the ruined village. "Though there is peace now, I fancy we should not get much farther than that fort ahead, if they guessed that we were the fellows who gave them such trouble two years and a half ago."

"There is no fear of our being recognised," Surajah said. "The guard has probably been changed long ago; besides, they never once caught sight of our faces."

"Oh, no; we are safe enough," Dick agreed. "If I had not been sure of that we would have gone up one of the passes to the south that has been ceded to us, though it would have been a great deal longer round to Bangalore—unless, indeed, we had gone by Kistnagherry, and that would have been too dangerous to attempt, for the officers on the frontier would probably have recognised us."

It was late in the afternoon before they arrived at the gate. It stood open, and there was no sentry on duty. A few soldiers could be seen loitering about in the street, but it was evident that now the war was over and everything finally settled, it was considered that all occasion for vigilance was at an end. Upon making inquiries they soon found a house where they could put up for the night. They had, as is the custom in India, brought their provisions with them, and after leaving their goods in the house, and seeing that the horse was fed, Ibrahim set to work to cook a meal, while the others opened one of the packs and went round the village, where they disposed of a few small articles. They arrived without any adventure at Bangalore. There, as soon as they had established themselves at one of the caravanseries for travellers, Dick and Surajah went to the house of the trader to whom Pertaub had promised to consign their goods.

"We have come for some packs that have been sent by friends of ours at Seringapatam to your care," Dick said, making as he spoke the sign that Pertaub had taught him, as enabling those who were Hindoos to recognise each other at once. "We were to use the word 'Madras' as a sign that we were the parties to whom they were consigned."

"The goods arrived a week ago," the trader said, "and are lying for you at my warehouse. I will hand them over to you to-morrow morning."

"Thank you. We may not come early, for we have to purchase two pack-horses to carry them, and three tats for ourselves and our man. This may take us some time, and it will be perhaps better for us to come to you early the next morning, and we can then start away direct."

This was arranged, and on the following day two strong animals were bought for the packs, and three tats or ponies for their own riding; Dick had disposed of the horse he had ridden down to Tripataly for a good price, and had also been supplied with funds by his mother, although, as he said, the contents of their packs ought to suffice to pay all their expenses for a long time. Then they purchased some provisions for the journey. The pack-horse they had brought with them was laden with these and the goods brought up from Amboor. The new pack-horses were taken round to the trader's, and the goods sent from Seringapatam packed on them. Then they mounted and rode off at a walk, the pack-animals following Ibrahim's horse, tied one behind the other.

They had already debated upon the course to pursue, and finally decided that they would, in the first place, again visit Savandroog; for the conviction Dick had entertained that there was at least one white captive there had increased rather than diminished.

"I can't give any good reason for it, Surajah," he had admitted when they talked it over before starting, "but it is just because I have no good reason to give that I want to go there again. Why should I have such a strong conviction without a good cause? One has heard of a presentiment of evil—I can't help feeling that this is a presentiment of good. The question is, how can we best go there again? I don't think it is in the least likely that the governor will have heard of our flight, as this would be the last direction any one would think of our taking, for had we done so we might have met the Sultan on his way back from Bangalore. It will naturally be supposed that we have made for the frontier, and have descended the Western or Southern Ghauts. The affair will, of course, seem a mystery to them altogether; for why should two young fellows, so recently promoted, and in such high favour, desert Tippoo's service? If they do not associate Annie's disappearance with our flight—and there is no reason on earth why they should do so, as no one ever saw us speaking to her—they will most likely think that we have fallen into the hands of the Dacoits, or Thugs, and have been murdered. Numbers of people do disappear every year, and are, as every one supposes, victims of that detestable sect. My uncle has told me of Thugs. He warned me to be very careful if I travelled with strangers, for that these men travel in all sorts of disguises. So I think, that, as far as that goes, we could boldly put on our uniforms and badges again, and ride into Savandroog. The disadvantage of doing so is, however, plain.

The commander would remain with us all the time. We should get no opportunity of speaking privately with any of the soldiers, and, taking us to be in Tippoo's confidence, he would, as before, shirk the question of prisoners. On the other hand, if we can get in as traders we shall be able to move about unwatched—to go to the soldiers' huts and offer goods to their wives, and be able to find out to a certainty if there is a prisoner there, and, if so, where he is kept. We may even see him; for while, if the governor wished to keep his existence a secret, he would have shut him up when he heard that two of Tippoo's officers were coming, he would not trouble about it one way or the other in the case of a couple of traders. The only objection to that course is that we were here but two or three months since, and he and his servants and that artillery officer we went round with would know us at once. If we go we shall have to alter our appearance completely. At any rate, we had better provide means for disguise, and we can use them or not, as we please."

While they were at Tripataly, therefore, they had two false beards made for themselves, and tried many experiments in the way of painting their faces, and found that by tracing light lines on their foreheads and at the corners of their eyes, they were able, by the help of beards, to counterfeit the appearance of old age so well that it could only be detected on close observation.

Dick, too, had purchased a pair of native spectacles, with large round glasses and broad black-horn rims, that made him look, as he said, like an astonished owl. It was agreed that Surajah should wear, under his dress, a very thickly padded vest, which would give him the appearance of being fat as well as elderly.

They proceeded for seven or eight miles at a walking pace, and when the heat of the day rendered it necessary for them to stop, turned into a grove by the roadside, as they had no intention of going on to Savandroog that day, intending to halt some miles short of it, and to present themselves there the next afternoon. They therefore prepared for a stay of some hours. The pack-horses were unloaded, and the saddles taken off the other animals. Half-an-hour later a party of twelve men, travelling in the same direction as themselves, also halted and turned in among the trees. The man who was apparently the leader of the party came across to where they were sitting.

"We do not disturb you, I hope, brothers?" he said. "The grove is large enough for us all. I see that you are traders like myself."

"By no means," Surajah replied. "The wood is open to all, and even were it not, we should be discourteous indeed did we refuse to share our shade with others. Sit down by us, I beg of you, while your people are unloading your animals."

"I marked you as you left Bangalore," the trader said, as he seated himself beside them, "and when I saw that you were taking the same route that we should follow, I wondered how far our roads might lie together."

"We are travelling west," Surajah replied. "It may be that we shall stop at Magree, and there, or at Outradroog, stop for a day or two to trade. Thence we may go north."

"Then as far as Outradroog our paths will lie together," the merchant said. "There we shall strike the river and turn south to Seringapatam. I am sorry that you will not be going farther in our direction, for the roads are far from safe; since the war with the Feringhees ended, there are many disbanded soldiers who have taken to dacoity, and it is always better to travel with a strong band. I wonder that you venture with three loaded animals and only one man beside yourselves."

Surajah was about to speak; but a quick glance from Dick stopped him.

"We think there is less danger in travelling in a small body than there is with a large one," the latter said; "there is less to tempt any one to interfere with us. Moreover, we could not travel with a caravan, because the greater part of our goods are such as would tempt the peasantry only. We therefore stop at small villages to trade, leaving the towns to those who travel with more valuable merchandise."

After chatting for some minutes, the traveller got up and joined his party.

"I don't much like that fellow's looks," Dick said, when they were alone.

"Why? He looks a very respectable man."

"Oh, yes, he looks respectable enough, but for all that I don't fancy him. It may be that he regards us as rivals, and was only trying to find out where we intended to stop, and whether we were likely to spoil his trade. That was why I said what I did, so that he might perceive that we were not likely to interfere with him. Then again, Surajah, I remembered my uncle's warning against joining other travellers, as these Thugs, who, they say, commit so many murders, generally travel in bands, disguised sometimes as traders, sometimes as men seeking work, sometimes as disbanded soldiers. Anyhow, it is as well to be careful. We have each got a brace of double-barrelled pistols in our girdles, in addition to these old single-barrelled Indian ones that we carry for show, and our swords are leaning against the tree behind us, so we can get hold of them in a moment. I know, of course, that the betting is all in favour of these people being peaceful traders, but I don't want to leave anything to chance, and there is nothing like being prepared for whatever may happen."

Presently Dick got up and sauntered across to Ibrahim, who was engaged in cooking. "Ibrahim," he said, "don't look round while I speak to you, but go on with your cooking. I don't like the look of the leader of this party, He may be a respectable trader, he may be a Dacoit or a Thug. I want you to keep a sharp look-out without seeming to do so. See that your pistols will come out of your girdle easily. Keep your sword handy for use; if you see anything suspicious, come over and tell me, and if there is not time for that, shout."

M 84

DICK AND SURAJAH ARE ATTACKED BY THUGS.

"I will watch, Sahib," Ibrahim said. "But they seem to me peaceable men like ourselves. Of course they carry weapons; no one would travel about with merchandise without doing so."

"They may be all right, Ibrahim, but I have a sort of feeling that they are not, and at any rate it is best to be cautious."

The other party did not light a fire, but sat down and ate some provisions they carried with them. When Surajah and Dick had finished their meal, the leader again strolled over to them. He asked whether they intended to sleep, and on hearing that they did not, he again sat down with them. He proceeded to discuss trading matters, to describe the goods he carried, the places where he had purchased them, and the prices he had given. As he talked, Dick noticed that three or four of the others came across. They did not sit down, but stood round listening to the conversation, and sometimes joining in. Dick's feeling of uneasiness increased, and thrusting one hand carelessly into his girdle, he grasped the butt of one of his hidden pistols.

Suddenly a loud cry came from Ibrahim; at the same moment something passed before Dick's face. He threw himself backwards, drawing his pistol as he did so, and fired into the body of the man behind him. A second later he shot another, who was in the act of throwing a twisted handkerchief round Surajah's neck. Then he leapt to his feet, delivering as he did so a heavy blow with the barrel of his pistol on the head of the trader who had been sitting between him and Surajah. It had all passed in a few seconds, and the other men started back in their surprise at this unexpected failure of their plan. Surajah was on his feet almost as quickly as Dick. Even yet he did not understand what had happened. At this moment there was the crack of another pistol, and then Ibrahim came running towards them, having shot a man who had suddenly drawn his sword, and tried to cut him down. At his heels came the six men who had, up to this point, been standing in a group near their horses. Without hesitation

Dick drew out one of his single-barrelled pistols and shot the pretended trader, whose turban had saved him from the effect of the blow, and who, shouting loudly to his companions, was struggling to his feet. The remaining eight men had all drawn their swords, and were rushing upon them.

"Fire, Surajah!" Dick shouted. "Are you asleep, man?"

Surajah was not asleep, but he was confused by the suddenness of the fray, and was still doubtful whether Dick had not made an entirely unprovoked attack upon the strangers. However, he perceived that it was now too late to discuss that point, and was a question of fighting for his life. Accordingly, he fired both barrels of one of his pistols. One of the men dropped.

"Your sword, Surajah!" Dick exclaimed, as he grasped the scabbard of his own weapon in his left hand, while in his right he held his other double-barrelled pistol. Their antagonists, with yells of fury, were now upon them. Dick shot one, but the next man he aimed at darted suddenly aside when he fired. Dick dropped his pistol, and grasped the hilt of his sword just in time to ward off a blow aimed at his head. Blow after blow was showered upon him so quickly that he could do no more than ward them off and wait his opportunity. He heard Surajah fire two more shots in quick succession; then Ibrahim suddenly dashed forward and cut down his opponent, and then furiously engaged another who was on the point of attacking him from behind. Dick drew his remaining pistol, and shot the man through the head.

He had then time to look round.

Both Surajah's shots had told, and he was now defending himself against the assaults of two others who were pressing him hard, while a third stood irresolute a short distance away. Dick rushed to Surajah's assistance; as he did so, the third man fled.

"After him, Ibrahim!" Dick shouted. "Not one of them must get away."

The two Thugs defended themselves, with cries of fanatical

fury, but their opponents were far better swordsmen, and, fighting coolly, were not long before they cut them both down.

"What on earth is it all about, Dick?" Surajah asked, as, panting with his exertions, he looked round after cutting down his opponent.

"Thugs," Dick said briefly.

"Are you sure, Dick?" Surajah asked presently. "It may be a terrible business for us if there is any mistake."

For answer Dick pointed to the bodies of the two men he had first shot. One still grasped the roomal, or twisted silk sash, while a like deadly implement lay by the side of the other.

"Thank Heaven!" Surajah ejaculated. "I was afraid there might have been a mistake, Dick, but I see that you were right, and that it was a party of Thugs. If it had not been that you were on the watch for them and had your pistol ready, we should have lost our lives."

"It was a close shave as it was, Surajah. One second later and you and I should both have been strangled. I had my hand on my pistol and felt so sure that an attack was intended that the moment something passed before my face, although I had no idea what it was, I threw myself back and fired at the man behind me, with an instinctive feeling that my life depended on my speed. But it was only when, on looking at you, I saw a man in the act of throwing a noose round your neck, that I knew exactly what I had escaped."

"It was fortunate that they had not pistols," Surajah said. "We should have had no chance against them if they had had fire-arms."

"No; they could have shot us the moment I first fired. But uncle said, when he was talking to me one day, that he had heard that the Stranglers did not carry fire-arms, because the reports might attract attention, and that it was a matter of religion with them to kill their victims by strangling, but that if the Strangler failed, which he very seldom did, the other men would then despatch the victims with their swords and knives. Ah! here comes Ibrahim."

"I caught him just outside the trees, Sahib. He will strangle no more travellers."

"Well, what had we better do?" asked Surajah.

"I should say we had better make off as fast as we can. Of course if we were really traders, able to prove who we are, we should go back to the town and report the affair, but as we can't do that we had better be moving on at once, before any other party of travellers comes up. That was why, when we had killed several of them, I was anxious that none should get away, for they might have gone and accused us of slaughtering their companions."

"That would be too unlikely a story to be believed. No one would credit that three men would attack twelve."

"But there would be no one to prove that there were only three. The fellows would naturally swear that there were a score of us, and that after murdering their companions the rest had made off with the booty.

"Ibrahim, load the pack-animals at once. We will saddle the horses. I think, Surajah, we had better leave everything just as it is. It is now getting on for the afternoon. It is likely enough that no other travellers will enter the grove to-day. By to-morrow at the latest some one will come in, and will of course go and report at once in Bangalore what he has found, and they will send out here to examine into it. When they find that the men have all fallen sword in hand, that two of them are evidently Stranglers, and that their girdles have not been searched nor the packs on their horses opened, it will be seen that it was not the work of robbers. I don't suppose they will know what to make of it, but I should think they would most likely conclude that these men have been attacked by some other party, and that it is a matter of some feud or private revenge—though, even then, the fact that the bodies have not been searched for valuables, or the baggage or animals carried off, will beat them altogether."

By this time the horses were ready for the start, and after looking up and down the long, straight road, to see that no one was in sight, they issued from the wood and continued their journey. Being anxious now to get away as far as possible from the scene of the struggle, instead of going on to Magree as they had intended, they turned off by the first country road on the left-hand side and made for Savandroog, which they could see towering up above the plain. When within three miles of it they halted in a large wood. Here, as soon as the horses had been unsaddled and the fire lighted, their talk naturally turned to the fight they had gone through.

"I cannot make out how you came to suspect them, Dick."

"I can hardly account for it myself, but, as I told you, I did not like the look of that man, and I had an uneasy sort of feeling, which I could not explain even to myself, that there was danger in the air."

"But what made you think of these Stranglers? I had heard some talk about them, but never anything for certain."

"The Rajah told me, when he was warning me against joining parties of travellers, that although very little was known about the organisation, it was certain that there was a sect who strangled and robbed travellers in great numbers. He said that he was aware that complaints had been made to princes all over India of numbers of persons being missing, and that it was certain that these murders were not the work of ordinary dacoits, but of some secret association, and that even powerful princes were afraid to take any steps against it, as one or two, who had made efforts to investigate the affair, had been found strangled in their beds. Therefore, no one cared to take any steps to search into the matter. It was not known whether these Stranglers, scattered as they were very widely, obeyed one common chief, or whether they acted separately; but all were glad to leave this mysterious organisation alone, especially as they preyed only on travellers. and in no case meddled in any way with rajahs, or officials, who did not interfere with them. Consequently, the idea occurred to me directly that these men who seemed like traders might be a party of these Stranglers; and when the others came up while the leader was sitting talking to us, I felt as if cold water was running down my back, and that some one was whispering to me, 'Be on your guard, be on your guard!' Therefore, the moment something passed before my face I threw myself back and fired at the man behind me without a moment's thought as to what it was."

"Well, certainly you saved our lives by doing so, Dick; for I suppose if that man behind me had once got his silk scarf round my neck, he would have choked me before I had time to so much as lift my hand."

"I have not the least doubt that he would, and I feel thankful indeed that I had such a strange feeling that these men were dangerous. Do you know, Surajah, it seems to me that it was just the same sort of feeling that my mother tells me she has, whenever my father is in danger, and I shall be curious to know when we get back whether she had the same feeling about me. Anyhow, I shall in future have even more faith than I had before in her confidence that she would have certainly known if any evil had happened to my father."

CHAPTER XIX.

FOUND AT LAST.

THE next morning, early, Dick and Surajah set to work to perfect their disguises. They had before appeared simply as two young traders, well to do, and of a class above the ordinary peddling merchant. They now fitted on the ample beards that had been made at Tripataly. These were attached so firmly to their faces by an adhesive wax that they could not be pulled off without the use of a good deal of force. With the same stuff, small patches of hair were fastened on, so as to hide the edge of the foundation of the beard. Tufts of short grey hair were attached to their eyebrows; a few grey lines were carefully drawn at the corner of the eyes, and across the foreheads; and when this was done, they felt assured that no one was likely to suspect the disguise.

Ibrahim, who had assisted in the operation, declared that he should take them for men of sixty-five, and as, before beginning it, both of them had darkened their faces several shades, they felt confident that no one at the fort was likely to recognise them. When Surajah had put on the padded under-garment and converted himself into a portly-looking old man, and Dick the great horn spectacles, they indulged in a burst of laughter at their changed appearance, while Ibrahim fairly shouted with amusement. He was to stay behind in the wood when they went on, for it would but have added to the risk had he accompanied them, as, unless also completely disguised, he would have been recognised by the soldiers with whom he had talked during his twenty-four hours' stay inside the Tower walls. He was in the evening to proceed along the road, to encamp in the last grove he came to, at a distance of a quarter of a mile from the gates, and to remain there until they returned.

Under his garments Dick had wound a thin, but very strong, silken cord that he had purchased at Bangalore. It was four hundred feet in length, and considerably increased his apparent bulk, although he was still far from emulating the stoutness of Surajah. The halters of the pack-horses were attached to the cruppers of the riding-ponies, and after a final instruction to Ibrahim that if at the end of four days they had not returned, he was to endeavour to find out what had happened to them, and was then to carry the news to Tripataly, they started for the fort. When they approached the gate, they were, as before, hailed by the sentry.

"We are merchants," Surajah said, "and we have with us a rich assortment of goods of all descriptions—silks and trinkets for the ladies of the governor's harem, and handkerchiefs, scarves, silver ornaments, and things of all kinds suitable for the wives of those of lower rank. We pray for permission to enter and exhibit our wares, which have been collected by us in the cities where they were manufactured and which we can therefore sell at prices hitherto unheard of."

"I will send word up to the governor," the officer said. "It is a long time since we have been visited by traders, and maybe he will grant you permission. You had best go back to the shade of those trees. It will be a good hour before the answer comes."

"I think it likely they will let us in," Dick said, as they moved away towards the trees. "It is but a short time since things were sufficiently settled for traders to venture up here, and as Savandroog lies altogether off the roads between large towns, it is possible that none with such goods as we have, have come this way since the garrison took over Savandroog from the British detachment that occupied it."

In little over an hour there was a shout from the walls, and on approaching the gate again, they were told that the governor had given permission for them to enter.

"You are to be blindfolded," the officer said, as the gate closed behind them. "No one may ascend the rock unless he consents to this. Your horses will be led, and beware that you do not attempt to remove the bandages until you have permission to do so."

It took nearly an hour to mount the steep road, and when they came to a standstill and the sub-officer who had accompanied them told them they could now remove their bandages, they found themselves in front of a small building, close to the commander's quarters. The packs were, by the order of the officer, taken off the horses by the soldiers who had led them up, and carried into the house; the horses were fastened in the shade to rings in the wall, and on Surajah pointing out the packs containing goods he wished to show to the ladies, two of the soldiers carried them across to the governor's house. The old officer himself came to the door.

"Enter, my friends," he said. "You are the first traders who have come up here since we took over the fort, some six months ago, and methinks you will do a brisk business if your wares are, as you sent up to say, good and cheap."

The bales were taken into a room, the soldiers retired, and in a minute the commander's wife, accompanied by three or four other ladies, entered. Dick and Surajah, after salaaming profoundly to the veiled figures, at once began to unpack their bales. The assortment had been very judiciously made, and to women who had for more than six months been deprived of the pleasure of shopping, the display was irresistible. In their desire to examine the goods, the ladies speedily lifted their veils, and, seating themselves on cushions they had brought in with them, chattered unrestrainedly, examining the quality of the silks which Surajah and Dick, squatting behind their wares, handed for their inspection, comparing the colours, asking each other's advice, and endeavouring to beat down the terms Surajah named. In the first place he asked the prices marked on small labels attached to each article, but suffered himself, after the proper amount of reluctance and protests that he should be a ruined man, to abate his terms considerably, although the ladies were evidently well satisfied that the goods were indeed bargains.

It was a long time before the ladies could make up their minds which to choose among the many silks exhibited for their selections. When this had been settled, the pack containing delicate muslins was opened, and the same scene gone through. It was altogether four hours before the purchases were all made, and even then the boxes of trinkets remained unopened, the governor's wife saying, "No we will not look at them. We have ruined ourselves already. To-morrow, when our husbands know how much we have spent, you can show the trinkets to them, and try your best to get them to buy. These things we have been getting are our own affair. It is for them to make us presents of ornaments if they are disposed to. This evening you must come in again. The ladies from the other fort will be here then."

The purchases made were paid for, the bales again fastened

up and carried across to their room. The governor met them as they went out.

"I suppose you have been ruining us all?" he said good-humouredly. "Well, it is a dull life up here, and the ladies have but few chances of spending money.'

"We are to see the ladies from the other fort this evening, my lord," Surajah said. "Have we your permission in the meantime to go and sell in the soldiers' quarters? We have goods suited to the needs of their wives also, as well as those for the ladies."

"Certainly. You can go about as you please up here; it is only as to the approaches that we have to be careful. But wait in your room for a short time; I will have food sent over to you."

In a few minutes a servant brought across a large dish of pillau and several cakes of sweetmeats, the latter being, as he informed them, the special gift of the governor's wife. There was no occasion for them to start, as they had intended, after their meal, for the news of their coming had spread, and by the time they had finished, a number of women were waiting outside; until sunset they were busily engaged in selling their goods—for the most part bright cotton cloths, red silk handkerchiefs, and cheap silver trinkets. Soldiers sauntered in and out: for these they had provided a store of pipes, tobacco, tobacco-boxes, knives, and muslins for turbans; and as the news spread that these were to be obtained, the number of soldiers increased, until the room was quite crowded with them as well as by many natives engaged in the work of rebuilding the fortifications. Surajah did the selling, while Dick's part of the work was receiving the money and giving change.

As he was stooping over a tray in front of him, piled with copper, picking up the change for silver coin, he heard a man ask Surajah for a pound of his best tobacco and a pipe. There was something in the accent that caused him to look up sharply. As he did so he started; the blood rushed to his head so violently that a mist seemed to pass across his eyes, and

M 84

DICK AND SURAJAH VISIT THE FORT DISGUISED AS MERCHANTS.

his hand shook so that he dropped the coins he was counting. Forgetful of the dark stain on his face, he bent forward over the tray again to conceal his emotion, forced himself to pick out the right change, and then, handing it to its owner, again looked up.

The man who was standing before Surajah was broader and taller than those around him. The sun had darkened his face until its shade approached those of his companions, and yet there was no mistaking the fact that he was a European. A heavy moustache and beard, streaked with grey, concealed the lower part of his face. Dick dared not gaze on the man too earnestly, and could see no likeness to the picture on the wall at Shadwell; but, allowing for the effects of hardship and suffering, he judged him to be about the age of his father.

The man was evidently on good terms with the soldiers, one or two of whom were chaffing him on his purchase.

"Will nothing but the best tobacco satisfy you?" one laughed.

"Nothing; and even that won't really satisfy me. This stuff is good enough, when rolled up, for cigars, and it does well enough in hookahs; but I would give all this pound for a couple of pipes of pigtail, which is the tobacco we smoked at sea."

Again Dick's heart beat rapidly. This man must have been a sailor. He could not restrain himself from speaking.

"Have you been a sailor, then?" he asked.

"Ay, I was a sailor, though it is many years ago now since I saw the sea."

"We got some English tobacco at Madras," Dick said, not hesitating for once at telling an untruth. "We sold most of it to the Feringhee soldiers on our way up, but I think I have got a little of it still left somewhere in the pack. I am too busy to look for it now, and we shall soon be going to show our goods to the officers' wives; but if you can come here at nine o'clock I may have looked it out for you."

"I can't come at nine," the man said, "for at half-past eight I am shut up for the night."

"Come at eight, then," Dick said. "If I am not back, come the first thing in the morning, before we get busy."

"I will come sure enough," the man said. "I would walk a hundred miles, if they would let me, for half a pound of pigtail."

"Get rid of them, Surajah," Dick whispered, as the man shouldered his way through the crowd; "make some excuse to send them off."

"Now, my friends," Surajah said, "you see it is getting dusk. It will soon be too dark to see what you are buying, and we have been selling for eight hours, and need rest. At eight o'clock to-morrow we will open our packs again, and every one shall be served; but I pray you excuse us going on any longer now. As you see, we are not as young as we once were, and are both sorely weary."

As time was no object, and the work of purchasing would relieve the tedium of the following day, the crowd good-humouredly dispersed.

Surajah rose and closed the door after the last of them, and then turned to Dick. He had himself been too busily engaged in satisfying the demands of the customers to look up, and had not noticed that one of them was a white man.

"What is it?" he asked, as he looked round. "Has the heat upset you?" Then, as his eye fell on Dick, his voice changed, and he hurried towards him, exclaiming anxiously, "What is it, Dick? What has happened?"

For Dick was leaning against a bale by the side of him, and had hidden his face in his arms. Surajah saw that his whole frame was shaking with emotion.

"My dear lord," Surajah said, as he knelt beside him and laid his arm across his shoulder, "you frighten me. Has aught gone wrong? Are you ill?"

Dick slightly shook his head, and, lifting one of his hands, made a sign to Surajah that he could not at present speak. A minute or two later he raised his head.

"Did you not see him, Surajah?"

"See who, Dick?"

"The white man you last served."

"I did not notice any white man."

"It was the one you gave a pound of the best tobacco to. Did you not hear me speak to him afterwards?"

"No. I was so busy and so fearfully hot with this padded thing, it was as much as I could do to attend to what they said to me. A white man, did you say? Oh, Dick!" And as the idea struck him he rose to his feet in his excitement. "Do you think—do you really think he can be your father?"

"I do think so, Surajah. Of course I did not recognise his face; nine years must have changed him greatly, and he has a long beard. But he is about the right age, and, I should say about the same figure, and he has certainly been a sailor, for he said to one of the soldiers that he would give that pound of tobacco for a couple of pipes of pigtail, which is the tobacco sailors smoke. I told him that perhaps I might be able to find him some in my packs, and asked him to come here at eight o'clock this evening; if I was not in then he was to come the first thing to-morrow morning; but of course I shall be in at eight. You must make some excuse to the ladies. Say that there are some goods you wish to show them in one of the other packs, and ask me to go and look for it."

"Oh, Dick, only to think that after all our searching we seem to have come on him at last! It is almost too good to be true."

Great as was Surajah's confidence in Dick, he had never quite shared his faith that he would find his father alive, and his non-success while with the army, and since, had completely extinguished any hopes he had entertained. His surprise, therefore, equalled his delight at finding that, after all, it seemed probable that their search was likely to be crowned with success.

"Of course we will manage it," he said. "I will put aside that narrow Benares cloth-of-gold work for trimmings, and you can be as long as you like looking for it. They will be too busy examining the other things to give it a thought after you have gone out."

"I can be back at half-past eight," Dick said, "for the man told me he was locked up at that hour. If it had not been for that, I should have arranged for him to come a little later. But of course I shall have opportunities for talking to him to-morrow. There is some one at the door."

Surajah opened it, and a soldier entered with their evening meal and a request that they would go across to the governor's as soon as they had finished it, as the ladies had already assembled there. They hurried through their food, and then went across. There was quite a large gathering, for not only had the wives of the officers in the other fort come over, but all those who had been there in the morning were again present, several of them prepared to make further purchases. Trade was as actively carried on as it had been before. When he judged it to be nearly eight o'clock, Dick nudged Surajah, who said, a minute afterwards, "We have forgotten the Benares cloth-of-gold. I am sure that will please the ladies for waist-bands or for trimmings. It must have got into the other bales by mistake."

"I will go and fetch it," Dick said, and, rising, left the room. A figure was standing at the door when he reached the house.

"I was afraid you had forgotten me," the man said. "It is not quite eight o'clock yet, but as I found that you were both out, I began to be afraid that you might be detained until after I had to go; and you don't know how I long for a pipe of that tobacco: the very thought of it seems to bring old days back again."

By this time they had entered the house, and Dick shut the door behind him. He had left a light burning when they went out. Dick was so agitated that he felt unable to speak, but gazed earnestly in the man's face.

"What is it, old chap?" the latter said, surprised at the close scrutiny. "I anything wrong with you?'

Dick took off his spectacles, rather to gain time than to see more clearly, for a plain glass had been substituted for the lenses.

"I want to ask you a question," he said. "Is your name Holland?"

The man started. "My name is Jack Holland," he said, "sure enough; though how you come to know it beats me altogether, for I am always called Jack, and except the governor, I don't think there is a man here knows my other name."

"You were captain of the *Hooghley*, wrecked on the Malabar coast nine years ago," Dick said, this time speaking in English.

After an exclamation of startled surprise, the man stared at him in an astonishment too great for words.

"Are you English?" he said slowly, at last. "Yes, I was in command of the *Hooghley*. Who, in God's name, are you?"

Dick took his two hands. "Father," he said, "I am your son Dick."

The sailor gazed at him with a stupified air. "Are you mad, or am I?" he said hoarsely.

"Neither of us, father. I am disguised as an old man, but really I am little more than eighteen. I have been searching for you for more than two years, and, thank God, I have found you at last;" and, bursting into tears, Dick would have thrown his arms round his father's neck, but the latter pushed him off with one hand, and held him at arm's distance, while his other hand plucked at his own throat, as if to loosen something that was choking him.

"It can't be true," he muttered to himself. "I am dreaming this. I shall wake presently and you will be gone."

"It is quite true, father. Mother is down at Tripataly waiting for me to bring you to her."

With a hoarse cry the sailor reeled, and would have fallen had not Dick caught him and allowed him to sink gradually to the ground, where he lay half-supported by one of the bales. Dick ran to one of the saddle-bags, where he carried a flask of brandy in case of emergencies, poured some into a cup and held it to his father's lips. The sailor gasped.

"It is brandy," he said suddenly. "I can't have dreamt that."

Then he broke into a violent sobbing. Dick knelt by his side and took his hand.

"It is assuredly no dream, father," he said gently. "I am really your son Dick. I am here with a trusty friend, and now we have found you, you may be sure that we will in some way manage your escape. There is no time now to tell you all that has happened; that I can do afterwards. All that is important for you to know, is, that mother is quite well. She has never given up hope, and has always insisted that you were alive, for she said that she should surely have known if you had died. So she taught me her language, until I could speak like a native, and two years and a half ago she came out here with me. I accompanied the army with my uncle's troop, and searched every hill-fort they took, for you. Since they went back I have been up in Mysore with my friend Surajah, and, thank God, at last we have found you!"

"Thank God, indeed, my boy. I do thank Him, not only that you have found me, but that your mother, whom I had never hoped to see again, is alive and well, and also that He has given me so good a son."

"And now, father, about your escape. In the first place, have you given your parole not to try to get away?"

Captain Holland was himself now.

"No lad, no. At the fort, where I was for six years, there was no possibility of escape, and as I was a long time before I began to speak the language, even if I had got away I could never have made my way through the country. Then the governor—it was the same we have here—took me with him to Kistnagherry. I was the only white captive who went there with him. At Kistnagherry there were five or six others, but when Tippoo heard that an English army was coming up the ghauts, an order came that they were to be killed; but the governor is a kind-hearted old fellow, and as I had become almost a chum of his he chose to consider that the order did not apply to me, but only to those he had found at Kistnagherry—for I fancy my existence had been forgotten altogether. I had great hopes that the British would take the place. I think that is the only time I have hoped since I was made prisoner; but the old man is a good soldier, and beat them off.

"When peace was made, Kistnagherry was, as you know, given up, and the governor was ordered to evacuate the place and to come here. He brought me with him, making me dye my face before I started, so that in my native dress it would not be noticed in any town we passed through that I was a white; for had this been done, the news might have come to Tippoo's ears, and there would have been an end of me. Except that I am locked up at night, I am not treated as a prisoner; but the governor, who has a strong sense of duty, has a certain watch kept over me. He has a real friendship for me, and would do all in his power to save my life, short of disobedience to an actual order. But his view is that I have been confided to his care, and that if at any moment the Sultan should write to demand me of him, he would be bound to produce me."

"Well, father, it must be nearly half-past eight. I will go with you and see where you are confined—that is the first step. We will both, to-night, think over the best way of attempting your escape, and in the morning, when your guard is removed, if you will come straight here we will talk it over. I am afraid you will have to wait for your pigtail till we get to Madras."

Captain Holland laughed.

"I can afford to wait for that now. God bless you, my boy! I have never looked for such happiness as this again. But, as you say, it is time for me to be off. I have never been late yet, and if it were reported to the governor that I was so to-night, he might think that there was something in the wind.'

Dick walked with his father across the fort.

"That is the house, in the corner," the captain said, pointing to one before which a group of soldiers were standing; "don't come any farther."

Dick stood looking after him, and heard a voice say,—

"You are late, Jack; I was beginning to wonder what had become of you."

"I don't think it is past the hour yet," Captain Holland replied. "I have been with those traders. They told me this afternoon they might be able to find me some English tobacco in their pack; but they have been too busy to look for it. I hope they will light on it to-morrow. If they do, I will give you half a pipeful; I won't give you more, for it is strong enough to blow your head off, after this tasteless stuff you smoke here."

Then Dick hurried off to the house, snatched up the stuff he was supposed to be looking for, and joined Surajah at the governor's.

It was another hour before the ladies had completed their purchases. Dick, on entering, had given a little nod to Surajah, to let him know that it was really his father whom he had discovered, and had then tried to keep his attention upon his work as a salesman; and Surajah, as he handed him the goods, had given a furtive squeeze to his hand in token of his sympathy.

"So it is really your father?" he said, as, carrying their greatly diminished pack, they walked across to their house.

"It is, indeed. You may imagine his surprise and joy when I told him who I was. Now we have got to talk over the best plan of getting him out."

When the door was shut, and they had seated themselves on two of the bales, Dick first repeated all that his father had told him, and then, for a long time, they discussed the best plan of attempting an escape. Both agreed at once that it would be next to impossible to get him down the road and out of the gate. In the first place, they would have to leave by daylight; and even could a disguise be contrived that would deceive the sentries and guard at the gate, all of whom were well acquainted with Captain Holland's figure and appearance, it was certain that as but two had come up the rock, a third would not be allowed to leave, unless he had a special order from the governor. They agreed, therefore, that the escape must be made over the precipice. That this was a matter of great difficulty was evident from the fact that the captain had made no attempt to get away in that manner. Still, there was hope that, with the assistance of the silk rope Dick had brought with them, it might be managed

There was, too, the initial difficulty of getting out from the fort to be faced.

"We can do nothing till we have had a long talk with my father," Dick said. "I have no doubt that he has thought all these things over, and has, long before this, made up his mind as to the point at which a descent would be easiest. As at present we know little except by the casual examination we made last time, we can decide on nothing by ourselves."

"I hope it won't be a long way to let oneself down," Surajah said, "for I am quite sure I could not hold on by that thin rope for any distance."

"Nor could I, Surajah, if I had to trust only to my hands. My father, as a sailor, will be able to put us up to the best way to do it. But at any rate he might let you down first; and I think that by twisting the rope two or three times round my body, and then holding it between my knees and feet, I might manage. But I dare say my father will hit on some better plan than that. And now we will lie down. I am so stiff that I can hardly stand, from squatting for so many hours behind those things of ours. I thought that I had got pretty well accustomed to it, but I never calculated on having to do it from ten in the morning until ten at night, with only two half-hours off."

Dick, however, had little sleep that night. He was too excited over the glorious success he had obtained to be capable of closing an eye, and it was not until day was breaking that he fell into a doze.

An hour later he started to his feet at a knock at the door. He was wide awake in a moment, and on running to it his father entered.

"You look older to-day than you did yesterday," the latter said, as he held his hand and gazed into Dick's face. "I fancy that neither of us has had any sleep to speak of. As for myself, I have not closed an eye."

"Nor did I, father, until day began to break. Now please let us talk over our plan of escape first, for we may be interrupted at any moment."

"Right you are, lad. Does your friend here speak English?—for I have never got to be a good hand at their lingo. I want to thank him too, but, as you say, time is precious, and we must postpone that."

"He understands it, father, and can talk it pretty fairly. We have been constantly together for nearly two years. Now, in the first place, is there any place where we can get down from the top here with the aid of a rope?"

"It would be a pretty tough job, anyhow, but at the farthest end of the rock is a place where it goes sharp down, as if cut with a knife; that would be the best place to try. I take it to be about two hundred feet deep; beyond, the ground seems to slope regularly away. If I could have got a rope I should have tried it, but they are pretty scarce commodities up here—in fact, I have never seen a piece twenty feet long since we came. What sort of rope have you got?"

Dick opened the front of his garment, and showed the rope round his body. Captain Holland gave a low whistle of dismay.

"I should not like to trust a child with that thing, Dick, much less a grown man. It is no thicker than a flag-halliard."

"It is thin, father, but there is no fear as to its strength. I tested every yard of it, and found it would bear six hundred-weight."

"Well, that is ample; but how is one to hold on to a cord that like?"

"That is just what we want you to tell us, father. There must be some way of managing it, if one could but hit upon it."

"Yes, that is so, lad," the sailor said thoughtfully. "I will think it over. Anyhow, I think I could lower you both down, and by knotting it I might get hold enough to come down after you; but even the knots would be precious small."

"One might get over that, father, by fastening a short stick across every five or six feet, or every two or three feet if you like."

"Good, Dick. That would prevent one's coming down with a run certainly, and by keeping it between one's legs one could always get a rest. Yes, that will do, lad, if I can think of nothing better. There are a lot of spears stowed away in the room adjoining mine; if we were to cut them up into six-inch lengths, with one of a foot long to each ten, for sitting on, they would be just the thing."

"That is capital, father. I had a lot of practice in rope climbing before I came out, and I am sure that I could manage with the help that would give. I don't think Surajah could, but we could let him down first easily. Now as to your prison."

"There are bars to the windows," the captain said, "and a sentry is always on duty outside. The only way would be to escape at the rear. I have often thought it over, but it was of no use breaking out there if I could not get any farther. The wall is built of loose stone, without mortar. You see, it would have been a big job to bring up either mortar or bricks from down below, so most of the buildings are entirely of stone. The wall is two feet thick, but there would be no great difficulty in getting out the stones, and making a hole big enough to crawl through. I could not do it in my room, because they always look round to see that everything is safe before they lock me up, and it would take so long to do it noiselessly that half the night would be wasted before I could get out; but the magazine, where the spears are kept, communicates with my room, and I could slip in there in the daytime when no one was looking, get behind the spears, which are piled against the wall, and work hidden by them. No one would be likely to go into my room during the day, and if he did he would not expect to find me there, as I am generally about the place. In that way I could get out enough stones to render it an easy job to finish it after I was locked up. A spear-head is as good a thing to help me prize them out as one could wish for."

"Very well, father. Then we had better settle that you shall get out in that way. Now, shall we go round on the outside and help you."

"No; I don't say but that your help would make it easier to get the stones out without making a noise; still, your going round might be noticed."

"Well, then, father, shall we seize and gag the sentry? We have done such a thing before successfully."

"No, that wouldn't do, Dick; the guard-house is hard by, and the slightest noise would destroy us all. Besides, as they have not many sentries posted up here, they relieve guard every hour, so that the thing would be discovered in no time. No. When I get out I will creep along noiselessly by the wall. There are houses in the yard almost all along, and though the sentry would not be likely to see me in the shade of the wall, I will take care to cross the open spaces when his back is turned. I will then come straight here for you, and we will make for the wall behind the governor's house. There is no sentry on that side, for that steep ravine covers it from attack there; however, there are six or eight feet of level ground between the foot of the wall and the edge of the ravine. The walls are twenty feet in height. With fifty feet of that rope I will make a ladder, and will get hold of a piece of iron to make a grapnel of. How much time can you give me?"

"I should think we could stay here to-day and to-morrow without seeming to be dawdling without reason. Do you think you could get ready by to-morrow night, father?"

"Yes, that will give me plenty of time. Let me see, there is the short ladder to make; that won't take me over an hour. There are a hundred bits to cut for the long ladder, putting them about two feet apart; that will be a longish job, for the spear-shafts are of very tough wood. However, I have a saw, and some oil, which will prevent it making a noise, and can make fairly quick work of it. I have several tools, for I very often do carpentering jobs of all sorts—that is what first made the governor take to me. I can get all that part of the work done to-day; to-night I will do the knotting. Of course I shall make it a goodish bit over two hundred feet long, for it may turn out that I have not judged the depth right, and that the cliff is higher than I thought it was. I don't think sawing up the spear-shafts will take more than an hour or two, so I shall be able to show myself about the place as usual; I will go over and take a good look at the rock again, and stick a spear-head into the ground at the point where it seems to me that it goes down straightest, and where there is the least chance of the rope getting rubbed against a sharp edge. I sha'n't begin at the wall until to-morrow, for I don't suppose I shall be able to get out the first few stones without making a bit of a noise, and it would not do to work at night.

"Now, lad, I think we can consider that as all settled, and I won't come near you again unless there is some change of plan. I shall be here to-morrow evening, I hope it will be by ten o'clock—that must depend upon how long it takes me to get down the outside layer of stone. If you should hear a sudden row, make at once for the wall behind the governor's house, and wait there for me to join you. You see, some of the stones may come down with a run, and if they do I shall give the rest a shove, and be out like a shot. I shall hear which side the sentry is running round the house, and shall bolt the other way. Of course he will see the stones and give the alarm; but in the darkness I have not much doubt of being able to slip away, and I will then make my way straight to the wall.

Of course I shall have the ladders tied up into bundles, and shall take care not to leave them behind me."

"All right, father; we will be ready to-morrow evening. We shall wait quietly for you until you come, unless we hear a sudden alarm. If we do, we will go round behind the governor's house and wait there for your coming."

"That is it, my lad. Now I will be going. I am glad that no one has come in while I have been here."

CHAPTER XX.

THE ESCAPE.

SOON after eight o'clock customers began to drop in, and throughout the day a brisk trade was carried on. Surajah was sent for in the course of the morning by the governor, who bought several silver bracelets, brooches, and ear-rings, for his wife. Most of the other officers came in during the day, and made similar purchases, and many trinkets were also sold to the soldiers, who considered them a good investment for their money; indeed, no small portion of the earnings of the natives of India are spent upon silver ornaments for their women, as they can at any time be converted into cash. The commoner cloths, knives, beads, and trinkets, were almost all disposed of by the end of the day, for as no traders had come up for six months, and as a long time might elapse before others did so, the garrison were glad to lay in a store of useful articles for themselves and families, especially as the prices of all the goods were at least as low as they could have been bought in a town.

"We sha'n't leave much behind us," Dick said, as he looked round after the last customer had left, and they had sat down to their evening meal. "Almost all the silver work and the better class of goods have gone, and I should say three-quarters of the rest; I daresay we shall get rid of the remainder to-morrow. I don't suppose many of the soldiers stationed down by the gate have come up yet; but when they hear that we sell cheaply, some of them will be here to-morrow. We have made no money by the transaction, but at any rate we shall have got back the outlay. Of course, I should not have cared if we had got nothing back; still, it is satisfactory to have cleared oneself. I wonder how Ibrahim is getting on down in the wood."

"He won't be expecting us to-day," Surajah replied, "but I have no doubt he will begin to feel anxious by to-morrow night. I wish we could have seen some way of getting the horses down; it will be awkward doing without them."

"Yes. I hope we shall get a good start. Of course, we must put on our peasant's dresses again. I am glad enough to be rid of that rope, though I have had to put on two or three additional things to fill me out to the same size as before. Still, I don't feel so bound in as I did, though it is horribly hot."

"I am sure I shall be glad to get rid of all this stuffing," Surajah said. "I felt ready to faint to-day when the room was full."

"Well, we have only one more day of it," Dick said. "I do hope father will be able to get out by ten o'clock; then, before eleven we shall be at the edge of the rock. Say we are two hours in getting down and walking round to join Ibrahim. That will take us till one, and we shall have a good five hours before father's escape will be discovered. They will know that he can't have gone down the road, and it will take them fully two hours to search the fort, and all over the rock. It will be eight o'clock before they set out in pursuit, and by that time we ought to be well on the road between Cenopatam and Anicull. If we can manage to buy horses at Cenopatam, of course we will do so. We shall be there by five o'clock, and ought to be able to get them in a couple of hours. Once on horseback, we are safe. I don't think they will pursue very far—perhaps not even so far as Cenopatam; for the governor will see that he had better not make any fuss about a white captive having escaped, when it was not known that he had one there at all. I think it more likely that when he finds father has got fairly away, he will take no steps at all. They have no cavalry here, and he will know well enough that there will be no chance of our being tracked and overtaken by footmen if we had but a couple of hours' start."

"I think that is so, Dick. He has done his duty in keeping your father a prisoner, but I don't think he will be, at heart, at all sorry that he has made his escape."

"I think, Surajah, I will write a letter to him, and leave it here, to be found after we have got away, thanking him in father's name for the kindness that he has always shown him, saying who I am, why I came here, and asking his pardon for the deception that I have been obliged to play upon him. He is a good old fellow, and I should think it would please him."

"I should think it would," Surajah agreed.

"I will do up my brace of pistols in a packet and put them with the note," Dick went on, "and will say in it that I hope he will accept them as a token of our esteem and gratitude. They are well-finished English pistols, and I have no doubt he will prize them. I will mention, too, that we shall have made our escape at eleven o'clock, and therefore, by the time he receives my letter, we shall be far beyond the reach of pursuit. I daresay that will decide him upon letting the matter pass quietly, and he will see himself that, by making no fuss over it, no one outside the fortress will ever know that a prisoner has escaped."

The next day passed comparatively quietly. A good many soldiers and women came up from below, and before sunset their goods were completely cleared out. The governor came over in the afternoon and had a talk with them; they expressed their satisfaction at the result of their trading, and said that they should be off before sunrise.

"I hope you will come again," he said; "but not for another six months, for assuredly you will take away with you pretty nearly every rupee in the fortress. My wife and the other ladies are all well content with their purchases, and agree that they would not have got them cheaper at Seringapatam or Bangalore."

"We try to buy cheaply and sell cheaply," Surajah said modestly. "In that way we turn over our money quickly. But it is seldom indeed that we find so good a market as we have done here. When we left Bangalore we thought that it might be a month before we should have to go back there to replenish our packs from our magazine; but we shall only have been away five or six days."

"I am glad that you are content, for you are honest traders, and not like some of the rascals that have come up to the forts I have commanded, and fleeced the soldiers right and left."

Although not given to blushing, Dick felt that he coloured under his dye at the praise; for although they had certainly sold cheaply, he doubted whether the term honest could be fairly applied to the whole transaction.

As ten o'clock approached, the two friends sat with open door listening intently for every sound. Conversation was still going on in the houses, and occasionally they could make out a dark figure crossing the yard. It was not yet ten when a light footfall was heard, and a moment later Captain Holland appeared at the door.

"It is all right so far," he said, "but wait five minutes, to give me time to get the ladder fixed. You had better come one by one and stroll quietly across the yard. It is too dark for any one to recognise you, unless they run right against you; and even if they do so, they will not think it strange you should be out, after having been cooped up all the day."

In another moment he was gone. They had each during the day gone out for a time, and had walked round through the narrow lane behind the governor's house to see that there were no obstructions that they might fall over in the dark. They agreed, on comparing notes, that Captain Holland had chosen the best possible place for scaling the wall, for the lane was evidently quite unused, and the house, which was higher than the wall, would completely screen them from observation. In five minutes Dick followed his father, leaving Surajah to come on in a minute or two. They had secured about them the gold and silver they had received for their purchases, but they left behind a large heap of copper coins, on the top of which Dick had placed his letter to the governor, and the parcel containing the brace of pistols. He met no one on his way to the rendezvous, but almost ran against his father in the dark.

"Steady, Dick, or you will run me down," Captain Holland said. "I have got the ladder fixed, so you had better go up at once. Take these three spears with you. I will bring the long ladder."

"We sha'n't want the spears, father; we have a brace of double-barrelled pistols and two brace of single-barrels."

"Never mind that, Dick; you will see that they will come in useful."

Dick took the spears, and mounted the ladder without further question. His father then came up and placed the long rope, which, with the pieces of wood, was a bulky bundle, on the wall and then descended again. It was another five minutes before Surajah came up.

"I was stopped on the way," he said, "and had to talk with one of the officers."

He and the captain were soon by Dick's side. The ladder was then pulled up and lowered on the other side of the wall; they were soon standing at its foot.

"Shall I jerk the ladder down, father?"

"I think not, Dick; it would only make a clatter, and it is no matter to us whether they find it in the morning or not. You had better follow me; I know every foot of the ground, and there are some nasty places, I can tell you."

They had to make several *détours*, to avoid ravines running deep into the plateau, and for a time Captain Holland walked very cautiously. When he had passed these he stepped out briskly, and in less than an hour from starting they were near the edge of the precipice. Their eyes had by this time become accustomed to the darkness.

"We are just there now," Captain Holland said; "but we must go very cautiously, for the rock falls sheer away, without warning. Ah! there is the edge a few yards ahead of me. Now, do you stay where you are, while I feel about for that spear-head I put in to mark the place. It had about three feet of the staff on it. If it were not for that, there would be small chance of finding it. I know it is somewhere close here."

In a few minutes he returned to them. "I have found it," he said. "Keep close behind me." After walking for fifty yards he stopped. "Here it is, lads. Now give me those spears, Dick." He thrust them firmly into the ground, a few inches apart, "Throw your weight on them too," he said. "That is right. Now they will stand many times the strain we shall put on them. I have chosen this place, Dick, for two reasons. In the first place, because it is the most perpendicular, and in the second, because the soil and grass project slightly over the edge of the rock. There is a cushion in that bundle, and four spear-heads. I will peg it down close to the edge, and the rope will run easily over it. Now, Surajah, we had better let you down first; you will be tied quite securely, and there will be no risk whatever, as you know, of the rope giving way. I should advise you to keep your eyes shut till you get to the bottom, for the rope will certainly twist round and round; but keep your arms well in front of you, and whenever you feel the rock, open your eyes, and send yourself off with your arms and legs. I don't think you will touch, for at this point it seemed to me, as I looked down, that the rock projects farther out than anywhere else on the face of the precipice, and that a stone dropped straight down would fall some fourteen or fifteen feet from its foot. Would you like me to bandage your eyes?"

"No, thank you; I will keep my eyes closed."

"That is the best thing you can do," Captain Holland said, "though it is so dark that you would not be able to see if you did. When you get to the bottom, untie the rope, pull it gently down, and call out to me whether the lowest piece of stick touches the ground. If it does not, I will pull it up again and fasten on some more. I have got a dozen spare ones with me."

Captain Holland then told Surajah and Dick to take off their upper garments. These he wound round and round the lower four feet of the rope, increasing its diameter to over two inches."

"There," he said, as he fastened this round Surajah's body, under the arms; "it won't hurt you now. That silk rope would have cut in an inch deep before you got to the bottom, if it had not been covered." Then he took off his own garment, made it up into a roll, lashed one end to the rope in the centre of Surajah's back, passed it between his legs and fastened it to the knot at his chest."

"There," he said; "that will prevent any possibility of the thing slipping up over your shoulders, and will take a lot of the strain off your chest." Then he lay down and crawled forward to the edge, pegged the cushion down, and then, turning to Surajah, said, "All is ready now."

Surajah had felt rather ashamed that all these precautions should be taken for him, while the others would have to rely solely upon their hands and feet, and, sternly repressing any sign of nervousness, he stepped forward to the side of Captain Holland.

"That is right," the captain said approvingly. "Now lie down by my side and work yourself backwards. Go over on one side of the cushion, for you might otherwise displace it. I will hold your wrists and let you over. Dick will hold the rope; I will put it fairly on the cushion. Then I shall take it and stand close to the edge, and pay it out gradually as you go down. If you should find any projecting piece of rock, call out 'Stop!' I will hold on at once. We can then talk over how we can best avoid the difficulty. When you are down, and I tell you Dick is coming, take hold of one of the steps, and hold the

M 84

DICK AND HIS FRIENDS ESCAPE FROM THE HILL-FORTRESS.

ladder as firmly as you can, so as to prevent it from swaying about. Now, are you ready?"

"Quite ready," Surajah said, in a firm voice.

Dick, who was standing five or six yards back, tightened the rope. Gradually he saw Surajah's figure disappear over the edge.

"Slack out a little bit," his father said. "That is right; I have got it over the cushion. Now hold it firmly until I am on my feet. That is right. Now pay it out gradually."

It seemed an endless time to Dick before his father exclaimed,—

"The strain is off! Thank God he has got down all right!"

A minute later there was a slight pull on the rope, and the captain paid it out until he heard a call from below.

"Have you got to the lowest stick?" he asked, leaning over.

"Yes; it is just touching the ground."

"Not such a bad guess," the captain said, as he turned to Dick. "There are about twenty feet left."

He now fastened the rope round the spears in the ground.

"I will lower you down, if you like, Dick. You are half as heavy again as that young native, but I have no doubt that I can manage it."

"Not at all, father; I am not a bit nervous about it. If it was light, I should not feel so sure of myself, for I might turn giddy; but there is no fear of my doing so now."

"Well, lad, it is as well to be on the safe side, and I manufactured this yesterday."

He put a loop, composed of a rope some four feet long, over Dick's shoulders and under his arms. To each end was attached a strong double hook, like two fingers.

"There, lad! Now, if you feel at all tired or shaky, all you have got to do is to hook this on to one of the steps. Do you see?—one hook on each side of the cord. That way you can rest as long as you like, and then go on again. You say you can go down a rope with your hands only; I should advise you to do that, if you can, and not to use your legs unless you want to sit down on one of the long steps, for, as you know, if you use your feet the rope will go in till they are almost level with your head, while, if you use your arms only, it will hang straight down."

"I know, father. And I don't suppose I shall have to rest at all, for these cross-sticks make it ten times as easy as having to grip the rope only."

Dick laid himself down as Surajah had done, and crawled backwards until he was lying half over the edge; then he seized the rope and began to descend, hand over hand. He counted the rungs as he went down, and half way he sat down on one of the long pieces, hitched the hooks on to the one above, and rested his arms. After a short pause he continued until he reached the bottom.

The captain, who was stooping with his hand on the rope, felt the vibration cease, and as he leaned over he heard Dick call out,—

"I am all right, father. Those bits of wood make easy work of it."

Then the captain at once began to descend, and was soon standing beside his son and Surajah.

"Thank God that job is finished! How do you both feel?"

"My arms feel as if they had done some work, father. I have been four or five months without practice, or I should hardly have felt it."

"And how are you, Surajah?"

"I feel ashamed at having been let down like a baby, Captain Holland, and at being so nervous."

"There is nothing to be ashamed of," Captain Holland said. "Rope-climbing is a thing that only comes with practice; and as to nervousness, most landsmen are afraid to trust themselves to a rope at all. Did you open your eyes?"

"Not once, Sahib. I kept my arms out, as you told me, but I did not touch anything. I could feel that I was spinning round and round, and was horribly frightened just at first. But I went down so smoothly and quietly that the feeling did not last long; for I knew that the rope was very strong, and as I did not touch anything, it seemed to me that there could be no fear of it being cut against the rock."

The clothes were soon unwound from the rope, and put on again. Captain Holland cut off all the slack of the rope and made it into a coil.

"The slope is all right, as far as I could see from the top," he said; "but we may come across nasty bits again, and this will stand in useful if we do."

They went down cautiously, but at a fair rate of speed, until, without meeting with any serious difficulty, they arrived on the plain. Four miles' brisk walking brought them to the grove where Ibrahim had been left, and they had scarce entered among the trees when he asked,—

"Who is it that is coming?"

"It is us, Ibrahim. We have got my father!"

Ibrahim gave an exclamation of joy, and a minute later they joined him.

"You were not asleep, then, Ibrahim?" Dick said.

"No, my lord. I have slept during the day, and watched at night; but I did not sleep yesterday, for I was growing sorely anxious, and had begun to fear that harm had befallen you."

"Well, let us be off at once. Of course we have had to leave the horses behind us, and I want to be at Cenopatam by daybreak; we will buy horses there."

They struck across the country to the south-west, until they came on a road between Magree and Cenopatam, and arrived within sight of the latter town just at daybreak. As they walked, Dick and Surajah had, with no small amount of pain, removed their beards and the patches of hair.

"You ought both to have shaved before you put those things on," Captain Holland said, as they muttered exclamations of pain. "You see, cobbler's wax, or whatever it is, sticks to what little down there is on your cheeks and chin, and I don't wonder that it hurts horribly, pulling it off. If you had shaved first, you would not have felt any of that."

"I will remember that, father, if I ever have to disguise myself again," Dick said. "I feel as if I were pulling the whole skin off my face."

The painful task was at last finished.

"I shall be glad to have a look at you in the morning, Dick," his father said, "so as to see what you are really like, of which I have not the least idea at present. You must feel a deal more comfortable now that you have got rid of the rope."

"I am, indeed. I am sure Surajah must be quite as much pleased at leaving his padding behind."

They stopped half a mile from the town, which was a place of considerable size. Dick took from the saddle-bag of the horse Ibrahim was leading the bottle of liquid with which he was in the habit of renewing his staining every few days, and darkened his father's face and hands. Then they took off their costumes as merchants, and put on their peasants' attire. Dick directed Ibrahim to make a *détour*, so as to avoid the town and come down on the road half a mile beyond it, and there wait until they rejoined them—for his father was to accompany Ibrahim.

It was growing light as Dick and Surajah entered the town, and in half-an-hour the streets became alive with people. After some search they found a man who had several horses to sell, and, after the proper amount of bargaining, they purchased three fairly good animals. Another half-hour was occupied in procuring saddles and bridles, and, after riding through quiet streets to avoid questioning, they left the town, and soon rejoined their companions.

"Now, Surajah," Dick said, "we will be colonels again for a bit."

The saddle-bags were again opened, and in a few minutes they were transformed.

"Why, where on earth did you get those uniforms?" Captain Holland asked, in surprise. "Those sashes are the signs that their wearers are officers of the Palace, for I have seen them more than once at Kistnagherry; and the badges are those of colonels. There is nothing like impudence, Dick, but it seems to me it would have been safer if you had been contented with sub-officers' uniforms."

Dick laughed.

"We are wearing them because we have a right to them," Dick laughed. "We are both colonels in Tippoo's army, and officers of the Palace—that is, we were so until a month ago, though I expect since then our names have been struck off their army list. I will tell you about it as we ride."

"You had better tell me afterwards, Dick. I have never ridden a horse in my life, except when they were taking me from the coast to Mysore, and I shall have enough to do to keep my seat and attend to my steering, without trying to listen to you."

They rode all day, passed through Anicull and Oussoor, and halted for the night in a grove two or three miles farther on. They had not been questioned as, at a walk, they went through the town. Captain Holland had ridden behind with Ibrahim, and the latter had stopped and laid in a stock of provisions at Anicull.

"Thank goodness that is over!" Captain Holland said, as they dismounted. "I feel as if I had been beaten all over with sticks, and am as hungry as a hunter."

"Ibrahim will have some food ready in half-an-hour, father, and I shall be glad of some myself; though, you know, we all had some chupatties he bought."

"They were better than nothing, Dick, but a pancake or two does not go very far with men who have been travelling since ten o'clock last night. Well, lad, I am glad that you have got rid of your beard, and that, except for that brown skin, I am able to have a look at you as you are. You will be bigger than I am, Dick—bigger by a good bit, I should say, and any father might be proud of you, much more so one who has been fetched out from a captivity from which he had given up all hope of escaping. As it is, lad, words can't tell how grateful I feel to God for giving me such a son."

"My dear father, it is mother's doing. It has been her plan, ever since she heard that you were wrecked, that we should come out here to find you, and she has had me regularly trained for it. I had masters for fencing and gymnastics, we always talked Hindustani when we were together, and she has encouraged me to fight with other boys, so that I should get strong and quick."

That evening by the fire, Dick told his father the whole story of his life since he had been in India.

"Well, my lad, you have done wonders," his father said, when he had finished, "and if I had as much enterprise and go as you have, I should have been out of this place years ago. But in the first place, I was very slow in picking up their lingo. You see, until within the last three or four years there have always been other Englishmen with me. Of course we talked together, and as most of them were able to speak a little of the lingo, there was no occasion for me to learn it. Then I was always, from the first, when they saw that I was handy at all sorts of things, kept at odd jobs, and so got less chance of picking up the language than those who were employed in drilling, or who had nothing to do but talk to their guards. But most of all, I did not try to escape because I found that if I did so it would certainly cost my companions their lives.. That was the way that scoundrel Tippoo kept us from making attempts to get off.

"Well, soon after the last of the other captives was murdered, we moved away to Kistnagherry, which was a very difficult place to escape from; and besides, very soon after we got there, I heard of the war with our people, and hoped that they would take the place. It was, as you may suppose, a terrible disappointment to me when they failed in their attack on it. Still, I hoped that they would finally thrash Tippoo, and that, somehow, I might get handed over to them. However, as you know, when peace was made, and Kistnagherry had to be given over, the governor got orders to evacuate it, without waiting for the English to come up to take possession. Well, since I have been at Savandroog I have thought often of trying to get away. By the time I got there I had learned to speak the language fairly enough to make my way across the country, and I have been living in hopes that, somehow or other, I might get possession of a rope long enough to let myself down the rocks. But, as I told you, I have never so much as seen one up there twenty feet long.

"I did think of gradually buying enough cotton cloth to twist up and make a rope of; but you see, when one has been years in captivity, one loses a lot of one's energy. If I had been worse off, I should have set about the thing in earnest, but you see, I was not badly treated at all. I was always doing odd carpentering jobs for the colonel and officers, and armourer's work at the guns. Any odd time I had over, I did jobs for the soldiers and their wives. I got a good many little presents, enough to keep me in decent clothes and decent food—if you can call the food you have up there decent—and to provide me with tobacco, so that, except that I was a prisoner, and for the thought of my wife and you, I had really nothing to grumble about, and was indeed better off than any one in the fortress, except the officers. So you see, I just existed, always making up my mind that some day I should see a good chance of making my escape, but not really making any preparations towards casting off my moorings. Now, Dick, it must be past twelve o'clock, and I am dog-tired. How far have we to ride to-morrow?"

"It is thirty-five miles from Oussoor to Kistnagherry, which will be far enough for us to go to-morrow, and then another five-and-twenty will take us down to Tripataly. As the horses have gone about forty miles, it would be a long journey for them to go right through to-morrow."

"I don't think I could do it, Dick, if they could. I expect

I shall be stiffer to-morrow than I am now. Eager as I am to see your dear mother, I don't want to have to be lifted off my horse when I arrive there, almost speechless with fatigue."

The next day they rode on to Kistnagherry, passing a small frontier fort without question. They slept at the post-house there, Dick and Surajah having removed their scarves and emblems of rank as soon as they passed the frontier, in order to escape all inquiries. They started next morning at day-break, and arrived within sight of Tripataly at ten o'clock.

"Now, father, I will gallop on," Dick said. "I must break the news to mother before you arrive."

"Certainly, Dick," his father, who had scarcely spoken since they started, replied. "I have been feeling very anxious about it all the morning; for though, as you tell me, she has never lost faith in my being alive, my return cannot but be a great shock to her."

Dick rode on, and on arriving at the palace was met in the courtyard by the Rajah, who was on the point of going out on horseback. He dismounted at once.

"I am truly glad to see you back, Dick, for your mother has been in a sad state of anxiety about you. Eight days ago she started up from a nap she was taking in the middle of the day, and burst out crying, saying that she was certain you were in some terrible danger, though whether you were killed or not she could not say. Since then she has been in a bad state; she has scarcely closed an eye, and has spent her whole time in walking restlessly up and down."

"It is quite true that I was in great danger, uncle, and I am sorry indeed that she is in this state, for my coming home will be a shock to her; and she has an even greater one to bear. Surajah and I have rescued my father, and he will be here in a few minutes."

"I congratulate you," the Rajah said warmly. "That is news, indeed—news that I, for one, never expected to hear. It is simply marvellous, Dick. However, I am sure that your mother is not fit to bear it at present. I will go up now, and tell Gholla to break your return gradually to her. I will say nothing about your father to your aunt. As soon as the news that you are here is broken, you must go to your mother. Tell her as little as possible. Pretend that you are hungry, and have a meal sent up, and persuade her to take some nourishment; then declare positively that you won't tell her anything about your adventures until she has had a long sleep. Gholla will prepare a sleeping-draught for her. In the meantime, I will ride off, directly I have seen my wife, to meet Surajah and your father, and bring him on here. I sha'n't tell any one who he is, in case a chance word should come to your mother's ears. If she wakes up again this evening, and asks for you, you must judge for yourself whether to tell her anything or to wait until morning. You might, perhaps, if she seems calm, gladden her with the news that, from what you have heard, you have very strong hopes that a prisoner in keeping at one of the hill-forts is your father. Then to morrow morning you can tell her the whole truth. Now I will run up to Gholla; there is no time to be lost."

"I shall be in the dining-room, uncle, when I am wanted."

A few minutes later Gholla came in hastily.

"Your mother has fainted, Dick. I broke the news to her very gently, but it was too much for her in her weak state. When she comes round again, and is able to talk, I will fetch you; in the meantime, I will send Annie in to you."

Two minutes later the girl ran in with a flushed face, threw herself into Dick's arms, and kissed him.

"I can't help it, Dick," she said, "so it is of no use your scolding me. This is a surprise. Who would have thought of your coming back so soon? But it is lucky you did; your mother has been in a sad way, and she was so sure that you had been in some terrible danger that I have been almost as anxious as she has. And now it seems that I need not have frightened myself at all."

"I was in great danger, Annie. Just at the time my

mother dreamt about me, Surajah, Ibrahim, and I, were attacked by a party of Stranglers, disguised as merchants, and if it had not been that I had some strange suspicion of them, we should all have been murdered. As it was, we shot the whole gang, who, fortunately for us, had no fire-arms."

"It must have been your mother who warned you," Annie said gravely. "She told us that she dreamt you were in some terrible danger, though she could not remember what it was, and she tried with all her might to warn you."

"Perhaps it was that, Annie. I don't know why I suspected them so strongly—Surajah quite laughed at the idea. Anyhow it saved our lives. And how are you getting on, Annie? Are you happy?"

"Oh, so happy!" she exclaimed. "At least, I was until your mother got ill, and I was working very hard at my lessons; but of course that has all been stopped, as far as taking them from her is concerned. But I have gone on working, and the Rajah's sons have been very good and helped me sometimes, and I begin to read words of two letters. And what has brought you back so soon?"

"That I can't tell you yet, Annie. I will only tell you that it is not bad news; and no one but my uncle will know more than that till I have told my mother—even my aunt won't hear it."

"Has Surajah come back too, Dick?"

"Yes; I heard horses in the courtyard just now, and I have no doubt it was him. I rode on first, being anxious to see my mother."

They chatted for a few minutes; then the Rajah came to the door and called Dick into the next room.

"I have settled your father in the room at the other end of the gallery, Dick. He agreed with me that it was better for him to keep there by himself until you have told your mother that he is here. I have just ordered a meal to be sent, and after that will send my barber in to shave him; he says your mother will never recognise him with all that hair on his face.

I am going to see if something cannot be done to take the stain off his face, and shall then set half a dozen tailors to work on some dark blue cloth, to turn him out a suit before to-morrow morning, in what he calls sailor fashion, so that he may appear before your mother in something like the style in which she remembers him."

A few minutes later Gholla came in, and said that Mrs. Holland was ready for Dick to go in to her.

Dick found his mother looking pale and weak; but the joy of his coming had already brightened her eyes and given a faint flush to her cheeks.

"I have been so dreadfully anxious, Dick," she said, after the first embrace. "I was certain you had been in some terrible danger."

"I have been, but thank God I escaped, owing, I think, to the warning Annie says you tried to give me. But we must not talk about that now. I will tell you all the story to-morrow; you are not fit to talk. You must take some broth, and some wine, and a sleeping-draught, and I hope you will go off and not wake up till to-morrow morning. Now, you do as I tell you. While you are drinking your broth I will go in and take something to eat, for I have had nothing to-day, and am as hungry as a hunter; then I will come back and sit by you till you go off to sleep."

He was not long away, but he was met at the door by his aunt, who said,—

"She has gone off already, Dick. I have no doubt that she will sleep many hours, but if she wakes I will let you know at once."

"If that is the case, Gholla," the Rajah, who had come in at the same moment, said, "I can let you into a secret which no one but myself knows yet, but which, now that Margaret is asleep, can be told."

Gholla was very pleased when she heard the news, and Dick went off at once to his father. It was a great relief to the latter to know that his wife had gone off to sleep and would probably be well enough to have the news broken to her in the morning.

"I hear that you are preparing for the meeting, father, by getting yourself shaved, and having a blue cloth suit made?"

"Yes, Dick; I should like to be as much like my old self as possible."

"I don't think mother will care much what you look like, father. Still, it is very natural that you should want to get rid of all that hair."

"What bothers me, lad," Captain Holland went on, putting his hand to the back of his neck, "is this shaved spot here. Of course, with the turban on and the native rig, it was all right, but it will look a rum affair in English clothes."

Dick could not help laughing at his father's look of perplexity.

"Well, father, it is just the same with myself. I have not changed yet, but when I do, the hair above, which is now tucked up under the turban, will be quite long enough to come down to the nape of the neck, and hide that bare place till the hair grows again."

"Yes; I did not think of that. My hair is long enough to come down over my shoulders. I was going to tell the barber to cut it short all over, but I will see now that he allows for that."

"Now, father, do you mind my bringing in Annie Mansfield? I know she will be wanting to keep close to me all day, and I should never be able to get rid of her without telling her about you."

"Bring her in by all means, Dick; she must be a plucky young girl, by what you said about her."

"Where have you been, Dick?" Annie inquired, when Dick went out a few minutes later. "I have been looking for you everywhere; nobody had seen you, unless it was the Rajah. I asked him, and he said that little girls must not ask questions, and then laughed. You have not brought home another white girl?" she exclaimed suddenly.

"Would it not be very nice for you to have a companion, Annie?"

"No," she said sharply; "I should not like it at all."

"Well, I will take you in to see her, and I think you will like her. No; I am only joking," he broke off, as he saw tears start into her eyes; "it is not another girl. But you shall see for yourself."

He took her hand and led her to his father's room.

"There, Annie, this is the gentleman who has come back with me this time."

Annie looked at Captain Holland in surprise, and then turned her eyes to Dick for an explanation.

"He is a respectable-looking old native, isn't he, Annie?"

"Yes, he looks respectable," Annie said gravely; "but he doesn't look very old. Why has he come down with you, Dick? He can't have been a slave."

"But I have, lass," the captain said, in English, to Annie's intense astonishment. "I have been in their hands a year or so longer than you were."

Annie turned impulsively to Dick, and grasped his arm.

"Oh, Dick," she said, in an excited whisper. "Is it—is it your father, after all?"

"Ay, lass," the captain answered for him. "I am the boy's father, and a happy father, too, as you may guess, at finding I have such a son. And I hear he has been a good friend to you, too."

"Oh, he has, he has indeed!" Annie cried, running forward and seizing his hands in both of hers. "I don't think there ever was any one so kind and good."

"What bosh, Annie?" Dick exclaimed, almost crossly.

"Never mind what he says, my dear; you and I know all about it. Now we can do very well without him for a time; he can go and tell his uncle and cousins all about his adventures, which, I have no doubt, they are dying to hear. and you and I can sit here and exchange confidences until my barber comes. I don't look much like an Englishman now, but I hope that they will be able to get me something that will take this stain off my face."

Mrs. Holland did not wake till evening; she seemed very much better, and had a short chat with Dick. She would have got up had he not told her that he should be going to bed himself in a short time, and that all his story would keep very well until the morning, when he hoped to find her quite herself again.

By dint of the application of various unguents and a vast amount of hard scrubbing, Captain Holland restored his face to its original hue.

"I look a bit sunburnt," he said, "but I have often come back browner than this from some of my voyages."

"You look quite like yourself in your portrait at home, father," Dick said. "It is the shaving and cutting your hair, even more than getting off the dye, that has made the difference. I don't think you look much older than you did then, except that there are a few grey hairs."

"I shall look better to-morrow, Dick, when I get these outlandish things off. I have been trying on my new suit, and I think it will do first-rate. Those clothes that you wore on board ship, and handed to them as a model, gave them the idea of what I wanted."

And indeed, the next morning, when Captain Holland appeared in his new suit, Dick declared that he looked jus as if he had walked down from his picture.

The ranee had agreed to break the news to Mrs. Holland as soon as she was dressed; she came into the room where the others were waiting for breakfast, and said to Captain Holland,—

"Come. She knows all, and has borne it well."

She led him to the door of Mrs. Holland's room, and opened it. As he entered there was a cry of,—

"Oh Jack! my Jack!" Then she closed it behind him, and left husband and wife together.

A few days afterwards there was a family consultation.

"Now, Dick," his father said, "we must settle about your plans. You know we have decided upon going home by the next ship, and taking Annie with us, without waiting for her father's letter. Of course I shall have no difficulty in finding out, when I get there, what his address is. I have promised your mother to give up the sea, and settle down again at Shadwell, where I can meet old friends and shall feel at home. We have had a long talk over what you said the other night, about your insisting that we should take the money those jewels of yours fetch. Well, we won't do that."

"Then I will sell them, father," Dick said positively, "and give the money to a hospital!"

"I have not finished yet, Dick. We won't take all the money, but we have agreed that we will take a quarter of it. Of course we could manage on my savings as your mother did when I was away. We shall lose the little allowance the Company made her, but I shall buy a share in a ship with my money, which will bring in a good deal better rate of interest than she got for it in the funds, so we could still manage very well. Still, as we feel that it would please you, we agree to take a quarter of the money the jewels fetch; and that, with what I have, will give us an income well beyond our wants. So that is settled. Now about yourself: I really don't think that you can do better than what you proposed when we were talking of it yesterday. You would be like a fish out of water in England if you had nothing to occupy your time, and therefore can't do better than enter the Service here, and remain at any rate for a few years.

"As your commission was dated from the time you joined Lord Cornwallis, two and a half years ago, you won't be at the bottom of the tree, and while you are serving you will want no money here, and the interest of your capital will be accumulating. If I invest it in shipping for you, you will get eight or ten per cent. for it; and as I shall pick good ships, commanded by men I know, and will divide the money up in small shares, among half a dozen of them, there will be practically no risk—and of course the vessels will be insured. So that, at the end of ten years, by re-investing the profits, your money will be more than doubled, and you will have a nice fortune when you choose to come home, even if the jewels do not fetch anything like what you expect."

A week later the party journeyed down to Madras, where they stayed for a fortnight. Dick, on his arrival, called upon the governor, who congratulated him most heartily when he heard that he had succeeded in finding and releasing his father, and at once appointed him to one of the native cavalry regiments; and his parents had the satisfaction of seeing him in uniform before they started. Annie showed but little interest in the thought of going to England and being restored to her parents, being at the time too much distressed at parting from Dick to give any thought to other matters. But at last the good-byes were all said, and as the anchor was weighed Dick returned on shore in a surf-boat, and next day joined his regiment.

Surajah had wanted to accompany him to Madras, and to enlist in any regiment to which he might be appointed, and the assurance that it might be a long time before he became a native officer, as these were always chosen from the ranks, except in the case of raising new regiments, had little influence with him. The Rajah, however, had finally persuaded him to stay, by the argument that his father, who was now getting on in years, would sorely miss him, that the captain of the troop would also be retiring shortly, and that he should, as a reward for his faithful services to his nephew, appoint him to the command as soon as it was vacant. Ibrahim entered the Rajah's service, preferring that to soldiering.

CHAPTER XXI.

HOME.

It was early in December, 1792, that Dick Holland joined his regiment, which was stationed at Madras. There were but five other officers, and Dick found, to his satisfaction, that the junior of them had had four years' service; consequently, he did not step over any one's head, owing to his commission being dated nearly three years previously. As there were in the garrison many officers who had served on the general staff in the last war, Dick soon found some of his former acquaintances, and the story of his long search for his father, and its successful termination, soon spread, and gained for him a place in civil as well as military society. The next year passed peacefully, and was an unusually quiet time in India. That Tippoo intended to renew the war as soon as he was able was well known to the government, and one of its chief objects of solicitude was the endeavour to counteract the secret negotiations that were constantly going on between him, the Nizam, and the Mahrattis.

Tippoo was known to have sent confidential messengers to all the great princes of India—even to the ruler of Afghanistan—inviting them to join the confederacy of the Mahrattis, the Nizam, and himself, to drive the English out of India altogether. Still greater cause for uneasiness was the alliance that Tippoo had endeavoured to make with the French, who, as he had learned, had gained great successes in Europe; and, believing from their account that their country was much stronger than England, he had sent envoys to the Mauritius to propose an offensive and defensive alliance against England. The envoys had been politely received, and some of them had proceeded to France, where Tippoo's proposal had been accepted. They committed France, indeed, to nothing, as she was already at war with England; but the French were extremely glad to embrace the proposal of Tippoo, as they overrated his power, and believed that he would prove a formidable opponent to the English, and would necessitate the employment of additional troops and ships there, and so weaken England's power at home. To confirm the alliance, some sixty or seventy Frenchmen, mostly adventurers, were sent from the Mauritius as civil and military officers.

Tippoo's council had been strongly opposed to this step on

his part. They had pointed out to him that their alliance with a power at war with the English would render war between the English and him inevitable, and that France was not in a position to aid them in any way. The only benefit, indeed, that he could gain, was the possibility that the fourteen thousand French troops in the service of the Nizam might revolt and come over to him; but even this was doubtful, as these were not troops belonging to the French government, but an independent body, raised and officered by adventurers, who might not be willing to imperil their own position and interests by embarking on a hazardous war at the orders of a far-distant government.

These events happened soon after Dick's return, but nothing was generally known of what was passing, although reports of Tippoo's proceedings had reached the government of India. The party of Frenchmen arrived at Seringapatam and were at first well received by Tippoo; but they had soon disgusted him by their assumption of dictatorial powers; while they, on their part, were disappointed at not receiving the emoluments and salaries they had expected. Most of them very speedily left his service. Some of the military men were employed at Bangalore and other towns in drilling the troops, and a few remained at Seringapatam, neglected by Tippoo, whose eyes were now open to the character of these adventurers. But this in no way shook his belief that he would obtain great aid from France, as he had received letters from official personages there, encouraging him to combine with other native powers, to drive the English out of India, and promising large aid in troops and ships.

When the Earl of Mornington—afterwards the Marquis of Wellesley—arrived at Calcutta as Governor-General of India, in May 1798, the situation had become so critical that although war had not been absolutely declared on either side, Tippoo's open alliance with the French rendered it certain that hostilities must commence ere long, and Lord Mornington lost no time in proceeding to make preparations for war. As

Lord Cornwallis had done, he found the greatest difficulty in inducing the supine government of Madras to take any steps. They protested that were they to make any show of activity, Tippoo would descend the ghauts and at once ravage the whole country, and they declared that they had no force whatever that could withstand him. They continued in their cowardly inactivity until the governor-general was forced to override their authority altogether, and take the matter into his own hands.

The first step was to curb the Nizam's power, for everything pointed to the probability that he intended to join Mysore, being inclined so to do by Tippoo's promises, and by the influence of the officers of the strong body of French troops in his service. Negotiations were therefore opened by Lord Mornington, who offered to guarantee the Nizam's dominions if he would join the English against Tippoo, and promised that after the war he should obtain a large share of the territory taken from Mysore. The Nizam's position was a difficult one. On one side of him lay the dominions of his warlike and powerful neighbour Tippoo; on the other he was exposed to the incursions of the Mahrattis, whose rising power was a constant threat to his safety. He had, moreover, to cope with a serious rebellion by his son Ali Jah.

He was willing enough to obtain the guarantee of the English against aggressions by the Mahrattis, but he hesitated in complying with the preliminary demand that he should dispense with the French. The fighting powers of this body rendered them valuable auxiliaries, but he secretly feared them, and resented their pretensions, which pointed to the fact that ere long, instead of being his servants, they might become his masters. When, therefore, the British government offered him a subsidiary force of six battalions, and to guarantee him against any further aggression by the Mahrattis, he accepted the proposal, but in a half-hearted way, that showed he could not be relied upon for any efficient assistance in disarming his French auxiliaries.

No time was lost by the government in marching the promised force to Hyderabad. The French, 14,000 strong, refused to disband, and were joined by the Nizam's household force, which was in the French interest. The Nizam, terrified at the prospect of a contest the success of which was doubtful, abandoned the capital and took refuge in a fortress, there to await the issue of events, but positively refused to issue orders to the French to disband. Two of the English battalions, which were on the other side of the river to that on which the French were encamped, opened a destructive fire upon them, and with red-hot shot set fire to their magazines and storehouses, while the other four battalions moved into position to make a direct attack.

The Nizam now saw that he had no alternative but to declare openly for the French or to dismiss them. He preferred the latter alternative. Peron, who commanded the French, saw that unless he surrendered, the position of his force was desperate. Accordingly, on receipt of the order, he and his officers expressed their readiness to accept their dismissal. Their men were, however, in a state of mutiny, and the officers were compelled to make their escape from the camp under cover of night. The next morning the camp was surrounded by the English and the troops of the Nizam, and the French then surrendered without a shot being fired.

While the Nizam was thus rendered powerless, negotiations had been going on with the Mahrattis; but owing to the quarrels and jealousies of their chiefs, nothing could be done with them. It was, however, apparent that for the same reason Tippoo would equally fail in his attempt to obtain their alliance against us, and that therefore it was with Mysore alone that we should have to deal. In the meantime, though preparing for war, Lord Mornington was most anxious to avoid it. When Tippoo wrote to complain that some villages of his had been occupied by people from Coorg, the governor-general ordered their immediate restoration to him. In November he sent the Sultan a friendly letter, pointing out that he could look for no efficient aid from France, and that any auxiliaries who might possibly join him would only introduce the principles of anarchy and the hatred of all religion that animated the whole French nation; that his alliance with them was really equivalent to a declaration of war against England; and as he was unwilling to believe that Tippoo was actuated by unfriendly feelings, or desired to break the engagements of the treaty entered into with him, he offered to send an officer to Mysore to discuss any points upon which variance might have arisen, and to arrange a scheme that would be satisfactory to them both.

To this letter no answer was received for five weeks, by which time Lord Mornington had arrived at Madras. He then received a letter containing a tissue of the most palpable lies concerning Tippoo's dealings with the French.

Two or three more letters passed, but as Tippoo's answers were all vague and evasive, the governor-general issued a manifesto, on the 22nd of February, 1799, recapitulating all the grievances against Mysore, and declaring that though the allies were prepared to repel any attack, they were equally anxious to effect an arrangement with him. But Tippoo still believed that a large French army would speedily arrive. He had received letters from Buonaparte in person, written from Egypt, and saying that he had arrived on the borders of the Red Sea, "with an innumerable and invincible army, full of the desire to deliver you from the iron yoke of England." Tippoo well knew also that although the governor-general spoke for himself and his allies, the Nizam was powerless to render any assistance to the English, and that the Mahrattis were far more likely to join him than they were to assist his foes.

The manifesto of Lord Mornington was speedily followed by action, for at the end of January an army of nearly 37,000 men had been assembled at Vellore. Of these some 20,000 were the Madras force; with them were the Nizam's army, nominally commanded by Meer Alum, but really by

Colonel Wellesley—afterwards Duke of Wellington—who had with him his own regiment, the 33rd; 6,500 men under Colonel Dalrymple; 3,621 infantry, for the most part French troops who had re-enlisted under us; and 6000 regular and irregular horse.

Dick, who had now attained the rank of captain, had been introduced by one of Lord Cornwallis's old staff-officers to General Harris, who, as general of the Madras army, was in command of the whole. On hearing of the services Dick had rendered in the last war, and that his perfect acquaintance with the language, and with the ground over which the army would pass, would enable him to be equally efficient on the present occasion, General Harris at once detached him from service with the regiment, and appointed him to a post on his own staff.

Had it not been that Dick had seen for the last two years that hostilities must ere long be commenced with Tippoo, he would, before this, have left the army and returned home. He was heartily tired of the long inaction. When the regiment was stationed at Madras, life was very pleasant; but a considerable portion of his time was spent at out-stations, where the duties were very light, and there was nothing to break the monotony of camp life. He received letters regularly from his mother, who gave him full details of their home life. The first that he received merely announced their safe arrival in England. The second was longer and more interesting; they had had no difficulty in discovering the address of Annie's father, and on writing to him he had immediately come up to town. He had lost his wife on his voyage home from India, and was overjoyed at the discovery of his daughter, and at her return to England.

"He is," Dick's mother wrote, "very much broken in health. Annie behaved very nicely. Poor child, it was only natural that after what you did for her, and our being all that time with her, the thought of leaving us for her parent, of whom she had no recollection, was a great grief. However, I talked it over with her many times, and pointed out to her that her first duty was to the father who had been so many years deprived of her, and that, although there was no reason why she should not manifest affection for us, she must not allow him to think for a moment that she was not as pleased to see him as he was to welcome her. She behaved beautifully when her father arrived, and when he had been in the house five minutes, and spoke of the death of his wife, his bitter regret that she had not lived to see Annie restored to them, the loneliness of his life and how it would be brightened now that she was again with him, his words so touched her that she threw herself into his arms and sobbed out that she would do all she could to make his life happy. He had, of course, received the letter we had written to him from Tripataly, and quite pained me by the gratitude he showed for what he called my kindness to his daughter.

"He said that by this post he should write to endeavour to express some of his feelings to you. Annie went away with him the next day to a place he has bought near Plymouth. He has promised to let us have her for a month every year, and we have promised to go down for the same time every summer to stay with her. He asks numberless questions about you, which neither I nor Annie are ever tired of answering. Even with a mother's natural partiality, I must own that her descriptions are almost too flattering, and he must think that you are one of the most admirable of men. Next as to the jewels. Your father took them to be valued by several diamond merchants, and accepted the highest offer, which was £16,000, of which he has already invested twelve in your name in shares in six ships. Four of these are Indiamen; the other two are privateers. He said that he did not think you would object to a quarter of the money being put into a speculative venture, and that they were both good craft, well armed and well commanded, with strong crews, and would, if successful, earn as much in a year as a merchantman would in ten."

Since then the letters had been of a uniform character. The

shares in the Indiamen were giving a good and steady return. The privateers had been very fortunate, and had captured some rich prizes. Annie had been up, or they had been down at Plymouth. The letters during the last three years had reported her as having grown into a young woman, and, as his mother declared, a very pretty one. After that the allusions to her were less frequent, but it was mentioned that she was as fond of them as ever, and that she was still unmarried.

"She always asks when you are coming home, Dick," Mrs. Holland said, in the last letter he had received before accompanying General Harris to Vellore. "I told her, of course, that your last letter said that war was certain with Tippoo, that you hoped this time to see Seringapatam taken and the tyrant's power broken, and that after it was over you would come home on leave and perhaps would not go out again."

During the six years that he had been in the army, Dick had very frequently been at Tripataly, as there was little difficulty in getting leave for a fortnight. His cousins had now grown up into young men; Surajah commanded the troop; and his stays there were always extremely pleasant. The troop now numbered two hundred, for with quiet times the population of the territory had largely increased, and the Rajah's income grown in proportion. The troop was now dressed in uniform, and in arms and discipline resembled the irregular cavalry in the Company's service, and when Dick arrived at Vellore he found his uncle and cousins there with their cavalry.

"I thought, Dick, of only sending the boys," the Rajah said, "but when the time came for them to start, I felt that I must go myself. We have suffered enough at the hands of Mysore, and I do hope to see Tippoo's capital taken, and his power of mischief put an end to for good and all."

"I am glad indeed that you are coming, uncle. You may be sure that whenever I can get away from my duties with the general, I shall spend most of my time in your camp, though I must occasionally drop in on my own regiment."

The Rajah had already been down to Madras a month before, and with his sons had been introduced to General Harris, by the latter's chief of the staff, as having been always, like his father before him, a faithful ally of the English, and as having accompanied Lord Cornwallis on the occasion of the last campaign in Mysore. The general had thanked him heartily for his offer to place his two hundred cavalry at the disposal of the government, and had expressed a hope that he, as well as his sons, would accompany it in the field.

On the 11th of February, 1799, the army moved from Vellore, but instead of ascending by the pass of Amboor, as had been expected, it moved south-west, ascended the pass of Paliode, and on the 9th of March was established, without opposition, in Tippoo's territory, at a distance of eighty miles east of his capital. They then marched north until they reached a village ten miles south of Bangalore. This route, although circuitous, was chosen, as the roads were better, the country more level, and cultivation much more general, affording far greater facilities for the collection of forage for the baggage animals. Hitherto nothing had been seen of the Mysorean army. It had been confidently expected that Tippoo would fight at least one great battle to oppose their advance against his capital, but so far no signs had been seen of an enemy, and even the Mysore horse, which had played so conspicuous a part in the last campaign, in no way interfered with the advance of the army, or even with the foraging parties.

A despatch that reached them by a circuitous route explained why Tippoo had suffered them to advance so far unmolested. While the Madras army had advanced from the south-east, a Bombay force, 6,500 strong, was ascending the Western Ghauts. As the advance brigade, consisting of three native battalions, under Colonel Montresor, reached Sedaseer, Tippoo, with 12,000 of his best troops, fell upon it suddenly. His force had moved through the jungle, and attacked the brigade in front and rear. Although thus surprised by an enemy nearly six times their superior in force, the Sepoys behaved with a calmness and bravery that could not have been surpassed by veteran troops. Maintaining a steady front, they repulsed every attack, until a brigade, encamped eight miles in their rear, came up to their assistance; and Tippoo was then forced to retreat, having suffered a loss of 1,500 men, including many of his best officers. This proof of the inferiority of his troops, even when enormously outnumbering the English and fighting with all the advantages of surprise, profoundly impressed Tippoo, and from this time he appeared to regard the struggle as hopeless, and displayed no signs whatever of the dash and energy that had distinguished him when leading one of the divisions of his father's army.

He marched with his troops straight to Seringapatam, and then moved out with his whole force to give battle to the main body of the invaders. The antagonists came within sight of each other at the village of Malavilly, thirty miles east of the capital. For some time an artillery fire on both sides was kept up. Gradually the infantry became engaged, and the Mysoreans showed both courage and steadiness until a column of two thousand men moved forward to attack the 33rd Regiment. The British troops reserved their fire until the column was within fifty yards of them; then they poured in a withering volley and charged. The column fell back in disorder. General Floyd at once charged them with five regiments of cavalry, sabred great numbers of them, and drove the remainder back in headlong rout. The whole British line then advanced, cheering loudly. The first line of Tippoo's army fell back upon its second, and the whole then marched away at a speed that soon left the British infantry far behind them.

Instead of continuing his march straight upon the capital, General Harris, learning from spies that Tippoo had wasted the whole country along that line, moved south-west, collecting as he went great quantities of cattle, sheep, and goats, and an abundance of grain and forage, crossed the Cauvery at a ford at Sosilay, and on the 5th of April took up his position at a distance of two miles from the western face of the fort of Seringapatam. This movement completely disconcerted Tippoo. He had imagined that the attack would, as on the previous occasion, take place on the northern side of the river, and had covered the approaches there with a series of additional fortifications, while on the other side he had done but little. So despondent was he that he called together his principal officers, and said to them, "We have arrived at our last stage. What is your determination?"

His advisers took no brighter view of the prospect than he did himself. They had unanimously opposed the war, had warned Tippoo against trusting to the French, and had been adverse to measures that could but result in a fresh trial of strength with the English. The Sultan, however, while not attempting to combat their opinion, had gone on his own way, and his officers now saw their worst fears justified. They replied to his question, "Our determination is to die with you."

On the day after arriving before Seringapatam, the British attacked the villages and rocky eminences held by the enemy on the south side of the river, and drove them back under the shelter of their guns. General Floyd was sent with the cavalry to meet the Bombay force and escort it to Seringapatam. This was accomplished, and although the whole of the Mysore cavalry and a strong force of infantry hovered round the column, they did not venture to engage it, and on the 14th the whole arrived at the camp before Seringapatam.

The Bombay force, which was commanded by General Stuart, crossed to the north bank of the river, and took up a position there which enabled them to take in flank the outlying works and trenches with which Tippoo had hoped to prevent any attack upon the western angle of the fort, where the river was so shallow that it could be easily forded.

Tippoo now endeavoured to negotiate, and asked for a conference. General Harris returned an answer, enclosing the draft of a preliminary treaty with which he had been supplied before starting. It demanded one-half of Tippoo's territories, a payment of two millions sterling, and the delivery of four of his sons as hostages. Tippoo returned no reply, and on the 22nd the garrison made a vigorous sortie, and were only repulsed after several hours' fighting.

For the next five days the batteries of the besiegers kept up a heavy fire, silenced every gun in the outlying works, and compelled their defenders to retire across the river into the fort. Tippoo now sank into such a state of despondency that he would listen to none of the proposals of his officers for strengthening the position, and would not even agree to the construction of a retrenchment, which would cut off the western angle of the fort, against which it was evident that the attack would be directed.

He knew that if captured there was little chance of his being permitted to continue to reign, and had, indeed, made that prospect more hopeless by massacring all the English prisoners who had, by his order, been brought in from the hill-forts throughout the country on his return to Seringapatam, after the repulse he had suffered in his attack on the Bombay force. On the 2nd of May the batteries opened on the wall of the fort near its north-west angle, and so heavy was their fire that by the evening of the 3rd a breach of sixty yards long was effected. General Harris determined to assault on the following day. General Baird, who had for four years been a prisoner in Seringapatam, volunteered to lead the assault, and before daybreak 4,376 men took their places in the advance trenches, where they lay down. It was determined that the assault should not be made until one o'clock, at which time Tippoo's troops, anticipating no attack, would be taking their food, and resting during the heat of the day. The troops who were to make the assault were divided into two columns which, after mounting the breach, were to turn right and left, fighting their way along the ramparts until they met at the other end. A powerful reserve under Colonel Wellesley was to support them after they had entered.

When the signal was given the troops leapt from the

trenches, and, covered by the fire of the artillery which at the same moment opened on the ramparts, dashed across the river, scaled the breach, and, in six minutes from the firing of the signal gun, planted the British flag on its crest. Then the heads of the two columns at once started to fight their way along the ramparts. At first the resistance was slight; surprised and panic-stricken, the defenders of the strong works at this point offered but a feeble resistance. Some fled along the walls; some ran down into the fort; many threw themselves over the wall into the rocky bed of the river. The right column in less than an hour had won its way along the rampart to the eastern face of the fort, but the left column met with a desperate resistance, for as each point was carried, the enemy, constantly reinforced, made a fresh stand. Most of the officers who led the column were shot down, and so heavy was the fire that several times the advance was brought to a standstill. It was not until the right column, making their way along the wall to the assistance of their comrades, took them in the rear, that the Mysoreans entirely lost heart.

Taken between two fires they speedily became a disorganised mass. Many hundreds were shot down, either in the fort or as, pouring out through the river gate, they endeavoured to cross the ford and escape to the north. As soon as the whole rampart was captured, General Baird sent an officer with a flag of truce to the Palace, to offer protection to Tippoo and all its inmates, on condition of immediate surrender. Two of Tippoo's younger sons assured the officer that the Sultan was not in the Palace. The assurance was disbelieved, and, the princes being sent to the camp under a strong escort, the Palace was searched. The officer in command, on being strictly questioned, declared that Tippoo, who had in person commanded the defence made against the left column, had been wounded, and that he had heard he was lying in a gateway on the north side of the fort. A search was immediately made, and the information proved correct. Tippoo was found lying there, not only wounded, but dead. He had indeed received several wounds, and was endeavouring to escape in his palanquin, when this had been upset by the rush of fugitives striving to make their way through the gate.

The gateway was, indeed, almost choked up with the bodies of those who had been either suffocated in the crush or killed by their pursuers. On his palanquin being overturned, Tippoo had evidently risen to his feet, and had at the same moment been shot through the head by an English soldier, ignorant of his rank. In the evening he was buried with much state by the side of his father, in the mausoleum of Lal Bang, at the eastern extremity of the island. It was with great difficulty that, when the British soldiers became aware of the massacre of their countrymen a few days before, they were restrained from taking vengeance upon his sons and the inmates of the Palace. In the assault 8000 of the defenders were killed, while the loss of the British during the siege and in the assault amounted to 825 Europeans and 639 native troops. An enormous quantity of cannon, arms, and ammunition was captured, and the value of the treasure and jewels amounted to considerably over a million pounds, besides the doubtless large amount of jewels that had, in the first confusion, fallen into the hands of the soldiers.

As Dick, after the fighting had ceased, went, by order of the general, to examine the prisoners and ascertain their rank, his eye fell upon an old officer whose arm hung useless by his side, broken by a musket-ball. He went up to him and held out his hand. "Mirzah Mahomed Buckshy!" he exclaimed, "I am glad to meet you again, although sorry to see that you are wounded."

The officer looked at him in surprise. "You have spoken my name," he said, "but I do not know that we have ever met before."

"We have met twice. The first time I was, with a friend, dressed as one of Tippoo's officers, and came to examine the state of Savandroog; the second time we were dressed as merchants, and I succeeded in effecting the liberation of my father. Both times I received much kindness at your hands. But far more grateful am I to you for your goodness to my father, whose life you preserved. I see you still carry the pistols I left for you, and doubtless you also received the letter I placed with them."

"Thanks be to Allah," the old colonel said, "that we have thus met again! Truly I rejoiced, when my first anger that I had been fooled passed away, that your father had escaped, and that without my being able to blame myself for carelessness. Your letter to me completed my satisfaction, for I felt that Heaven had rightly rewarded the efforts of a son who had done so much and risked his life for a father. Is he alive? Is he here? I should be glad to see him again; and indeed, I missed him sorely. I have been here for two years, having been appointe to a command among the troops here."

"My father is well, and is in England. He will, I know, be glad indeed to hear that I have met you, for he will ever retain a grateful remembrance of your kindness. Now I must finish my work here and will then go to the general and beg him to give me an order for your release."

An hour later Dick returned with the order, and carried Mahomed Buckshy off to the Rajah's camp. Here his arm was set by one of the surgeons, and he was so well cared for by the Rajah, Dick, and Surajah, that a fortnight later he was convalescent, and was able to join his wife in the town. "I am thankful," he said, on leaving, "that my life as a soldier is over, and that I shall never more have to fight against the English. Tippoo was my master, but it is he who, by his cruelty and ambition, has brought ruin upon Mysore. I have saved enough to live in comfort for the rest of my life, and to its end I shall rejoice that I have again met the son of my friend Jack."

The capture of Seringapatam was followed at once by the entire submission of the whole country. A descendant of the old Rajah of Mysore was placed upon the throne. His rule was, however, but a nominal one. A very large amount of territory was annexed; the island of Seringapatam was permanently occupied as a British possession; the new rajah was bound to receive and pay a large military force for the defence of his territories, not to admit any European foreigners into his dominions, to allow the Company to garrison any fort in Mysore that might seem advisable to them, and to pay at all times attention to such advice as might be given him as to the administration of his affairs. He was, in fact, to be but a puppet, the British becoming the absolute rulers of Mysore. The family of Tippoo, and the ladies of the harem, were removed to Vellore, where they were to receive a palace suitable to their former rank and expectations, and allowances amounting to £160,000 a year.

Thus Mysore, one of the most ancient and powerful of the kingdoms of India, fell into the hands of the English, owing to the ambition, bigotry, and besotted cruelty of the son of a usurper.

Dick's part in all these operations had been a busy, although not a very dangerous one. The only share he had taken in the active fighting had been in the battle at Malavilly, where having been sent with a message to Colonel Floyd, just before he led the cavalry to the assault of the column that had attacked the 33rd, he took his place by the side of the Rajah and his cousins, whose troop formed part of Floyd's command, and joined in the charge on the enemy. He had, however, rendered great services in the quartermasters' department, was very highly spoken of in the despatches of General Harris, and his name appeared, as promoted to the rank of major, in the list of honours promulgated by Lord Mornington at the termination of the campaign.

His regiment was among those selected for the occupation of Mysore, and, a month after the capture of the city, he obtained leave to return to England. He stayed for a week at Tripataly, and then took an affectionate farewell of his uncle, the ranee, his cousins, and Surajah, and sailed from Madras a fortnight later.

M84

A HEARTY WELCOME AWAITS DICK ON HIS RETURN.

The ship in which he was a passenger was accompanied by two other Indiamen, and when a fortnight out they encountered a French frigate, which, however, they beat off, and arrived in England without further adventure.

As soon as he landed, Dick drove to the house where his father and mother had taken up their residence on their arrival in England; but he found to his surprise that, eight months before, they had moved to another, in the village of Hackney. He proceeded there, and found it to be a considerably larger one than that they had left, and standing in its own grounds, which were of some extent.

He had written to them after the fall of Seringapatam, and told them that he should probably sail for England about six weeks later.

As the vehicle drove to the door, his father and mother ran out. His father grasped his hand, and his mother threw her arms round his neck with tears of joy.

As soon as the first greeting was over, Dick saw a young lady in deep mourning standing on the steps. He looked at her for a moment in surprise, and then exclaimed,—

"It is Annie Mansfield!"

Annie held out her hand and laughed.

"We are both changed almost beyond recognition, Dick." Then she added demurely, "The last time, I had to ask you——"

"You sha'n't have to ask me again, Annie," he said, giving her a hearty kiss. "My first impulse was to do it, but I did not know whether your sentiments on the subject had changed."

"I am not given to change," she said. "Am I, Mrs. Holland?"

"I don't think you are, my dear. I think there is a little spice of obstinacy in your composition. But come in, Dick; don't let us stand talking here at the door when we have so much to say to each other."

He went into the sitting-room with his father and mother, where Annie presently left them to themselves.

"Why, father, the privateers must have done well indeed!" Dick said, looking round the handsome room.

"I have nothing to grumble at on that score, Dick, though they have not been so lucky the last two years. But it is not their profits that induced us to move here. You saw Annie was in mourning. Her father died nearly a year ago, and at her earnest request, as he said in his will, appointed us her guardians until she came of age, which will be in a few months now. As he had no near relations, he left the whole of his property to her, and having been in India in the days when, under Warren Hastings, there were good pickings to be obtained, it amounted to a handsome fortune. She said that she should come and live with us, at any rate until she became of age; and as that house of ours, though a comfortable place, was hardly the sort of house for an heiress, she herself proposed that we should take a larger house between us. And so here we are. We shall stay here through the winter, and then we are going down to her place at Plymouth for the summer. What we shall do afterwards, is not settled. That must depend upon a variety of things."

"She has grown much prettier than I ever thought she would do," Dick said. "Of course I knew she would have grown into a woman, but somehow I never realised it until I saw her, and I believe I have always thought of her as being still the girl I carried off from Seringapatam."

In a few minutes Annie joined them, and the talk then turned upon India, and many questions were asked as to their friends at Tripataly.

"I suppose by this time, Annie—at least, I hope I may still call you Annie?"

"If you call me anything else, I shall not answer," she said indignantly.

"Well, I was going to say, I suppose you have got a good deal beyond words of two letters now?"

"I regard the question as an impertinent one. I have even mastered geography, the meaning of which word you may remember you explained to me, and I have a partial knowledge of history."

The next day Dick met an old friend, Ben Birket. Dick had kept his promise and had written to him as soon as he returned to Tripataly with his father, and a few weeks after Captain Holland's return, his old shipmate came to see him and his wife. Ben had for some time thought of retiring, and he now left the sea and settled down in a little cottage near. Captain Holland insisted upon settling a small pension upon him, and he was always a welcome guest at the house. His delight at Dick's return was extreme.

"I never thought you would do it, Master Dick, never for a moment, and when on coming home I got your letter, and found that the Captain and your mother were in England, it just knocked me foolish for a bit."

Three weeks later, Dick told Annie that he loved her. He spoke without any circumlocution, merely taking her hand one evening, when they happened to be alone together, and telling her so in plain words. "I know nothing of women, Annie," he said, "or their ways. I have been bothering myself how to set about it, but though I don't know how to put it, I do know that I love you dearly. All these years I have been thinking about you—not like this, you know, but as the dear, plucky little girl of the old days."

"The little girl of old days, Dick," she said quietly, "is in no way changed. I think you know what I thought of you then; I have never for a moment wavered. I gave you all the love of my heart, and you have had it ever since. Why, you silly boy," she said, with a laugh, a few minutes later, "I had begun to think, that, just as I had to ask you for a kiss in the old times, and again when you met me, I should have to take this matter in hand. Why, I never thought of anything else. Directly I got old enough to look upon myself as a woman, and young men began to come to the house, I said to my dear father,—

"'It is of no use their coming here, father. My mind has been made up for years, and I shall never change.'

"He knew at once what I meant.

"'I don't blame you, my dear,' he said. 'Of course you are young at present but, he has won you fairly, and if he is at all like what you make him out to be, I could not leave you in better hands. He will be home in another three or four years, and I shall have the comfort of having you with me until then. But you must not make too sure of it. He may fall in love out there; you know that there is plenty of society at Madras.'

"I laughed at the idea.

"'All the pretty ones either come out to be married, or get engaged on the voyage or before they have been there a fortnight. I have no fear, father, of his falling in love out there, though I don't say he might not when he gets home, for of course he thinks of me only as a little girl.'

"'Well, my dear,' he said, 'we will get him and his father and mother to come down as soon as he gets home. As you have made up your mind about it, it is only right that you should have the first chance.'

"It was not to be as he planned, Dick, but you see I have had the first chance, and it is well it was so, for no one can say how matters would have turned out if I had not been on the spot. Do you know, Dick, I felt that when you rescued me from slavery, you became somehow straightway my lord and master. As you carried me that night before you, I said to myself I should always be your little slave; and you see it has come quite true."

"I don't know about that, Annie. We are in England now, and there are no slaves; you will be the mistress now, and I your devoted servant."

"It will be as I say, Dick," she said tenderly. "I feel that to the end of my life I shall remain your willing slave."

There was nothing to prevent an early marriage. It was settled that Captain and Mrs. Holland should retain the house, which indeed they could well afford to do, and that Dick and Annie should reside there whenever they were in town, but that, as a rule, they would live at the estate her father had purchased, near Plymouth. Their means were ample, for during the eight years he was in the Service Dick's £12,000, had, as his father had predicted, doubled itself, and Annie's fortune was at least as large as his own. Dick had good reason to bless to the end of his life his mother's plan, that had resulted in the double satisfaction of restoring his father to her, and in winning for himself the woman whom he ever regarded as the dearest and best wife in the world.

THE END.

BLACKIE & SON'S
BOOKS FOR YOUNG PEOPLE.

BY G. A. HENTY.

The Tiger of Mysore: A Story of the War with Tippoo Saib. By G. A. HENTY. With 12 Illustrations by W. H. MARGETSON, and a Map. Crown 8vo, cloth elegant, olivine edges, 6s.

Dick Holland's father is supposed to be one of the English captives in the hands of that bloodthirsty tyrant, Tippoo Saib, who is known in history as "The Tiger of Mysore". So Dick, who is a spirited lad, resolves to proceed to India, gain tidings of his father, and help him to escape, if possible. Accordingly he sails for Madras, joins the army under Lord Cornwallis, and takes part in a campaign against Tippoo. Afterwards, he assumes a disguise; enters Seringapatam, the capital of Mysore; rescues Tippoo's harem from a tiger; and is appointed to high office by the tyrant. In this capacity Dick visits the hill fortresses, still in search of his father, and at last he discovers him in the great stronghold of Savandroog. The hazardous rescue which Dick attempts, and the perilous night ride through the enemy's country are at length accomplished, and the young fellow's dangerous mission is done. And the end comes all too soon—so clever, and plucky, and daring are the devices and adventures of gallant Dick Holland.

A Knight of the White Cross: A Tale of the Siege of Rhodes. By G. A. HENTY. With 12 full-page Illustrations by RALPH PEACOCK. Crown 8vo, cloth elegant, olivine edges, 6s.

Gervaise Tresham, the hero of this story, is determined to follow a military career, and from his father's friendship to the Grand Prior of the Knights of St. John, he is enabled to join that famous Order. Leaving England he proceeds to the island stronghold of Rhodes, and becomes a page in the household of the Grand Master. Subsequently, Gervaise is made a Knight of the White Cross for valour in a sea-fight with pirates, while soon afterwards he is appointed commander of a war-galley, and in his first voyage destroys a fleet of Moorish corsairs. During one of his cruises the young knight is attacked on shore, captured after a desperate struggle, and sold into slavery in Tripoli. He succeeds in escaping, however, and returns to Rhodes in time to take part in the splendid defence of that fortress when it was besieged by all the might of the Turks. Altogether a fine chivalrous tale, of varied interest, and full of noble daring.

BY G. A. HENTY.

"Mr. Henty is one of the best of story-tellers for young people."—*Spectator.*

When London Burned: A Story of Restoration Times and the Great Fire. By G. A. HENTY. With 12 page Illustrations by J. FINNEMORE. Crown 8vo, cloth elegant, olivine edges, 6*s.*

"One of the best stories Mr. Henty has written."—*The Times.*

"No boy needs to have any story of Henty's recommended to him, and parents who do not know and buy him for their boys should be ashamed of themselves. Those to whom he is yet unknown could not make a better beginning than with *When London Burned.*"—*British Weekly.*

Beric the Briton: A Story of the Roman Invasion. By G. A. HENTY. With 12 page Illustrations by W. PARKINSON. Crown 8vo, cloth elegant, olivine edges, 6*s.*

"We are not aware that any one has given us quite so vigorous a picture of Britain in the days of the Roman conquest. Mr. Henty has done his utmost to make an impressive picture of the haughty Roman character, with its indomitable courage, sternness, and discipline. *Beric* is good all through."—*Spectator.*

Through the Sikh War: A Tale of the Conquest of the Punjaub. By G. A. HENTY. With 12 page Illustrations by HAL HURST, and a Map. Crown 8vo, cloth elegant, olivine edges, 6*s.*

"The picture of the Punjaub during its last few years of independence, the description of the battles on the Sutlej, and the portraiture generally of native character, seem admirably true. . . . On the whole, we have never read a more vivid and faithful narrative of military adventure in India."—*The Academy.*

With Lee in Virginia: A Story of the American Civil War. By G. A. HENTY. With 10 page Illustrations by GORDON BROWNE, and 6 Maps. Crown 8vo, cloth elegant, olivine edges, 6*s.*

"The story is a capital one and full of variety, and presents us with many picturesque scenes of Southern life. Young Wingfield, who is conscientious, spirited, and 'hard as nails', would have been a man after the very heart of Stonewall Jackson."—*Times.*

With Wolfe in Canada: Or, The Winning of a Continent. By G. A. HENTY. With 12 page Illustrations by GORDON BROWNE. Crown 8vo, cloth elegant, olivine edges, 6*s.*

"A model of what a boys' story-book should be. Mr. Henty has a great power of infusing into the dead facts of history new life, and as no pains are spared by him to ensure accuracy in historic details, his books supply useful aids to study as well as amusement."—*School Guardian.*

The Dash for Khartoum: A Tale of the Nile Expedition. By G. A. HENTY. With 10 page Illustrations by J. SCHÖNBERG and J. NASH, and 4 Plans. Crown 8vo, cloth elegant, olivine edges, 6*s.*

"It is literally true that the narrative never flags a moment; for the incidents which fall to be recorded after the dash for Khartoum has been made and failed are quite as interesting as those which precede it."—*Academy.*

BY G. A. HENTY.

"Surely Mr. Henty should understand boys' tastes better than any man living."
—*The Times.*

Reduced Illustration from "Wulf the Saxon".

Wulf the Saxon: A Story of the Norman Conquest. By G. A. Henty. With 12 page Illustrations by Ralph Peacock. Crown 8vo, cloth elegant, olivine edges, 6*s*.

"The story shows Mr. Henty at his best." —*Daily Chronicle.*

"*Wulf the Saxon* is second to none of Mr. Henty's historical tales, and we may safely say that a boy may learn from it more genuine history than he will from many a tedious tome. The points of the Saxon character are hit off very happily, and the life of the period is ably reconstructed."—*The Spectator.*

By Pike and Dyke: A Tale of the Rise of the Dutch Republic. By G. A. Henty. With 10 page Illustrations by Maynard Brown, and 4 Maps. Crown 8vo, cloth elegant, olivine edges, 6*s*.

"The mission of Ned to deliver letters from William the Silent to his adherents at Brussels, the fight of the *Good Venture* with the Spanish man-of-war, the battle on the ice at Amsterdam, the siege of Haarlem, are all told with a vividness and skill which are worthy of Mr. Henty at his best."—*Academy.*

BY G. A. HENTY.

"Among writers of stories of adventure for boys Mr. Henty stands in the very first rank."—*Academy.*

The Lion of St. Mark: A Tale of Venice in the Fourteenth Century. By G. A. HENTY. With 10 page Illustrations by GORDON BROWNE. Crown 8vo, cloth elegant, olivine edges, 6*s.*

"Every boy should read *The Lion of St. Mark*. Mr. Henty has never produced any story more delightful, more wholesome, or more vivacious. From first to last it will be read with keen enjoyment."—*The Saturday Review.*

By England's Aid: The Freeing of the Netherlands (1585-1604). By G. A. HENTY. With 10 page Illustrations by ALFRED PEARSE, and 4 Maps. Crown 8vo, cloth elegant, olivine edges, 6*s.*

"The story is told with great animation, and the historical material is most effectively combined with a most excellent plot."—*Saturday Review.*

Under Drake's Flag: A Tale of the Spanish Main. By G. A. HENTY. Illustrated by 12 page Pictures by GORDON BROWNE. Crown 8vo, cloth elegant, olivine edges, 6*s.*

"There is not a dull chapter, nor, indeed, a dull page in the book; but the author has so carefully worked up his subject that the exciting deeds of his heroes are never incongruous or absurd."—*Observer.*

Bonnie Prince Charlie: A Tale of Fontenoy and Culloden. By G. A. HENTY. With 12 page Illustrations by GORDON BROWNE. Crown 8vo, cloth elegant, olivine edges, 6*s.*

"Ronald, the hero, is very like the hero of *Quentin Durward*. The lad's journey across France with his faithful attendant Malcolm, and his hairbreadth escapes from the machinations of his father's enemies make up as good a narrative of the kind as we have ever read. For freshness of treatment and variety of incident, Mr. Henty has here surpassed himself."—*Spectator.*

"A historical romance of the best quality. Mr. Henty has written many more sensational stories, but never a more artistic one."—*Academy.*

For the Temple: A Tale of the Fall of Jerusalem. By G. A. HENTY. With 10 page Illustrations by S. J. SOLOMON, and a Coloured Map. Crown 8vo, cloth elegant, olivine edges, 6*s.*

"Mr. Henty's graphic prose pictures of the hopeless Jewish resistance to Roman sway adds another leaf to his record of the famous wars of the world. The book is one of Mr. Henty's cleverest efforts."—*Graphic.*

True to the Old Flag: A Tale of the American War of Independence. By G. A. HENTY. With 12 page Illustrations by GORDON BROWNE. Crown 8vo, cloth elegant, olivine edges, 6*s.*

"Does justice to the pluck and determination of the British soldiers. The son of an American loyalist, who remains true to our flag, falls among the hostile redskins in that very Huron country which has been endeared to us by the exploits of Hawkeye and Chingachgook."—*The Times.*

BY G. A. HENTY.

"Mr. Henty is the king of story-tellers for boys."—*Sword and Trowel.*

Reduced Illustration from "St. Bartholomew's Eve".

St. Bartholomew's Eve: A Tale of the Huguenot Wars. By G. A. HENTY. With 12 page Illustrations by H. J. DRAPER, and a Map. Crown 8vo, cloth elegant, olivine edges, 6s.

"A really noble story, which adult readers will find to the full as satisfying as the boys. Lucky boys! to have such a caterer as Mr. G. A. Henty."—*Black and White.*

With Clive in India: Or, The Beginnings of an Empire. By G. A. HENTY. With 12 page Illustrations by GORDON BROWNE. Crown 8vo, cloth elegant, olivine edges, 6s.

"Among writers of stories of adventure for boys Mr. Henty stands in the very first rank. Those who know something about India will be the most ready to thank Mr. Henty for giving them this instructive volume to place in the hands of their children."—*Academy.*

BY G. A. HENTY.

"Mr. Henty is one of our most successful writers of historical tales."—*Scotsman.*

The Lion of the North: A Tale of Gustavus Adolphus and the Wars of Religion. By G. A. Henty. With 12 page Pictures by J. Schönberg. Crown 8vo, cloth elegant, olivine edges, 6*s.*

"A praiseworthy attempt to interest British youth in the great deeds of the Scotch Brigade in the wars of Gustavus Adolphus. Mackay, Hepburn, and Munro live again in Mr. Henty's pages, as those deserve to live whose disciplined bands formed really the germ of the modern British army."—*Athenæum.*

The Young Carthaginian: A Story of the Times of Hannibal. By G. A. Henty. With 12 page Illustrations by C. J. Staniland, R.I. Crown 8vo, cloth elegant, olivine edges, 6*s.*

"The effect of an interesting story, well constructed and vividly told, is enhanced by the picturesque quality of the scenic background. From first to last nothing stays the interest of the narrative. It bears us along as on a stream whose current varies in direction, but never loses its force."—*Saturday Review.*

Redskin and Cow-boy: A Tale of the Western Plains. By G. A. Henty. With 12 page Illustrations by Alfred Pearse. Crown 8vo, cloth elegant, olivine edges, 6*s.*

"It has a good plot; it abounds in action; the scenes are equally spirited and realistic, and we can only say we have read it with much pleasure from first to last. The pictures of life on a cattle ranche are most graphically painted, as are the manners of the reckless but jovial cow-boys."—*Times.*

In Freedom's Cause: A Story of Wallace and Bruce. By G. A. Henty. With 12 page Illustrations by Gordon Browne. Crown 8vo, cloth elegant, olivine edges, 6*s.*

"His tale of the days of Wallace and Bruce is full of stirring action, and will commend itself to boys."—*Athenæum.*

By Right of Conquest: Or, With Cortez in Mexico. By G. A. Henty. With 10 page Illustrations by W. S. Stacey, and 2 Maps. Crown 8vo, cloth elegant, olivine edges, 6*s.*

"*By Right of Conquest* is the nearest approach to a perfectly successful historical tale that Mr. Henty has yet published."—*Academy.*

In Greek Waters: A Story of the Grecian War of Independence (1821–1827). By G. A. Henty. With 12 page Illustrations by W. S. Stacey, and a Map. Crown 8vo, cloth elegant, olivine edges, 6*s.*

"There are adventures of all kinds for the hero and his friends, whose pluck and ingenuity in extricating themselves from awkward fixes are always equal to the occasion. It is an excellent story, and if the proportion of history is smaller than usual, the whole result leaves nothing to be desired."—*Journal of Education.*

BY G. A. HENTY.

"No more interesting boys' books are written than Mr. Henty's stories."—*Daily Chronicle.*

Through the Fray: A Story of the Luddite Riots. By G. A. Henty. With 12 page Illustrations by H. M. Paget. Crown 8vo, cloth elegant, olivine edges, 6*s.*

"Mr. Henty inspires a love and admiration for straightforwardness, truth, and courage. This is one of the best of the many good books Mr. Henty has produced, and deserves to be classed with his *Facing Death.*"—*Standard.*

Captain Bayley's Heir: A Tale of the Gold Fields of California. By G. A. Henty. With 12 page Illustrations by H. M. Paget. Crown 8vo, cloth elegant, olivine edges, 6*s.*

"A Westminster boy who makes his way in the world by hard work, good temper, and unfailing courage. The descriptions given of life are just what a healthy intelligent lad should delight in."—*St. James's Gazette.*

Through Russian Snows: A Story of Napoleon's Retreat from Moscow. By G. A. Henty. With 8 Illustrations by W. H. Overend, and a Map. Crown 8vo, cloth elegant, olivine edges, 5*s.*

The hero of this story, Julian Wyatt, is a careless, good-natured youth, who becomes, quite innocently, mixed up with smugglers—when smuggling was common in the south coast of England. The smugglers carry him to France, and hand him over as a prisoner to the French; but he subsequently regains his freedom by joining Napoleon's army in the campaign against Russia. The young Englishman takes part in the great battles of Smolensk and Borodino, arriving at Moscow with the victorious Emperor. Then, when the terrible retreat begins, Julian finds himself in the rear-guard of the French army, fighting desperately, league by league, against famine, snow-storms, wolves, and Russians. Ultimately he escapes, after rescuing the daughter of a Russian Count; makes his way to St. Petersburg; and then returns to England. A story this with an excellent plot, exciting adventures, and splendid historical interest.

In the Heart of the Rockies: A Story of Adventure in Colorado. By G. A. Henty. With 8 page Illustrations by G. C. Hindley. Crown 8vo, cloth elegant, olivine edges, 5*s.*

"Few Christmas books will be more to the taste of the ingenuous boy than *In the Heart of the Rockies.*"—*Athenæum.*

"Mr. Henty is seen here at his best as an artist in lightning fiction."—*Academy.*

One of the 28th: A Tale of Waterloo. By G. A. Henty. With 8 page Illustrations by W. H. Overend, and 2 Maps. Crown 8vo, cloth elegant, olivine edges, 5*s.*

"Written with Homeric vigour and heroic inspiration. It is graphic, picturesque, and dramatically effective . . . shows us Mr. Henty at his best and brightest. The adventures will hold a boy of a winter's night enthralled as he rushes through them with breathless interest 'from cover to cover'."—*Observer.*

BY G. A. HENTY.

"Ask for Henty, and see that you get him."—*Punch.*

The Cat of Bubastes: A Story of Ancient Egypt. By G. A. HENTY. With 8 page Illustrations by J. R. WEGUELIN. Crown 8vo, cloth elegant, olivine edges, 5*s.*

"The story, from the critical moment of the killing of the sacred cat to the perilous exodus into Asia with which it closes, is very skilfully constructed and full of exciting adventures. It is admirably illustrated."—*Saturday Review.*

Maori and Settler: A Story of the New Zealand War. By G. A. HENTY. With 8 page Illustrations by ALFRED PEARSE, and a Map. Crown 8vo, cloth elegant, olivine edges, 5*s.*

"It is a book which all young people, but especially boys, will read with avidity."—*Athenæum.*

"A first-rate book for boys, brimful of adventure, of humorous and interesting conversation, and of vivid pictures of colonial life."—*Schoolmaster.*

St. George for England: A Tale of Cressy and Poitiers. By G. A. HENTY. With 8 full-page Illustrations by GORDON BROWNE. Crown 8vo, cloth elegant, olivine edges, 5*s.*

"A story of very great interest for boys. In his own forcible style the author has endeavoured to show that determination and enthusiasm can accomplish marvellous results; and that courage is generally accompanied by magnanimity and gentleness."—*Pall Mall Gazette.*

The Bravest of the Brave: With Peterborough in Spain. By G. A. HENTY. With 8 full-page Pictures by H. M. PAGET. Crown 8vo, cloth elegant, olivine edges, 5*s.*

"Mr. Henty never loses sight of the moral purpose of his work—to enforce the doctrine of courage and truth, mercy and lovingkindness, as indispensable to the making of an English gentleman. British lads will read *The Bravest of the Brave* with pleasure and profit; of that we are quite sure."—*Daily Telegraph.*

For Name and Fame: Or, Through Afghan Passes. By G. A. HENTY. With 8 full-page Illustrations by GORDON BROWNE. Crown 8vo, cloth elegant, olivine edges, 5*s.*

"Not only a rousing story, replete with all the varied forms of excitement of a campaign, but, what is still more useful, an account of a territory and its inhabitants which must for a long time possess a supreme interest for Englishmen, as being the key to our Indian Empire."—*Glasgow Herald.*

A Jacobite Exile: Being the Adventures of a Young Englishman in the Service of Charles XII. of Sweden. By G. A. HENTY. With 8 page Illustrations by PAUL HARDY, and a Map. Crown 8vo, cloth elegant, olivine edges, 5*s.*

"Incident succeeds incident, and adventure is piled upon adventure, and at the end the reader, be he boy or man, will have experienced breathless enjoyment in a romantic story that must have taught him much at its close."—*Army and Navy Gazette.*

BY G. A. HENTY.

"Mr. Henty's books are always alive with moving incident."—*Review of Reviews.*

Condemned as a Nihilist: A Story of Escape from Siberia. By G. A. HENTY. With 8 page Illustrations by WALTER PAGET. Crown 8vo, cloth elegant, olivine edges, 5*s.*

"The best of this year's Henty. His narrative is more interesting than many of the tales with which the public is familiar, of escape from Siberia. Despite their superior claim to authenticity these tales are without doubt no less fictitious than Mr. Henty's, and he beats them hollow in the matter of sensations."—*National Observer.*

Orange and Green: A Tale of the Boyne and Limerick. By G. A. HENTY. With 8 full-page Illustrations by GORDON BROWNE. Crown 8vo, cloth elegant, olivine edges, 5*s.*

"The narrative is free from the vice of prejudice, and ripples with life as vivacious as if what is being described were really passing before the eye. . . . Should be in the hands of every young student of Irish history."—*Belfast News.*

Held Fast for England: A Tale of the Siege of Gibraltar. By G. A. HENTY. With 8 page Illustrations by GORDON BROWNE. Crown 8vo, cloth elegant, olivine edges, 5*s.*

"Among them we would place first in interest and wholesome educational value the story of the siege of Gibraltar. . . . There is no cessation of exciting incident throughout the story."—*Athenæum.*

In the Reign of Terror: The Adventures of a Westminster Boy. By G. A. HENTY. With 8 full-page Illustrations by J. SCHÖNBERG. Crown 8vo, cloth elegant, olivine edges, 5*s.*

"Harry Sandwith, the Westminster boy, may fairly be said to beat Mr. Henty's record. His adventures will delight boys by the audacity and peril they depict. The story is one of Mr. Henty's best."—*Saturday Review.*

By Sheer Pluck: A Tale of the Ashanti War. By G. A. HENTY. With 8 full-page Pictures by GORDON BROWNE. Crown 8vo, cloth elegant, olivine edges, 5*s.*

"Morally, the book is everything that could be desired, setting before the boys a bright and bracing ideal of the English gentleman."—*Christian Leader.*

The Dragon and the Raven: Or, The Days of King Alfred. By G. A. HENTY. With 8 page Illustrations by C. J. STANILAND, R.I. Crown 8vo, cloth elegant, olivine edges, 5*s.*

"A story that may justly be styled remarkable. Boys, in reading it, will be surprised to find how Alfred persevered, through years of bloodshed and times of peace, to rescue his people from the thraldom of the Danes. We hope the book will soon be widely known in all our schools."—*Schoolmaster.*

A Final Reckoning: A Tale of Bush Life in Australia. By G. A. HENTY. With 8 page Illustrations by W. B. WOLLEN. Crown 8vo, cloth elegant, olivine edges, 5*s.*

"All boys will read this story with eager and unflagging interest. The episodes are in Mr. Henty's very best vein—graphic, exciting, realistic; and, as in all Mr. Henty's books, the tendency is to the formation of an honourable, manly, and even heroic character."—*Birmingham Post.*

BY G. A. HENTY.

"As publishers of books of adventure for boys Messrs. Blackie & Son have no superiors."—*St. James's Gazette.*

Facing Death: Or, The Hero of the Vaughan Pit. A Tale of the Coal Mines. By G. A. HENTY. With 8 page Pictures by GORDON BROWNE. Crown 8vo, cloth elegant, olivine edges, 5*s.*

"If any father, godfather, clergyman, or schoolmaster is on the look-out for a good book to give as a present to a boy who is worth his salt, this is the book we would recommend."—*Standard.*

A Chapter of Adventures: Or, Through the Bombardment of Alexandria. By G. A. HENTY. With 6 page Illustrations by W. H. OVEREND. Crown 8vo, cloth elegant, 3*s.* 6*d.*

"Jack Robson and his two companions have their fill of excitement, and their chapter of adventures is so brisk and entertaining we could have wished it longer than it is."—*Saturday Review.*

Two Thousand Years Ago: Or, The Adventures of a Roman Boy. By Professor A. J. CHURCH. With 12 page Illustrations by ADRIEN MARIE. Crown 8vo, cloth elegant, olivine edges, 6*s.*

"Adventures well worth the telling. The book is extremely entertaining as well as useful, and there is a wonderful freshness in the Roman scenes and characters."—*The Times.*

The Clever Miss Follett. By J. K. H. DENNY. With 12 page Illustrations by GERTRUDE D. HAMMOND. Crown 8vo, cloth elegant, olivine edges, 6*s.*

"Just the book to give to girls, who will delight both in the letterpress and the illustrations. Miss Hammond has never done better work."—*Review of Reviews.*

BY ROSA MULHOLLAND.

Banshee Castle. By ROSA MULHOLLAND. With 12 page Illustrations by JOHN H. BACON. Crown 8vo, cloth elegant, olivine edges, 6*s.*

"One of the most fascinating of Miss Rosa Mulholland's many fascinating stories. . . . The charm of the tale lies in the telling of it. The three heroines are admirably drawn characters."—*Athenæum.*

"Is told with grace, and brightened by a knowledge of Irish folk-lore, making it a perfect present for a girl in her teens."—*Truth.*

Giannetta: A Girl's Story of Herself. By ROSA MULHOLLAND. With 8 page Illustrations by LOCKHART BOGLE. Crown 8vo, cloth elegant, olivine edges, 5*s.*

"Giannetta is a true heroine—warm-hearted, self-sacrificing, and, as all good women nowadays are, largely touched with the enthusiasm of humanity. One of the most attractive gift-books of the season."—*The Academy.*

BY KIRK MUNROE.

At War with Pontiac: Or, The Totem of the Bear. By KIRK MUNROE. With 8 page Illustrations by J. FINNEMORE. Crown 8vo, cloth elegant, olivine edges, 5*s*.

This is a story of old colonial days in America, when Detroit was a frontier fort, and the shores of Lake Erie were held by hostile Indians under Pontiac, their famous chief. The hero is Donald Hester, a young English officer, who goes in search of his sister Edith, she having been captured by the redskins. Strange and terrible are his experiences; for he is wounded, taken prisoner, condemned to be burned, contrives to escape, and is again captured. In all his adventures he finds a magic talisman in the Totem of the Bear, which was tattooed on his arm in his childhood by a friendly Indian; while in the end there is peace between Pontiac and the English, and Donald marries the great chief's daughter. One dares not skip a single page in this most enthralling tale.

The White Conquerors of Mexico: A Tale of Toltec and Aztec. By KIRK MUNROE. With 8 page Illustrations by W. S. STACEY. Crown 8vo, cloth elegant, olivine edges, 5*s*.

"Mr. Munroe gives most vivid pictures of the religious and civil polity of the Aztecs, and of everyday life, as he imagines it, in the streets and market-places of the magnificent capital of Montezuma."—*The Times.*

Highways and High Seas: Cyril Harley's Adventures on both. By F. FRANKFORT MOORE. With 8 page Illustrations by ALFRED PEARSE. Crown 8vo, cloth elegant, olivine edges, 5*s*.

"This is one of the best stories Mr. Moore has written, perhaps the very best. The exciting adventures are sure to attract boys."—*Spectator.*

"It is pleasant to come across such honest work as F. Frankfort Moore's *Highways and High Seas.* Captain Chink is a real achievement in characterization." —*Scots Observer.*

A Fair Claimant: Being a Story for Girls. By FRANCES ARMSTRONG. With 8 page Illustrations by GERTRUDE D. HAMMOND. Crown 8vo, cloth elegant, olivine edges, 5*s*.

"As a gift-book for big girls it is among the best new books of the kind. The story is interesting and natural, from first to last."—*Westminster Gazette.*

The Heiress of Courtleroy. By ANNE BEALE. With 8 page Illustrations by T. C. H. CASTLE. Crown 8vo, cloth elegant, olivine edges, 5*s*.

"We can speak highly of the grace with which Miss Beale relates how the young 'Heiress of Courtleroy' had such good influence over her uncle as to win him from his intensely selfish ways."—*Guardian.*

BY GEORGE MAC DONALD.

A Rough Shaking. By GEORGE MAC DONALD. With 12 page Illustrations by W. PARKINSON. Crown 8vo, cloth elegant, olivine edges, 6*s.*

"One of the very best books for boys that has been written. It is full of material peculiarly well adapted for the young, containing in a marked degree the elements of all that is necessary to make up a perfect boys' book."—*Teachers' Aid.*

At the Back of the North Wind. By GEO. MAC DONALD. With 75 Illustrations by ARTHUR HUGHES. Crown 8vo, cloth elegant, olivine edges, 5*s.*

"The story is thoroughly original, full of fancy and pathos. . . . We stand with one foot in fairyland and one on common earth."—*The Times.*

Ranald Bannerman's Boyhood. By GEO. MAC DONALD, With 36 Illustrations by ARTHUR HUGHES. Crown 8vo, cloth elegant, olivine edges, 5*s.*

"The sympathy with boy-nature in *Ranald Bannerman's Boyhood* is perfect. It is a beautiful picture of childhood, teaching by its impressions and suggestions all noble things."—*British Quarterly Review.*

The Princess and the Goblin. By GEORGE MAC DONALD. With 32 Illustrations. Crown 8vo, cloth extra, 3*s.* 6*d.*

"Little of what is written for children has the lightness of touch and play of fancy which are characteristic of George Mac Donald's fairy tales. Mr. Arthur Hughes's illustrations are all that illustrations should be."—*Manchester Guardian.*

The Princess and Curdie. By GEORGE MAC DONALD. With 8 page Illustrations. Crown 8vo, cloth extra, 3*s.* 6*d.*

"There is the finest and rarest genius in this brilliant story. Upgrown people would do wisely occasionally to lay aside their newspapers and magazines to spend an hour with Curdie and the Princess."—*Sheffield Independent.*

BY HARRY COLLINGWOOD.

The Pirate Island: A Story of the South Pacific. By HARRY COLLINGWOOD. With 8 page Pictures by C. J. STANILAND and J. R. WELLS. Crown 8vo, cloth elegant, olivine edges, 5*s.*

"A capital story of the sea; indeed in our opinion the author is superior in some respects as a marine novelist to the better known Mr. Clark Russell."—*The Times.*

The Log of the "Flying Fish": A Story of Aerial and Submarine Adventure. By HARRY COLLINGWOOD. With 6 page Illustrations by GORDON BROWNE. Crown 8vo, cloth elegant, 3*s.* 6*d.*

"The *Flying Fish* actually surpasses all Jules Verne's creations; with incredible speed she flies through the air, skims over the surface of the water, and darts along the ocean bed. We strongly recommend our school-boy friends to possess themselves of her log."—*Athenæum.*

*** For other Books by Harry Collingwood, see pages 21 and 23.

BY GEORGE MANVILLE FENN.

"Mr. Fenn stands in the foremost rank of writers in this department."—*Daily News.*

Quicksilver: Or, A Boy with no Skid to his Wheel. By GEORGE MANVILLE FENN. With 10 page Illustrations by FRANK DADD. Crown 8vo, cloth elegant, olivine edges, 6*s.*

"*Quicksilver* is little short of an inspiration. In it that prince of story-writers for boys—George Manville Fenn—has surpassed himself. It is an ideal book for a boy's library."—*Practical Teacher.*

Dick o' the Fens: A Romance of the Great East Swamp. By G. MANVILLE FENN. With 12 page Illustrations by FRANK DADD. Crown 8vo, cloth elegant, olivine edges, 6*s.*

"We conscientiously believe that boys will find it capital reading. It is full of incident and mystery, and the mystery is kept up to the last moment. It is rich in effective local colouring; and it has a historical interest."—*Times.*

Devon Boys: A Tale of the North Shore. By G. MANVILLE FENN. With 12 page Illustrations by GORDON BROWNE. Crown 8vo, cloth elegant, olivine edges, 6*s.*

"An admirable story, as remarkable for the individuality of its young heroes as for the excellent descriptions of coast scenery and life in North Devon. It is one of the best books we have seen this season."—*Athenæum.*

The Golden Magnet: A Tale of the Land of the Incas. By G. MANVILLE FENN. Illustrated by 12 page Pictures by GORDON BROWNE. Crown 8vo, cloth elegant, olivine edges, 6*s.*

"There could be no more welcome present for a boy. There is not a dull page in the book, and many will be read with breathless interest. 'The Golden Magnet' is, of course, the same one that attracted Raleigh and the heroes of *Westward Ho!*"—*Journal of Education.*

In the King's Name: Or, The Cruise of the *Kestrel.* By G. MANVILLE FENN. Illustrated by 12 page Pictures by GORDON BROWNE. Crown 8vo, cloth elegant, olivine edges, 6*s.*

"The best of all Mr. Fenn's productions in this field. It has the great quality of always 'moving on', adventure following adventure in constant succession."—*Daily News.*

Nat the Naturalist: A Boy's Adventures in the Eastern Seas. By G. MANVILLE FENN. With 8 page Pictures. Crown 8vo, cloth elegant, olivine edges, 5*s.*

"This sort of book encourages independence of character, develops resource, and teaches a boy to keep his eyes open."—*Saturday Review.*

Bunyip Land: The Story of a Wild Journey in New Guinea. By G. MANVILLE FENN. With 6 page Illustrations by GORDON BROWNE. Crown 8vo, cloth elegant, 4*s.*

"Mr. Fenn deserves the thanks of everybody for *Bunyip Land*, and we may venture to promise that a quiet week may be reckoned on whilst the youngsters have such fascinating literature provided for their evenings' amusement."—*Spectator.*

BY GEORGE MANVILLE FENN.

"No one can find his way to the hearts of lads more readily than Mr. Fenn."—*Nottingham Guardian.*

Brownsmith's Boy: A Romance in a Garden. By G. MANVILLE FENN. With 6 page Illustrations. Crown 8vo, cloth elegant, 3*s.* 6*d.*

"Mr. Fenn's books are among the best, if not altogether the best, of the stories for boys. Mr. Fenn is at his best in *Brownsmith's Boy.*"—*Pictorial World.*

*** For other Books by G. MANVILLE FENN, see page 22.

BY ASCOTT R. HOPE.

Young Travellers' Tales. By ASCOTT R. HOPE. With 6 Illustrations by H. J. DRAPER. Crown 8vo, cloth elegant, 3*s.* 6*d.*

"Possess a high value for instruction as well as for entertainment. His quiet, level humour bubbles up on every page."—*Daily Chronicle.*

"Excitement and cheerful enjoyment run through the book."—*Bookman.*

The Seven Wise Scholars. By ASCOTT R. HOPE. With nearly 100 Illustrations by GORDON BROWNE. Cloth elegant, 5*s.*

"As full of fun as a volume of *Punch*; with illustrations, more laughter-provoking than most we have seen since Leech died."—*Sheffield Independent.*

Stories of Old Renown: Tales of Knights and Heroes. By ASCOTT R. HOPE. With 100 Illustrations by GORDON BROWNE. Crown 8vo, cloth elegant, 3*s.* 6*d.*

"A really fascinating book worthy of its telling title. There is, we venture to say, not a dull page in the book, not a story which will not bear a second reading."—*Guardian.*

Under False Colours: A Story from Two Girls' Lives. By SARAH DOUDNEY. With 6 page Illustrations by G. G. KILBURNE. Crown 8vo, cloth elegant, 4*s.*

"Sarah Doudney has no superior as a writer of high-toned stories—pure in style and original in conception; but we have seen nothing from her pen equal in dramatic energy to this book."—*Christian Leader.*

"This is a charming story, abounding in delicate touches of sentiment and pathos. Its plot is skilfully contrived."—*Scotsman.*

The Universe: Or The Infinitely Great and the Infinitely Little. A Sketch of Contrasts in Creation, and Marvels revealed and explained by Natural Science. By F. A. POUCHET, M.D. With 272 Engravings on wood, of which 55 are full-page size, and 4 Coloured Illustrations. Twelfth Edition, medium 8vo, cloth elegant, gilt edges, 7*s.* 6*d.*; also morocco antique, 16*s.*

"We can honestly commend Professor Pouchet's book, which is admirably, as it is copiously illustrated."—*The Times.*

"Scarcely any book in French or in English is so likely to stimulate in the young an interest in the physical phenomena."—*Fortnightly Review.*

BY DR. GORDON STABLES.

For Life and Liberty: A Story of Battle by Land and Sea. By Dr. Gordon Stables, R.N. With 8 Illustrations by Sydney Paget, and a Map.

When in 1861 war was declared in America between the North and South, the news greatly interested Osmond Lloyd, who was at school in England. Being of an adventurous spirit, and having relations in the States, the lad ran away from home with his chum Kenneth Reid, and the two made their way to America in the *Mosquito*. Here Osmond joined the Southern army, while Kenneth entered the navy, and their various adventures in that great conflict are vigorously set forth in this narrative. Osmond was in the army of the Potomac, took part in all the campaigns, and won praise for his valour from the famous general, "Stonewall" Jackson.

Reduced Illustration from "To Greenland".

To Greenland and the Pole. By Gordon Stables, M.D. With 8 page Illustrations by G. C. Hindley, and a Map. Crown 8vo, cloth elegant, olivine edges, 5*s*.

"His Arctic explorers have the verisimilitude of life. It is one of the books of the season, and one of the best Mr. Stables has ever written."—*Truth.*

Westward with Columbus. By Gordon Stables, M.D. With 8 page Illustrations by A. Pearse. Cloth elegant, 5*s*.

"We must place *Westward with Columbus* among those books that all boys ought to read."—*The Spectator.*

'Twixt School and College: A Tale of Self-reliance. By Gordon Stables, C.M., M.D., R.N. With 8 page Illustrations by W. Parkinson. Crown 8vo, cloth elegant, olivine edges, 5*s*.

"One of the best of a prolific writer's books for boys, being full of practical instructions as to keeping pets, and inculcates in a way which a little recalls Miss Edgeworth's 'Frank' the virtue of self-reliance."—*Athenæum.*

BY ROBERT LEIGHTON.

Olaf the Glorious. By ROBERT LEIGHTON. With 8 page Illustrations by RALPH PEACOCK, and a Map. Crown 8vo, cloth elegant, olivine edges, 5*s*.

"Is as good as anything of the kind we have met with. Mr. Leighton more than holds his own with Rider Haggard and Baring Gould."—*The Times.*

"Among the books best liked by boys of the sturdy English type few will take a higher place than *Olaf the Glorious*. . . . ."—*National Observer.*

The Wreck of "The Golden Fleece": The Story of a North Sea Fisher-boy. By ROBERT LEIGHTON. With 8 page Illustrations by F. BRANGWYN. Crown 8vo, cloth elegant, 5*s*.

"This story should add considerably to Mr. Leighton's high reputation. Excellent in every respect, it contains every variety of incident. The plot is very cleverly devised, and the types of the North Sea sailors are capital."—*The Times.*

The Pilots of Pomona: A Story of the Orkney Islands. By ROBERT LEIGHTON. With 8 page Illustrations by JOHN LEIGHTON, and a Map. Crown 8vo, cloth elegant, olivine edges, 5*s*.

"A story which is quite as good in its way as *Treasure Island*, and is full of adventure of a stirring yet most natural kind. Although it is primarily a boys' book, it is a real godsend to the elderly reader."—*Glasgow Evening Times.*

The Thirsty Sword: A Story of the Norse Invasion of Scotland (1262-63). By ROBERT LEIGHTON. With 8 page Illustrations by A. PEARSE. Crown 8vo, cloth elegant, 5*s*.

"This is one of the most fascinating stories for boys that it has ever been our pleasure to read. From first to last the interest never flags. Boys will worship Kenric, who is a hero in every sense of the word."—*Schoolmaster.*

BY G. NORWAY.

A Prisoner of War: A Story of the Time of Napoleon Bonaparte. By G. NORWAY. With 6 page Illustrations by ROBT. BARNES, A.R.W.S. Crown 8vo, cloth elegant, 3*s*. 6*d*.

"More hairbreadth escapes from death by starvation, by ice, by fighting, &c., were never before surmounted. . . . It is a fine yarn."—*The Guardian.*

The Loss of John Humble: What Led to It, and What Came of It. By G. NORWAY. With 8 page Illustrations by JOHN SCHÖNBERG. Crown 8vo, cloth elegant, olivine edges, 5*s*.

"This story will place the author at once in the front rank. It is full of life and adventure. The interest of the story is sustained without a break from first to last."—*Standard.*

A True Cornish Maid. By G. NORWAY. With 6 page Illustrations by J. FINNEMORE. Crown 8vo, cloth elegant, 3*s*. 6*d*.

"There is some excellent reading. . . . Mrs. Norway brings before the eyes of her readers the good Cornish folk, their speech, their manners, and their ways. *A True Cornish Maid* deserves to be popular."—*Athenæum.*

With the Sea Kings: A Story of the Days of Lord Nelson. By F. H. WINDER. With 6 page Illustrations by W. S. STACEY. Crown 8vo, cloth elegant, 4*s.*

"Just the book to put into a boy's hands. Every chapter contains boardings, cuttings out, fighting pirates, escapes of thrilling audacity, and captures by corsairs, sufficient to turn the quietest boy's head. The story culminates in a vigorous account of the battle of Trafalgar. Happy boys!"—*The Academy.*

Grettir the Outlaw: A Story of Iceland. By S. BARING-GOULD. With 6 page Illustrations by M. ZENO DIEMER, and a Coloured Map. Crown 8vo, cloth elegant, 4*s.*

"Is the boys' book of its year. That is, of course, as much as to say that it will do for men grown as well as juniors. It is told in simple, straightforward English, as all stories should be, and it has a freshness, a freedom, a sense of sun and wind and the open air, which make it irresistible."—*National Observer.*

Gold, Gold, in Cariboo: A Story of Adventure in British Columbia. By CLIVE PHILLIPPS-WOLLEY. With 6 page Illustrations by G. C. HINDLEY. Crown 8vo, cloth extra, 3*s.* 6*d.*

"It would be difficult to say too much in favour of *Gold, Gold, in Cariboo.* We have seldom read a more exciting tale of wild mining adventure in a singularly inaccessible country. There is a capital plot, and the interest is sustained to the last page."—*The Times.*

A Champion of the Faith: A Tale of Prince Hal and the Lollards. By J. M. CALLWELL. With 6 page Illustrations by HERBERT J. DRAPER. Crown 8vo, cloth elegant, 4*s.*

"Will not be less enjoyed than Mr. Henty's books. Sir John Oldcastle's pathetic story, and the history of his brave young squire, will make every boy enjoy this lively story."—*London Quarterly.*

BY ALICE CORKRAN.

Meg's Friend. By ALICE CORKRAN. With 6 page Illustrations by ROBERT FOWLER. Crown 8vo, cloth extra, 3*s.* 6*d.*

"One of Miss Corkran's charming books for girls, narrated in that simple and picturesque style which marks the authoress as one of the first amongst writers for young people."—*The Spectator.*

Margery Merton's Girlhood. By ALICE CORKRAN. With 6 page Pictures by GORDON BROWNE. Cr. 8vo, cloth extra, 3*s.* 6*d.*

"Another book for girls we can warmly commend. There is a delightful piquancy in the experiences and trials of a young English girl who studies painting in Paris."—*Saturday Review.*

Down the Snow Stairs: Or, From Good-night to Good-morning. By ALICE CORKRAN. With 60 Illustrations by GORDON BROWNE. Crown 8vo, cloth elegant, olivine edges, 3*s.* 6*d.*

"A gem of the first water, bearing upon every page the mark of genius. It is indeed a Little Pilgrim's Progress."—*Christian Leader.*

BY HUGH ST. LEGER.

Hallowe'en Ahoy! Or, Lost on the Crozet Islands. By HUGH ST. LEGER. With 6 Illustrations by H. J. DRAPER. Crown 8vo, cloth elegant, 4*s.*

This is the strange history of the derelict *Hallowe'en*, in which is set forth: How she was found on the high-seas beyond the equator; how it befell that there was only a ghost on board; how the ghost was captured; how the vessel was cast ashore on a desert island in the Southern Ocean; how the crew, being Englishmen, took the disaster cheerily; and how at length, after many hardships and hairbreadth escapes, they floated their stout craft, bringing her back safe again to old England. And in this wonderful tale there is such wealth of fine enchantment that it will warp the hungry school-boy from remembrance of his dinner.

Sou'wester and Sword. By HUGH ST. LEGER. With 6 page Illustrations by HAL HURST. Crown 8vo, cloth elegant, 4*s.*

"As racy a tale of life at sea and war adventure as we have met with for some time. . . . Altogether the sort of book that boys will revel in."—*Athenæum.*

BY EDGAR PICKERING.

Two Gallant Rebels: A Story of the Great Struggle in La Vendée. By EDGAR PICKERING. With 6 Illustrations by W. H. OVEREND. Crown 8vo, cloth elegant, 3*s.* 6*d.*

These two rebels are two English youths who are shipwrecked and cast ashore in La Vendée, a province of France. Here they are rescued by the inhabitants, and in gratitude for this assistance they join the Vendéans in their revolt against the French Republic. The two young fellows maintain the English character for pluck in the various ambushes and battles in which they take part; and even when captured and condemned to the guillotine they contrive to escape by sheer reckless daring.

In Press-Gang Days. By EDGAR PICKERING. With 6 Illustrations by W. S. STACEY. Crown 8vo, cloth elegant, 3*s.* 6*d.*

"It is of Marryat we think as we read this delightful story; for it is not only a story of adventure with incidents well conceived and arranged, but the characters are interesting and well-distinguished."—*Academy.*

An Old-Time Yarn: Wherein is set forth divers desperate mischances which befell Anthony Ingram and his shipmates in the West Indies and Mexico with Hawkins and Drake. By EDGAR PICKERING. Illustrated with 6 page Pictures drawn by ALFRED PEARSE. Crown 8vo, cloth elegant, 3*s.* 6*d.*

"And a very good yarn it is, with not a dull page from first to last. There is a flavour of *Westward Ho!* in this attractive book."—*Educational Review.*

Silas Verney: A Tale of the Time of Charles II. By EDGAR PICKERING. With 6 page Illustrations by ALFRED PEARSE. Crown 8vo, cloth elegant, 3*s.* 6*d.*

"Altogether this is an excellent story for boys."—*Saturday Review.*

BY CHARLES W. WHISTLER.

A Thane of Wessex: Being the Story of the Great Viking Raid of 845. By CHARLES W. WHISTLER. With 6 Illustrations by W. H. MARGETSON. Crown 8vo, cloth elegant, 3*s.* 6*d.*

The story of young Heregar, a thane in the old kingdom of Wessex. Wherein is finely set forth,—how he was falsely accused, and unfairly outlawed as a traitor; how in his wanderings he discovered the war-galleys of the Vikings, and carried the War-arrow; how he withstood the raiding Danes at Bridgwater, and gathered the levies at Glastonbury; how he contrived an ambush, and completely defeated the Vikings at Parret mouth; and how, at length, he was inlawed again, and in reward of his valour made the King's Standard-Bearer. That is the noble story of Heregar.

His First Kangaroo: An Australian Story for Boys. By ARTHUR FERRES. With 6 Illustrations by PERCY F. S. SPENCE. Crown 8vo, cloth elegant, 3*s.* 6*d.*

This is a story of adventure on an Australian cattle-station. Dick Morrison accepts an invitation to spend a holiday in the bush, and has a good time. A band of bush-rangers also make things lively, for on one occasion the station is "stuck up", while a young Scotsman is kidnapped and rescued with difficulty. The story is full of healthy out-of-doors adventure, in fresh and attractive surroundings.

Three Bright Girls: A Story of Chance and Mischance. By ANNIE E. ARMSTRONG. With 6 page Illustrations by W. PARKINSON. Crown 8vo, cloth elegant, 3*s.* 6*d.*

"Among many good stories for girls this is undoubtedly one of the very best." —*Teachers' Aid.*

A Very Odd Girl: or, Life at the Gabled Farm. By ANNIE E. ARMSTRONG. Illustrated. Crown 8vo, cloth elegant, 3*s.* 6*d.*

"The book is one we can heartily recommend, for it is not only bright and interesting, but also pure and healthy in tone and teaching."—*The Lady.*

The Captured Cruiser: By C. J. HYNE. Illustrated by FRANK BRANGWYN. Crown 8vo, cloth elegant, 3*s.* 6*d.*

"The two lads and the two skippers are admirably drawn. Mr. Hyne has now secured a position in the first rank of writers of fiction for boys."—*Spectator.*

Afloat at Last: A Sailor Boy's Log of his Life at Sea. By JOHN C. HUTCHESON. Crown 8vo, cloth elegant, 3*s.* 6*d.*

"As healthy and breezy a book as one could wish to put into the hands of a boy."—*Academy.*

Picked up at Sea: Or, The Gold Miners of Minturne Creek. By J. C. HUTCHESON. With 6 page Pictures. Cloth extra, 3*s.* 6*d.*

Brother and Sister: Or, The Trials of the Moore Family. By ELIZABETH J. LYSAGHT. Crown 8vo, cloth elegant, 3*s.* 6*d.*

The Search for the Talisman: A Story of Labrador. By HENRY FRITH. With 6 page Illustrations by J. SCHÖNBERG. Crown 8vo, cloth elegant, 3*s.* 6*d.*

"Mr. Frith's volume will be among those most read and highest valued. The adventures among seals, whales, and icebergs in Labrador will delight many a young reader."—*Pall Mall Gazette.*

Reefer and Rifleman: A Tale of the Two Services. By Lieut.-Col. PERCY-GROVES. With 6 page Illustrations by JOHN SCHÖNBERG. Crown 8vo, cloth elegant, 3*s.* 6*d.*

"A good, old-fashioned, amphibious story of our fighting with the Frenchmen in the beginning of our century, with a fair sprinkling of fun and frolic."—*Times.*

Dora: Or, A Girl without a Home. By MRS. R. H. READ. With 6 page Illustrations. Crown 8vo, cloth elegant, 3*s.* 6*d.*

"It is no slight thing, in an age of rubbish, to get a story so pure and healthy as this."—*The Academy.*

Storied Holidays: A Cycle of Red-letter Days. By E. S. BROOKS. With 12 page Illustrations by HOWARD PYLE. Crown 8vo, cloth elegant, 3*s.* 6*d.*

"It is a downright good book for a senior boy, and is eminently readable from first to last."—*Schoolmaster.*

Chivalric Days: Stories of Courtesy and Courage in the Olden Times. By E. S. BROOKS. With 20 Illustrations by GORDON BROWNE and other Artists. Crown 8vo, cloth extra, 3*s.* 6*d.*

"We have seldom come across a prettier collection of tales. These charming stories of boys and girls of olden days are no mere fictitious or imaginary sketches, but are real and actual records of their sayings and doings."—*Literary World.*

Historic Boys: Their Endeavours, their Achievements, and their Times. By E. S. BROOKS. With 12 page Illustrations by R. B. BIRCH and JOHN SCHÖNBERG. Crown 8vo, cloth extra, 3*s.* 6*d.*

"A wholesome book, manly in tone, its character sketches enlivened by brisk dialogue and high-class illustrations; altogether one that should incite boys to further acquaintance with those rulers of men whose careers are narrated. We advise teachers to put it on their list of prizes."—*Knowledge.*

Dr. Jolliffe's Boys: A Tale of Weston School. By LEWIS HOUGH. With 6 page Pictures. Crown 8vo, cloth extra, 3*s.* 6*d.*

"Young people who appreciate *Tom Brown's School-days* will find this story a worthy companion to that fascinating book. There is the same manliness of tone, truthfulness of outline, avoidance of exaggeration and caricature, and healthy morality as characterized the masterpiece of Mr. Hughes."—*Newcastle Journal.*

The Bubbling Teapot. A Wonder Story. By MRS. L. W. CHAMPNEY. With 12 page Pictures by WALTER SATTERLEE. Crown 8vo, cloth extra, 3*s.* 6*d.*

"Very literally a 'wonder story', and a wild and fanciful one. Nevertheless it is made realistic enough, and there is a good deal of information to be gained from it."—*The Times.*

Thorndyke Manor: A Tale of Jacobite Times. By MARY C. ROWSELL. With 6 page Illustrations by L. LESLIE BROOKE. Crown 8vo, cloth elegant, 3*s.* 6*d.*

"Miss Rowsell has never written a more attractive book than *Thorndyke Manor.*"—*Belfast News-Letter.*

Traitor or Patriot? A Tale of the Rye-House Plot. By MARY C. ROWSELL. Illustrated. Crown 8vo, cloth, 3*s.* 6*d.*

"Here the Rye-House Plot serves as the groundwork for a romantic love episode, whose true characters are lifelike beings."—*Graphic.*

BLACKIE'S NEW THREE-SHILLING SERIES.

Beautifully Illustrated and Handsomely Bound.

Hussein the Hostage: Or, A Boy's Adventures in Persia. By G. NORWAY. With 6 page Illustrations by JOHN SCHÖNBERG. *New Edition.* Crown 8vo, cloth elegant, 3*s.*

"*Hussein the Hostage* is full of originality and vigour. The characters are lifelike, there is plenty of stirring incident, the interest is sustained throughout, and every boy will enjoy following the fortunes of the hero."—*Journal of Education.*

Reduced Illustration from "Cousin Geoffrey".

Cousin Geoffrey and I. By CAROLINE AUSTIN. With 6 page Illustrations by W. PARKINSON. *New Edition.* Crown 8vo, cloth extra, 3*s.*

"Miss Austin's story is bright, clever, and well developed."—*Saturday Review.*

The Congo Rovers: A Story of the Slave Squadron. By HARRY COLLINGWOOD. With 6 page Illustrations by J. SCHÖNBERG. Crown 8vo, cloth elegant, 3*s.*

"No better sea story has lately been written than the *Congo Rovers.* It is as original as any boy could desire."—*Morning Post.*

THREE-SHILLING SERIES—Continued.

Under Hatches: or, Ned Woodthorpe's Adventures. By F. FRANKFORT MOORE. With 6 page Illustrations by A. FORESTIER. Crown 8vo, cloth elegant, 3*s.*

"The story as a story is one that will just suit boys all the world over. The characters are well drawn and consistent; Patsy, the Irish steward, will be found especially amusing."—*Schoolmaster.*

Menhardoc: A Story of Cornish Nets and Mines. By G. MANVILLE FENN. With 6 page Illustrations by C. J. STANILAND, R.I. Crown 8vo, cloth extra, 3*s.*

"They are real living boys, with their virtues and faults. The Cornish fishermen are drawn from life, and stand out from the pages in their jerseys and sea-boots all sprinkled with silvery pilchard scales."—*Spectator.*

Yussuf the Guide: or, The Mountain Bandits. A Story of Strange Adventure in Asia Minor. By G. MANVILLE FENN. With 6 page Illustrations by J. SCHÖNBERG. Crown 8vo, cloth extra, 3*s.*

"Told with such real freshness and vigour that the reader feels he is actually one of the party, sharing in the fun and facing the dangers."—*Pall Mall Gazette.*

Robinson Crusoe. With 100 Illustrations by GORDON BROWNE. Crown 8vo, cloth extra, 3*s.*

"One of the best issues, if not absolutely the best, of Defoe's work which has ever appeared."—*The Standard.*

Gulliver's Travels. With 100 Illustrations by GORDON BROWNE. Crown 8vo, cloth extra, 3*s.*

"Mr. Gordon Browne is, to my thinking, incomparably the most artistic, spirited, and brilliant of our illustrators of books for boys, and one of the most humorous also, as his illustrations of 'Gulliver' amply testify."—*Truth.*

Patience Wins: or, War in the Works. By GEORGE MANVILLE FENN. With 6 page Illustrations. Cr. 8vo, cloth extra, 3*s.*

"Mr. Fenn has never hit upon a happier plan than in writing this story of Yorkshire factory life. The whole book is all aglow with life."—*Pall Mall Gazette.*

Mother Carey's Chicken: Her Voyage to the Unknown Isle. By G. MANVILLE FENN. With 6 page Illustrations by A. FORESTIER. Crown 8vo, cloth extra, 3*s.*

"Undoubtedly one of the best Mr. Fenn has written. The incidents are of thrilling interest, while the characters are drawn with a care and completeness rarely found in a boy's book."—*Literary World.*

The Wigwam and the War-path: Stories of the Red Indians. By ASCOTT R. HOPE. With 6 page Illustrations. Crown 8vo, cloth elegant, 3*s.*

"Is notably good. It gives a very vivid picture of life among the Indians, which will delight the heart of many a schoolboy."—*Spectator.*

THREE-SHILLING SERIES—Continued.

The Missing Merchantman. By HARRY COLLINGWOOD. With 6 page Illustrations by W. H. OVEREND. Cloth extra, 3*s.*

"One of the author's best sea stories. The hero is as heroic as any boy could desire, and the ending is extremely happy."—*British Weekly.*

The Rover's Secret: A Tale of the Pirate Cays and Lagoons of Cuba. By HARRY COLLINGWOOD. With 6 page Illustrations by W. C. SYMONS. Crown 8vo, cloth elegant, 3*s.*

"*The Rover's Secret* is by far the best sea story we have read for years, and is certain to give unalloyed pleasure to boys."—*Saturday Review.*

Perseverance Island: or, The Robinson Crusoe of the 19th Century. By DOUGLAS FRAZAR. With 6 page Illustrations. Crown 8vo, cloth extra, 3*s.*

"This is an interesting story, written with studied simplicity of style, much in Defoe's vein of apparent sincerity and scrupulous veracity; while for practical instruction it is even better than *Robinson Crusoe.*"—*Illustrated London News.*

Girl Neighbours: or, The Old Fashion and the New. By SARAH TYTLER. With 6 page Illustrations by C. T. GARLAND. Crown 8vo, cloth elegant, 3*s.*

"One of the most effective and quietly humorous of Miss Sarah Tytler's stories. It is very healthy, very agreeable, and very well written."—*The Spectator.*

BLACKIE'S HALF-CROWN SERIES.

Illustrated by eminent Artists. In crown 8vo, cloth elegant.

A Musical Genius. By the Author of the "Two Dorothys". Illustrated by JOHN H. BACON.

Hugo Ricardo has a genius for the violin, and is adopted by a wealthy musical amateur who has discovered his special gift. The lad studies hard, and fulfils the highest expectations of his new friend. But he never quite forgets his humble, unselfish brother the conjurer; and when he is called upon to make choice between affection for his brother and a wealthy home, he quickly chooses the former. The charm of this tale is in its naturalness, and in the engaging self-sacrifice of the two noble brothers.

For the Sake of a Friend: A Story of School Life. By MARGARET PARKER. Illustrated by G. DEMAIN HAMMOND.

Stories of school life are common enough, but this tale of a girls' school in Melbourne is quite new. The vivacity of these Australian girls is not less attractive than the home-like brightness and freedom of the school. The heroine, Susie Snow, and her friend, Trixie Beresford, are the sweetest and cleverest of girls, and although there are jealousies, mistakes, and misunderstandings among the pupils at Stormont House, yet all comes right in the end.

HALF-CROWN SERIES—Continued.

Under the Black Eagle. By ANDREW HILLIARD. Illustrated by W. BOUCHER.

Ernest Wentworth is an English lad resident in Russia, and his great chum is a student called Gregorieff. As this student has secret dealings with Nihilists, the two friends become suspected of plots, and the final result is that both are apprehended, and exiled to Siberia. On the journey they contrive to leap from the convict-steamer, swim ashore in the darkness, escape from their pursuers, and make their way across "the Roof of the World" into Northern India.

The Secret of the Australian Desert. By ERNEST FAVENC. With 4 Illustrations by PERCY F. S. SPENCE.

Three white men, and a blackfellow called Billy Buttons, start on an expedition into the great Australian desert. Strange, uncanny, and terrible are their experiences in that vast wilderness. They meet with the cannibal Warlattas; find a mysterious burning mountain; discover traces of the lost explorer, Dr. Leichhardt; and only arrive back at their cattle-station after long and grievous wandering in the waterless desert. The vivid actuality of this enthralling narrative is due to the fact that the author has taken the material from his own thrilling experiences.

A Little Handful. By HARRIET J. SCRIPPS.

"He is a real type of a boy."—*The Schoolmaster.*

A Golden Age: A Story of Four Merry Children. By ISMAY THORN. Illustrated by GORDON BROWNE.

"Ought to have a place of honour on the nursery shelf."—*The Athenæum.*

A Rough Road: or, How the Boy Made a Man of Himself. By Mrs. G. LINNÆUS BANKS.

"Mrs. Banks has not written a better book than *A Rough Road.*"—*Spectator.*

The Two Dorothys. By Mrs. HERBERT MARTIN.

"A book that will interest and please all girls."—*The Lady.*

Penelope and the Others. By AMY WALTON.

"This is a charming book for children. Miss Walton proves herself a perfect adept in understanding of school-room joys and sorrows."—*Christian Leader.*

A Cruise in Cloudland. By HENRY FRITH.

"A thoroughly interesting story."—*St. James's Gazette.*

Marian and Dorothy. By ANNIE E. ARMSTRONG.

"This is distinctively a book for girls. A bright wholesome story."—*Academy.*

Stimson's Reef: A Tale of Adventure. By C. J. HYNE.

"It may almost vie with Mr. R. L. Stevenson's *Treasure Island.*"—*Guardian.*

Gladys Anstruther. By LOUISA THOMPSON.

"It is a clever book: novel and striking in the highest degree."—*Schoolmistress.*

HALF-CROWN SERIES—Continued.

BY BEATRICE HARRADEN.

Things Will Take a Turn. By BEATRICE HARRADEN. With 44 Illustrations by JOHN H. BACON. Crown 8vo, cloth elegant, 2*s*. 6*d*.

"Perhaps the most brilliant is *Things Will Take a Turn*. . . . A tale of humble child life in East London. It is a delightful blending of comedy and tragedy, with an excellent plot."—*The Times*.

From "Things will Take a Turn". (Reduced.)

The Whispering Winds, and the Tales that they Told. By MARY H. DEBENHAM. With 25 Illustrations by PAUL HARDY. Crown 8vo, cloth elegant, 2*s*. 6*d*.

"We wish the winds would tell *us* stories like these. It would be worth while to climb Primrose Hill, or even to the giddy heights of Hampstead Heath in a bitter east wind, if we could only be sure of hearing such a sweet, sad, tender, and stirring story as that of Hilda Brave Heart, or even one that was half so good."—*Academy*.

Hal Hungerford. By J. R. HUTCHINSON, B.A.

"Altogether, Hal Hungerford is a distinct literary success." *Spectator*.

The Secret of the Old House. By E. EVERETT-GREEN.

"Tim, the little Jacobite, is a charming creation."—*Academy*.

The Golden Weathercock. By JULIA GODDARD.

"A cleverly conceived quaint story, ingeniously written."—*Saturday Review*.

White Lilac: or, The Queen of the May. By AMY WALTON.

"Every rural parish ought to add *White Lilac* to its library."—*Academy*.

Miriam's Ambition. By EVELYN EVERETT-GREEN.

"Miss Green's children are real British boys and girls." *Liverpool Mercury*.

The Brig "Audacious". By ALAN COLE.

"Fresh and wholesome as a breath of sea air."—*Court Journal*.

HALF-CROWN SERIES—Continued.

The Saucy May. By HENRY FRITH.

"Mr. Frith gives a new picture of life on the ocean wave."—*Sheffield Independent.*

Jasper's Conquest. By ELIZABETH J. LYSAGHT.

"One of the best boys' books of the season."—*Schoolmaster.*

Little Lady Clare. By EVELYN EVERETT-GREEN.

"Reminds us in its quaintness of Mrs. Ewing's delightful tales."—*Liter. World.*

The Eversley Secrets. By EVELYN EVERETT-GREEN.

"Roy Eversley is a very touching picture of high principle."—*Guardian.*

The Hermit Hunter of the Wilds. By G. STABLES, R.N.

"Will gladden the heart of many a bright boy."—*Methodist Recorder.*

Sturdy and Strong. By G. A. HENTY.

"A hero who stands as a good instance of chivalry in domestic life."—*The Empire.*

Gutta Percha Willie. By GEORGE MAC DONALD.

"Get it for your boys and girls to read for themselves."—*Practical Teacher.*

The War of the Axe: Or, Adventures in South Africa. By J. PERCY-GROVES.

"The story is well and brilliantly told."—*Literary World.*

The Lads of Little Clayton. BY R. STEAD.

"A capital book for boys."—*Schoolmaster.*

Ten Boys who lived on the Road from Long Ago to Now. By JANE ANDREWS. With 20 Illustrations.

"The idea is a very happy one, and admirably carried out."—*Practical Teacher.*

A Waif of the Sea: Or, The Lost Found. By KATE WOOD.

"Written with tenderness and grace."—*Morning Advertiser.*

Winnie's Secret. By KATE WOOD.

"One of the best story-books we have read."—*Schoolmaster.*

Miss Willowburn's Offer. By SARAH DOUDNEY.

"Patience Willowburn is one of Miss Doudney's best creations."—*Spectator.*

A Garland for Girls. By LOUISA M. ALCOTT.

"These little tales are the beau ideal of girls' stories."—*Christian World.*

Hetty Gray: Or, Nobody's Bairn. By ROSA MULHOLLAND.

"Hetty is a delightful creature—piquant, tender, and true."—*World.*

Brothers in Arms: A Story of the Crusades. By F. BAYFORD HARRISON.

"Sure to prove interesting to young people of both sexes."—*Guardian.*

Miss Fenwick's Failures. By ESMÉ STUART.

"A girl true to real life, who will put no nonsense into young heads."—*Graphic.*

Gytha's Message. By EMMA LESLIE.

"This is the sort of book that all girls like."—*Journal of Education.*

HALF-CROWN SERIES—Continued.

Hammond's Hard Lines. By SKELTON KUPPORD. Illustrated by HAROLD COPPING.

"The story is very clever and provocative of laughter." —*Standard.*

"It is just what a boy would choose if the selection of a story-book is left in his own hand."—*School Guardian.*

Reduced Illustration from "Hammond's Hard Lines".

Dulcie King: A Story for Girls. By M. CORBET-SEYMOUR. Illustrated by GERTRUDE D. HAMMOND.

"An extremely graceful, well-told tale of domestic life. . . . The heroine, Dulcie, is a charming person, and worthy of the good fortune which she causes and shares."—*Guardian.*

Hugh Herbert's Inheritance. By CAROLINE AUSTIN. With 4 page Illustrations by C. T. GARLAND.

"Will please by its simplicity, its tenderness, and its healthy interesting motive. It is admirably written."—*Scotsman.*

Nicola: The Career of a Girl Musician. By M. CORBET-SEYMOUR. Illustrated by GERTRUDE D. HAMMOND.

Jack o' Lanthorn: A Tale of Adventure. By HENRY FRITH.

My Mistress the Queen. By M. A. PAULL.

The Stories of Wasa and Menzikoff.

Stories of the Sea in Former Days.

Tales of Captivity and Exile.

Famous Discoveries by Sea and Land.

Stirring Events of History.

Adventures in Field, Flood, and Forest.

"It would be difficult to place in the hands of young people books which combine interest and instruction in a higher degree."—*Manchester Courier.*

BLACKIE'S TWO-SHILLING SERIES.

Illustrated by eminent Artists. In crown 8vo, cloth elegant.

NEW VOLUMES.

In the Days of Drake. Being the Adventures of Humphrey Salkeld. By J. S. Fletcher. With Illustrations by W. S. Stacey.

Wilful Joyce. By W. L. Rooper. Illustrated by Harold Copping.

Proud Miss Sydney. By Geraldine Mockler. Illustrated by G. Demain Hammond.

The Girleen. By Edith Johnstone. Illustrated by Paul Hardy.

The Organist's Baby. By Kathleen Knox.

School-Days in France. By An Old Girl.

The Ravensworth Scholarship: A High School Story for Girls. By Mrs. Henry Clarke.

Queen of the Daffodils: A Story of High School Life. By Leslie Laing.

Raff's Ranche: A Story of Adventure among Cow-boys and Indians. By F. M. Holmes.

An Unexpected Hero. By Eliz. J. Lysaght.

The Bushranger's Secret. By Mrs. Henry Clarke, M.A.

The White Squall. By John C. Hutcheson.

The Wreck of the "Nancy Bell". By J. C. Hutcheson.

The Lonely Pyramid. By J. H. Yoxall.

Bab: or, The Triumph of Unselfishness. By Ismay Thorn.

Brave and True, and other Stories. By Gregson Gow.

The Light Princess. By George Mac Donald.

Nutbrown Roger and I. By J. H. Yoxall.

Sam Silvan's Sacrifice. By Jesse Colman.

Insect Ways on Summer Days in Garden, Forest, Field, and Stream. By Jennett Humphreys. With 70 Illustrations.

Susan. By Amy Walton.

A Pair of Clogs. By Amy Walton.

The Hawthorns. By Amy Walton.

Dorothy's Dilemma. By Caroline Austin.

TWO-SHILLING SERIES—Continued.

Marie's Home. By CAROLINE AUSTIN.

A Warrior King. By J. EVELYN.

Aboard the "Atalanta". By HENRY FRITH.

The Penang Pirate. By JOHN C. HUTCHESON.

Teddy: The Story of a "Little Pickle". By JOHN C. HUTCHESON.

A Rash Promise. By CECILIA SELBY LOWNDES.

Linda and the Boys. By CECILIA SELBY LOWNDES.

Swiss Stories for Children. From the German of MADAM JOHANNA SPYRI. By LUCY WHEELOCK.

The Squire's Grandson. By J. M. CALLWELL.

Magna Charta Stories. Edited by ARTHUR GILMAN, A.M.

The Wings of Courage; AND THE CLOUD-SPINNER. Translated from the French of GEORGE SAND, by Mrs. CORKRAN.

Chirp and Chatter: Or, LESSONS FROM FIELD AND TREE. By ALICE BANKS. With 54 Illustrations by GORDON BROWNE.

Four Little Mischiefs. By ROSA MULHOLLAND.

New Light through Old Windows. By GREGSON GOW.

Little Tottie, and Two Other Stories. By THOMAS ARCHER.

Naughty Miss Bunny. By CLARA MULHOLLAND.

Adventures of Mrs. Wishing-to-be. By ALICE CORKRAN.

The Joyous Story of Toto. By LAURA E. RICHARDS.

Our Dolly: Her Words and Ways. By MRS. R. H. READ.

Fairy Fancy: What she Heard and Saw. By MRS. READ.

BLACKIE'S EIGHTEENPENNY SERIES.

With Illustrations. In crown 8vo, cloth elegant.

NEW VOLUMES.

The Little Girl from Next Door. By GERALDINE MOCKLER.

Uncle Jem's Stella. By Author of the "Two Dorothys".

The Ball of Fortune. By C. PEARSE. *New and Cheaper Edition.*

The Family Failing. By DARLEY DALE. *New and Cheaper Edition.*

Warner's Chase: Or, The Gentle Heart. By ANNIE S. SWAN. *New Edition.*

Climbing the Hill. By ANNIE S. SWAN. *New Edition.*

Into the Haven. By ANNIE S. SWAN.

THE EIGHTEENPENNY SERIES.—Continued.

Olive and Robin: or, A Journey to Nowhere. By the author of "The Two Dorothys".

Mona's Trust: A Story for Girls. By PENELOPE LESLIE.

Wild Meg and Wee Dickie. By MARY E. ROPES.

Grannie. By ELIZABETH J. LYSAGHT.

The Seed She Sowed. By EMMA LESLIE.

[*Reduced Specimen of the Illustrations.*]

From "Pleasures and Pranks".

Unlucky: A Fragment of a Girl's Life. By CAROLINE AUSTIN.

Everybody's Business: Or, A Friend in Need. By ISMAY THORN.

Tales of Daring and Danger. By G. A. HENTY.

The Seven Golden Keys. By JAMES E. ARNOLD.

The Story of a Queen. By MARY C. ROWSELL.

Edwy: Or, Was he a Coward? By ANNETTE LYSTER.

The Battlefield Treasure. By F. BAYFORD HARRISON.

Joan's Adventures at the North Pole. By ALICE CORKRAN.

Filled with Gold. By J. PERRETT.

Our General: A Story for Girls. By ELIZABETH J. LYSAGHT.

Aunt Hesba's Charge. By ELIZABETH J. LYSAGHT.

By Order of Queen Maude: A Story of Home Life. By LOUISA CROW.

The Late Miss Hollingford. By ROSA MULHOLLAND.

Our Frank. By AMY WALTON.

A Terrible Coward. By G. MANVILLE FENN.

Little Jimmy: A Story of Adventure. By Rev. D. RICE-JONES, M.A.

Pleasures and Pranks. By ISABELLA PEARSON.

In a Stranger's Garden: A Story for Boys and Girls. By CONSTANCE CUMING.

A Soldier's Son: The Story of a Boy who Succeeded. By ANNETTE LYSTER.

Mischief and Merry-making. By ISABELLA PEARSON.

Littlebourne Lock. By F. BAYFORD HARRISON.

Yarns on the Beach. By G. A. HENTY.

Tom Finch's Monkey. By J. C. HUTCHESON.

Miss Grantley's Girls, and the Stories she Told Them. By THOS. ARCHER.

The Pedlar and his Dog. By MARY C. ROWSELL.

Town Mice in the Country. By M. E. FRANCIS.

Phil and his Father. By ISMAY THORN.

Prim's Story. By L. E. TIDDEMAN.

EIGHTEENPENNY SERIES—Continued.

Down and Up Again. By GREGSON GOW.

Madge's Mistake. By ANNIE E. ARMSTRONG.

The Troubles and Triumphs of Little Tim. By GREGSON GOW.

The Happy Lad: A Story of Peasant Life in Norway. By B. BJÖRNSON.

A Box of Stories. Packed for Young Folk by HORACE HAPPYMAN.

The Patriot Martyr, and other Narratives of Female Heroism.

LIBRARY OF FAMOUS BOOKS FOR BOYS AND GIRLS.

In Crown 8vo. Illustrated. Cloth extra, 1*s.* 6*d.* each.

The Cruise of the Midge. M. SCOTT.
Lives and Voyages of Drake and Cavendish.
Edgeworth's Moral Tales.
Marryat's The Settlers in Canada.
Michael Scott's Tom Cringle's Log.
White's Natural History of Selborne.
Waterton's Wanderings in S. America.
Anson's Voyage Round the World.
Autobiography of Franklin.
Lamb's Tales from Shakspeare.
Southey's Life of Nelson.
Miss Mitford's Our Village.
Two Years Before the Mast.
Marryat's Children of the New Forest.
Scott's The Talisman.
The Basket of Flowers.
Marryat's Masterman Ready.
Alcott's Little Women.
Cooper's Deerslayer.
The Lamplighter. By Miss Cummins.
Cooper's Pathfinder.
The Vicar of Wakefield.
Plutarch's Lives of Greek Heroes.
Poe's Tales of Romance and Fantasy.

Also a large selection of Rewards at a Shilling, Ninepence, Sixpence, and Fourpence. A complete list will be sent post free on application to the Publishers.

The Best Book for Children.

Laugh and Learn: The Easiest Book of Nursery Lessons and Nursery Games. By JENNETT HUMPHREYS. Profusely Illustrated. Square 8vo, cloth extra, 3*s.* 6*d.*

"One of the best books of the kind imaginable, full of practical teaching in word and picture, and helping the little ones pleasantly along a right royal road to learning."—*Graphic.*

LONDON:
BLACKIE & SON, LIMITED, 50 OLD BAILEY, E.C.